TAMIZDAT

A volume in the NIU Series in

Slavic, East European, and Eurasian Studies
Edited by Christine D. Worobec

For a list of books in the series, visit our website at cornellpress.cornell.edu.

TAMIZDAT

CONTRABAND RUSSIAN LITERATURE IN THE COLD WAR ERA

YASHA KLOTS

NORTHERN ILLINOIS UNIVERSITY PRESS
AN IMPRINT OF CORNELL UNIVERSITY PRESS
Ithaca and London

First published 2023 by Cornell University Press

Library of Congress Cataloging-in-Publication Data

Names: Klots, Yasha, author.
Title: Tamizdat : contraband Russian literature in the
    Cold War era / Yasha Klots.
Description: Ithaca [New York] : Northern Illinois
    University Press, an imprint of Cornell University
    Press, 2023. | Includes bibliographical references
    and index.
Identifiers: LCCN 2022036248 (print) |
    LCCN 2022036249 (ebook) | ISBN 9781501768958
    (hardcover) | ISBN 9781501768965 (epub) |
    ISBN 9781501768989 (pdf)
Subjects: LCSH: Russian literature—Foreign
    countries—20th century—History and criticism. |
    Prohibited books—Soviet Union. | Underground
    literature—Soviet Union—History and criticism. |
    Russian literature—Publishing—Foreign countries—
    History—20th century.
Classification: LCC PG3515 K576 2023 (print) |
    LCC PG3515 (ebook) | DDC 891.709/004—dc23/
    eng/20221121
LC record available at https://lccn.loc.gov/2022036248
LC ebook record available at https://lccn.loc.gov/
    2022036249

CONTENTS

Acknowledgments

In his speech "In Memory of Carl Proffer" (1984), Joseph Brodsky noted, "Normally, when one reads a book, one seldom thinks of its publisher: one is grateful to its author. The specifics of Russian history, however, made a publisher no less an important figure than a writer; made this distinction shrink considerably—the way distinctions do in adversity."[1] It is these publishers of "contraband" Russian literature abroad to whom I owe my inspiration—without always agreeing, however, with their ideological agendas and editorial practices—for this book.

The idea of writing a book on this topic emerged in 2012, when I taught a seminar, "Russian Literature behind Bars," at Williams College. I am indebted to Lysander Jaffe, a student in my class, who noticed the odd discrepancies between two English translations of Varlam Shalamov's short story "The Snake Charmer," one by John Glad done in 1980, the other by Robert Chandler more recently.[2] Lysander's paper sent me on an exciting journey through archives and libraries around the world that promised to shed some light on the wondrous and previously undocumented adventures of Russian literature smuggled out of the Soviet Union for publication abroad. The first archive I visited was in Amherst, Massachusetts: the former director of the Amherst Center for Russian Culture, Stanley Rabinowitz, made my explorations there possible and fruitful, accompanied by many meaningful conversations about *tamizdat* and its subjects. In Amherst I have also had the chance to discuss tamizdat with William and Jane Taubman, Catherine Ciepiela, Viktoria Schweitzer, Polina Barskova, and other colleagues from the Five Colleges.

Between 2014 and 2016 my project was supported by a research fellowship from the Alexander von Humboldt Foundation, which enabled me to work with the archives at the Center for East European Studies (Forschungsstelle Osteuropa) in Bremen, Germany. I thank its director,

Sussanne Schattenberg, for hosting me and Maria Klassen, the archivist, for her generous help with my research. My stay in Bremen would not be nearly as memorable, and this book would not be the same, without the eye-opening conversations I had with Gabriel Superfin, as well as with Tatiana Dviniatina, Nikolai Mitrokhin, Manuela Putz, and Felix Herrmann. I am grateful to Lazar Fleishman for introducing me to the Bremen archives and its staff back in 2011. In 2015, as a Humboldt fellow, I was able to work with other archives elsewhere in Europe, particularly the Bibliothèque de Documentation Internationale Contemporaine (BDIC) in Nanterre and the Instytut Literacki (Kultura Paryska) in Maison Lafitte outside Paris. I am deeply indebted to Claire Niemkoff (Nanterre) and Anna Bernhardt (Maison Lafitte) for accommodating me in my archival pursuits.

Central to my research on tamizdat and the Russian emigration more broadly have been the archival collections at the Beinecke Rare Book and Manuscript Library at Yale and at the Hoover Institution at Stanford, both of which have awarded me visiting fellowships. I thank Allison Van Rhee and Edwin Schroeder, former director of the Beinecke, for making it a place I find myself ever drawn to, and Carol A. Leadenham for her permission to publish my findings from the invaluable Gleb Struve Collection at Stanford. I am also grateful to Tanya Chebotarev from the Bakhmeteff Archive at Columbia University; Anna Gavrilova and Sergei Soloviev for familiarizing me with some sources from the Russian State Archive of Literature and Art (RGALI); and Pavel Tribunsky from the Alexander Solzhenitsyn Dom Russkogo Zarubezh'ia in Moscow for his help and collaboration.

While many of its ideas and preliminary research took shape earlier and elsewhere, this book was written after I joined Hunter College of the City University of New York in 2016. It was here that my project met the greatest enthusiasm and support, including two PSC-CUNY Enhanced Research Awards and several other grants and fellowships. Most importantly, it is my students and colleagues at Hunter and the CUNY Graduate Center I have to thank. All chapters of this book were read and thoroughly discussed at the Hunter Faculty Writing Seminar, spearheaded by Robert Cowan and Andrew Polsky, dean of the School of Arts and Sciences; it was at Hunter that in December 2018 I was able to organize an international conference and book exhibition, "Tamizdat: Publishing Russian Literature in the Cold War," cosponsored by the Harriman Institute of Columbia University and the Department of Russian and Slavic Studies of NYU. I thank Polina Barskova, the conference co-organizer, and Alla Roylance, the book exhibition cocurator, for all their thoughts and energy. I thank, too, the conference guests and participants: Olga Matich, Ronald Meyer, Elizabeth Beaujour, Nadya Peterson, Katerina Clark, Rossen Djagalov, Olga Voronina, Philip Gleissner, Erina Megowan, Ann Komaromi, Ilja Kukuj, Benjamin Nathans, Roman Utkin, Jessie Labov, Siobhan Doucette, Irena Grudzinska Gross, Robin Feuer Miller, Michael Scammell, Pavel Litvinov, Irina Prokhorova, and Ellendea Proffer Teasley.[3] Three years later, an edited volume based on the tamizdat conference at Hunter was published, thanks to Ilja Kukuj's heroic efforts.[4] It was also at Hunter that Tamizdat Project, a digital extension of this book, was conceived and grew into a public scholarship initiative.[5] I thank the New York Public Library and Bogdan Horbal, curator for the Slavic and East European Collections, for his support of Tamizdat Project and my work on this book by providing access to valuable databases, as well as for his own perspective on tamizdat as a librarian. As the director of Tamizdat Project, I thank all its numerous volunteers, as well as the National Endowment for the Humanities for its summer stipend (2020), which allowed me to promote the project and tamizdat as a topic among students worldwide. From December 2020 to August 2021, I was honored to hold the James Billington Fellowship from the Kennan Institute of the Wilson Center, which allowed me time off from teaching and made it possible to finish the book that spring.

I have presented parts of my project at multiple conferences, guest lectures, and other venues, to whose organizers, fellow panelists, and audiences I am forever indebted: Boris Belenkin, Paolo Fasoli, Edwin Frank, Tomas Glanc, Yelena Kalinsky, Peter Kaufman, Ann Komaromi, Ilya Kukulin, Bettina Lerner, Mark Lipovetsky, Misha Melnichenko, Elena Mikhailik, Elena Ostrovskaya, Nina Popova, Tatiana Pozdniakova, Mathew Rojansky, Irina Sandomiskaja, Klavdia Smola, Alex Spektor, Leona Toker, Zara Torlone, Birutė Vagrienė, Matvei Yankelevich, Elena Zemskova, and countless others.

This book would not have been possible without hours, days, and years of conversations with Tomas Venclova, who taught me the life of books when I was his graduate student at Yale and who has remained an inexhaustible source of knowledge and inspiration thereafter.

Finally, this book would never have been written without the love and encouragement of my friends Polina Barskova, Anna Bespiatykh and Max Paskal, Rossen Djagalov, Nora Gortcheva, Barbara Harshav, Denise Marquez, Anna Nizhnik, Alexander Pau Soria, Ross Ufberg, Roman Utkin, Yulia Volfovich, and Gregorio, whose faith in my project inspired each page. I owe this book to my mother, whose typewriter's clatter would lull me to sleep as a child blissfully ignorant of what she was secretly typing and why; this book is a belated answer to my uncle's impassionate question, year after year, about how my manuscript was progressing; it is what my then-teenage son grew so used to discussing with me from dinner to dinner that "Pkhentz," an alien from Tertz's short story, has become one of our codewords and nearly part of the family.

Parts of the following articles previously published elsewhere have been reworked and expanded in this book: "Tamizdat as a Practice and Institution," in *Tamizdat: Publishing Russian Literature across Borders.* Special issue of *Wiener Slawistischer Almanach* Band 86, edited by Yasha Klots, 9–23. Berlin: Peter Lang, 2021; "Lydia Chukovskaia's *Sofia Petrovna* Is *Going Under* and Abroad," in *Tamizdat: Publishing Russian Literature across Borders*, 87–118; "Tamizdat as a Literary Practice and Political Institution," in *The Oxford Handbook of Soviet Underground Culture*, edited by Mark Lipovetsky, Ilja Kukuj, Tomas Glanc, and Klavdia Smola (New York: Oxford University Press; forthcoming); "Varlam Shalamov between Tamizdat and the Soviet Writers' Union (1966–1978)," in *Russia—Culture of (Non)Conformity: From the Late Soviet Era to the Present.* Special issue of *Russian Literature* 86–98C (2018), edited by Klavdia Smola and Mark Lipovetsky, 137–66; "From Avvakum to Dostoevsky: Varlam Shalamov and Russian Narratives of Political Imprisonment," *Russian Review* 75, no. 1 (2016): 1–19. I thank the editors of these publications for allowing me to use them.

My special thanks to both reviewers of my manuscript and Amy Farranto at Cornell University Press who helped make this book a reality.

Note on Transliteration and Translation

A simplified version of the Library of Congress transliteration system is used throughout the main text, notes, and bibliography. Original Cyrillic is preserved in block quotations from poetry, but not in run-on quotations, where it is transliterated and italicized. Unless spelled otherwise in the quoted source, first and last names ending in "-ий" are transliterated with a "-y" (Georgy, Rzhevsky), but not other words (*sovetskii*). Soft and hard sign indicators are usually dropped. Unless quoted from an existing source in English, all translations are mine, including the titles.

TAMIZDAT

Introduction
Tamizdat as a Literary Practice and Political Institution

In the early 1920s, observing the life of the Russian literary diaspora in Berlin and pondering whether he should go back or stay in exile, the renowned formalist critic Viktor Shklovsky lamented, "Poor Russian emigration! It has no heartbeat. . . . Our batteries were charged in Russia; here we keep going around in circles and soon we will grind to a halt. The lead battery plates will turn into nothing but sheer weight."[1] This book revisits Shklovsky's apprehension by situating it in another historical context: it explores the patterns of circulation, first publications, and reception abroad of contraband manuscripts from the Soviet Union in the 1950–1980s, covering the period from Khrushchev's Thaw to the Stagnation era under Brezhnev. Since Shklovsky's sojourn in Berlin, texts produced in Russia but denied publication at home had indeed continued to modulate the "heartbeat" of the Russian literary diaspora. But in the post-Stalin years, they also served as a weapon on the cultural fronts of the Cold War, laying bare the geographical, stylistic, and ideological rift between two seemingly disparate yet inextricably intertwined fields of Russian literature at home and abroad, a fracture that resulted from the political upheavals of the first half of the twentieth century. Tracing the outbound itineraries of individual manuscripts across Soviet state borders, as well as their "repatriation" back home in printed form, this book is devoted to the history of literary exchanges between publishers, critics, and readers in the West with writers in Russia, whose clandestine texts bring the dynamics of these intricate relationships into focus. This is a cultural history of the "irregular heartbeat" of Russian literature on opposite sides of the Iron Curtain, desynchronized as it were for political reasons and diagnosed on the basis of aesthetic and sociocultural symptoms caused by the dispersal of texts across different geographies and time zones.

What Is *Tamizdat*?

A derivative of *samizdat* (self-publishing) and *gosizdat* (state publishing), tamizdat refers to publishing "over there," i.e., abroad. Comprising manuscripts rejected, censored, or never submitted for publication at home but smuggled through various channels out of the country and printed elsewhere with or without their authors' knowledge or consent, tamizdat contributed to the formation of the twentieth-century Russian literary canon: suffice it to say that the majority of contemporary Russian classics, with few exceptions, first appeared abroad long before they could see the light of day in Russia after perestroika. As the chapters of this book demonstrate, tamizdat mediated the relationships of authors in Russia with the local literary establishment on the one hand and the nonconformist underground on the other, while the very prospect of having their works published abroad, let alone the consequences of such a transgression, affected these authors' choices and ideological positions. As a practice and institution, tamizdat was, consequently, as emblematic of Russian literature after Stalin as its more familiar and better-researched domestic counterparts, samizdat and gosizdat. This study aims to revisit the traditional notion of late-Soviet culture as a dichotomy between the official and underground fields by viewing it instead as a transnationally dynamic, three-dimensional model.

Historically and terminologically, "tamizdat" is younger than "samizdat," a neologism that goes back to Nikolai Glazkov's self-manufactured books of poetry from as early as the 1940s: typed by the author on his own typewriter, the title pages of these handmade editions were marked *samsebiaizdat* ("myself—by myself—publishing") to mock the standard abbreviations of "Gosizdat," "Goslitizdat," and so on, that appeared invariably on officially sanctioned publications in Soviet Russia. Since the late 1950s Glazkov had become an officially recognized poet, but his pioneering practice, poignantly captured by the term "samsebiaizdat," later contracted to "samizdat," became a true token of twentieth-century Russian literary history.[2] But while "samizdat" suggests a handwritten or typed text that circulates locally without official sanction among a relatively narrow circle of initiated readers who continue to reproduce and disseminate it further, "tamizdat" implies a text with all the official attributes of a print edition that is published extraterritorially after it crosses the border of its country of origin. To be considered tamizdat, the text thus must enter a foreign literary jurisdiction where it assumes a new life (at least until it makes it back home in print form). Narrowly defined, "tamizdat" stands for texts that have twice crossed the geographical border: on the way out as a manuscript and on the way back in as a publication. Such was the fate of all texts analyzed in this book (with the exception of Solzhenitsyn's *One Day in the Life of Ivan Denisovich*, whose role in the drain of other manuscripts abroad, including Solzhenitsyn's own, is explored in the first chapter). The vicissitudes of these texts' travels varied, as did the actors involved.

The roundtrip journey of contraband Russian literature abroad and back home, from manuscript to print edition, involved many actors: an author whose name may or may not have been indicated on the cover and title pages, whether or not the publication was authorized; one or more couriers who smuggled the manuscript abroad manually or via a diplomatic pouch, with or without the help of the author's local friends or foreign diplomats with mail privileges; an editor who received the manuscript once it had crossed the border and who prepared it for publication by their or someone else's press or periodical; critics, who included Russian émigrés, Western Slavists, scholars, and journalists; émigré and Western readers—the first audience of the fugitive manuscript; then another courier (usually an exchange scholar, a graduate student, or a journalist), who smuggled the print edition back to the Soviet Union via embassy channels or otherwise, with or without an honorarium for the author; and finally, the reader back home, who may or may not have been already familiar with the text in question through samizdat (or even from an earlier publication in gosizdat).

Tamizdat thus combined elements of both the official and unofficial fields insofar as it attached a legal status to a manuscript that had been deemed illegal or refused official circulation at home. Although the etymological meaning of "tamizdat" may appear quite innocent, referring simply to a place of publication that lies elsewhere in relation to where the work was created, the political function of tamizdat was fully realized only when the text reunited with its author and readers

back home, thus completing the cycle. It is this dimension of tamizdat that made it a barometer of the political climate during the Cold
War. Depending on the author's standing with the Soviet authorities,
the ideological profile and repertoire of the publisher abroad and its
sources of funding, the international atmosphere in general, and the
relationships between the two countries in particular, tamizdat often
incriminated the author of a runaway manuscript to an even greater
extent than had that same manuscript not leaked abroad but remained
confined to the domestic field of samizdat. Operating from opposite
sides of the state border, samizdat and tamizdat amplified one another
and, at the end of the day, were bound to fuse into an ever more potent
alternative for nonconformist Russian literature to find its way to the
reader, albeit in a roundabout way.

The distinctive feature of tamizdat, however, remains geographic
rather than political since the very climate of the Cold War almost irreparably blurred the line between the political and the artistic. Likewise, drawing a line between official and underground literary fields,
including sam- and tamizdat, on the basis of aesthetic merit or "quality factor" hardly appears productive today, much as it may have been
tempting decades earlier, when Dimitry Pospielovsky, the author of one
of the first articles on tamizdat, claimed that "samizdat and tamizdat
[include] the greatest writers and poets—both living and dead—of the
Soviet era, while the bulk of the contemporary gosizdat output is grey
mediocrity at best."[3] Such a politically driven approach, understandable at the time, is clearly shortsighted if only because the same authors
sometimes published in both gosizdat and tamizdat (the former rarely
precluding the latter, but not vice versa). Moreover, tamizdat critics
themselves often praised and were eager to republish a work that had
passed Soviet censorship and appeared in gosizdat, as was the case with
Solzhenitsyn's *Ivan Denisovich*, Vladimir Dudintsev's *Not by Bread Alone*,
and Mikhail Bulgakov's *The Master and Margarita*, to name but a few.[4]

Although the author's physical whereabouts were not always a de-
finitive factor for the readers of tamizdat in Russia in the 1950s–1980s
(what mattered was that the edition itself came from abroad), the geographic principle adopted in this study does not allow émigré literature
to be regarded as tamizdat, since it was both written *and* published
abroad, within one geopolitical field. This terminological problem per-
sisted long after tamizdat became a reality. For example, as late as 1971,
Gleb Struve defined tamizdat as "*émigré* books by non-*émigré* writers,"
thus highlighting the role of Russian emigration in channeling the

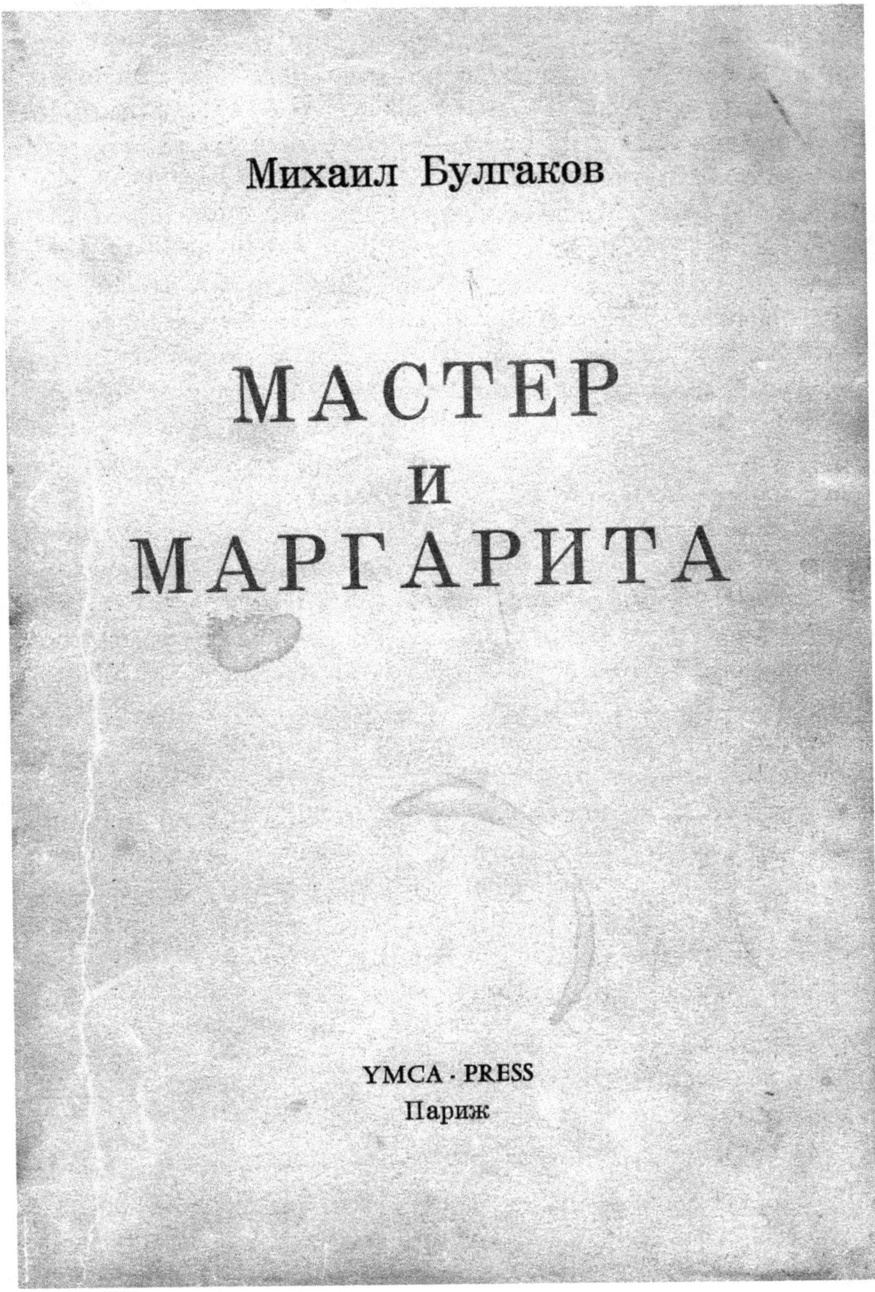

Михаил Булгаков

МАСТЕР
и
МАРГАРИТА

YMCA · PRESS
Париж

FIGURE 0.1. Mikhail Bulgakov. *Master i Margarita. Roman*. Foreword by Archpriest Ioann San-Frantsissky. Paris: YMCA-Press, 1967. Cover of the first book edition.

contraband traffic of manuscripts from the Soviet Union but avoiding the term that by that time was already widespread among "non-émigré" authors in Russia.[5] Although the vast majority of émigré publishers and critics were poets and prose writers in their own right, their roles in publishing authors from behind the Curtain should be regarded as separate from their original contributions to Russian literature as writers and poets. Vladimir Nabokov's fiction may have indeed been as forbidden a fruit in Soviet Russia as Boris Pasternak's novel *Doctor Zhivago*, first printed in Italy in 1957 and believed to be the first tamizdat publication. But the reason the latter is tamizdat and the former is not has less to do with the subject matter of the two writers' oeuvre (deceptively apolitical in Nabokov's case and somewhat more poignant in Pasternak's) than with their geographical whereabouts in relation to those of their publishers. For the sake of consistency, when the author emigrated—as did Joseph Brodsky in 1972, Andrei Sinyavsky in 1973, and Aleksandr Solzhenitsyn in 1974—only their publications abroad *before* emigration, not after, are considered tamizdat in this study.

Although historically and etymologically related, samizdat and tamizdat were, in more ways than one, mirror opposites. Apart from the obvious differences in their form of reproduction and circulation (handmade versus industrially published; distributed illegally to a limited underground audience versus readily available "aboveground" from bookshops and libraries), what sets them apart are their respective readers. True, both samizdat and tamizdat "offered authors two legitimate routes to audiences,"[6] but the audiences themselves, especially in the early years of tamizdat, were geographically, politically, and culturally perhaps as divided as the authors of contraband manuscripts in Soviet Russia and their publishers, critics, and readers abroad. A remarkable example is the epigraph of Akhmatova's *Requiem*:

Нет, и не под чуждым небосводом,
И не под защитой чуждых крыл—
Я была тогда с моим народом,
Там, где мой народ, к несчастью, был.[7]

[No, not under foreign skies, / Nor under the protection of foreign wings— / I was then with my people, / There, where my people, unfortunately, were.]

The lines articulate the void between the "two Russias" after the Revolution, as well as the author's unequivocal position vis-à-vis those who found themselves elsewhere geographically, ideologically, and stylistically as a result. The authors in Soviet Russia, including Akhmatova, could even be viewed by some of the émigrés as ideological opponents. Their life experiences and, more importantly, their means of registering the Soviet reality in their texts often evoked suspicion and misunderstanding on the opposite side of the Curtain. Over time, as tamizdat was gradually rejuvenated by new arrivals from the Soviet Union who came to replace the older generation, these differences would wear off, though they never entirely disappeared. But until the Third Wave of the Russian emigration took over the tamizdat publishing scene in the 1970s, the temperature of relationships between publishers, critics, and readers in the West with the authors in Russia was often quite hot.

The attitudes of the authors in Russia to tamizdat were also often mixed. The lack of direct communication between them and their publishers abroad could not but produce letters of protest and public renunciations of tamizdat publications (one such example is addressed in the last chapter on Shalamov). Indeed, few authors in the 1960s remained fully content with the handling of their manuscripts abroad. Their frustration was caused not only by editorial flaws, including the typographical errors that infested tamizdat, but also by the shortsighted reception of their works in Western and émigré media, to say nothing of the reluctance or inability of most tamizdat publishers to pay their authors royalties or honoraria. Much depended on the current standing of the author in Russia with the local establishment, which could range from official to semiofficial to underground. That said, tamizdat never limited itself to dissident writers only, although nonconformist literature was its main fuel. As it happened, most notably with Solzhenitsyn, the same author could stand at the vanguard of gosizdat before falling from favor and finding himself forced out into the unofficial fields of samizdat and tamizdat. Or one might be active as an official and even high-ranking Soviet editor or critic but not as a prose writer, as was the case with Lydia Chukovskaia or Andrei Sinyavsky (until his second identity as Abram Tertz was exposed). The author might have been able to publish lyrical verses but not works on less innocent subjects, such as Akhmatova's "Poem without a Hero" and *Requiem*. Thus, the conventional distinction between the official and nonofficial spheres is hardly applicable to tamizdat, given its inherently dual nature, which combined elements of both.

Unsurprisingly, tamizdat jeopardized or altogether aborted one's chances of being published in gosizdat, but it could also cast a shadow onto an author's reputation among like-minded nonconformist audiences and fellow authors in the underground, especially when political changes raised hopes that the grip of censorship would abate, as was the case during the Thaw and in particular after the Twenty-second Congress of the Communist Party in October 1961, when Stalin's crimes were for the first time publicly exposed. One might say that, at least during the formative years of tamizdat in the late 1950s and early 1960s, samizdat and tamizdat derived from a different ethos: while releasing one's manuscript to samizdat and circulating it in the underground locally was considered an act of civic solidarity, courage, and even heroism, letting it leak abroad and (not) seeing it published in tamizdat could be viewed as a disgrace or even a betrayal of one's civic duty as a writer and citizen. Far from the rule, and perhaps even an exception, but on December 28, 1963, when Akhmatova showed Chukovskaia a copy of *Requiem* that had just been published in Munich, the latter's reaction was rather ambiguous: "Here is enough shame for us," Chukovskaia wrote that day, "that the great 'Requiem' rang out in the West before it did so at home."[8] Sure enough, Chukovskaia soon found that her own novella *Sofia Petrovna*, which shares the subject matter and much of its setting with *Requiem*, was also published in tamizdat despite all her efforts to have it first published in Russia.

Whether anonymous, pseudonymous, or under the real name of the author, tamizdat included both works by authors who were no longer alive (e.g., poets of the Silver Age)[9] and works produced more recently by those still around to face the likely consequences of such a transgression. It is the latter category that I have chosen to focus on in this study in order to trace, on the one hand, the full spectrum of authors' relationships with their tamizdat publishers, and, on the other, the effect of their publications abroad on their careers at home. Although a direct punishment for publishing in tamizdat was not always guaranteed, and the extent of the punishment varied from light reprimand to years of hard labor, the painful memory of the affair of *Doctor Zhivago* affected authors' choices as they dared to consider, let alone pursue, the opportunity offered them overtly or indirectly by tamizdat or when they simply learned that their works had appeared abroad "without their knowledge or consent." (This standard disclaimer was widely used by tamizdat publishers to protect the authors in Russia from the authorities.)[10]

While the story of the first publication of Pasternak's novel abroad remained the indelible background for tamizdat throughout the rest of the Soviet era, I have chosen another milestone of twentieth-century Russian literary history to explore tamizdat of the Thaw through the prism and in part as a consequence of the publication of Solzhenitsyn's *One Day in the Life of Ivan Denisovich* in Russia in gosizdat. As I argue in the first chapter, it was this gosizdat publication in 1962 that generated a virtually uninterrupted traffic of clandestine manuscripts from the Soviet Union to the West in the years to follow and that helped shape tamizdat as a practice and institution that relied on literary and political developments at home. Solzhenitsyn's groundbreaking novella also shapes the thematic framework of my study: narratives of Stalinism and the gulag. The gulag was, no doubt, the "hottest" topic of the Cold War, but it also called for a new form of linguistic representation of the catastrophic reality, which resisted verbalization and rendered human language inadequate to the inhuman experiences. Whether first published at home, like Solzhenitsyn's *Ivan Denisovich*, or abroad, like Shalamov's *Kolyma Tales*, gulag narratives revealed an especially profound dissonance in their reception on either side of the Curtain. While censored for political reasons at home, their highly codified language often proved aesthetically inaccessible abroad, since the émigrés' historical and personal backgrounds, including their trauma of exile, did not match those of the authors who had stayed behind and lived through whatever the Soviet century had to offer. The gulag posed a linguistic, epistemological, and communicative problem, which tamizdat both attempted to resolve and is itself derived from.

Bridging the Divide

The subject matter of this book is inherently liminal historically and geographically, domestically and transnationally, aesthetically and institutionally. In the aftermath of the October Revolution and throughout the Soviet era, Russian literature remained split into "two Russian literatures": one at home, the other abroad. Inside Russia, and especially after the death of Stalin in 1953, it also remained subdivided into official and unofficial fields, although even during the harshest (or, for that matter, the most sluggish) years of Soviet history, the cultural scene was never as binary as it has been traditionally portrayed, with the line between official and underground spheres ever permeable and never entirely clear-cut.[11]

It was the Thaw of the late 1950s and early 1960s that first lifted the fear and broke the silence that had reigned in the country for decades under Stalin, producing hopes and burgeoning opportunities to verbalize the traumas of the still recent past, such as the Great Terror and the gulag, WWII and the siege of Leningrad. This turbulent decade also brought into focus the stylistic consequences of the ideological bifurcation of Russian literature into its Soviet and émigré branches, on the one hand, and into the official and underground ones inside Russia, on the other. It was then that these doctrinally demarcated "fields of cultural production," to use Pierre Bourdieu's term, hitherto perceived as autonomous, started to overlap, creating a contact zone of double political and aesthetic magnitude, with more and more authors, readers, publishers, and critics from either side of the Curtain, drawn in. It is this contact zone, or area of overlap, in which the Thaw era operated, paving the way for a future reunification of Russian literature both domestically and globally during perestroika, when the Iron Curtain began to rust.[12]

On March 5, 1953, Soviet society experienced what Irina Paperno has described as "a Nietzschean moment of the death of God . . . (tears were convulsively shed both by those who loved Stalin and those who did not)." For the Soviet intelligentsia, the death of Stalin meant a radical shift in their perception of history and time itself: "It was not so much their sense of the past that changed after Stalin's death as the sense of the future. Throughout the years of the terror they had carefully preserved memories for future use. But, as it now became clear, they had not really believed that this future would ever come—at least not in their lifetime."[13] Memory of the recent past was activated, and the still open wounds began to heal, three years later, in 1956, when Khrushchev delivered his "secret speech" against Stalin at the Twentieth Congress of the Communist Party. Part of the de-Stalinization campaign that followed was the rehabilitation of political prisoners, whether or not posthumous. Gulag survivors were now returning from the camps not only to reunite with their families, if they still had any, but also to face those who had thrown them behind the barbed wire years or decades earlier. They were also coming back to record their experiences, an endeavor that for a while the state even officially encouraged.[14] On March 4, 1956, a week after the Twentieth Congress, Anna Akhmatova told Chukovskaia: "Now the prisoners will return, and two Russias will look each other in the eyes: the one that pronounced sentences, and the one that served them. A new epoch has begun. You and I have lived to see it."[15] This divide between "two Russias," articulated as a sign of transition from one era to the next, ran through the entire Soviet society:

there was hardly any family in the country unaffected by collectivization, the purges of the 1930s, and subsequent political persecution.
Both groups found it "easy, even comforting, to think—as Akhmatova
then did—of 'two Russias,'" while Akhmatova, who had lived long
enough to have witnessed the entire spectrum of twentieth-century upheavals, now "longed not only for a clear sense of historical divide, but
also for a sense of a clear division in the community." One may argue
that such a division, or at least an awareness of it, was necessary for a
society coming to terms with the traumas of its past by putting them
down in words. "In 1956 the future began once again," Paperno concludes, no matter how short-lived it proved to be in reality.[16]

Regained faith in the future was entrusted to manuscripts emancipated as a result of the Thaw, which came to an end much sooner than
hoped for, only to be replaced by a new cold spell, to use another meteo-
rological metaphor. Yet in the relatively short time that spring was still
in the air, the experiences of the gulag survivors recorded in their firsthand accounts, fiction and poetry, amounted to a true monument to
those who did not live to record theirs. "It was the text that served as the
ultimate monument to the year 1937," Paperno writes of this remarkable "culture of texts" that transformed the Russian literary landscape
on both sides of the Curtain.[17] Whether newly written or salvaged from
the past, first published at home or abroad, texts that floated to the
surface from the rubble of history during these liminal years became
the holy scriptures of the overwhelmingly secular Soviet intelligentsia.
It was the sacred status of these manuscripts that may help explain the
ferocious persecution of their authors by the state, on the one hand,
and the immense moral and social value that the authors themselves
attached to their writings, on the other. To impart such a value to a literary text—to proclaim that "manuscripts do not burn," as one Russian
author put it,—meant belonging to the intelligentsia.[18]

Translating the memory of the past into a narrative took time. The
country had to wait several more years until its awakened memory
found an outlet in several groundbreaking publications in the wake of
the Twenty-second Party Congress. The night the congress adjourned
on October 31, 1961, Stalin's body was taken out of the mausoleum.
Streets and cities that bore his name were soon renamed. It was then,
too, that a great many literary manuscripts, including those discussed
in this book, were emancipated and declassified. Submitted to Soviet
publishing houses and periodicals, most of them were rejected, and
some were then leaked abroad, where they were first published. One

manuscript, however, managed to pass censorship and appeared in the official Soviet press a year later, with the personal sanction of Khrushchev: Aleksandr Solzhenitsyn's *One Day in the Life of Ivan Denisovich*.[19] There was little disagreement at the time about the importance of its timely breakthrough, but this gosizdat publication only exacerbated the deep-seated rift between the intelligentsia and "the people," the social class clearly favored by the authorities (as they favored Solzhenitsyn's male protagonist versus the female perspective in Akhmatova's *Requiem* and Chukovskaia's *Sofia Petrovna*, explored in the second and third chapters). Despite the enormous social value that the intelligentsia bestowed upon Solzhenitsyn, *Ivan Denisovich* outlined the ultimate limits of the admissible in the official Soviet press and thus, inadvertently, forced out other manuscripts about the gulag, first into the underground at home and then abroad.

Apart from the uneasy split between the intelligentsia and the people, the Thaw introduced yet another dimension to the newly reawakened historical self-awareness of the Soviet intelligentsia after Stalin: for the first time in decades, the country opened its borders to foreign scholars and students arriving in the USSR on academic and cultural-exchange programs, as well as to Western writers and journalists.[20] Although closely monitored, their very presence on Soviet territory and their contacts with Russian writers, artists, and intellectuals served as a reminder of an alternative life elsewhere, including the opportunity, no matter how surreal at first sight, of having one's manuscript sent for publication abroad. Contacts with foreigners, who served as physical proof that state borders could now be crossed, if only in one direction, also impelled the intelligentsia to realize its "foreignness" in its own country. This realization, in other words, fostered the identity of nonconformist Russian authors as "internal émigrés," or simply as outcasts, an inalienable trait of the late-Soviet intelligentsia. It was through foreign scholars, journalists, and diplomats that, from the late 1950s on, much of contemporary Russian literature traveled abroad to be first published in tamizdat.

Naturally foreigners caused suspicion and fear among even the bravest members of the underground literary circles in Russia, especially among the older generation. When Carl and Ellendea Proffer, cofounders of the now legendary Ardis Publishers in Ann Arbor, Michigan, first visited Nadezhda Mandelshtam, the poet's widow, in 1969, she told them that, a few years earlier, when she first met Clarence Brown, a Mandelshtam scholar from Princeton, "she hid behind the door at Akhmatova's, afraid to show herself. . . . She often peered out the front windows after we arrived, checking to see if we were being followed."[21] Needless to say, fear accompanied even the bravest foreigners throughout their stays in the Soviet Union as well. "Repeatedly during our six-month stay in 1969," Carl Proffer recalled, "we had the jarring experience of going to a new home, asking about a photograph on a wall or table, and getting the answer: that's my father, he was shot in 1937. (The relation and year might change, but the formula and the shock were always the same.) Yes, we agreed, this was the kind of thing that could make one afraid for a long time." The Proffers, too, were often afraid, "so much so that we had stomach pains for days, caused by the stories we were hearing and by the illegal things we were doing—such as getting and giving away large numbers of books, including especially dangerous ones such as the Russian *Doctor Zhivago*, Solzhenitsyn's novels, Orwell, Bibles, and so on. Arrests and searches of foreign students were common. . . . Fear was logical even for us, so why shouldn't N.M. and so many others be afraid after the carnivorous age they had been through" (20–21).[22]

Proffer's account goes back to his second (and his wife's first) trip to Russia in 1969, five years after the infamous show trial of Joseph Brodsky in 1964, followed by the arrest and imprisonment of Andrei Sinyavsky and Yuli Daniel in 1965–1966. Indeed, in the minds of the older generation, the persecution of younger writers sparked a painful flashback to the years of high Stalinism, in other words, to that very past from which the "future" that had begun after Stalin's death was meant to depart. On March 14, 1964, the day after Brodsky's verdict was announced, sentencing the poet to five years of internal exile for "social parasitism," Chukovskaia wrote: "It seemed to me all along as if I were back in Leningrad, as if it was the year 1937 yet again. The same feeling of humiliation and ineffaceable insult." "Of course," she added, "1964 is nothing compared to 1937; no more Special Sessions or military tribunals, sentencing thousands and thousands of people to instant or slow death every day, but there is still no truth, and the same impenetrable wall. The same habitual . . . hatred toward the intelligentsia."[23] Much like the affair of Sinyavsky and Daniel, "the Brodsky case in 1964," Paperno concludes, "brought back old patterns. . . . The 1930s and the 1960s were connected by emotions."[24] This emotional connection between two distinct epochs, however, was not limited to the historical consciousness of the intelligentsia in Russia. It manifested itself in the responses of publishers and critics abroad to the same events unfolding in the USSR. As if they were two interconnected vessels, the pattern was clear: the higher the political pressure inside the country, the higher the cultural output abroad.[25] Indeed, Brodsky's first book of poetry came out in the United States in 1965 as a direct consequence of his trial in Leningrad.[26]

Triggered by fluctuations of the political climate during the Thaw and in its immediate aftermath, historical memory (or rather, its idiosyncratic aberrations on either side of the Curtain) proved to defy geography while at the same time relying on it. Tamizdat publishers' unflagging interest in the gulag, along with the paramount significance bestowed upon this hot topic by the writers in Russia, invites a comparison of the contraband traffic of manuscripts across Soviet state borders to the escape of prisoners from the camps, very seldom successful in the case of the latter. Tamizdat, thus, seemed to fulfil one of the morphological features of gulag narratives as a genre, insofar as gulag authors, according to Leona Toker, tended to "view the whole of the USSR as the 'Larger Zone,' . . . a giant prison house with but different degrees of illusory freedom of movement."[27] But the textual freedom promised by tamizdat to the runaway manuscripts often led to imprisonment for the authors. The specifics of twentieth-century Russian literature made geography as tangible as history to the writers.

As Soviet society grappled with the flywheel of history set in motion by the Thaw, the West was preoccupied with what has been referred to as "the spatial turn," a movement in the social sciences and the humanities that stressed the role of geography, cartography, and mapping in the production of discourse and cultural identity. In 1967 Michel Foucault proclaimed that while "the great obsession" of the nineteenth century—and, belatedly, of much of the twentieth century in Russia—was history, "with its themes of development and of suspension, of crisis, and cycle, themes of the ever-accumulating past, . . . the present epoch will perhaps be above all the epoch of space. We are," Foucault claimed, "in the epoch of juxtaposition, the epoch of the near and far, of the side-by-side, of the dispersed. We are at a moment . . . when our experience of the world is less that of a long life developing through time than that of a network that connects points and intersects with its own skein."[28] As a literary practice and political institution that relied on deterritorialization, tamizdat, according to Olga Matich, presumed that "the spatial *there* often began, so to speak, as a foreign *here*, fusing the near and far by transforming them into a peculiar Cold War side-by-side, which might be identified as another kind of in-betweenness."[29] This movement of contraband texts across state borders in both directions meant to step out, transgress, break away from the boundaries that were both geographically demarcated and historically internalized. Tamizdat may have offered nonconformist manuscripts a chance to escape the panopticon of Soviet censorship, understood in Foucauldian terms as total surveillance achieved through spatial ordering.[30] However, confined to the Soviet territory as the only geography their authors could physically afford, these texts often migrated abroad only to find themselves girdled by a new kind of horizon of expectations, to use a key term of reception theory.

For the purposes of reconstructing the sociopolitical and aesthetic milieu in which texts produced in Russia were first published abroad, reception theory serves as an apt prism. It postulates that a literary work "is not an object that stands by itself and that offers the same view to each reader in each period." Instead, according to Hans Robert Jauss, a text is a priori dialogical, since its reception "is unthinkable without the active participation of its addressees."[31] Except for the rather narrow circle of samizdat readers who may have been familiar with contraband Russian literature locally, the first audience of tamizdat consisted of Western publishers, critics, and general readers, above all Russian émigrés, i.e., an interpretive community with its own variety of personal and socially conditioned reflexes. The responses of Western readers to contraband manuscripts from the USSR shaped tamizdat as an alternative "field of cultural production," to cite Bourdieu's term once again, which like Jauss's "horizons of expectations," is also a spatial metaphor. In keeping with Bourdieu's model, this field involved a network of "agents" (or "actors") and institutions, and it was fueled by a conversion of symbolic capital (manuscripts) into economic goods (books). Yet even this socioeconomic dimension of tamizdat, which will be addressed in detail in the case studies below, was also contingent upon geography, deterritorialization, and the migration of texts from one field to the other. That said, insofar as tamizdat represented an alternative field of cultural production, set up in stark opposition to the Soviet regime and the literary dogma of socialist realism in particular, it was not devoid of its own hierarchy and ideological agenda. It also had a prehistory that shaped tamizdat as a practice and institution of the late-Soviet era.

Historical Precedents of Tamizdat

It was Pasternak's *Doctor Zhivago* and its first publication in Italy in 1957, orchestrated in part by the American secret services, that poked the first hole in the Curtain for numerous other manuscripts to leak through it in the years to follow and instituted tamizdat as a late-Soviet phenomenon.[32] The *Zhivago* affair, however, was not entirely unprecedented in the history of Russian letters and thought; nor was the Cold War the first time Russian literature had had to migrate abroad or go underground at home. To bypass state censorship poetry, fiction, plays, and autobiographies were passed from hand to hand and circulated through various channels locally for as long as modern Russian literature has existed, making censorship as old as Russian literary culture itself. This practice can be traced back as early as the seventeenth century, when Archpriest Avvakum (1620–1682), an Old Believer burned at the stake for his schismatic views on the Orthodox Church, wrote what is considered to be the first autobiographical account of political imprisonment in the Russian language. A text that marked a transition from the ecclesiastical genre of hagiography to that of a genuine autobiography (and by extension to secular literature), *The Life of Protopop Avvakum* was "copied out by hand and passed from one Old Believer community to the other," earning, for lack of a better term, the status of "the first significant Russian samizdat text."[33]

In the nineteenth century "unacceptable" texts from tsarist Russia started to find their way to Western Europe, beyond the reach of the Third Section of His Imperial Majesty's Own Chancellery instituted by Nicolas I in the wake of the Decembrist uprising as the central organ for state censorship, surveillance, and propaganda. Mikhail Lermontov's "Demon" (1829–1839), of all examples, was first published in 1856 in Karlsruhe, Germany, before seeing the light of day in Russia four years later. State control of literary production in the Russian empire, as in the Soviet Union a century later, extended from overtly subversive political writing to frivolous texts on subjects that had little if anything to do with politics, such as the pornographic poems (*sramnye stikhi*) by Mikhail Longinov, once a freethinker (*vol'nodumets*) and friend of Nikolai Nekrasov, Ivan Turgenev, and other members of the liberal *Sovremennik* circle, and later, ironically, Russia's censor-in-chief:

Пишу стихи я не для дам,
Все больше о пизде и хуе;

Я их в цензуру не отдам,
А напечатаю в Карлсруэ.[34]

[I write my verses not for the ladies, / But more about vaginas and dicks; / I won't give them to the censor, / But will publish instead in Karlsruhe.]

The main point of reference for tamizdat of the Soviet era was Alexander Herzen's monthly *Kolokol* (*The Bell*), published in London and Geneva over the course of ten years (1857–1867) by the Free Russian Press, which had been established a few years earlier. In his call "To Our Brethren in Russia" ("Brat'iam na Rusi,") dated February 21, 1853, Herzen wrote: "At home there is no place for free Russian speech, but it can ring out elsewhere if only its time has come. I know how hard it is for you to keep silent, what it costs you to conceal every feeling, every thought, every impulse." Indeed, according to Herzen, in 1853 "the time has come to publish in Russian outside of Russia," but the success of his cause depended on the writers in Russia. "It is your job to come up with material and get involved," Herzen admonished. "Send what you wish, and everything written in a spirit of freedom will be printed, from scientific and fact-based articles on statistics and history to novels, stories, and verse. We are even ready to print these materials for free. . . . Whether you want to make use of it or not will be on your conscience. If we receive nothing from Russia it will not be our fault. If tranquility is dearer to you than free speech—keep silent."[35]

The establishment of Herzen's London-based publishing house was made possible by the experience and encouragement of his Polish comrades-in-arms, including Adam Mickiewicz and Joachim Lelewel, whose slogan "For our freedom and yours" (*Za naszą i waszą wolność*), coined during the Polish-Lithuanian uprising of 1830–1831 against Russian rule, inspired Herzen to adopt it as the political credo of his own oppositionist activity two decades later.[36] In his call "To Our Brethren in Russia," Herzen turns to the Polish example: "Ask what is being done by our Polish brothers, who are more oppressed than we are. Haven't they sent everything they wanted to Poland for the past twenty-five years, avoiding the lines of police and the nets of informers? And now, true to their great banner on which is written: 'For our freedom and yours,' they extended a hand to us."[37] For his call to be heard and produce an effect in Russia, Herzen had to wait two years for the new monarch, Alexander II, to succeed Nicholas I, who died on March 2, 1855: until then, few Russian writers, intellectuals, or political thinkers dared send their manuscripts abroad for publication. "The operations of the new Press," wrote Martin Malia, himself an active contributor to tamizdat operations a century later, "were at first modest. There was almost nothing to publish but Herzen's own productions, and very little got through to Russia before 1856. Still, the essential had been accomplished: a free forum for Russian opinion had at least been established, and it would grow into a major political force under the more liberal conditions of the next reign."[38] Of course, it was not only political freedom but also economic opportunities in Europe, especially in Paris and London, the main hub of the Polish political opposition throughout the nineteenth and twentieth centuries, that facilitated the operations of Herzen's Free Russian Press, until *Kolokol* and the rest of its publications gradually lost popularity in Russia and by 1867 ceased to exist.[39] This remarkable alliance of Russian and Polish publishers in exile, assisted by institutions of their host countries in Europe, was destined to play out on a much larger scale a hundred years later.

Herzen could not have imagined, of course, what resonance his name and the title of his monthly *Kolokol* were fated to acquire for the Soviet intelligentsia in the second half of the twentieth century, to say nothing of the roles of Nicholas I and Stalin in suppressing the freedom of speech in their respective Russias. On January 9, 1963, suspecting a change for the worse in the political climate after a few "warm" years, an old literary scholar and former political prisoner Yulian Oksman lamented in a letter to Gleb Struve, an émigré professor of Russian literature at Berkeley, "What had been needed in 1937–42 was 'another Kolokol' (The Bell). Perhaps an organ of this type . . . is what we need now, too. But there is no Herzen and no Ogarev, nor any of that intelligentsia who supported them so generously on the continent."[40] As a focal point of both historical nostalgia and academic research, Herzen loomed large in the consciousness of both the older and younger generations of Soviet intellectuals and dissidents, as suggested by the title of a samizdat journal in Leningrad in 1965 (*Kolokol*),[41] and by the following passage from the memoirs of Anatoly Marchenko, who describes a night transfer to the Vladimir prison where in the early 1960s he went on his first in a series of hunger strikes: "I remembered reading how Herzen, before his departure abroad, used to stand on the balcony of his house here in Vladimir and watch the convicts, all in chains, being driven along the famous 'Vladimir road'—'from Russia to the wastes of Siberia.' I remembered Levitan's 'Vladimir Road,'" Marchenko added. "Probably that well-beaten road, trodden down by the feet of convicts, no longer existed. Nor did the chains. Nobody would see us and no one remember us, except for our jailers. And there was no contemporary Levitan or Herzen to tell the world about our prison convoys in the year 1961."[42]

The reasons for Herzen's popularity in Soviet Russia during and after the Thaw had as much to do with his political and publishing activity abroad as with the genre of his own magnum opus, *Byloe i Dumy* (*My Past and Thoughts*, 1852–1868). As Paperno points out, Herzen's autobiography "has been evoked as an immediate inspiration and a model for imitation by practically every Soviet memoirist [who] thought of his or her autobiographical writings as *My Past and Thoughts* or has read the writings of another in this key."[43] Conceived of as a life journey through nineteenth-century Russia unconfined to its geographical borders, Herzen's autobiography "helped to create . . . an intimate circle of intellectuals alienated from the state and society who felt bound by a sense of their social and historical mission," which defined the identity of the Russian intelligentsia.[44] Moreover, the form of *My Past and Thoughts* seemed "easy to imitate" and offered "an illusion of conversation that involves the reader."[45] Herzen's role in giving a voice to his like-minded contemporaries in tsarist Russia, and by historical proxy to the Soviet generation of nonconformist writers and intellectuals, paved the way for a remarkable revival of documentary prose, so much so that from the 1960s forward the Russian literary landscape, both official and underground, became flooded with memoirs and other autobiographical texts, including diaries, whether retrieved from the past or newly written. It was then, at the juncture of the Thaw and the Stagnation eras, that the Soviet intelligentsia, reawakened by the inescapable parallels between Herzen's times and its own, yet again realized its momentous entanglement in history and found itself at a crossroads.[46]

Yet the differences between Herzen's times and the Soviet era were also obvious. After defecting to the West in 1968, Arkady Belinkov, a writer, literary scholar, and former political prisoner, embarked on compiling *Novyi kolokol* (*The New Bell*), a publication initially conceived as a periodical.[47] Two years after the first and only issue of *Novyi kolokol* finally came out in 1972, however, Gleb Struve questioned the validity of the historical lineage suggested by the almanac's title and claimed that *Novyi kolokol* "was inexpertly edited, was rather uneven, and did not resemble a journal, let alone Herzen's *Kolokol*, thus perhaps confirming Oksman's bitter earlier statement about the absence of Herzens in our days."[48] Not that the editors of *Novyi kolokol* had such aspirations.

Admitting how far "we have departed from Herzen's times," the editorial preface states, "We are aware of the extent to which our edition differs from its famous precursor. . . . We are continuing the tradition of *Kolokol* only as far as free press without censorship beyond the confines of our homeland is concerned."[49] While the formal aspects of tamizdat in the Soviet era continued to be inflected with Herzen's nineteenth-century example, it was obvious that "what has been and is happening in Soviet Russia . . . is an entirely new phenomenon."[50] Indeed, according to Andrei Sinyavsky, the very notion of dissidence "grew directly from the soil of the Soviet reality," so much so that even though Akhmatova, Pasternak, and Mandelshtam were "heretics in Soviet literature" and thus "anticipated dissent," "one cannot call them dissidents for the simple reason that their roots go back to bygone, prerevolutionary traditions of Russian culture."[51] Still, it was precisely the bygone, prerevolutionary precedent of Herzen that inspired authors in Soviet Russia and their tamizdat publishers in the West.

An entire publishing house that bore Herzen's name, the Alexander Herzen Foundation, was established in 1969 in Amsterdam by Karel van het Reve, Peter Reddaway, and Jan Willem Bezemer. Its mission "to publish manuscripts written in the USSR which cannot be published there because of censorship" was "a much needed response . . . to the wishes of various Soviet citizens who would like their manuscripts to be published under independent and scholarly auspices."[52] Unlike most émigré publishers, who were reluctant or unable to pay honoraria to their authors in Russia, the Herzen Foundation, run by Western Slavists, promised that "two thirds of the money received from royalties is used to pay the Foundation's authors when possible, to keep in trust for them when necessary."[53] Far from being financially lucrative (except perhaps for such literary sensations as Solzhenitsyn's *The Gulag Archipelago*), tamizdat was nevertheless an opportunity to convert the symbolic capital of contraband manuscripts to economic gain. Whether the authors in Russia received any remuneration was another matter: copyright, like other property, belonged to the state, and international money wires to the Soviet Union were hardly an option, which meant that tamizdat yielded only symbolic capital, unless the author subsequently emigrated or received royalties illegally.[54] In fact, financial gain often brought its authors material losses, social ostracism, and even prison time. Still, the economic potential of tamizdat depended on the symbolic capital the author had managed to accumulate back home as an outspoken dissident or a classic whose works were banned or otherwise unavailable.

The economic opportunity of what would become tamizdat was pursued by none other than Lev Tolstoy, whose novel *Resurrection* (illustrated, incidentally, by Leonid Pasternak, father of the author of *Doctor Zhivago*) was first published in uncensored form in England in 1899.[55] The publication was handled by the writer's friend and editor, Vladimir Chertkov, who had been exiled from Russia a few years earlier and settled in London, where he founded his publishing house Free Word (Svobodnoe slovo) in part as a fundraising campaign to help the Dukhobors, a religious community supported by Tolstoy and persecuted by the tsarist government for its members' rejection of the Orthodox Church and refusal to serve in the army.[56] Tolstoy's decision to abort the publication of his unorthodox novel in the Petersburg journal *Niva*, where it was serialized in a heavily censored form from March through December 1899, was informed not only by financial but also by ideological considerations. But it took a writer like Tolstoy to align the symbolic and the economic capitals by publishing abroad, an accomplishment matched in the twentieth century perhaps only by Solzhenitsyn. In London (and then in Christchurch, where he moved in 1890), Chertkov, assisted by Tolstoy's biographer Pavel Biriukov, published ten volumes of *Collected Works by Lev Tolstoy Banned in Russia*, as well as two periodicals, *Svobodnoe slovo* (Free Word, 1901–1905) and *Svobodnaia mysl'* (Free Thought, 1899–1901). Unlike Herzen, who died in Paris in 1870 without living to see his name rehabilitated in Russia, Chertkov returned from exile in 1908 to be lauded a decade later by the new regime for his anti-tsarist activity.[57] In 1918, as the sole heir of Tolstoy's copyright, Chertkov embarked on the state-sponsored project of publishing Tolstoy's ninety-volume complete works, overseen by the People's Commissariat for Education and Anatoly Lunacharsky personally. Chertkov died in 1936. At the suggestion of Stalin his funeral was organized by the Politburo of the VKP(b). Ironically, the anti-tsarist activity of the Decembrists, Herzen, Chertkov, and Tolstoy were now celebrated by the new regime.

A year after the first volume of Tolstoy's complete works came out in Soviet Russia in 1928, two other writers, Boris Pilniak and Evgeny Zamiatin, came under attack for allowing their works to be published in Europe. By 1921 the state had monopolized book publishing in the newly charted Soviet territory. It successfully maintained this policy until perestroika, except for the years of NEP (New Economic Policy) in the 1920s, when private entrepreneurship, including book publishing, was briefly allowed. Needless to say, this monopoly entailed not only ideological but also economic consequences for the writers. As Zamiatin put it in his 1921 confrontational article "I Am Afraid" ("Ia boius'"), the choice he and his fellow Russian writers were now facing was between becoming "nimble" (*iurkii*), like the Futurists, or loyally serving the state. "Today," Zamiatin wrote, "Gogol would have to run with a briefcase to the theater section; Turgenev would, no doubt, be translating Balzac and Flaubert for 'World Literature'; Herzen would teach at Baltflot; Chekhov would work for Komzdrav. Or else, . . . Gogol would have to write four 'Inspectors General' a month, Turgenev—three 'Fathers and Sons' every two months, and Chekhov—a hundred short stories a month." Under such circumstances, he concluded, "I am afraid that Russian literature has only one future: its past."[58] Of course, state control of book publishing in Russia in 1921 could not be compared to the One State's total control of all spheres of life in Zamiatin's famous dystopian novel *We* (*My*), which was banned in Russia at its completion the same year.

Meanwhile, NEP and the consolidated endeavors of the Russian diaspora in Berlin, the busiest outpost of Russian literature at the time, made it possible for Soviet writers to publish abroad (while the émigrés could, conversely, publish in Russia). As rumor had it, there were more Russian than German publishing houses and periodicals in post–World War I Berlin, due to the unprecedented inflation that made publishing cheap. Moreover, writers who had fled the Bolshevik terror were now free, for a while, to go back, as did Victor Shklovsky, for example, when he sensed that the "heartbeat" of the Russian emigration was dying out. What mattered was not where the writers published or even lived but the political content of what they wrote. If the term had existed then, tamizdat as such was hardly a transgression during NEP.

The storm broke in August 1929, when Pilniak and Zamiatin were assaulted on the pages of *Literaturnaia gazeta* (*The Literary Gazette*) by Boris Volin, a member of the Russian Association of Proletarian Writers (RAPP), who proclaimed those writers' publications abroad "unacceptable phenomena" (the title of Volin's feuilleton).[59] Pilniak's novella *Krasnoe derevo* (*Mahogany*) was printed in Berlin in 1929 by Petropolis, a publishing house that specialized in works by Soviet authors. As for Zamiatin's *We*, by that time it had already appeared in foreign-language translations, but in the spring of 1927, excerpts from the original

FIGURE 0.2.   Evgeny Zamiatin. *My*. New York: Izdatel'stvo imeni Chekhova, 1952. Cover of the first book edition.

Russian were published in the Prague-based émigré monthly *Volia Rossii* (Russia's Will).[60] In his introduction the journal editor, Mark Slonim, stated that he was publishing *We* in reverse translation from Czech (evidently, to protect Zamiatin against the authorities in Russia). Moreover, as Slonim confessed decades later, to make his statement more credible, "I had deliberately changed and rewritten a few passages" from the original manuscript at his disposal.[61] Unlike Pilniak's *Mahogany*, this publication of *We* was, strictly speaking, unauthorized, and so the main target of Volin's attack was not Zamiatin but Pilniak. Besides, Pilniak's rank in the Soviet literary establishment as chairman of the All-Russia

Union of Writers was higher than Zamiatin's, who was merely the secretary of its Leningrad branch.

Volin's invective in 1929 would set the tone for later Soviet condemnations of tamizdat. He lamented that "émigré newspapers and petty journals are preying on our literature" and was indignant at the fact that "Soviet writers, whose works are reprinted by the White Guard press, have never bothered to protest it. . . . How could Pilniak have given them his novel? Did he not realize he was thus striking up a relationship with an organization that is evil and hostile to the land of Soviets? And if the émigrés published his novel without his knowledge or against his will, why did Pilniak, head of the All-Russia Union of Writers, not protest?" Volin concluded that "this series of absolutely unacceptable phenomena, which compromise Soviet literature," should be unconditionally condemned by "the entire Soviet society."[62]

A public condemnation of the "unacceptable phenomena" immediately ensued, prompting Vladimir Mayakovsky to claim a week later that although he "has read neither *Mahogany* nor any other works by Pilniak," he considered his novel to be "a weapon," and the fact that Pilniak had "surrendered" it to the émigrés—an act of "strengthening the enemy's arsenal." "Today," Mayakovsky added, "when the clouds are getting thicker and thicker, it equals treason on the frontlines. . . . Who gave him confidence that a genius has the right to class exterritoriality [*eksterritorial'nost'*]?"[63] As a key concept of the newly instituted ideology, class consciousness thus acquired a geographical dimension that could henceforth incriminate any author who dared publish abroad, violating the state's monopoly on publishing. Mayakovsky's bashing critique of Pilniak would be repeated almost verbatim three decades later during the campaign against Pasternak in 1958, when the author of *Doctor Zhivago* was expelled from the Soviet Writers' Union and narrowly escaped being physically banished from the country, having been awarded the Nobel Prize, which he was pressed to reject.[64] In 1929, however, Pilniak remained a widely published Soviet writer. This changed in 1937, when he was arrested, tried as a Japanese spy, and shot on April 21, 1938. As for Zamiatin, he published an open letter to the editor of *Literaturnaia gazeta* in which he refused "to be part of a literary organization that persecutes its own members."[65] Two years later he was allowed to emigrate (the permission was granted by Stalin personally, after Maksim Gorky interceded on his behalf). Zamiatin died in exile in Paris in 1937, having never renounced or been stripped of Soviet citizenship, unlike numerous authors of the post-Stalin period, who would also find themselves in exile as a consequence of publishing their "slanderous" works in tamizdat and expressing disagreement with the Soviet regime. The vicissitudes of the first publications of Zamiatin's dystopian novel abroad were such that one may go so far as to name it the first example of tamizdat as a literary practice and political institution of the Soviet era.

Anticipating predicaments of tamizdat in the late-Soviet era, the Pilniak and Zamiatin affair was, nevertheless, eclipsed by the more distant and hence romanticized example of Herzen from the mid-nineteenth century. In the consciousness of the Soviet intelligentsia of the Thaw, it was Herzen, not Pilniak or Zamiatin, who served as a source of inspiration and nursed historical nostalgia, as described in Zygmunt Bauman's terms as a variety of "retrotopia."[66]

Tamizdat from the Thaw to Stagnation

The manuscripts explored in this book were first published abroad before the dissident movement was born in Russia, i.e., before samizdat crystallized into a tool of political opposition largely in response to the trial of Sinyavsky and Daniel. The dissident movement was born on December 5, 1965, at the first Glasnost meeting on Pushkin Square in Moscow, when it was demanded that the trial of the two writers be made public.[67] As a result, nonconformist Russian literature was married to the dissident movement, so much so that in the public imagination they remained virtually inseparable from each other for the rest of the Soviet era, both in Russia and abroad. By 1968, when Solzhenitsyn's novels *Cancer Ward* and *In the First Circle* were published abroad after the author fell out of favor with the authorities at home, after Aleksandr Ginzburg and his "accomplices" were arrested and tried for circulating materials on the trial of Sinyavsky and Daniel in samizdat and publishing them in Germany,[68] after seven other dissidents walked onto Red Square to protest the Soviet invasion of Czechoslovakia on August 25, 1968—by this time, the dissident movement had matured and spread to the West (its main bulletin, *The Chronicle of Current Events*, founded in 1968, was reprinted in tamizdat beginning in 1974).[69] Yet until the dissidents entered the political arena with leaflets and public appeals, fact-based reports, open letters, and signed petitions, it was fiction and poetry that served not only as a means of coming to terms with the Stalinist past (and of trying to prevent the country from slipping back into it after the overthrow of Khrushchev in 1964), but also as the main tool of political opposition through literary means. In other words, un-til the late 1960s, the hottest books of the Cold War were fiction and poetry, including, oddly, Brodsky's lyrical verses and the "fantastic" prose of Sinyavsky and Daniel. The writings of such heavyweights as Akhmatova, Chukovskaia, and Shalamov, for that matter, cannot be described as dissident literature either, despite their enormous politi-cal import.

However influential the example of Herzen's nineteenth-century autobiography had been even earlier, the unprecedented popularity of memoirs during the Thaw was also sparked indirectly by the trial of Sinyavsky and Daniel and can, therefore, be ascribed to the rise of the dissident movement. According to Benjamin Nathans, who treats Soviet dis-sident life writing as "a transnational platform for the presentation of an alternative Soviet self on a global stage,"[70] the memoirs by dissidents and gulag survivors in particular that engulfed the Russian literary land-scape in the late 1960s on, "faced a dual estrangement: from the author's native land and from a Western readership eager to extract familiar Cold War lessons from the unfamiliar landscape of post-totalitarian social-ism."[71] The increasing popularity of the autobiographical genre fueled the tendency of tamizdat publishers and readers to treat fiction and even poetry from the USSR as nonfiction at best or as mere sources of information on life behind bars at worst, a tendency that revealed itself perhaps most vividly in the history of the first publication and reception of Shalamov's Kolyma Tales abroad (see chapter 4).

In his Nobel lecture in 1970, which he was unable to deliver in per-son, Solzhenitsyn declared that "today there is a mutual reaction be-tween the writers of one country and the readers and writers of another, which if not immediate is at least close to it."[72] In the early 1960s, how-ever, this "mutual reaction" between writers in Russia and their pub-lishers, readers, and fellow authors in the West was not so much weaker as it was of a different institutional nature. Until the 1970s there were hardly any Russian publishing houses abroad that were not financed by the CIA and its covert projects, whose role in orchestrating tamiz-dat was perhaps matched only by the role of the KGB in keeping the Soviet literary canon politically upright.[73] There were, likewise, virtu-ally no publishing houses independent of the political agenda of the old emigration, whose horizons of expectations affected the manner in which manuscripts from the Soviet Union were first published and read. In truth, it was only via the joint operations of Russian emigration and Western institutions, including the secret services, that tamizdat took shape. But it was not until the early 1970s that the paradigms of reception of Russian literature from behind the Iron Curtain began to shift in the West, when the Third Wave began to arrive, bringing with it not only new manuscripts but also a profoundly different, firsthand knowledge of Soviet literature, language, and culture, including experiences in the gulag where much of this language and culture had been tempered.

The most significant tamizdat press of the new generation was Ardis, founded by Carl and Ellendea Proffer in Ann Arbor, Michigan, in the spring of 1971, two years after their trip to Russia where the idea to start the publishing house was conceived. Ardis was not only the first American publishing house of caliber that printed works of Russian literature without the direct support of federal or even academic institutions; it was also the first tamizdat press that specialized in Russian literature but was not run by émigrés.[74] In Brodsky's words, Carl Proffer, a native of the American Midwest, "did to Russian literature what the Russians themselves would have liked to do but could not," an achievement the Russian poet compared to Gutenberg's invention.[75] Unlike its older émigré counterparts, such as the YMCA-Press in Paris and Possev in Frankfurt, Ardis had neither a religious nor a political bend, which often repelled younger authors like Brodsky. Thanks to Ardis and its network of couriers and professional editors, some of whom had recently emigrated from Russia, tamizdat became not only textually more reliable but also "psychologically infinitely more appealing, trustworthy and intimate to the remaining writers and readers in the USSR"[76] than it had ever been under the auspices of the old generation of publishers. From its inception in 1971 and throughout the rest of the Soviet period, Ardis provided a more attractive alternative for those authors in Russia who no longer entertained the idea of publishing in gosizdat, partly because the regime under Brezhnev and then Andropov was increasingly tightened, partly because it was simply official.

The name of the publishing house came from Nabokov's novel *Ada*, which the Proffers had read during their stay in Russia in 1969: "*Ada* had a special place in our memories, tied to that hotel, that winter, and our desperate desire to read something new in English to offset the power of the Russian world we were exploring. Something to remind us, perhaps, that we came from the English language—the irony being that the novel was written by a Russian émigré."[77] Apart from inheriting the name of Nabokov's fictional estate, that "mythical place blending features of both Russia and America . . . transformed by Nabokov's own love for the estates of his childhood,"[78] Ardis reprinted Nabokov's works originally written in Russian, which were the most sought-for literary contraband in the Soviet Union. Lev Loseff, himself an Ardis editor following his emigration from Russia in 1976, remarked that, indeed, "for the Russian intelligentsia, this real Ardis would take on the same mythical stature as Nabokov's imaginary estate,"[79] a junction of the writer's two countries, languages, and careers.

The logo of a horse-drawn carriage on the title pages of Ardis books, adopted from a woodcut by Vladimir Favorsky, alluded to Pushkin's famous definition of translators as the "post horses of enlightenment." In the case of Ardis, however, the image acquired more literal meaning than Pushkin could have intended: before they could be even published, let alone translated, the manuscripts first had to be smuggled out, and in this sense, "Ardis indeed became a stage-coach covering a vast, at times very hostile territory."[80] As before, in the 1970s tamizdat involved an entire network of actors "harnessed" to the affair (which now included, as Brodsky joked, the Proffers' own children who "confused the KGB surveillance by running in all possible directions, hiding important mail in their parkas and in general creating a great commotion"). But the way Ardis handled this multistage operation was different from how it was done by the majority of its older émigré peers not only financially but also ideologically. Ardis's mission to publish Russian literature as works of art, not anti-Soviet propaganda, coupled with the cultural baggage of the Third Wave with which it allied and historically overlapped, derived from a different sociopolitical impulse compared to what motivated even the most sensible tamizdat publishers of the old generation. In January 1969, preparing for their trip to Russia, the Proffers "stopped in New York City on the way and had a series of crucial meetings in Manhattan bars. Gleb Struve, a famous émigré literary scholar, met us in the first bar," Ellendea Proffer Teasley recalls, "and declared that we should abandon our trip because the Soviets had violently repressed the revolt in Czechoslovakia the previous year: it was immoral, in his view, to even visit the Soviet Union. But nothing could change our minds. We were tired of the polarities of the Cold War, we wanted to see the Soviet Union and decide for ourselves. We were not proud of our own country as it struggled with civil rights for African-Americans and bombed civilians in Cambodia and Vietnam, and this had the effect of making us question Cold War attitudes."[81]

While the older generation of tamizdat publishers often refused to acknowledge Ardis as its ally or legitimate heir and saw it instead as a competitor, it was then that the ideological and stylistic binaries of the Cold War started giving way.[82] The confrontations of Ardis and the Third Wave with the older tamizdat ventures, e.g., Boris Filippov's Inter-Language Literary Associates, were not only ideological and generational, but also aesthetic. The tensions reached their climax in the 1970s, when the old Russian emigration faced newcomers from the Soviet Union, such as Brodsky, some of whose manuscripts they had first published only a few years prior but who were now reluctant to remain their "clientele" and adulterously defected to Ardis; others established their own publications, such as Sergei Dovlatov's *Novyi amerikanets* (*The New American*), a rival to the oldest Russian émigré newspaper *Novoe russkoe slovo* (*New Russian Word*), which had been in business since 1910.[83] Still others, like Solzhenitsyn, stayed faithful to the old YMCA-Press in Paris, which, it should be noted, published both émigré and non-émigré authors alike regardless of their generation or aesthetics.[84] An even more varied repertoire of titles was offered by the Frankfurt-based Possev and its journal *Grani* (*Facets*), which was affiliated with the National Alliance of Russian Solidarists (NTS), the most odious anticommunist organization.

In the eyes of the Soviet establishment, Ardis, on the other hand, was a more innocent enterprise partly because nearly half its titles were in English, including translations of works by "reliable" Soviet authors and scholarly monographs on Russian literature. "Although confrontations with the Soviet authorities were obviously unavoidable, Ardis nevertheless did not fit the paradigm of Russian-language publishing houses in the West, most of which were products of the Cold War."[85] According to Ellendea Proffer's own account, "the English translations were what made the authorities hesitate to ban us, because we were translating works by Soviet writers (Trifonov, Nagibin, Rasputin, etc.), something they very much valued; thus we were labeled a 'complex phenomenon,' which meant we were to be watched but not interfered with."[86] This meant that, unlike the émigrés who left Russia with a one-way ticket, the Proffers could travel to the Soviet Union and even participate in Moscow book fairs. It was thanks to their personal friendships and direct contacts with the authors in Russia that Ardis "absorbed influences from several informal literary circles in Moscow and Leningrad."[87] However, this changed in 1979 when Ardis brought out *Metropol*, an almanac that "was not meant to be political, but its very nature marked it as such in the Soviet context."[88] From then and until perestroika, the Proffers' visa applications were denied. Carl, who died in 1984, never saw Russia again. But the inflow of manuscripts they continued to receive from the Soviet Union was neither interrupted nor even reduced.

The *Metropol* affair unearthed a new attitude among Russian authors to the artificial bifurcation of Russian literature into the official and underground fields, a division they no longer considered valid and were ready to challenge. While the dissident movement since its inception in the late 1960s, according to Serguei Oushakine's diagnosis, was remarkable, among other things, "not only because of [its] dissent but also because of the very Soviet expression of [the dissidents'] political disagreement,"[89] Evgeny Popov, one of the editors of *Metropol*, claimed that "for him, much dissident literature was just 'socialist realism in reverse,' and equally bad, and that he found dissidents to be 'characters'

FIGURE 0.3. *Metropol'. Literaturnyi al'manakh.* Ann Arbor, MI: Ardis, 1979.

just as much as dedicated Communists were."[90] To break away from the Cold War binaries, Popov, who "never had any desire to identify as a dissident and never wanted to leave the Soviet Union [or] publish abroad, because he was afraid of becoming a typical tamizdat writer," coined a new term to refer to *Metropol*: *zdes'izdat* ("here-publishing"), which stood for "legitimate publishing within the Soviet Union but outside the boundaries set by censors, editors, the Writers' Union, and dissidents."[91] In the words of *Metropol*'s other editor, Vasily Aksenov, the "authorities were far less upset by the content of the almanac than by our action, our solidarity, and our disregard for the usual official channels."[92] Ironically, however, despite the editors' "desire to assume a third position in a world of binaries," today *Metropol* is still "remembered less for its artistic quality than for the challenge it posed to the literary ecosystem."[93] Indeed, when it was brought out by Ardis, first in Russian and then in the English translation,[94] its claim to fame was based, by inertia, on its contributors' reputations as dissidents silenced at home.[95] But while the West praised *Metropol* contributors for their courage and nonconformism, the old generation of Russian émigrés refused to acknowledge even that. Instead, they branded the almanac as obscene and vulgar. "The émigré newspaper *Russian Thought* [*Russkaia mysl'*]," Popov concluded, "made the same criticism of the collection that Feliks Kuznetsov [at the time, first secretary of the Moscow branch of the Writers' Union] had made, only from the other side; while for Kuznetsov the almanac was anti-Soviet, for *Russian Thought* it was Soviet, base, soulless, not in line with the émigré idea of 'good' literature, which had to adhere to specific aesthetic as well as political standards."[96] At the end of the day, "*Metropol*'s emphasis on openness, free speech, and the letter of the law, and its attempt, however quixotic, to achieve official publication . . . was very much in keeping with the practices of political dissidents of the 1970s." The démarche of *Metropol* can even be traced back to the origins of the dissident movement, with its call for *glasnost'* (publicity) in the affair of Sinyavsky and Daniel and demand to "Respect the Soviet constitution!"[97] Against its editors' better judgment, *Metropol* became, nonetheless, the most politically scandalous publication by Ardis.

And yet, compared to the early 1960s, the opportunities offered by Ardis and other tamizdat publishing houses of the new generation a decade later allowed, as Brodsky put it, "greater stylistic or philosophical maneuver in literature."[98] As a result, the line between "Soviet" and "émigré" Russian literature, on the one hand, and that between "official" and "underground" literature, on the other, became rather blurred. Although tamizdat always rendered these binaries more complex, it was not until Ardis and the new era in tamizdat publishing that it heralded that Russian literary criticism on both sides of the Curtain began to shift from playing up ideological differences to focusing on stylistic ones. In the early 1980s Sinyavsky claimed, half in jest, that his "disagreements with the Soviet government were basically aesthetic,"[99] while Brodsky intuited that "Russian literature gradually ceases to be divided into official and underground, and the former becomes somewhat modified by the very palpable pressure from the latter."[100] Only then did the literary climate, according to Brodsky, become "healthier" and start to "resemble the last quarter of the XIX century when there was no distinction between Russian books published abroad and inside the country. They were regarded as one literature—which they were."[101] The question of "one or two Russian literatures" raised in the 1920s by the First Wave of Russian emigration in Berlin and Paris became rhetorical: the answer was one. In 1978 the question inspired the eponymous conference in Geneva, where Maria Rozanova, Sinyavsky's wife and publishing partner, pointed out that what mattered now was no longer the ideological or geographical division of Russian literature into Soviet and émigré, but the "linguistic, stylistic barrier" between the old and the new generations of the Russian emigration, on the one hand, and the old (prerevolutionary) and the new (Soviet) Russian literatures inside the country, on the other.[102] Three years later the same question was discussed at another conference of the Third Wave in Los Angeles, where Carl Proffer, who published émigré and non-émigré authors alike, as well as reprint editions of the Silver Age classics, spoke of "the remarkable decade that destroyed Russian émigré literature," implying that in the 1980s the Russian literary landscape should be categorized not as "émigré literature, and not Soviet literature, but simply Russian literature."[103]

A joint venture of Russian emigration and Western institutions, tamizdat remained firmly inscribed in Soviet literary history until the Curtain was lifted. The political mission of tamizdat then became obsolete. Having lost much of its politically oriented readership, tamizdat has retreated into history, prompting the writer Zinovy Zinik to claim that it is only now, beyond the political context, that the genuine literary motifs of exile and emigration (and, by extension, of tamizdat) have started floating to the surface: "In this sense, Russian émigré literature is only starting."[104] There is, however, another reason to look back at the years when tamizdat took shape: today, more than thirty years after the end of the Cold War, we are witnessing a resurgence of its rhetoric and, worse, reenactments of some of its most austere policies on both the international and local scales, culminating with the war in Ukraine.

Still, the post-Soviet "thaw" of the 1990s, as it may now be called, made tamizdat obsolete not only politically but also technologically. It introduced an entirely new path, or technique, for clandestine texts to "go live" bypassing not only state censorship, but also geographical borders, however open they may have become by the 1990s. From then on, geography and space itself seem to have hardly mattered as they have become virtual, while the time previously required by a typical tamizdat operation has also shrunk to just a few clicks. Yet while in the early days of the Internet "cyberspace seemed to be free and open" (the ultimate freedom of speech incarnate), today "it is being fought over, divided up, and closed off behind protective barriers,"[105] suggesting an eerie return to the geopolitical realities of the Cold War, when the world was divided. Tamizdat serves as a reminder that "the power of print could be as threatening as cyberwarfare."[106] In fact, it was more.

CHAPTER 1

Aleksandr Solzhenitsyn's *One Day in the Life of Ivan Denisovich* at Home and Abroad

The battle for salvaging the long-muffled voices of the gulag victims during the Thaw played out on domestic grounds, exposing the inherent indebtedness of tamizdat as a practice and institution to the political and cultural climate in Russia. Sparked by Khrushchev's "secret speech" in 1956 and fueled by the de-Stalinization campaign that followed, this battle reached its peak in the wake of the Twenty-second Party Congress in October 1961, culminating in the publication of Solzhenitsyn's *One Day in the Life of Ivan Denisovich* in the progressive Soviet journal *Novyi mir* the following year. The official publication of this sensational text became a turning point for Russian literary culture both at home and abroad, a crossroads of sorts between gosizdat, samizdat, and tamizdat. Revisiting this historical junction, which numerous Russian authors faced in 1961–1962, this chapter situates the success of *Ivan Denisovich* vis-à-vis the shared failure of other gulag narratives to see the light of day in Russia around the same time. Solzhenitsyn's breakthrough in the official Soviet press not only "emancipated" many other manuscripts on the subject, whether written before or after *Ivan Denisovich*, but also precluded them from being published at home, forcing them out of the official literary field first into the underground at home and eventually abroad, to tamizdat. The incontestable achievement of Solzhenitsyn, who managed to reach out to the general Soviet reader but did not have the means to tell the whole truth about the camps, was largely shaped by his text's ostensible conformity to socialist realism and Soviet mythology on the whole, whereby the key to the feat of *Ivan Denisovich* lay not in its subject matter, as was customary to think, but in its social and allegorical orchestration, as well as in the author's and his advocates' failsafe strategy to make the novella publishable, and the publication possible.

The Solzhenitsyn Momentum (1961–1962)

The life of Solzhenitsyn's most celebrated protagonist proved to be much longer than one day, a day that was meant to embrace his entire ten-year sentence in the gulag: "Just one of the 3,653 days of his sentence, from bell to bell. The extra three were for leap years."[1] It stretched, indeed, beyond the entire era of which this ordinary day in the life of one ordinary prisoner was designed to be both an artistic image and eyewitness testimony. A former peasant and Red Army soldier, Ivan Denisovich Shukhov was conceived in captivity in 1951, when his author was still serving his own term at the Ekibastuz camp for political prisoners in northern Kazakhstan. Shukhov, who left for the front on the first day of war only to be sentenced to ten years of hard labor for the sole "crime" of being captured by the Germans, saw the light of day on the pages of the eleventh issue of *Novyi mir* on November 17, 1962. His birth, according to Kornei Chukovsky, was a "literary miracle."[2] This miracle was assisted, first and foremost, by the journal's editor in chief, Aleksandr Tvardovsky; by Lev Kopelev and Raisa Orlova, who passed Solzhenitsyn's manuscript on to Tvardovsky through their mutual friend and editor Anna Berzer; by Khrushchev's personal assistant Vladimir Lebedev, who agreed to familiarize the First Secretary with this unusual text; and by Khrushchev himself, who personally sanctioned the publication. In his interview to the BBC on the occasion of the twentieth anniversary of *Ivan Denisovich*, Solzhenitsyn spoke of that historic moment as a matter of physics rather than history or literature: "The publication of my novella in the Soviet Union in 1962 defied the laws of physics, as if, for example, objects would start taking off from the ground by themselves, or cold stones would start by themselves heating up and glowing. It was impossible, absolutely impossible."[3] One wonders, however, why it was in fact possible for *Ivan Denisovich* to be published at home, and why only then, and what made it *impossible* for other nonconformist Russian authors to see their works on the same subject published in Russia around the same time?

Apart from its exploits at home, the publication of *Ivan Denisovich* generated a steady, virtually uninterrupted flow of contraband manuscripts from the Soviet Union to the West—so much so that tamizdat as a bridge between "two Russian literatures" (one at home, the other abroad), as well as a weapon on the literary fronts of the Cold War, took shape in earnest not after the publication of Pasternak's *Doctor Zhivago* in Italy in 1957, but after the publication of Solzhenitsyn's *Ivan Denisovich* in Russia five years later.[4] "Had this not happened," Solzhenitsyn confessed years later, "I would have sent a microfilm with my camp writings abroad under the pen name Stepan Khlynov, and such a microfilm had indeed been prepared."[5] But this scenario could not possibly have produced the effect that the publication of *Ivan Denisovich* had at home. That Solzhenitsyn's manuscript had not leaked abroad in the course of almost a year from its submission to *Novyi mir* until its publication in November 1962, was, in the author's words, "a miracle of no smaller significance than its publication in the USSR itself."[6] Soon enough, however, Solzhenitsyn's other works, including his novels *Cancer Ward* (*Rakovyi korpus*) and *In The First Circle* (*V kruge pervom*), as well as his magnum opus *The Gulag Archipelago* (*Arkhipelag GULag*), had to be smuggled out of Russia for publication abroad. Yet back in the early 1960s it was the semiliterate peasant Ivan Denisovich who was entrusted with the sacred mission of giving voice to the gulag topic. To translate the famous nineteenth-century adage into the Soviet context, Russian literature about the camps came out from Solzhenitsyn's padded jacket.[7]

According to yet another physics-inspired metaphor coined by Vladimir Voinovich, in 1961–1962 the events evolved as if by the laws of a pendulum: "Stalin's terror was one side of the amplitude, Khrushchev's Thaw gravitated towards the other. . . . The pendulum still moved in the direction of liberalization, but it was clear that it would soon reach its limit, and this limit—if published—would be Solzhenitsyn's anti-Stalinist work. Which is exactly what happened."[8] Indeed, the sweep of the pendulum was such that the dynamic within its field of operation was truly unprecedented. The Twenty-second Congress of the Party, with Khrushchev's critique of Stalin made public for the first time since 1956, took place on October 17–31, 1961. On November 10, 1961, Solzhenitsyn's manuscript was handed to Anna Berzer at the office of *Novyi*

FIGURE 1.1. Aleksandr Solzhenitsyn. *Arkhipelag GULAG. Opyt khudozhestvennogo issledovaniia. 1918–1956*. Vol. 1. Paris: YMCA-Press, 1973.

mir by Lev Kopelev's wife, Raisa Orlova. The manuscript was signed "A. Ryazansky," since Solzhenitsyn was still living and working at the time as a school teacher in Ryazan. It was titled *Shch-854*, Ivan Denisovich's number in his special camp for political prisoners. The manuscript was a "lightened" version of the original text, self-censored by the author earlier that year.[9] On December 8, 1961, when Tvardovsky was finally back from vacation, Berzer, bypassing the editor's deputies, handed him two manuscripts: *Sch-854* by Solzhenitsyn-Ryazansky and *Sofia Petrovna* by Lydia Chukovskaia. While the author of the latter work needed no introduction (everyone knew Chukovskaia's father, the famous critic, translator, and children's author Kornei Chukovsky), Solzhenitsyn's manuscript was presented to the editor as a "very national," or "plain-folk," work (*ochen' narodnaia veshch*), "the camps through the eyes of a peasant" (*lager' glazami muzhika*).[10] According to Solzhenitsyn, Berzer "could not have aimed more accurately at Tvardovsky's heart than she did in those few words," the reason being that "the muzhik Ivan Denisovich was bound to arouse the sympathy of the superior muzhik Tvardovsky and the supreme muzhik Nikita Khrushchev. . . . It was not poetry and not politics that decided the fate of my story, but that unchanging peasant nature, so much ridiculed, trampled underfoot and vilified in our country since the Great Break, and indeed earlier."[11]

Tvardovsky read the manuscript overnight. The next day, Kopelev wrote to Solzhenitsyn in Ryazan: "Aleksandr Trifonovich is delighted with the article" (a euphemism they devised to refer to the manuscript).[12] On December 11, 1962, Solzhenitsyn turned forty-three. That day, he received Tvardovsky's telegram with an invitation to come to Moscow, all expenses paid. They met at the office of *Novyi mir* the following day and signed the contract, with the advance payment alone exceeding two years' worth of Solzhenitsyn's salary as a math teacher.[13] (On his way to meet Tvardovsky in Moscow, Solzhenitsyn "superstitiously paused by Pushkin's statue . . . —partly to beg for his support, and partly to promise that I knew the path I must follow and would not stray from it.")[14] Although Tvardovsky had to warn the author that the publication was not yet set in stone, this first meeting between author and editor resulted in several changes to the already "lightened" version of *Shch-854*, including the title, which Solzhenitsyn regretted but had to accept.[15]

For the next nine months Tvardovsky secured support for the manuscript from such influential figures as Kornei Chukovsky, Samuil Marshak, Konstantin Paustovsky, and Konstantin Simonov, to name but a few. On August 6, 1962, accompanied by Tvardovsky's introduction and his personal letter to Khrushchev, the manuscript was handed over to Vladimir Lebedev, the First Secretary's personal assistant, who informed Tvardovsky on September 15 that Khrushchev had approved the publication, although the official decision still had to wait until the presidium of the Supreme Soviet convened a month later. On October 20, 1962, Khrushchev received Tvardovsky to tell him of the favorable outcome of the campaign, adding that although he found the text unusual, the manuscript did not leave him with a heavy feeling despite all the bitterness it contained: "I think this is a life-affirming piece [*zhizneutverzhdaiushchaia veshch*]," the First Secretary concluded.[16] On November 15, 1962, Tvardovsky received the advance copy of the eleventh issue of *Novyi mir*, and in two more days *One Day in the Life of Ivan Denisovich* was out, heralded by Konstantin Simonov's glowing prepublication review in the newspaper *Izvestiia* under the title "About the Past in the Name of the Future" ("O proshlom vo imia budushchego"). The print run of the *Novyi mir* issue was 96,900 copies, two thousand of which were delivered to the Kremlin for the participants of the plenum of the Central Committee scheduled to open in several days. Twenty-five thousand additional copies were printed at the request of the Supreme Soviet. Early the following year the novella appeared in two separate editions of 700,000 and 100,000 copies.[17] When Solzhenitsyn fell out of favor with the authorities and was exiled from Russia in February 1974, all publications of *Ivan Denisovich*, as well as his other works, were withdrawn from official circulation. But in 1962 the total of nearly one million copies was still not enough to satiate the demand of Soviet readers, who began retyping the text of *Ivan Denisovich* on their personal typewriters.[18]

Despite its unfathomable success, the immediate effect of Solzhenitsyn's publication lasted less than two weeks: on December 1, 1962, Khrushchev made his famous appearance at the Manezh Exhibition of avant-garde artists in Moscow, where his pronouncements equaled a pogrom, which drew the Thaw to an end. Throwing obscenities at the artists and their canvases ("a donkey wags its tail better," were the words recalled by Ernst Neizvestnyi),[19] Khrushchev referred to *Ivan Denisovich* as the ultimate model for Soviet artists:

> Here is a work of literature. Solzhenitsyn did write about terrible things after all, didn't he? But he wrote from life-affirming perspectives. Here is a prisoner, their time is up, and they still have

not used up the mortar that had been prepared; they are called to leave, but he says: how can we leave, it will all go to waste, let's use everything and then leave. Here is a man who was unjustly convicted, rejected, battered, but he keeps thinking about life, about the mortar. What does he need this mortar for, when he himself has been turned into mortar? Here is a work about terrible things, about injustice, and this man still pays back with kindness. But he strained himself not for those who treated him like this; he strained himself for the future. He lived there as a prisoner, but looked with his eyes [sic!] onto the future.[20]

Equating the author with his fictional character, Khrushchev was enchanted by Solzhenitsyn's humble peasant Ivan Denisovich, whom he took for an ally in his crusade against Stalinism. On December 17, 1962, a month after *Ivan Denisovich* appeared in *Novyi mir*, Solzhenitsyn was invited to Khrushchev's meeting with the intelligentsia at the Kremlin "as the main birthday boy," though he was overcome with anxiety that the attack on the artists at the Manezh and "the inertia of the general turn would take a toll on camp literature too."[21] Indeed, after the next meeting of the Party officials with the intelligentsia in March 1963, and after the plenum of the Central Committee on ideology and culture in June, the gulag topic was no longer allowed in the Soviet press. On October 14, 1964, Khrushchev was ousted, and the Thaw was replaced by Stagnation.

Still, the events that took place in the immediate aftermath of Solzhenitsyn's publication transformed the Russian literary landscape beyond recognition. Suffice it to say that even Anna Akhmatova, who had never before written down her *Requiem* and only recited it out loud to her closest friends, now decided not only to "declassify" her poem and for the first time commit it to paper but also to send it to the same journal that had published Solzhenitsyn. Chukovskaia's efforts to publish *Sofia Petrovna*, which she had written in 1939–1940 but kept secret until after the Twenty-second Party Congress, were even more relentless than Akhmatova's, albeit equally futile. Skeptical of publishing abroad, both Akhmatova and Chukovskaia hoped that after *Ivan Denisovich*, the process of liberalization in Russia would continue and that their works would also find their way into print. The publication of Solzhenitsyn's novella, in other words, was taken for the beginning of a new road supposed to pave the way for other manuscripts on Stalinism and the gulag. However, the road soon came to a dead end. What the Soviet intelligentsia realized but underestimated was that Akhmatova's *Requiem*, Chukovskaia's *Sofia Petrovna*, Shalamov's *Kolyma Tales*, and other such works stood too far from Solzhenitsyn's novella both socially and stylistically and that the unprecedented achievement of Solzhenitsyn's publication "was due not so much to the work's informational content as to its narrative art."[22] Solzhenitsyn had adjusted groundbreaking content to official Soviet standards, as well as to Tvardovsky's personal and social background as a Soviet writer, editor, and citizen.

What stood behind Tvardovsky's infatuated support for *Ivan Denisovich* and his rejection of the manuscripts of Akhmatova, Chukovskaia, Ginzburg, Shalamov, and other authors that kept accumulating in the vault of his *Novyi mir* office? Unlike the protagonists of these texts, Solzhenitsyn's Ivan Denisovich was, no doubt, a closer progeny of Tvardovsky's own Vasily Terkin, a spirited and resourceful soldier who had earned his author a Stalin Prize for Literature in 1946. A "crafty and cunning but essentially moral picaresque hero in the Russian folk tradition (clearly a brother of Vasily Terkin)," as Michael Scammell defined him,[23] Ivan Denisovich resonated on an even deeper level with the reincarnated hero of Tvardovsky's anti-Stalinist sequel *Vasily Terkin in the Other World* (which, incidentally, could only be published after *Ivan Denisovich*).[24] By that time, Tvardovsky had finished another narrative poem, *Far Far Away* (*Za dal'iu dal'*, 1953–1960), with a separate chapter, "A Childhood Friend," devoted to the return of the gulag survivors from the camps. In this chapter, the narrator encounters a childhood friend with whom he used to "shepherd cattle in the field together" [*s kem my pasli skotinu v pole*], "light bonfires in the forest" [*palili v zales'e kostry*], and from whom, until a certain point, he was inseparable.[25] The two friends shared not only childhood memories but the entire period of Soviet history that came between them throughout their seventeen years apart: Tvardovsky's protagonist claims to have been with his friend "behind that wall" [*ia s drugom byl za toi stenoiu*], "known everything" [*i vedal vse*], and "eaten that bread" [*i khleb tot el*] (3: 261). He is certain that his friend, too, throughout his years in the gulag, had "known the same joys and miseries" [*i te zhe radosti i bedy / dushoi synovnei vedal on*] as the rest of the Soviet people, including the war and the victory, and that he had never blamed his motherland or fellow countrymen for what had happened to him [*Vinit' v svoei bede bezglasnoi / Stranu? / Pri chem zhe zdes' strana!*] (3: 262). Although Solzhenitsyn was not a childhood friend of Tvardovsky's, as one émigré critic assumed,[26] the fate of Solzhenitsyn's unjustly convicted protagonist

Ivan Denisovich could not but evoke Tvardovsky's personal and professional sympathy.

For Tvardovsky the terror of collectivization was inseparable from
the Great Terror of the late 1930s. To be fair, few gulag authors whose
manuscripts he rejected sufficiently emphasized the collectivization
campaign, while the plight of the peasants in Solzhenitsyn's novella,
"when they rounded everybody's horses up for the kolkhoz,"[27] serves
as the inescapable background of all Shukhov's misfortunes. It may be
for this reason that Tvardovsky rejected Evgenia Ginzburg's memoir
Journey into the Whirlwind, which opens with the sentence: "The year
1937 began, to all intents and purposes, at the end of 1934—to be exact, on the first of December,"[28] that is, the day of Kirov's assassination
in Leningrad, which triggered the Party purges and the Great Terror.
Driven by the moral imperative to rehabilitate the peasants, who were
not known for writing their own accounts of Stalinism despite being
the largest social group in the entire population of the gulag, Tvardovsky believed that Stalin's crimes should be traced back to the years of
collectivization, i.e., the late 1920s and early 1930s, not 1934. Having
himself come into literature "from the people," Tvardovsky looked for
new talents among authors who possessed "extensive life experience yet
[were] unengaged with the literary profession."[29] While this otherwise
noble mission may have stemmed from the classical nineteenth-century
Russian literary tradition, Tvardovsky only kept hushing authors who
had been condemned to silence in the 1930s. At the time he must
have read more manuscripts about the camps than anyone else in the
country, and he was especially attuned to so-called human documents
(*chelovecheskie dokumenty*), i.e., eyewitness accounts with a testimonial
quality. The essence of Tvardovsky's literary effort was "the search for
authenticity—historical, moral, and linguistic," and Solzhenitsyn's
work, as Denis Kozlov rightly noted, "set a standard below which the
editor did not want to descend," although this standard had clearly
been "set long before he read Solzhenitsyn."[30] Solzhenitsyn's choice of
a peasant to speak out on behalf of the victims of the gulag was more
than a mere reminder that, statistically, the peasants suffered more than
the intelligentsia under Stalin. "The focus on the peasant" was dictated
by "a narrative function: the character of Ivan Denisovich is perfectly
suited for the exploration of the tensions between the individual and
communal concerns,"[31] which lies at the heart of gulag narratives as a
genre. "Free of the eccentricities that might undermine his representative status . . ., this peasant-craftsman is sufficiently endearing to invite

the reader's empathy,"[32] a feature that seemed particularly promising to Tvardovsky as he contemplated the effect that Ivan Denisovich was bound to produce on Soviet readers. Thus, the task of bearing witness to the gulag could only be entrusted to a *muzhik*. The function of the *muzhik*, however, extends beyond social class to gender. While the male protagonists in Shalamov's *Kolyma Tales* failed to meet the social prerequisite by representing the intelligentsia, not the peasants, the works of Akhmatova, Chukovskaia, and Ginzburg, among other "flaws," violated the gender condition—not only did they feature female protagonists, they were authored by women.

Ivan Denisovich and the Limits of the Admissible

Solzhenitsyn was not the first Russian author to introduce the gulag topic to the Soviet press. In 1956 *Novyi mir*, at the time spearheaded by Simonov, serialized Vladimir Dudintsev's novel *Not by Bread Alone* (*Ne khlebom edinym*), which Tvardovsky considered "not that important, or rather not that artistic,"[33] despite its immense yet short-lived popularity.[34] Before *Ivan Denisovich*, the February issue of *Novyi mir* (1962) published Veniamin Kaverin's "Seven Pairs of the Unclean" ("Sem' par nechistykh"). Set in the north of Russia at the beginning of the war, Kaverin's novella features a transport of prisoners onboard a military ship on their way to the camp. When the prisoners realize that the ship is carrying firearms, they plot to hijack it to Norway, but when the Germans attack, they team up with the guards to fight the enemy. The camps as such are absent from Kaverin's text. But they are mentioned in Evgeny Evtushenko's celebrated poem "The Heirs of Stalin" ("Nasledniki Stalina"), published in *Pravda* on October 21, 1962, less than a month before *Ivan Denisovich*. Finally, on November 5, 1962, the newspaper *Izvestiia*, edited by Khrushchev's son-in-law Aleksei Adzhubei, ran a short story by Georgy Shelest, "The Nugget" ("Samorodok"), about four Party members in one of Kolyma's gold mines, who find a large nugget of gold, but instead of stashing it, deliver it straight to the camp authorities, showing true patriotism when the country most needed it (the story is set in 1942).[35] Unlike Dudintsev, Kaverin, or Evtushenko, Shelest was a longtime political prisoner himself, which raised the stakes for Adzhubei in his rivalry with Tvardovsky for publishing the first work about the camps in the Soviet press. Back in the 1950s, when the gulag topic was still strictly hushed, a text like Shelest's could have perhaps produced some effect. But in November 1962 it failed to draw the reader's attention and went virtually unnoticed: the competition between Shelest and Solzhenitsyn that Adzhubei tried to insinuate thus came to naught.

In 1962, when the pendulum of the Thaw was at its zenith, it seemed that *Ivan Denisovich* could pave the road to publication not only for manuscripts on the gulag but also for those that dealt with other traumatic issues of the still recent past, such as the Great Patriotic War and the siege of Leningrad. Until Solzhenitsyn the theme of the war was not to be soiled by that of the camps, as is apparent from Mikhail Sholokhov's *Fate of a Man* (*Sud'ba cheloveka*, 1956), a short story about a Russian soldier, Andrei Sokolov, who spends not "a couple of days," like Ivan Denisovich, but two years in German captivity. However, unlike Solzhenitsyn's protagonist, not only is Sholokhov's character spared the gulag for this sole "crime," but he is even nominated for a military decoration. And while Sholokhov's account of Sokolov's two years as a POW, followed by his heroic escape, makes up nearly the entire narrative, Solzhenitsyn's description of Ivan Denisovich's two days with the Germans, followed by his ill-fated encounter with the Soviet counterespionage officers, is crammed into less than a page and only as a flashback. Brutally beaten and forced to confess that he had surrendered to the Germans to betray his country, Ivan Denisovich is given a simple choice: "Don't sign and dig your own grave, or sign and live a bit longer."[36] Sholokhov's soldier, on the contrary, is treated like a hero for capturing a high-ranking German officer and delivering him to the Soviet commanders. He gratefully recalls being "fed, taken to the bathhouse, questioned, and given a new uniform," and when he "appeared before the colonel in good shape, clean in body and soul," the colonel "put his arms around me and said: 'Thank you, soldier, for the fine present you brought us from the Germans. . . . I'll recommend you for a military decoration!'"[37]

In 1959 Vasily Grossman, a frontline correspondent throughout the war, completed his magnum opus *Life and Fate* (*Zhizn' i sud'ba*), which ran over the edge of the admissible, as it not only portrayed the Battle of Stalingrad in a new light but also drew parallels between Nazism and Communism. In 1961, the "warmest" year of the Thaw, Grossman's novel was "arrested." One of the manuscripts was confiscated from the office of *Novyi mir*, where it had been submitted but denied publication. Frustrated with Tvardovsky's indecision, Grossman then took his work to another, more conservative journal, *Znamia*, whose editor Vadim Kozhevnikov is said to have personally delivered his copy of the manuscript directly to the KGB. Grossman died three years later, while his novel had to wait over twenty years more to appear in tamizdat—one of the manuscripts was preserved by Semyon Lipkin and, with the help of Vladimir Voinovich, was eventually smuggled abroad.[38] No parallels between the gulag and the Holocaust, or Stalinism and Nazism, were drawn explicitly in Evtushenko's poem "Baby Yar" published in *Literaturnaia gazeta* on September 19, 1961, or in the censored version of Anatoly Kuznetsov's documentary novel under the same title.[39]

Perhaps an even more sacred theme than the war itself was the siege of Leningrad, but even here the boundaries of the admissible seem to have given way in the wake of Solzhenitsyn's publication. When an abridged version of Lydia Ginzburg's *Blockade Diary*—which, like Akhmatova's *Requiem* and Chukovskaia's *Sofia Petrovna*, was written nearly two decades before *Ivan Denisovich*—was first published in Russia on the eve of perestroika, it had a triple date: "1942–1962–1983."[40] The year 1962 thus splits the history of Ginzburg's text into two equal halves. As Emily van Buskirk and Andrei Zorin explain, the publication of Solzhenitsyn's novella gave Ginzburg grounds to hope that her blockade narrative could also be published, although "she obviously did not want to be perceived as Solzhenitsyn's epigone and thus had to reject the form of 'one day in the life of the main character.'"[41] Much like *One Day in the Life of Ivan Denisovich*, the initial version of Ginzburg's text, titled *Otter's Day*, described the daily cycle of the protagonist, a cycle of three parts: morning, workday, and evening. Both Solzhenitsyn's and Ginzburg's characters are forty, in the middle of their life cycles. There is evidence that the early drafts of Ginzburg's text (commissioned to her in October 1941 for *A Day of the Besieged City*, a volume that remained unpublished) included "a description of the circle as a graphic metaphor for the hopelessness of the Siege days,"[42] not entirely unlike the one day of Ivan Denisovich's sentence in the gulag. Unlike Akhmatova and Chukovskaia, Ginzburg, it seems, did not submit her text for publication in Russia until the mid-1980s, nor did she ever allow it to circulate in samizdat or to be smuggled abroad. However, in the early 1960s, in one of her introductions to the new version, Ginzburg wryly remarked: "Compositions that lie ripening and decaying in the desk drawer for decades acquire literary predecessors just as naturally as published literature acquires followers."[43] Long before Harold Bloom's *The Anxiety of Influence* (1973), the effect of Solzhenitsyn's publication on Ginzburg was the opposite of what one could expect: driven by the necessity to liberate her text from *Ivan Denisovich*'s "influence," in 1962 Ginzburg began reworking it into a less "recognizable" form, thereby diminishing her chances of seeing it published in the official Soviet press.

The changes she introduced in 1962 dealt primarily with the title and composition of her earlier draft. *Otter's Day* became simply *Blockade*—evidently, to avoid the word "day," along with the name of the protagonist, in the title. Much like Solzhenitsyn, Ginzburg initially employed the form of "one day in the life of one character" to depict Otter's daily cycle as a circle in which the categories of time and space are brought to a common denominator. As in *Ivan Denisovich*, the cycle of Otter's day in the besieged city, from before sunrise until after sunset, was portrayed as a ritual: "It was a self-contained [*zamknutyi*] chain of entirely unfree ritualistic movements accurately flowing from the situation. They came in a cast-iron order. . . . It was impossible to make an unforeseen, non-ritualistic gesture."[44] Yet instead of simply enacting this ritual without ever questioning his experiences, Otter struggles to make sense of it, deconstructs and resists it, trying in vain to break away from the cycle (or circle). The more emaciated Otter's body becomes, the more cognitive exertion and willpower it takes him to maintain basic life functions: "During the period of greatest emaciation everything became clear: consciousness carries the body. Automatic movements, its reflexes, its inherent correlation with impulses of the psyche—none of that any longer existed. . . . And willpower interfered with things it never had anything to do with."[45] Otter's effort is, thus, essentially intellectual, based on the realization that his movements and his entire existence have ceased being automatic, as if in her clinical description of one day in the life of a siege man Ginzburg had invoked Shklovsky's famous definition of art as deautomatization (or defamiliarization).[46]

In the middle of *Otter's Day*, in the chapter called "Circle," which serves as the axis of the whole composition, Otter sits idly by the stove, sunk in thoughts. On the surface this delay in the narrative is vaguely reminiscent of the midday break in *Ivan Denisovich*, when the prisoners light their cigarettes and crowd around the stove. However, while Otter sits idly, the midday break in Solzhenitsyn's novella only spurs Shukhov on to begin working in earnest. Unlike Otter, Solzhenitsyn's protagonist is overcome by a true worker's zeal and by the end of the shift, even regrets that the day is over but the work is not finished:

> Off to a good start. . . . Haven't even got time to wipe my nose! . . .
> Shukhov and the other layers had stopped feeling the cold. . . . Set

a brisk pace and you become a sort of foreman yourself. Shukhov wasn't going to fall behind the other two: to hurry the mortar up that ramp, he'd have run the legs off his own brother. . . . The foreman laughed. "They'd be crazy to let you out! Any jail would be lost without you!" Shukhov laughed back at him. And went on laying. . . . "Bloody nuisance, these short working days," he called out jokingly, as the foreman strode down the ramp. "Just when you're beginning to enjoy yourself, it's quitting time."[47]

As Ginzburg continued to rework the initial version of her siege narrative to emancipate it from Solzhenitsyn's influence, there were a few things she did not need to worry about. It was hardly possible to mistake her aristocratic protagonist for Solzhenitsyn's peasant worker. Van Buskirk and Zorin observe that the name Otter derives simultaneously from the French *l'autre* ("the other") and *l'auteur* ("author") and thus serves as the alter ego of the author.[48] In 1962 Ginzburg renamed Otter "N," whereby as a character he became more "variable" and generic, defined as "a cumulative and provisional man" (*chelovek summarnyi i uslovnyi*), "an *intelligent* under special circumstances" (*intelligent v osobykh obstoiatel'stvakh*). In short, if there is a line between the people (*narod*) and the intelligentsia, Solzhenitsyn's Ivan Denisovich and Ginzburg's Otter / N stand on opposite sides of this difficult boundary.[49]

While acknowledging its social value, Ginzburg refused to applaud Solzhenitsyn's work for its artistic merit: "I cannot bring myself to accept this work as a work of literature; I cannot accept this unlikely and grimacing, anti-rational free indirect speech. . . . Of course, comparisons may be drawn between the circle of a hard-labor camp and the ring of the Siege. But my text is about something else."[50] Despite the rounded compositions of both texts ("the circle of a hard-labor camp and the ring of the Siege"), Ginzburg's narrative stands far apart from Solzhenitsyn's combination of peasant speech and folk wisdoms, often rhymed and thus "rounded," words from the Dal' Dictionary, and free indirect discourse, whereby the narrator assumes the perspective of the protagonist and speaks in the protagonist's fashion.[51] *Blockade Diary*, as van Buskirk and Zorin conclude, "resists the very idea of a final, canonical text. Rather, we are dealing here with a work that could not be finished in principle."[52] Solzhenitsyn's novella, conversely, appears to be almost perfectly rounded and resolved, although the reader is warned that Shukhov still has more than two years left of his sentence.

Ivan Denisovich and Socialist Realism

The day described in *One Day in the Life of Ivan Denisovich* is set in January 1951, two years before Solzhenitsyn was released from the Ekibastuz camp on February 13, 1953. Stalin died three weeks later, on March 5, 1953. Eight years had passed from the historical setting of the novella, and six years from Solzhenitsyn's release from the gulag, before he sat down to write it on May 18, 1959. That same day the Third Congress of the Soviet Writers' Union convened in Moscow.[53] The proceedings were broadcast on the radio and covered in major Soviet newspapers. On the third day of the Congress, Khrushchev appeared before the members of the Union with a speech titled "Serving the People Is a Lofty Calling of Soviet Writers":

> A good work of literature is when it shows a positive hero, but not everything is approved in this hero—he is seen as he appears in life. This is both natural and correct. After all, . . . some kind of heroes should be used to educate people, shouldn't they? And, evidently, the positive ones. I am for those writers and that method that take the positive facts in order to raise the pathos of labor, ignite people, call upon them, and show the way. Along the way, so to speak, the positive hero is stripped of everything that has gone into the past, everything that needs to be cut off.[54]

Three years later, in 1962, when Khrushchev gave his personal sanction to publish *Ivan Denisovich*, what he liked most about Solzhenitsyn's protagonist was his unshakeable working habits demonstrated in the scene of his laying bricks in the work zone, where Shukhov appears so "positively" different from Ginzburg's *intelligent* Otter. In Khrushchev's eyes Ivan Denisovich was the embodiment of a positive hero capable of "raising the pathos of labor, igniting people, and showing them the way." Moreover, Khrushchev's speech pointed back to the First Congress of Soviet Writers in 1934, when socialist realism was instituted as "the basic method of Soviet literature and literary criticism, which requires of the artist a truthful, historically concrete representation of reality in its revolutionary development" and pursues "the task of ideological transformation and education of the workers in the spirit of Socialism."[55] As a state-sponsored doctrine that "sought to create an exemplary society inspired by literary and artistic images,"[56] socialist realism remained officially prescribed for Soviet artists and writers until the late 1980s, without ever being ruled out even during the warmest years of Khrushchev's Thaw.

In his essay "What Is Socialist Realism?" (1957), Abram Tertz, aka Andrei Sinyavsky, treated the positive hero as the sanctum sanctorum of socialist realism, next to the mandate for a grand Purpose (understood as the ultimate triumph of Communism). Tertz claimed that, because of the ultimate Purpose, "each work of socialist realism, even before it appears, is thus assured of a happy ending. The ending may be sad for the hero, . . . but it is happy from the point of view of the superior Purpose."[57] The day described in Solzhenitsyn's novella turns out, accordingly, to be "unclouded," "almost a happy one,"[58] so much so that Chukovsky, whose review of the manuscript helped get it published, went as far as admitting that the "short story could be called 'A *Happy* Day in the Life of Ivan Denisovich' [Schastlivyi den' Ivana Denisovicha]."[59] Indeed, the day ends with a list of strokes of luck: Shukhov receives "two biscuits, two lumps of sugar, and one round chunk of sausage"[60] from the *intelligent* Tsezar, who has parcel privileges and always keeps warm at the camp office but is portrayed as morally inferior to Ivan Denisovich despite his higher social status.[61] The frost was "nowhere near forty today," only "twenty-seven and a half below" in the morning, and during the day, "eighteen below, no more. Good weather for bricklaying."[62] Shukhov's Gang 104 was luckier with their work assignment at the construction site than the prisoners in Gang 82, who were sent to dig holes in the frozen ground without anywhere to hide from the cold and the wind. On their way back to the barracks, Shukhov and his fellow prisoners felt "they were nearly home. Yes—that's what they all called it, 'home.' Their days were too full to remember any other home."[63] A small piece of bread in Shukhov's mattress "was still where he had put it that morning! Lucky he'd sewn it in!"[64] And the ration Shukhov earned that day was bigger than anyone else's: "Food today was according to the amount of work done—some had earned two hundred grams, some three hundred, and Shukhov four hundred," on top of another two hundred grams, "which was Tsezar's ration"; in short, "he was really living it up":[65]

> Shukhov felt pleased with life as he went to sleep. A lot of good things had happened that day. He hadn't been thrown in the hole. The gang hadn't been dragged off to Sotsgorodok. He'd swiped the extra gruel at dinnertime. The foreman had got a good rate for

the job. He'd enjoyed working on the wall. He hadn't been caught with the blade at the search point. He'd earned a bit from Tsezar that evening. He'd bought his tobacco. And he hadn't taken sick, had got over it.

The end of an unclouded day. Almost a happy one.[66]

On the surface, the day has indeed ended on a happy—or rather, "almost happy"—note. But if the driving vehicle of socialist realism, according to Tertz, is the positive hero in pursuit of a Purpose, then Ivan Denisovich should be more accurately described as a positive hero *without* a purpose (unless, like Khrushchev, we take him at his face value): his resourcefulness, peasant dignity, good spirits, and worker's zeal are not the tools for building socialism. Rather, they are his basic, instinctual means of self-preservation and an organic part of his identity as a worker and peasant. Ivan Denisovich is, thus, a socialist-realist character only halfway: born to join the ranks of positive heroes, he is deprived of their required socialist-realist gonfalon: the grand Purpose. The method is thus destabilized, to a point, from within.

A similar positive hero deprived of a purpose would soon appear in the Russian village prose, a movement linked with Solzhenitsyn's short story "Matrena's House" ("Matrenin dvor"), completed in the fall of 1960 and published in *Novyi mir* two months after *Ivan Denisovich*.[67] Although the "age difference" between Solzhenitsyn's two characters is not great, Matrena's positive qualities had in the meantime grown into righteousness: "None of us who lived close to her perceived that she was that one righteous person without whom, as the saying goes, no city can stand. Neither can the whole world."[68] Apart from the peasant martyr Matrena, who tragically dies in a train accident, the character of Ivan Denisovich also lurks behind Spiridon, a fifty-year-old peasant from Solzhenitsyn's *In the First Circle*, who speaks in rhymed, euphonically "rounded" folk wisdoms, e.g., "*Volkodav—prav, a liudoed—net* ("A wolf-hound is right, a cannibal—not").[69] And while it is more problematic to trace the selfless (and childless) Matrena to *Anna Karenina*, the only common characteristic between them being death on the train tracks, Solzhenitsyn's "positive heroes without a Purpose" appear as the Soviet offspring of the amiable Platon Karataev from *War and Peace*, whom Tolstoy defined a century earlier as "the embodiment of everything Russian, kindly and round."[70] As for the rounded composition of *Ivan Denisovich*, it may be traced back to Tolstoy's debut work, "A History of Yesterday" ("Istoriia vcherashnego dnia," 1851), written in the first person and employing the same composition of "one day" to zoom in on an entire life (or, in the case of Ivan Denisovich, on his entire ten-year sentence), a way "to trace the intimate side of life through an entire day," according to Tolstoy.[71]

Of course, proverbial Russian peasants reincarnated by Solzhenitsyn in the Soviet era were modified by the course of history itself, but so did socialist realism adjust classical realist paradigms to the demands of the Party and the historical moment (Tolstoy's Karataev, for one, was often frowned upon by Soviet critics as a "reactionary" and outdated example of passivity). One of the traits that distinguished socialist realism from its alleged nineteenth-century point of departure was its earnestness and austerity, which, according to Tertz, brought to mind not the nineteenth, but the eighteenth century, the age of classicism in Russia:

> As in the eighteenth century, we became severe and serious. This does not mean that we forgot how to laugh; but laughter ceased to be indecent and disrespectful; it acquired a Purpose. . . . Irony was replaced by pathos, the emotional element of the positive hero. We ceased to fear high-sounding words and bombastic phrases; we were no longer ashamed to be virtuous. The solemn eloquence of the ode suited us. We became classicists. . . . This is why socialist realism should really be called "socialist classicism."[72]

It would be a stretch to call Solzhenitsyn a classicist, although *One Day in the Life of Ivan Denisovich* does seem to be governed by the classical unities of time, place, and action, covering a period of less than a day, featuring one geographical setting, and following a single plotline with only occasional flashbacks and minimum digressions. By the same token, nothing is more alien to Ivan Denisovich than speaking in "high-sounding words and bombastic phrases." And yet, Samuil Marshak described the novella as "truthful, stern and serious" [*pravdiva, stroga i ser'ezna*],[73] while Chukovsky praised Solzhenitsyn's portrayal of Ivan Denisovich's rapture with physical labor as "classical" (not to say "classicist," as Tertz would have it).[74] His worker's zeal is, moreover, "transmittable" to other characters, stretching beyond the time-and-place setting of the novella. For example, the reader does not know whether Captain Buynovsky, Shukhov's old-school Communist camp-mate, would toil away at the construction site as zealously as Ivan Denisovich, since he is effectively "locked out" from the plot for a ten-day stretch in the punishment cell after insulting the chief of the guards early that morning. But years later, his real-life prototype, Captain Burkovsky, employed after his release from the camps by the Central Naval Museum at the Cruiser Aurora in Leningrad, expressed genuine admiration for the truthfulness of Solzhenitsyn's description of the work scene. In an interview to *Izvestiia*, Burkovsky said:

> It is a good, truthful work of literature. It is clear to anyone who has read the novella that, with some rare exceptions, people in the camps remained human precisely because they were Soviet in their hearts, because they never identified the evil done to them with the Party, with our regime. . . . There is another thing I value in Aleksandr Isaevich's novella: how truthfully our work (*trud*) is described. It was hard, exhausting, but it was never humiliating. After all, we realized, if only subconsciously, that even there, in the camps, we worked for our Motherland.[75]

Solzhenitsyn, however, was eager to exorcise the spirit of socialist realism from his reputation as a writer, having branded it a "solemn pledge to abstain from truth"[76] and refusing to admit that without this socialist-realist mask, which he had deftly tried on to stay in the game, he would not have been able to achieve what he did. In a letter to Kopelev from exile, Solzhenitsyn blamed his former friend, fellow prisoner at the Marfino *sharashka* and prototype for Lev Rubin in *In the First Circle*, for discarding his works as socialist realism. "But have you forgotten," Kopelev replied, "that for me, during those years, the notion of socialist realism was quite positive?"[77] Kopelev added that he was "neither alone nor original" in such an evaluation of Solzhenitsyn's writing: Heinrich Böll, Solzhenitsyn's proponent, referred to him as a "reformer of socialist realism," while Georg Lukács treated *Ivan Denisovich* as a socialist-realist novella par excellence, one that was capable of renewing and perfecting the socialist-realist method.[78] Not that such readers of Solzhenitsyn as Böll and Lukács "missed the joke,"[79] as Richard Tempest puts it, but underneath this mask of socialist realism—and in particular in the epithet "*almost* happy," as Shukhov's day is described—much more truth could be read about the camps than appeared on the surface. It was this Aesopian negotiation between what was true and what was allowed that lay at the heart of Solzhenitsyn's incontestable breakthrough, much as the novella itself "had such a shattering impact on Russian readers in part because its formats were so familiar," not to say formulaic or simply folkloric.[80] To be able to tell more, not only did the author himself have to have a different camp experience (for example, such as Shalamov's), but a different literary method, not so tightly bound by the conventions of socialist realism, had to be used.

Solzhenitsyn's affinities with socialist realism, according to Mark Lipovetsky, were such that he practiced it "aesthetically although he opposed it ideologically."[81] One problem with this otherwise elegant juxtaposition is that socialist realism is more than just an artistic method, which is why it has resisted an accurate definition and remained elusive despite being a key concept of Soviet culture. Commenting on Solzhenitsyn's triumphant entry into the literary establishment and his gradual falling out of favor only a few years later, Andrew Wachtel shrewdly observes that "for all the criteria scholars have advanced to describe what socialist realism was, the most important criterion was that it was always and only what the party said it was at any given time."[82] Built on models much older and more universal than the Soviet state or socialist ideology and stretching beyond the geographical confines of the USSR and the Socialist Blok (positive heroes and happy endings, for instance, are often the part and parcel of Hollywood Westerns), socialist realism was aptly incorporated into the Soviet mythology to serve not only creative, but also—primarily?—extraliterary, sociopolitical functions. According to Czesław Miłosz, socialist realism is "not merely a question of taste," i.e., not only a matter of aesthetics, but also an "anaesthetic" administered by the state to its subjects: "It is a philosophy, too, and the cornerstone of official doctrine worked out in Stalin's days," which "is directly responsible for the deaths of millions of men and women, for it is based on the glorification of the state by the writer and artist, whose task it is to portray the power of the state as the greatest good." Socialist realism, Miłosz concludes, "is thus an effective anaesthetic."[83]

Socialist realism, therefore, is not limited to the realm of art but extends—and derives from—the realm of myth. In the mid-1950s, Claude Lévi-Strauss pointed out that while "the purpose of myth is to provide a logical model capable of overcoming a contradiction" (such as coming to terms with the gulag, whose catastrophic reality resists a discrete explanation), the myth itself generates an "infinite number of slates" and "grows spiral-wise, until the intellectual impulse which has produced it is exhausted."[84] Charged with symbolic connotations of continuity and infinity, the spiral was ubiquitously used or implied in Soviet mythology in general and in socialist realism in particular, including in literature, the visual arts, and architecture, from as early as the avant-garde period of the 1920s throughout the rest of the Soviet century (with Tatlin's "Monument to the Third International" as one vivid example).[85] One might go so far as to say that the ever meandering shape of the spiral indeed came in handy as a model for the officially indoctrinated principle of total "replaceability" incorporated into the state ideology and ultimately responsible for the "replacement" of millions: "There are no irreplaceable ones," read the Soviet slogan, not entirely unlike each separate loop of the spiral is shaped by the previous one before being itself just as seamlessly replaced by the next.

If myth evolves spirally and the spiral consists of an infinite number of loops, enabling socialist realism "to produce new variations of the generic constant that defines it as a genre or subgenre,"[86] it appears that elements of mythology were built into the text of *Ivan Denisovich* from the outset. Its plot is set in motion when "the hammer banged reveille on the rail outside camp HQ at five o'clock as always,"[87] a blow that marks the beginning of the daily cycle, inscribed as it were into the closed circle of Shukhov's camp. In keeping with the geometric logic of the spiral, this cycle could theoretically be easily replaced by any another, and the more ordinary (generic) the day, the camp, and the protagonist, the more interchangeable (universal) they become in Solzhenitsyn's depiction of the monotonous reality and depersonalizing uniformity of the gulag.[88]

Much as Solzhenitsyn's text stood out for its unorthodox content, its publication was possible only insofar as it added yet another brick to the wall of the socialist-realist project. As it happened, the eleventh issue of *Novyi mir*, in which *Ivan Denisovich* appeared under Tvardovsky's preface, opens with a programmatically socialist-realist poem by Eduardas Mieželaitis, "Hymn to Morning" ("Gimn utru"), translated from Lithuanian by David Samoilov. According to Wachtel, who analyzed the reception of *Ivan Denisovich* in the context of other works included in the *Novyi mir* issue, this poem "gives the reader a vertiginous feeling of déjà vu" as it depicts the awakening of a Soviet man to the first rays of sun that come "knocking plangently against the glass, / the clearest morning sound / the sound of sun—like a bronze gong" [*luch, v stekla stuchashchiisia zvonko, / chisteishii i utrennii zvuk— / zvuk solntsa—mednogo gonga*].[89] Of course, the lyrical subject "awakened in Mieželaitis's hymn is not a *zek* in a Soviet prison camp but rather precisely the type of literary personage favored by contemporary socialist realist literature . . . who wants to 'build, create, and work' (*stroit', tvorit', rabotat'*)."[90] Yet these are precisely "the activities in which Shukhov will engage on his construction site. Even the actual work that Shukhov will do, laying bricks, is anticipated in a description of Mieželaitis's worker who reaches for 'clay and sand.' "[91] By contrast to the grim reality of Shukhov's camp, the ray of morning sun in Mieželaitis's poem brings light and happiness to the world, making the speaker smile and facilitating his rise to the socialist-realist moral standard: "When you want / to become a true person / you have to wake up and start smiling" [*Kogda chelovek / khochet stat' chelove-kom, / on dolzhen prosnut'sia i zaulybat'sia*].[92] While Mieželaitis's poem in the opening pages of the issue may have functioned as a "locomotive" to help pull Solzhenitsyn's not-so-radiant text through the cordons of censorship, it is hard to disagree with Wachtel that the poem

> was placed here precisely to emphasize the main point that Tvardovsky was so careful to make in his preface: *One Day* should not be read as a bitter and gloomy indictment of the Soviet system but rather as [a] somewhat unusual variant of the optimistic, properly Soviet attitude one finds in Mieželaitis's poems. After all, both works, though undoubtedly of different quality and in different genres, tell analogous stories. A symbolic Soviet "everyman" wakes up and faces resolutely and with a positive attitude the task of working and creating, regardless of whether he finds himself in a Vilnius writer's studio or in a Siberian prison camp.[93]

Much the same can be said about two other poems by Mieželaitis included in the same issue of the journal in order to channel the reader's and the censor's perception of *Ivan Denisovich* in the right direction. The first poem, "Rust" ("Rzhavchina"), zooms in on the image of a roll of barbed wire that the speaker, a prisoner in the past, stumbles upon while walking down the road. For a moment, he imagines it to be a rose that quickly blooms into the "rusty, metal crown of thorns" he had carried through life: "I confess, I have walked for a very long time / wrapped in barbed wire" [*priznaius', ia ochen' dolgo shel, / provolokoi opleten koliuchei*].[94] The next part, ten stanzas—which, in the context of Solzhenitsyn's novella on the pages to follow, may stand for a ten-year sentence—reads as an "anti-ode" of sorts to the barbed wire that had entangled not only the speaker but the entire country for decades: it had "grown everywhere higher than crops of rye / . . . / from the earth's blood-soothing wounds" [*vyrastala vsiudu vyshe rzhi / . . . / iz krovoto-chashchikh ran zemli*]. Yet, as he keeps treading down the road toward the bright future, the speaker starts to discern the "kind rays of sun bravely making their way through the wire" [*cherez provoloku smelo pronikaiut / solnechnye dobrye luchi*] and the green grass of spring "devouring" what remains of the "orange rusty drops" [*i ostatki ryzhikh rzhavykh kapel' / pozhiraet veshniaia trava*]. The "wicked shadows gradually recede" [*zlye teni postepenno otstupaiut*], and his "soul emerges from the night" [*i dusha moia vykhodit iz nochi*]. The poem concludes with the speaker's refusal to stir the painful memories of the past [*proshluiu bedu ne voroshu*], and he continues down the road in peaceful silence, joined by others like him (hence the sudden transition to the first-person plural): "Leaving the night behind, we walk out / onto the road lit by the sun" [*i ukhodim pokidaia noch' / na dorogu, solntsem zalituiu*].[95]

Miežxelaitis's final poem in the selection, titled "Air" ("Vozdukh"), features a speaker who seems to have walked into it directly from the two texts above, except that here his painful predicament with the past is finally resolved. Set straight as a model Soviet citizen, he enters the space of this poem as the ultimate moral terminus, the last station on his long and thorny way to happiness. He is greeted by fresh air and physical labor as a remedy against the traumas and unhealthy doubts of the past. The blood in his veins turns into "living water," and his rib cage expands "like an epic":

Пусть навалится бремя труда.
Я—творец. Мне ненадобно отдыха.
Только воздуха дайте сюда!
Больше воздуха! Свежего воздуха!

Растворяется воздух в крови,
как живая вода растворяется,
и становится тесно в груди,
и как эпос она расширяется.[96]

[Let the burden of labor overpower me. / I am a creator. I need no rest. / Only give me fresh air! / More fresh air! Fresh air! // The air dissolves in my blood, / like living water, / and I start feeling tight in my chest, / and my chest grows wide like an epic.]

It is hard to imagine Ivan Denisovich walking down the same road after his ten-year term in the camps. Nonetheless, there is much he could find in common with Miežxelaitis's narrator, be it the spiral-shaped clew of barbed wire conceived almost as the biblical crown of thorns, the road itself that keeps spiraling happily into the socialist-realist utopia, or the space of his lungs, contracting and expanding with fresh air to mythological size, like the ever-widening loops of the spiral. Having strategically hitched *Ivan Denisovich* to such uplifting, myth-driven images, Tvardovsky gave a powerful push to Solzhenitsyn's novella, which was bound to keep spiraling further, whether on the pages of *Novyi mir* or elsewhere, in Russia or abroad, always growing larger from the ground zero of Shukhov's camp and his day.

Cyclical structures with a potential to expand in general appear to be Solzhenitsyn's trademark. Reflective of the enclosed spaces described, they are planted throughout his texts and inform some of the titles: *In the First Circle*, which translates Dante's myth of the netherworld into the gulag context; *The Red Wheel*, a multivolume epic with separate "nodes" (*uzly*), each devoted to a historical milestone; *The Gulag Archipelago*, a metaphor for the system of camps conceived as islands. Not only *Ivan Denisovich* but most of Solzhenitsyn's other works of fiction tend to be rounded and resolved, distinguishing them from gulag narratives as a genre, whose constituent texts can never be exhaustive by definition if taken separately. Nor can they ever form a sufficient totality since there are always other firsthand accounts that remain unknown or whose authors did not live to write them. By contrast to the cyclical composition of *Ivan Denisovich*, many of Shalamov's *Kolyma Tales*, for instance, seem altogether unfinished and populated with characters who tend to be moving from point A to point B without much hope of return.

One cannot help but project cyclical structures onto Solzhenitsyn's biography and career as a writer. Unlike Shalamov, who died in poverty in a mental asylum in Moscow four years after his *Kolyma Tales* were first published as a book in London in 1978,[97] Solzhenitsyn returned triumphantly to Russia in 1994, after twenty years in exile. From Cavendish, Vermont, where he had lived and worked in seclusion since 1976, he flew to Alaska and on to Vladivostok, then crossed the country by train to Moscow. Several years later he was honored by President Putin, who had worked for the same organization that had thrown Solzhenitsyn and millions like him behind barbed wire half a century earlier, the same organization that had persecuted and exiled him in 1974. The symbolic itinerary of his roundtrip journey to exile and back home is in itself a full circle geographically and biographically. It may be traced back to the origins of the myth that gave birth to Ivan Denisovich in 1962, when this loaded spiral went off and, presumably, still spins to this day. One may wonder whether the "initial impulse" that produced the myth of *Ivan Denisovich* has by now been exhausted or whether we still find ourselves under its spell. But Solzhenitsyn can best be described as one of the greatest myth-makers of Soviet (or anti-Soviet) literature, whereas the majority of his fellow gulag authors, who raised similar issues but orchestrated them differently—to the effect that their works could only be published abroad—are myth-breakers. Denied publication at home and printed in tamizdat, their manuscripts failed to conform to the Soviet mythology that Solzhenitsyn, against his best intentions and better judgment, both relied on and himself helped to perpetuate. Those works either lacked a positive hero or other essentials of socialist realism or neglected its very morphology, or anatomical structure, such as the loops of the spiral in which myth nests.

Socialist Realism on the Other Shore: The West Reads Solzhenitsyn

As other gulag manuscripts were smuggled out of the Soviet Union, published, read, and reviewed abroad, many of them faced expectations that, upon closer look, were not all that different from the dictates of socialist realism at home. Not only in Russia but also abroad, *Ivan Denisovich* served as the ultimate yardstick to measure the artistic merit of clandestine manuscripts that started reaching the West after Solzhenitsyn's momentous publication in Russia. The resonance of Solzhenitsyn's bombshell novella was as strong abroad as it was at home, placing *Ivan Denisovich* at the junction of paths that Russian literature had allegedly followed previously and was bound to take thereafter. Years later Solzhenitsyn produced a major split in the community of Russian émigré writers and critics: while one group would continue to proclaim him as the greatest writer of the Soviet era and the key figure of the dissident opposition, the other would not only hold the opposite opinion but even claim that such a writer had never existed.[98] The breach between the two factions would only grow wider after Solzhenitsyn's arrival in the West in 1974. Alienated from the community of his fellow émigrés of the Third Wave, who refused to accept his increasingly nationalist, anti-Western, and antisemitic rhetoric and sardonically referred to his place of seclusion in Cavendish, Vermont, as the "Vermont *obkom*," Solzhenitsyn instead found support among the remaining figures of the First and the Second Waves, whose reception of *Ivan Denisovich* in 1962–1963, with few exceptions, was almost piously favorable and who continued to believe that "in Solzhenitsyn's writings, one can hear the voice of a prophet."[99]

The older émigrés' praise for Solzhenitsyn and his novella was backed up by Western media, academia, and other institutions, including major publishing houses. Not only did two pirate Russian editions appear in London immediately after the publication of *Ivan Denisovich* at home, but two competing English translations were also ready overnight, as were expedited translations into other languages.[100] To raise its sales on the wave of *Ivan Denisovich*'s unmatched popularity, Praeger Publishers went so far as to change the title of Fedor Abramov's novella about collectivization *Vokrug da okolo* (literally, *Around and Near*) into *One Day in the New Life*, as it came out in English translation in 1963, months after its first publication in a Soviet journal.[101] The manuscript of another author, Georgy Vladimov, making the rounds in Moscow samizdat, was ascribed to Solzhenitsyn by one émigré critic solely on the grounds of its subject matter.[102] All in all, as Polly Jones has noted, it was not until 1963, when *Ivan Denisovich* was published "in numerous translations and in huge print runs" in Europe and North America, that "soviet literature turned into a 'sensation'" for the Western reader.[103]

However, while in Russia it was a sensation first and foremost for its unorthodox content, Western readers of *Ivan Denisovich* tended to seek its significance in its form rather than its subject matter. One reviewer after another pointed out that "there is nothing new in the facts Solzhenitsyn has told us,"[104] "nothing we didn't know from the sad and horrible stories of people who endured [the camps] in Russia, in Germany, in all the other countries that ever existed."[105] In this sense, Solzhenitsyn's novella was even branded "extremely belated." "What does this work expose, after all? For us, people in the West, . . . it exposes nothing at all. In the West, people have known the truth about concentration camps and forced labor for several decades already."[106] Yet none of the "hundreds of books about the camps" that had appeared in the West since at least the 1920s could compare to Solzhenitsyn's as works of literature, as another émigré critic made clear.[107] In his review of the first two English translations, Franklin D. Reeve warned the Anglo-American audience against reading *Ivan Denisovich* "as another entry in the international political olympics," for "the book is not so much about history or politics as it is about men."[108] In the West the informational value of Solzhenitsyn's work may even have faded in comparison with the earlier firsthand accounts of the gulag by a few lucky fugitives or, more commonly, by émigrés of the Second Wave, who had "retreated" abroad with the Germans during the war.[109] Reviewing *Ivan Denisovich* in émigré periodicals years later, many of them, including former Nazi collaborators, could relate to the text on a personal level, since the fate of Ivan Denisovich, sentenced to ten years in the Gulag for as little as two days in German captivity, could easily have been their own, had they not escaped forced repatriation to Russia after the war. "Fugitives from a dystopia," the authors of "these memoirs were liable to represent a weapon at the service of the West in the Cold War, and indeed some of them may have fit that description," yet they must also have contributed to the climate in which Khrushchev "felt obliged not only to release most of the political prisoners in 1954–56 but also to allow a more or less inconspicuous repatriation of some foreign citizens among them,"[110] who also embarked on writing their testimonies. Before Solzhenitsyn, however, the gulag topic abroad seems to have been confined almost exclusively to the documentary genre, with hardly any significant works of fiction or poetry. In the West *Ivan Denisovich* became a sensation because it was fiction. "Its literary form," Gleb Struve confessed, "for me, came as a surprise. . . . I was expecting a truthful memoiristic story."[111] In short, it was the literary orchestration of *Ivan Denisovich*, rather than its subject matter, that prompted émigré critics, Western scholars, and journalists to inscribe it into the classical Russian literary tradition from which, they claimed, it derived.

In this age-old tradition driven essentially by humanistic values, compromised as they were by twentieth-century historical cataclysms including the gulag, the most immediate point of reference for Solzhenitsyn was Dostoevsky's *Notes from The House of the Dead* (*Zapiski iz mertvogo doma*), the first work of fiction about the prison experience in the Russian language. As it happened, the publication of *Ivan Denisovich* in 1962 marked the centennial of the first book edition of Dostoevsky's Siberian novel,[112] a coincidence that tamizdat critics picked up in an effort to establish a lineage between the nineteenth-century Russian classic and its Soviet literary offspring, in spite of the fact that tsarist *katorga* would often seem like a vacation resort to gulag prisoners a hundred years later. Next to Solzhenitsyn's, Dostoevsky's account of prison and forced labor indeed seemed "a little intellectualized, a little contrived"[113] (if only because Dostoevsky's quasi-autobiographical protagonist, Aleksandr Petrovich Gorianchikov, is a writer and nobleman, not a peasant). But the historical parallel between the two works a century apart gave grounds to hope that "perhaps Solzhenitsyn's next important book will be . . . the *Crime and Punishment* of our time," as one review, optimistically titled "The House of the Living," anticipated.[114] The émigré critic Viacheslav Zavalishin suggested that *Ivan Denisovich* was not only "a jubilee gift to Dostoevsky" but that it also "triggered a greater interest in *Notes from the House of the Dead*" in Russia, where a film adaptation of Dostoevsky's novel, with a script by Viktor Shklovsky, was apparently being shown "in overcrowded movie theaters" for the first time since the early 1930s when it was made.[115]

Such parallels between Solzhenitsyn's novella and its alleged nineteenth-century precursor should be viewed as part of the wider mission of the older generation of Russian émigrés to salvage prerevolutionary Russian culture from being repressed, defiled, or altogether extinguished at home throughout the Soviet era. To be fair, comparing Solzhenitsyn with Dostoevsky in the official Soviet press, even after the ban on Dostoevsky was lifted in Russia during the Thaw,[116] was still rather risky; tamizdat critics saw it as their civic duty to fill this gap, especially when it came to Dostoevsky's religious motifs and themes, which were downplayed in the Soviet Union. It was for much the same reason that Aleksandr Obolensky traced the genealogy of Aleshka-the-Baptist, a "sectarian" in Ivan Denisovich's camp, to the youngest and holiest of the brothers Karamazov, Alesha, whom the critic imagined "in the Soviet reality."[117] Perhaps a closer ancestor of Solzhenitsyn's Aleshka, however, is Dostoevsky's humble twenty-two-year-old Tatar Alei from *House of the Dead*; not only does he share the bunk with Dostoevsky's protagonist, as Aleshka does with Shukhov, but they are also near namesakes, and "have the same soul," pristine and untouched by the dehumanizing prison conditions, as another émigré critic asserted.[118]

In his comparative analysis of *Ivan Denisovich* and Dostoevsky's classic, Yugoslavian dissident Mihajlo Mihajlov pointed out a striking parallel not only between the respective dates of the two publications, but between such milestones of the nineteenth and twentieth centuries as the abolition of serfdom under Alexander II in 1861 and the release and rehabilitation of political prisoners under Khrushchev. "Of course," Mihajlov admits, "both writers needed to bring some kind of apology for the unusual and 'ticklish topic.' Dostoevsky underscores here and there that the kind of *katorga* he described no longer exists. . . . The same is done by Tvardovsky on Solzhenitsyn's behalf."[119] True, Tvardovsky's strategic preface to *Ivan Denisovich* opens with the disclaimer that while the novella "carries with it an echo of the painful phenomena in our development that dealt with the period of the cult of personality, now exposed and rejected by the Party," that period "appears to us today as distant past, despite having taken place not so long ago."[120]

Yet there were too many differences between Solzhenitsyn and Dostoevsky that disqualified the latter from serving as a point of reference for the former, starting with their titles: "life" versus "dead" (although "life" was not part of Solzhenitsyn's original Russian title, *Odin' den' Ivana Denisovicha*). These differences go beyond the two writers' choices of their protagonists, Dostoevsky's being "a nobleman and an *intelligent* capable of the deepest insights into the psychology of the crime, criminals and convicts," while Solzhenitsyn's "is a Russian peasant turned into a private in the Red Army and into a '*zek*' who sees the hell he is living in through the eyes of an average uneducated man."[121] Mihajlov rightly observes that Dostoevsky "speaks about the harshest *katorga* . . ., while the Special Camp of Ivan Denisovich was incomparably lighter than the camps he had been to before,"[122] such as the ominous Ust-Izhma, where he nearly died from scurvy. In other words, had Solzhenitsyn written a novel *à la* Dostoevsky, with an *intelligent* as the main character in a camp qualitatively harsher than Shukhov's, such a work would hardly have had any chance of seeing the light of day in Soviet Russia. As for the lengths of their prison sentences (four years for Dostoevsky and his semi-autobiographical protagonist; eight and ten years, respectively, for Solzhenitsyn and Shukhov), this, along with other "improvements" in the Soviet penal system, Mihajlov remarks, is just a sign of "modernization."

If there is anything in common between Solzhenitsyn's portrayal of Stalin's camps and Dostoevsky's psychological vivisection of prison as a human condition in the nineteenth century, it is their treatment of physical labor. Citing Solzhenitsyn's description of laying bricks in the zone as perhaps "the best [portrayal of physical labor] in Soviet literature because of the richness and truthfulness of its creative expression," Leonid Rzhevsky suggested that it stemmed not from the dictates of socialist realism, but from Dostoevsky's *House of the Dead*, for "it is unthinkable, after all, to attribute to prisoners the 'enthusiasm of a socialist construction process.'"[123] Unthinkable or not, the fact remains that what earned *Ivan Denisovich* Khrushchev's approval and the right to be published in gosizdat was precisely the protagonist's work enthusiasm. Solzhenitsyn, however, shares Dostoevsky's insight that "to crush and destroy a man completely and punish him with the most frightful possible penalty . . ., it would suffice to give the penal work the most completely and utterly useless and nonsensical character."[124] The reader may remember that Shukhov used to be a mason at his *kolkhoz* before the war and the camps, whereby bricklaying for him is but an "extension" of freedom, the only function of freedom he has retained, no matter that the work itself is compulsory. It is also true that just as Dostoevsky modeled *House of the Dead* on his own prison experience,

Solzhenitsyn, in his portrayal of Shukhov at the construction site, "dissolved" [*rastvoril*] his own firsthand experience as a prisoner in Ekibastuz.[125] The mortar [*rastvor*] that Shukhov and the rest of his gang use to lay bricks is, thus, as much construction material as Solzhenitsyn's creative material:

> How could Ivan Denisovich get through ten years if all he could do was curse his work day and night? After all, in that case he would have had to hang himself on the first handy hook! . . . Such is man's nature that even bitter, detested work is sometimes performed with an incomprehensible wild excitement. Having worked for two years with my hands, I encountered this strange phenomenon myself: suddenly you become absorbed in the work itself, irrespective of whether it is slave labor and offers you nothing. I experienced those strange moments at bricklaying (otherwise I wouldn't have written about it).[126]

While English-language reviews of *Ivan Denisovich*, especially in academic journals, tended to be more reserved and at times even derogatory,[127] there was hardly any critic in the Russian emigration who did not try to inscribe Solzhenitsyn into the classical literary tradition, through Dostoevsky or otherwise. A rare exception was Georgy Adamovich, who disagreed with "those who have found an incredible talent in the author" and treated *Ivan Denisovich* "not as a literary but rather as a social and political event."[128] Adamovich claimed that while "there are apt words [*metkie slovechki*] and vivid pages here and there, . . . the work on the whole is photographic, and the thousand separate strokes it is made of remain ever disjointed. There is no general picture, only hustle and jamming [*sutoloka, tolcheia*]." Solzhenitsyn's style reminded Adamovich not of the Russian classics, but of an "early Celine, modified in the Soviet style." A few years later, Adamovich, likewise, would stand out for praising Shalamov, whose literary talent he placed above Solzhenitsyn's, in what would become the only favorable review of *Kolyma Tales* in the same émigré newspaper.[129]

Acknowledging the social value of Solzhenitsyn's novella, Gleb Struve, on the other hand, suggested that rather than being photographic and bringing to mind Celine (or, for that matter, Dostoevsky), *Ivan Denisovich* "restores Soviet literature to its heyday period in the 1920s" and is heir to the traditions of Russian ornamental prose "so heavily influenced by Andrei Belyi and especially Remizov."[130] In his article "A. Solzhenitsyn, Socialist Realism, and the Remizov School,"

Roman Gul', the editor of the New York émigré journal *Novyi zhurnal*, went much further. Acknowledging the importance of Solzhenitsyn's work "not so much from the political perspective, but in the literary sense" (even though in Russia it "has become part of Khrushchev's propaganda"), Gul' claimed that *"Ivan Denisovich* crosses out the entire socialist realism, i.e., the entire Soviet literature," with which it "has absolutely nothing in common. . . . This work came into being bypassing Soviet literature, straight out of prerevolutionary literature. From the 'Silver Age.'"[131] Gul' treated *Ivan Denisovich* as a "harbinger" of Russian letters, a "sputnik" that "has pierced the airless space of Soviet literary propaganda in the past forty-five years." By equating socialist realism with Soviet literature, the critic betrayed his rather limited and biased notions of Russian literature of the Soviet period, which, needless to say, included not only "thousands of novels and novellas written for the demands of the state and the party"[132] but also works that, unlike Solzhenitsyn's, could only appear in tamizdat, having been rejected at home precisely for failing to comply with the socialist-realist standard. It is ironic that Gul', like Struve, associates the style of Solzhenitsyn's novella, including his use of *skaz*, with the "school" of Remizov, whose prose was not published in the Soviet Union during Remizov's lifetime, making it unlikely that Solzhenitsyn could be familiar with Remizov's oeuvre at the time (Remizov died in Paris in 1957).[133] Citing Zamiatin's "I Am Afraid" (1921), in which the author of the famous dystopia *We* claimed that "the future of Russian literature is actually its past," Gul' comes to the realization that *Ivan Denisovich*, accordingly, comes "entirely from 'the past of Russian literature'" and on these grounds alone "proves that the so-called Soviet literature is doomed."[134] Even the scene of bricklaying, according to Gul', is "not naturalistic at all, that is, not socialist-realist," but orchestrated instead "in the style of the Remizov school."[135] Gul' places Solzhenitsyn at the "classical junction" ("Go right, and you will perform the tasks of the Party, fall into the pit of socialist realism and disappear as a writer. Go left, along the artistic path, and you might not be as lucky the second time around") and concludes on a suspenseful note: "Will Solzhenitsyn produce anything large? One can hardly believe so, much as one would like to. The climate in the Soviet Union is difficult for a writer."[136]

Unfamiliar as they were with the catastrophic reality of the gulag, and not having yet been exposed enough to other, less "polished" accounts of this reality, including Solzhenitsyn's own *Gulag Archipelago*, émigré critics of the older generation read *Ivan Denisovich* as a revival of the classical humanistic values, blind to the fact that the more they insisted on such a reading, the more they mirrored the reception of Solzhenitsyn's novella at home, where it could only be published as long as it conformed, at least on the surface, to the prescribed socialist-realist ideology and mythology. No matter that the humanistic values read into the text of *Ivan Denisovich* both at home and abroad had once and for all become obsolete in the context of twentieth-century Soviet history and the gulag in particular. And yet, it was maintained that "the longer Shukhov stays behind bars, the kinder he becomes, and one can be sure that the corrupt regime of the camps would never turn him into a less worthy person."[137] With the void between the "two Russias" in the early 1960s being nearly soundproof, it was easy for tamizdat critics to fall into the same socialist-realist trap that Solzhenitsyn had attempted to undermine at home by tailoring *Ivan Denisovich* to the publishable standard and domesticating the gulag for the uninitiated reader, wherever that reader was geographically. Having adopted a line from the Soviet review of *Ivan Denisovich* as the title of his own ("it will never again be possible to write the way Soviet writers had until now," claimed the Soviet writer and World War II veteran Grigory Baklanov),[138] the émigré critic Evgeny Garanin also praised Solzhenitsyn's novella for its potential "to awaken good feelings in others, elevate people, make them more pure, better and freer."[139] Another anonymous émigré reviewer inadvertently echoed Khrushchev's reaction to *Ivan Denisovich* almost verbatim when he claimed that its "main idea is the spiritual firmness of man. Deep inside those prisoners live heartiness, comradely feelings and kind thoughts, in short, an undying human soul." "Mixed with those feelings [of horror and compassion] is the feeling of JOY," he continued, because, after all, "there, in our motherland, people are getting braver and braver."[140] Such heartening rhetoric mirrored the dozens of upbeat responses to *Ivan Denisovich* in Soviet criticism; the titles alone raised the novella to the heights of socialist realism as it was understood at the current historical moment.[141] Whether they were "friends" or "foes" of *Ivan Denisovich*, as Vladimir Lakshin referred to Solzhenitsyn's advocates and opponents, Soviet critics could not be that wrong, after all, when they praised *Ivan Denisovich* for high spirits, optimism, and resourcefulness, if their ideological opponents on the other side of the Curtain did essentially the same.

Lakshin predicted, "The novella about Ivan Denisovich Shukhov is bound to have a long life."[142] Its longevity was ensured less by historical authenticity, however, than by the universally worshiped "get-up-and-go" myth of hopefulness and sanguinity in the face of the dehumanizing reality of the gulag, a myth that informed "the tension between the ethical drive and the aesthetic impulse" in *Ivan Denisovich*, which, according to Toker, constitutes "the bi-functionality of Gulag narratives as acts of witness-bearing and as works of art."[143] Ironically, the homey garb of socialist realism that Ivan Denisovich had to wear in gosizdat, instead of his rough special-camp uniform, with the number Shch-854 replacing his name, was taken for bulletproof anti-Soviet armor by émigré critics abroad. The Russian emigration, joined by Western institutions, "echoed the discourse that greeted (and facilitated) its Soviet publication" because "redemption still had to form part of the reading experience," no matter where, and so "this redemptive, even 'triumphant,' trajectory, and the tropes of hope, survival, and victory" could not but fuel the success of *Ivan Denisovich* outside the Soviet literary jurisdiction, even making "this optimism central to the 'selling' of the works [of Soviet literature] to the Western audience."[144] In this sense, *Ivan Denisovich*, although first published in Russia, consolidated tamizdat not only as a literary practice and political institution but also as an industry, showing just how easily adaptable socialist realism was to capitalist reality.

The pathos of optimism built into the character of Ivan Denisovich—a positive hero without a Purpose, as he has been defined—proved highly mutable as it spread beyond Shukhov's native milieu to the transnational field of tamizdat. The moral "quest" of Ivan Denisovich, if he had any, was believed in the West to be "equally ours, our quest for our best selves, our real selves, our true selves." The pathos was quickly projected onto the sociopolitical value of Solzhenitsyn's novella as a whole, giving hope that it should "not preclude [other manuscripts on the gulag] yet to be written, as it does not excuse the prohibition of others already written but still unpublished."[145] Numerous other works by gulag survivors were indeed newly written or retrieved from the drawer in Russia in the wake of *Ivan Denisovich*'s success. Few of them, however, were published in the Soviet Union in spite of such hopes. Instead, until perestroika, they were destined to appear only abroad, where they were still haunted by the positive spirit of Solzhenitsyn's peasant protagonist. It was the rare gulag manuscript that escaped a comparison with the standard set by Solzhenitsyn.

Geographically removed from and ideologically opposed to the Soviet regime and its literary establishment, tamizdat accepted and even favored some of the basic principles of socialist realism on the formal

level—paradoxically, precisely because they were treated straightforwardly as "anti-Soviet" while in fact they remained irreducible to the
Soviet paradigm. This paradox is rooted in the innate mutability and
ever-evasive nature of socialist realism itself, as it has always stood for
more than just a creative method. In 1978, for instance, socialist realism was reformulated as a "historically open aesthetic system of the
truthful representation of life," differing only slightly from its original
definition in 1934 as "a truthful, historically concrete representation
of reality in its revolutionary development."[146] As Thomas Lahusen
has demonstrated in *Socialist Realism without Shores*, redefining socialist
realism as a "historically open aesthetic system" was, by and large, a
response to Western revisionism, including Roger Garaudy's *D'un réalisme sans rivages* (*Realism without Shores*), which appeared in France with
Louis Aragon's preface in 1963, the year the world celebrated the birth
of *Ivan Denisovich*. The reception of *Ivan Denisovich* at home and abroad
revealed that socialist realism was indeed "open" not only historically,
but also geographically: its "shores" could be found elsewhere, perhaps
everywhere, but it took half a century to come to terms with the fact
that "insofar as Solzhenitsyn's novella was officially published [in gos-
izdat], it . . . could be read and criticized only within the existing norms
of socialist realism," whether in Russia or abroad.[147] Like a myth that
lives longer than history and is by definition larger than the specific
reality it both derives from and formulates, *Ivan Denisovich*—or rather
its exploits at home and abroad—endowed socialist realism with a geographical dimension, having exposed its "shorelessness."[148]

CHAPTER 2

Anna Akhmatova's *Requiem* and the Thaw

A View from Abroad

Among the clandestine manuscripts emancipated by Solzhenitsyn in 1962, including those conceived much earlier, was Akhmatova's *Requiem*. Although it was not her first publication in tamizdat,[1] Akhmatova was the last living poet of the Silver Age, while the vast majority of representatives of bygone Russian culture either found themselves in exile or were annihilated in some way by the regime at home. After the execution of her first husband, Nikolai Gumilev, in 1921 and the repeated arrests of her son and her third husband, Nikolai Punin, Akhmatova's fate seemed sealed. But despite other ordeals, including Zhdanov's campaign against her and Mikhail Zoshchenko in 1946, she was spared the gulag. She resolved, however, to speak on behalf of those who were not, in her *Requiem*.

Akhmatova died on the same date as Stalin, thirteen years later. Her death on March 5, 1966, two weeks after the trial of Sinyavsky and Daniel, no doubt contributed to the general sense of the end of one era, still associated with the liberties of the Thaw, and the imminence of another epoch—the Stagnation, under Brezhnev. The last ten years of her life were "in many ways a sharp contrast to those [years] that had gone before."[2] Some of Akhmatova's works, although not *Requiem*, were finally published at home.[3] On September 4, 1962, she met Robert Frost during his visit to the Soviet Union.[4] In 1964 and 1965, more than fifty years after her last travel abroad in 1912, she was awarded and allowed to accept foreign literary prizes in Italy and England. But in 1966 Akhmatova's passing was regarded by the Russian diaspora mainly as the demise of prerevolutionary Russian culture. After Mandelshtam's death in a transit camp outside of Vladivostok in 1938, Tsvetaeva's suicide in Elabuga in 1941, and the persecution of Pasternak that led to his death in 1960, Akhmatova was the last poet of the great Silver Age quartet, invoked in her 1961 poem "The Four of Us" ("Nas chetvero"), as well as in her "Poem without a Hero."[5] Despite the fact that for over forty years—the longer part of her life—Akhmatova lived and worked in a country that could not be more different from the Russia they had known and remembered, the émigrés still regarded her as "one of their own" (*svoia*); it was not until *Requiem* appeared in tamizdat in 1963 that the view of Akhmatova from abroad began to change.

Congratulating Akhmatova on her seventy-fifth birthday, Yury Trubetskoi, a wartime émigré of dubious reputation, wrote, "On June 11 Akhmatova turned 75. What nonsense! She is not 75, but as young as she was when the brilliant maître of Symbolism, Viacheslav Ivanov, leaned over her narrow hand and said: 'My congratulations. Your poems are an event.'"[6] Trubetskoi may have meant it as a compliment to the "ever young" poetess, but he borrowed the phrase from Georgy Ivanov's highly fictitious memoir *Petersburg Winters* (*Peterburgskie zimy*), whose popularity abroad was matched only by Akhmatova's indignation at Ivanov's distortions of the facts of her early life, especially as regards her relationship with Nikolai Gumilev.[7] A week after Akhmatova died, another poet of the Second Wave, Nikolai Morshen, lamented, "I am not a fan of hers (in the sense that I consider myself a fan of Pasternak, Mandelshtam and Zabolotsky), but . . . now that she is gone, the Silver Age—the age of the giants [*vek bogatyrei*]—has also ended."[8] The reluctance of some of the émigré critics to admit that the Silver Age had ended much earlier than one wished, along with the implicit unwillingness to recognize that Akhmatova had survived as a poet in Russia after the Revolution, was part of the mission of the Russian diaspora to justify emigration as a civic and even heroic act, rather than mere escape, a justification both challenged and revitalized by *Requiem* once it was published abroad.

Comprising texts written years and decades apart and only much later brought together under one cover, *Requiem* was "woven" from the "poor words" of those whose lives and names were forever lost.[9] It was for this reason that *Requiem*, as Georgy Adamovich confessed, "resists a formal analysis," while "its contribution to Russian history eclipsed its importance for Russian poetry."[10] Indeed, both at home and abroad *Requiem* was read, above all, as an act of witness-bearing and a testimony to the victims of Stalinism and the gulag, rather than as a work of literature. Yet Akhmatova's way of speaking about the gulag and its victims in *Requiem* clashed with the émigrés' expectations of her as a Silver Age poet they remembered and worshiped. For all its apparent simplicity and formal transparency, distinguishing it from "Poem without a Hero," *Requiem* blurs the lines between literature and document, lyric and epic, the private and the public, the cry and the silence, bearing witness and suffering. It complicates the aesthetic and sociopolitical binaries and conventions that had shaped the identity of the Russian diaspora and blossomed in the climate of the Cold War. Meant for readers at home and inspired by their plight under Stalin, voiced as the poet's own predicament, *Requiem* did not immediately fit the horizons of expectations of its first readers abroad.

For her part, Akhmatova proudly confronted the status attached to her in Russian émigré circles as a victim of Stalin's terror, on the one hand, and a poet whose legacy was reduced to the Silver Age alone, on the other. For the last ten years of her life, when communication between Russia and abroad was partially restored, she insisted on being read as a poet, not as a martyr, and protested the widespread opinion that, from the mid-1930s until the Thaw she had remained silent and written nothing. In the 1960s her "Poem without a Hero" and *Requiem*, both written during the years of the so-called silence, emerged to challenge this popular misconception. Still, next to such Silver Age "matriarchs" in exile as Zinaida Gippius and Irina Odoevtseva, Akhmatova was viewed primarily as a poet of the past belle époque, a defender of Stalin's victims, and a martyr herself. The publication of *Requiem* in tamizdat revealed that for those who had found themselves "under foreign skies," as they are referred to in the epigraph, Akhmatova was increasingly becoming a "stranger," much as the emigration had likewise grown decidedly "alien" for Akhmatova. For half a century exile preoccupied Akhmatova as an alternative she proudly rejected in 1917. While in "Poem without a Hero," devoted to siege-time Leningrad (the true "hero" of the poem "missing" from the title), Akhmatova invokes her fellow poets, artists, and friends who had gone west after the Revolution, in *Requiem* she brings back the memory of those who had gone in the opposite direction.[11] The first publication of *Requiem* abroad was, thus, akin to a meeting of the "two Russias," much as they had, in the meantime, grown apart from each other geographically, aesthetically, and ideologically.

Prehistory: "Poem without a Hero"

The story of the first publication and reception of *Requiem* in tamizdat would be incomplete without taking a step back three years, when Akhmatova's "Poem without a Hero" first appeared in the New York almanac *Vozdushnye puti* edited by Roman Grynberg. An émigré of the First Wave with a passion for literature and the means to support it abroad, Grynberg embarked on his career as a publisher in 1953, when he cofounded another émigré journal, *Opyty* (*Experiments*), which remained in print until 1958.[12] Early the following year, Grynberg wrote to Sir Isaiah Berlin, one of the addressees and protagonists of "Poem without a Hero," that he had decided to put together an almanac in honor of Pasternak, who was turning seventy in 1960. Conceived as "a sign of our gratitude and recognition" to the poet, the almanac borrowed its title *Vozdushnye puti* (*Aerial Ways*) from Pasternak's eponymous short story of 1924, in order "to hint at our today's connection with him from over here."[13] In keeping with the editor's plan to make the almanac "not about Pasternak, but rather for him,"[14] its first issue did not feature Pasternak's own texts but opened instead with Akhmatova's "Poem without a Hero," accompanied by the disclaimer that it was being printed "without the author's knowledge."[15]

It remains unclear who smuggled out of Russia this early redaction of "Poem without a Hero," completed in 1946. According to Pavel Luknitsky, in 1962 Akhmatova recalled that it was "a certain literary scholar Iakovlev," to whom, however, she "had not given the manuscript" personally.[16] Roman Timenchik has suggested that "Iakovlev" could refer to no one other than Roman Jakobson, whose name Luknitsky could have either misheard or deliberately encrypted in his retelling of his conversation with Akhmatova. Before Jakobson emigrated to Prague in 1920, he studied together with Grynberg at Moscow State University (Grynberg left Russia two years later). Abroad, they stayed in touch and corresponded through the 1950s.[17] In 1956 Jakobson visited the Soviet Union for the first time since 1920. He did not see Akhmatova then, but they met twice several years later during Jakobson's subsequent trips to Russia in 1962 and 1964.[18] Thus, apart from the fact that Jakobson and Grynberg knew each other personally, and unless the assumption is based on the rather faint similarity between

Jakobson's name and "Iakovlev," Jakobson's involvement with the first publication of Akhmatova's "Poem without a Hero" appears to have little evidence. It could be, instead, that this earlier version of the poem was smuggled out—just in time to be included in the almanac—by another American Slavist, Charles Moser, who visited Akhmatova in February 1959 and was the first foreigner she had seen in the thirteen years since her fateful encounter with Isaiah Berlin in 1946, her "guest from the future" in "Poem without a Hero."[19] We do not know, however, if Grynberg and Moser were personally acquainted, although the timing of Moser's visit to Akhmatova—less than a year before "Poem without a Hero" appeared in Grynberg's almanac—is worth considering.[20]

A later version of "Poem without a Hero" appeared in the second issue of *Vozdushnye puti* in 1961 with the same disclaimer that it was being printed "without the author's knowledge" and a note from the editor that "the impossibility of getting in touch with the author is a great nuisance," making it difficult to know exactly "what refers to what in the 'stray' and often barely legible manuscripts."[21] This redaction of the poem, completed by 1959, was smuggled out by Grynberg's friend Evgenia (Zhenia) Klebanova, who visited Akhmatova in the fall of 1960 while on a business trip to Russia as an employee of the Cosmos Travel Agency in New York. In the disguise of "Nina," the first-person narrator of her memoir, Klebanova later recalled that when she entered Akhmatova's dacha (*budka*) in Komarovo, she saw lying on the poet's desk "in full view" a manuscript of "Poem without a Hero" opened to the first page. She remembered, however, that the poem had already been published in the first issue of Grynberg's almanac the previous year. The confusion was resolved when Akhmatova said she "was reworking it again, insisting that she was doing this for the last time."[22] According to Timenchik, Klebanova was introduced to Akhmatova by their mutual friend and translator Liubov' Bol'shintsova (referred to in Klebanova's memoir as "Vladimir"). Allegedly, Akhmatova invited them to come to Komarovo again the following day, "so that there are no strangers,"[23] and gave the newly reworked version of her "Poem without a Hero" to Bol'shintsova, who remembered her saying it was "for Zhenia."[24]

On October 14, 1960, after Klebanova returned to New York, Grynberg wrote to Georgy Adamovich in Paris: "Incidentally, I have received *the final* version of [Akhmatova's] poem. There is much new in it: corrections, another dedication (the third one) and an introductory letter to a certain N. N. All remarkably good." In this letter Grynberg also shared his joy about the success of the first issue of the almanac, which had not only "sold out completely" abroad but had also reached Russia, where Akhmatova, in the editor's words, was both "pleased" with the publication and even "grateful to us."[25] Much of what Grynberg communicated to Adamovich about Akhmatova coincides with Klebanova's account of visiting the poet in Komarovo just a few months earlier, although Klebanova says nothing of Akhmatova's reaction to seeing her "Poem without a Hero" published abroad. It could hardly be as rosy as Grynberg pretended it was.

Before the first issue of *Vozdushnye puti* reached her in Leningrad, Akhmatova had been familiar with the tamizdat publications of Mandelshtam, Gumilev, Pasternak, and Tsvetaeva. She had also been aware of some of the Western studies on Russian poetry, including her own. Moser recalls, for instance, that in February 1959 Akhmatova complained to him about Leonid Strakhovsky's monograph *Craftsmen of the Word: Three Poets of Modern Russia* (1949) and William E. Harkins's *Dictionary of Russian Literature* (1956), which "angered her more than Zhdanov's report" of 1946.[26] Besides, she was quite upset by the fact that Western publishers "were printing her works without permission and failed to pay her royalties."[27] When a year or so later Akhmatova received the first issue of Grynberg's almanac, where her "Poem without a Hero" had indeed been published without her permission, she called it a "theft" and threatened half-jokingly to "file a complaint to the bureau of copyright protection. Or write an insulting letter to Eisenhower." Nevertheless, despite Chukovskaia's apprehension that "everything is again as it once used to be with 'Zhivago,'" Akhmatova was "anxious, but not too much. . . . The times are special now."[28] Still, she was far from being "pleased" or "grateful" to her enterprising publisher, who also published his own review of "Poem without a Hero" in the same almanac a year later, signing it with his pen name "Erge" (that is, "R. G.," Roman Grynberg's initials).[29]

On October 24, 1961, while traveling in Italy, Grynberg sent Akhmatova a postcard, in which he apologized for the mistakes that had crept into both redactions of the poem in his almanac. "What happiness it would be," he added, "to hear what needs to be fixed—from you."[30] The postcard reached Akhmatova at the hospital, where she was recovering from her third heart attack. A friend who visited her on December 5, 1961, wrote down Akhmatova's words: "Sharks are also writing to me!" When he asked just what "sharks" Akhmatova had in mind, she smiled and showed him Grynberg's postcard: "The sharks of

capitalism, of course!"[31] Three and a half years later, upon returning
from Europe where she was awarded the honorary doctorate at Oxford
in June 1965, Akhmatova told Chukovskaia about her meeting with
Grynberg in London:

> I also met the shark of capitalism. It is a bad person. Sir Isaiah
> [Berlin] told him: "You have published Akhmatova's poetry and
> prose more than once. You have to pay her." He replied: "The law
> is on my side." Ever seen such a boor? [*Vidali khama?*] After a while,
> he nevertheless telephoned me and asked if I wanted him to de-
> liver the money in an envelope in person. I answered: "Good *for
> you* that you called and said these words. I don't need anything:
> neither your visit, nor the money, nor the envelope." And hung up
> without saying goodbye.[32]

However difficult it was for Grynberg to pay Akhmatova a honorarium before he could meet her in person in London, he valued her
"Poem without a Hero" not only as a literary sensation and "symbolic
capital" but also as a financial gain, which he, incidentally, planned
to distribute among other contributors to his almanac. On August 5,
1959, when the first issue of *Vozdushnye puti* was still in the making, he
wrote to Adamovich, expecting him both to contribute an article and
to review the almanac after it was published:

> But a miracle is also possible thanks to Akhmatova, and in that
> case the money [*barysh*] will go to the contributors. . . . Akhmato-
> va's poem is real gold [*nastoiashchee zoloto*]. Every word of it is a
> piece of this real metal. I have read nothing of the sort in years. . . .
> It should become an event, or rather it will become an event in our
> life, if I understand anything about it at all. However, the Russian
> émigrés are somehow completely indifferent to anything that is
> "not political." But there is this meaning in the poem too, much
> as I am reluctant to overemphasize it for obvious reasons. . . .
> I received the poem from "over there" [*ottudova*] so that I could
> publish and salvage it for everyone. You will understand right
> away just how I clung to it. It is both the gem of the almanac and
> the only artistic work in it, apart from half a dozen poems by lo-
> cal émigré authors. . . . And so I would like you to write a review
> of my volume.[33]

In his review Adamovich singled out Akhmatova's poem as the
"point of gravity" of the whole publication,[34] but focused on those of

the poem's parts that took the reader back to St. Petersburg before
World War I and the Revolution, the city that he and his fellow émigrés
of the First Wave had carried away into exile to preserve and immortal-
ize in their own writings. Author of the famous nostalgic lines about
Petersburg—"There used to be only one capital in the world. / Everything else—just cities" [*Na zemle byla odna stolitsa, / Vse drugoe—prosto
goroda*]—Adamovich refrained from discussing the siege of Leningrad
in Akhmatova's poem, which he did not feel entitled or even able to
comment upon from afar.[35] Instead, he chose to dwell on the Silver
Age setting of "Poem without a Hero," the year 1913, which came between the old and the new Russia and was the highlight of Acmeism
and Akhmatova's career in particular, her book *Chetki* (*Rosary*) having
been published in early 1914. Yet it was during the siege of Leningrad,
as Brodsky wrote years later, "that the name 'Leningrad' was finally
adopted by the inhabitants who survived, almost as a tribute to the
dead."[36] In June 1965, more than forty years since they had last seen
each other in Petrograd, Adamovich asked Akhmatova in Paris, "You
say Leningrad, not Petersburg?" "I say Leningrad," Akhmatova replied,
"because the city is called Leningrad." Two Russian poets of the same
generation born in the same city, since then thrice renamed, now spoke
a "different" language. "I understood," Adamovich confessed, "that it
was difficult and painful for her to speak about many things and immediately regretted having opened up such a subject. I thought I heard
a hint of reproach, even a challenge, in her voice: why ask me such
questions?"[37]

Linked to the siege in "Poem without a Hero" was the subject of
the gulag, the "stillness of Siberia's earth" [*tishina sibirskoi zemli*]. In
the poem's epilogue, written in Tashkent in 1942, Akhmatova outlined two opposite directions for Russia in the "real twentieth century": while the emigration, whether after the Revolution or during
the war, headed west, the Russia that Akhmatova refused to abandon
"walked east":

От того, что сделалось прахом,	From all that to ash is rendered,
Обуянна смертным страхом	Filled with moral dread yet
И отмщения зная срок,	Knowing the calendar
Опустивши глаза сухие	Of vengeance, having wrung her
И ломая руки, Россия	Hands, her dry eyes lowered, Russia
Предо мню шла на восток.	Walked before me towards the east.[38]

As for the Silver Age period of Petersburg culture, during their meeting in Paris in 1965, Akhmatova told Adamovich that it was being replaced by yet another "golden age," having in mind poets of the new generation, particularly her younger friend Joseph Brodsky, who was then serving time for "social parasitism" in the northern village Norenskaia after an infamous show trial in Leningrad in 1964. Akhmatova thus retorted to the émigrés' efforts to underplay or altogether discard poetry behind the Iron Curtain on the basis of its merely being "Soviet." She also showed Adamovich a recent issue of the New York émigré newspaper *Novoe russkoe slovo* with a laudatory article about her, whose message, however, she thought caused more harm than good: "Between the lines here you can read what a martyr I am, how much I've suffered, how I'm alien to everything and everyone in today's Russia, that everywhere I am lonely. . . . You have no idea how this has hurt me and how it can still hurt me!"[39] When asked if he could pass her words on to the editors of émigré journals and newspapers, Akhmatova told Adamovich that he would actually do her a big favor: "Let them forget about my suffering. . . . You don't have to make me your banner or mouthpiece."[40]

Nevertheless, one stanza in particular from the epilogue to "Poem without a Hero" could not but fuel the émigrés' pity for the poet-martyr in Russia, on the one hand, and their own civic pride in exile, on the other, laying bare the ideological bifurcation of Russian literature and culture after the Revolution:

А веселое слово—дома—
Никому теперь не знакомо,
Все в чужое глядят окно.

But the joyful word—home—
It is a word unknown to
All now, all look through
foreign panes.

Кто в Ташкенте, [а] кто в Нью-Йорке,
И изгнания воздух горький [—]
Как отравленное вино.

In New York, in Tashkent, the
Bitter air of exile
Is like a poisoned wine.[41]

Taking these lines as an example, Professor Helen Muchnic of Smith College referred to Akhmatova as an "exile in her own land" and read her "Poem without a Hero" as "a poem of exile" written "in appreciation of those who, whether in 'Tashkent or New York,' must look through strangers' windows and taste 'the air of banishment, bitter as poisoned wine.'"[42] Building on the deliberate ambiguity of the word "exile" [*izgnanie*] and stopping short of drawing a parallel between

Akhmatova's evacuation in Tashkent and the life of the Russian emigration abroad, Muchnic implied that "Poem without a Hero" and the tamizdat almanac that first published it served the same function: both were meant to prove "that the minds and the spirit of men communicate far above the barriers which are erected for them in vain by geography and politics."[43] Such an interpretation of "Poem without a Hero," suggested less by Akhmatova's text than by the title of Grynberg's almanac, paved the way abroad for a much more turbulent reception of *Requiem* three years later. While in "Poem without a Hero" it is Akhmatova's readers both in Russia and abroad, whether in New York or in Tashkent, who "look through foreign panes," the epigraph to *Requiem* addresses those who had found themselves "under foreign skies" as an antithesis to Akhmatova's audience in Russia and the author herself, who stayed "there, where my people, unfortunately, were."

Requiem Goes Public

Two weeks before Solzhenitsyn's *Ivan Denisovich* appeared in *Novyi mir*, Akhmatova told Chukovskaia, "Eleven people knew 'Requiem' by heart, and none of them had betrayed me."[44] This phrase marked the end of the long period of silence when *Requiem*, with its prologue dating back to 1935, had been confined to the memory of the author and her closest friends and existed only orally. Describing the "sad and beautiful" ritual of those years, Chukovskaia spoke of the atmosphere of fear and secrecy that *Requiem* both created and itself derived from:

> Anna Andreevna, when visiting me, recited parts of "Requiem" also in a whisper, but at home in Fontanny House did not even dare to whisper it; suddenly, in mid-conversation, she would fall silent and, signalling to me with her eyes at the ceiling and walls, she would get a scrap of paper and a pencil; then she would loudly say something very mundane: "Would you like some tea?" or "You're very tanned," then she would cover the scrap in hurried handwriting and pass it to me. I would read the poems and, having memorized them, would hand them back to her in silence. "How early autumn came this year," Anna Andreevna would say loudly and, striking a match, would burn the paper over an ashtray.[45]

Inspired by the success of *Ivan Denisovich*, Akhmatova decided not only to "declassify" her poem, as Timenchik has put it,[46] and for the first time commit it to paper, but also to send it to the same journal that had published Solzhenitsyn. On September 19, 1962, upon reading the manuscript of Solzhenitsyn's novella, Akhmatova famously proclaimed, "Each of the two hundred million citizens of the Soviet Union ought to read his novella and learn it by heart."[47] Solzhenitsyn and Akhmatova met on October 29, 1962, when *Ivan Denisovich* was only two weeks from being published. "Can you endure fame?" Akhmatova asked Solzhenitsyn. "I have strong nerves," he replied. "I have endured Stalin's camps."[48] Not long before, she had read his poetry, "which, as she justly and tactfully noted, was not his strength as a writer."[49] Now that she was meeting Solzhenitsyn in person, Akhmatova recited her *Requiem* to him. Kopelev, who had arranged their meeting, recalled Solzhenitsyn's reaction to the poem, no written copy of which yet existed, pointing out that it fully "coincided with any ideological criticism."

> I heard it through. Very attentively. And asked her to recite some of the poems again. Good poems, of course. Beautiful. Sonorous [*zvuchnye*]. But after all, a nation suffered, tens of millions, and it's a poem about an individual case, about one mother and son. . . . I said to her that the duty of a Russian poet is to write about the sufferings of Russia, to rise above personal grief and speak of the nation's grief. . . . She was silent, reflecting. Perhaps she didn't like that—she's accustomed to flattery, raptures. But she's a great poet. And a truly great theme. That imposes responsibility [*Eto obiazyvaet*].[50]

Ironically, Solzhenitsyn's reaction to *Requiem* anticipated some of the responses it would soon receive abroad. Still, it was largely thanks to his *Ivan Denisovich* and the hopes inspired by its sensational publication in gosizdat that the "emancipation" of *Requiem*—or its "second birth," in the author's own words,[51]—took place in early December 1962 at the Moscow apartment of Nika Glen, Akhmatova's literary secretary.

> The most important event of the months that Anna Andreevna spent on Sadovo-Karetnaia must have been the "emancipation" [*raskreposhchenie*] of "Requiem." Unfortunately, at the time I recorded nothing and remember it all only most generally: that Anna Andreevna was very nervous, and that I understood the importance of what was happening as I was typing these great poems

on my typewriter—after all, the full text of "Requiem" was for the first time being passed from memory on to paper. In those days (it must have been December 1962), Anna Andreevna expressed her personal desire to recite "Requiem" for an audio recording. I also remember a discussion of whether or not to submit "Requiem" for publication (the question was about *Novyi mir*).[52]

A more accurate date of the "emancipation" of *Requiem* can be restored from the diary of Yulian Oksman, an elderly literary scholar and political prisoner in the recent past, who played a key role in the first publication of *Requiem* abroad the following year. On December 9, 1962, Oksman wrote down that he had visited Akhmatova the day before at Glen's apartment.

> The conversation began when Anna Andreevna offered to take a look at her famous "Requiem," now for the first time brought together into a complete cycle. It was typed for the first time only yesterday, together with two introductions—one in prose, the other in verse. . . . But the strangest thing was A. A.'s desire to include the full text of "Requiem" in her new book of poetry. I struggled to convince A. A. that this poem could not be published just yet. . . . Its pathos goes beyond the problematics of fighting the cult of personality, its protest rises to the heights that no one will ever allow *her* to conquer. I even convinced her not to show it to the editors, who might destroy the whole book if they reported on "Requiem" to the higher authorities. She defended [herself and her poem] for a long time, claiming that Solzhenitsyn's novella and Boris Slutsky's poems about Stalin strike Stalin's Russia much harder than her "Requiem."[53]

The atmosphere was nevertheless festive: *Requiem* was no longer going to be lost "even if those seven or eleven people who . . . remembered it by heart all die in one go," and it was "no longer necessary to burn these words over an ashtray"; from now on, "they will themselves 'burn people's hearts.'"[54] However, Oksman's intuition proved right on both fronts. Contrary to Akhmatova's expectations, instead of paving the way for other manuscripts, Solzhenitsyn's novella only marked the ultimate limit of the admissible in the official Soviet press, causing these newly emancipated works, including *Requiem*, to go back underground. *Requiem* was rejected by Tvardovsky (instead, the January issue of *Novyi mir* printed two more short stories by Solzhenitsyn, followed by a few other poems by Akhmatova)[55] and excluded from her book *Beg vremeni*, which had already been scheduled for publication but was only brought out three years later.[56] Not that Akhmatova expected to compete for Tvardovsky's approval over *Ivan Denisovich*, as she later confessed to a friend: "Tvardovsky is worried about the peasants of Smolensk but is utterly indifferent to me."[57] Indeed, next to *Ivan Denisovich*, *Requiem* had too little, if anything, to do with the plight of the peasants during collectivization; it failed to comply with the socialist-realist mandate for a positive hero; and besides, it was written by—and about—a woman waiting in vain by the prison wall for her husband and son. Taken together, these factors disqualified *Requiem*, for Tvardovsky, from being a firsthand account of Stalin's atrocities, making it "secondary" to the suffering of those who had actually spent time behind bars.

Akhmatova's decision to submit *Requiem* for publication at home was dictated not only by hopes inspired by Solzhenitsyn's unmatched success. It was also driven by the fact that once it had been written down and began circulating in samizdat, it simply had to be made public and thus "legitimized." In other words, Akhmatova needed to demonstrate that she no longer considered her poem illegal, which does not mean, of course, that she was not afraid of becoming "the epicentre of the earthquake" once again, especially since it was almost inevitable that sooner or later *Requiem* was going to be leaked abroad without her even knowing.[58] Indeed, forced out of the official literary field, *Requiem* already circulated in samizdat in "thousands" of copies by the spring of 1963.[59] The new cold spell that descended on Russia soon after the publication of *Ivan Denisovich* meant that the number of unauthorized copies of *Requiem* circulating in samizdat would grow exponentially, generating a proportionately high number of discrepancies from the original typescript submitted to *Novyi mir*. These factors became a signal to transfer *Requiem* for publication abroad: the longer one waited, the more likely it was that another "stray" version of Akhmatova's poem would leak abroad instead of the authorized manuscript.

Requiem Goes West

The story behind the first publication of *Requiem* in 1963 was told for the first time six years later by its publisher, Gleb Struve, in his afterword to the second edition. Even then, three years after Akhmatova's death, Struve could only say so much to avoid incriminating the rest of those involved. Struve confessed that he first heard of *Requiem* at the

FIGURE 2.1.   Anna Akhmatova. *Rekviem*. Munich: Tovarishchestvo zarubezhnykh pisatelei, 1963.
Cover of the first book edition.

end of 1962 "from an acquaintance of mine (a foreigner)," who had
met Akhmatova in Russia and heard her recite the poem to him. There
was no hard copy of *Requiem* just yet, and it took another half a year for
the manuscript to reach Struve in California, "with a note that in January the poem had been submitted to *Novyi mir*, where it was rejected.
It must have been since then," Struve rightly assumed, "that *Requiem*
began circulating."[60]

Struve's clandestine correspondent in Moscow was Martin Malia, his
colleague at Berkeley and a professor of Russian history. In the beginning of 1962, Malia went as an exchange scholar to the Soviet Union,
where he struck up precious contacts with Akhmatova and other literary figures, including Chukovskaia and Oksman, whose correspondence with Struve he initiated and facilitated in the years to follow.[61]
Soon after his arrival in Moscow, on March 23, 1962, Malia informed

Struve, "You will no doubt receive for publication some unprinted materials of AAA (not from me directly but from Oksman),"[62] by which he meant materials for Akhmatova's collected works, which Struve had already been working on with Boris Filippov, the head of the émigré publishing house Inter-Language Literary Associates in Washington, DC.[63] But at the end of the year, awestruck by the publication of *Ivan Denisovich* and the escalation of the Caribbean crisis only weeks earlier,[64] Malia confidentially reported to Struve on December 6, 1962:

> [Akhmatova] for the first time wrote down a cycle of verses, "Requiem," composed in '37–'38, verses which for over 20 years had only been communicated orally to 11 of her closest friends, and some of which I have heard her recite . . . (these facts *not* for publication, or even for communication). . . . Hopes, thus, were immensely high—and then the чёрные сотни [black hundreds], with Фурцева's [Furtseva's] help, staged a провокацию [provocation] over abstract art, околпачили старого дурака Н<икиту> С<ергеевича> [hoodwinked the old fool Nikita Sergeevich Khrushchev], smashed modernism in art, and got Polikarpov reinstated at the head of the culture section of the ЦК [Central Committee of the Communist Party]. This probably means that AAA's Поэма [Poem] (it was given its final form, with new stanzas on the camps, etc., only after Сол<женицын> [Solzhenitsyn]), can't now be published. . . . However, . . . some of "Requiem" may set [sic!] into Нов<ый> Мир [*Novyi mir*] in Jan<uary>, together with two more stories of Сол<женицын> [Solzhenitsyn].[65]

It follows that *Requiem* was for the first time written down no later than December 6, 1962 (not December 8, as Oksman's diary entry suggested). But the "spring" that had been in the air since the Twenty-second Party Congress was already ending. On December 2, 1962, the day after Khrushchev's infamous "pogrom" at the Manezh Exhibition in Moscow, Oksman wrote to Struve (via Malia), "I suppose that the 'spring,' in which people believed after a few anti-Stalinist works in prose and poetry appeared in print, proved to be illusory. The story with the exhibition '30 Years of the Moscow Artists' Union' confirms my diagnosis."[66] Unlike the majority of the Soviet intelligentsia at the time, Oksman, "one of the first initiators of the process of surmounting the barriers between the émigré and the Soviet cultural life, . . . did not believe in the revival of intellectual freedoms in Soviet Russia without a dialogue or cooperation with the 'second' Russia abroad."[67] Struve realized that Oksman's perspective was rather an exception, and that the intelligentsia, including Akhmatova, was, on the contrary, wary of publishing abroad. Unlike his more opportunistic fellow tamizdat publishers, such as Grynberg, Struve tried to obey the will of the author for as long as was necessary: "I knew that the author was against publishing these poems abroad, I did not want to violate her will, was afraid to cause her harm, and did not rush to make this wonderful work public."[68]

Struve was also well aware that since at least the mid-1950s, his name was one of the most odious ones among Soviet authorities: Khrushchev's son-in-law Aleksei Adzhubei characterized him as an especially "malicious" émigré who "cooks up dirty articles about cultural life in the Soviet land,"[69] while another literary functionary, Nikolai Gribachev, wrote that "it was those like him who, in their own times, used to tear out the tongues of our Red Army soldiers, cut stripes of skin off their backs, and powder their wounds with salt."[70] In the same letter to Struve on December 6, 1962, Malia warned him of both considerations—that the intelligentsia, with the exception of Oksman, were largely against tamizdat, and that Struve's name was not to be uttered out loud in the official circles in Russia:

> Incidentally, if J.G.O.'s [Oksman's] *closest* friends knew what he is doing, I think they would be quite furious—and not a few doors would be closed to me too. . . . Part of this putative reaction to J.G.O.'s doings is the result of general attitudes towards publication of anything abroad—for instance AAA [Akhmatova] considers that Б.Л.П. [Pasternak] betrayed all his friends and Russian culture in general by publishing in Italy; part of this is due to attitudes towards you personally. It may interest you to know that you are a legend here, a hero to some, a dangerous enemy to others, but to all a power. On the whole, I think you will be "rehabilitated"—eventually.[71]

Malia's year-long sojourn in the USSR was up in January 1963, but the following month another colleague of Struve's from Berkeley, Lewis S. Feuer, a professor of sociology and philosophy took off for Moscow, accompanied by his fifteen-year-old daughter Robin Feuer. His wife, Kathryn Beliveau, joined them on March 14, 1963.[72] At the time, Kathryn was finishing her PhD thesis on Tolstoy at Columbia University; the official purpose of her trip was to work with the writer's manuscripts in Yasnaya Polyana. Before her departure she met with Struve in Berkeley to discuss her research and other issues related to her travel. Struve's choice of Kathryn for the role of courier, whom he entrusted with the mission of meeting Oksman in Moscow, obtaining from him the manuscript of *Requiem*, and sending it to California, was carefully thought through: a graduate student working on a nineteenth-century classic at a university other than his own, Kathryn was less likely to draw unnecessary attention from the authorities or pose a serious risk to Oksman than her husband or any senior colleague of Struve's, for that matter. Years later, Lewis recalled that by the time Oksman finally handed the manuscript of *Requiem* to her,

> Kathryn remembered that a former classmate of hers at the Russian Institute of Columbia University was now a foreign service officer at the American Embassy in Moscow. Besides being a scholar of literature, he was a keen political thinker. Of course, as an Exchange Scholar attached to the Soviet Academy, I had the privilege of sending my letters through the diplomatic pouch, but Kathryn's Columbia classmate kindly expressed a willingness to help send this new poem of Akhmatova's through an even more private pouch. Kathryn sealed and addressed *Requiem* to Gleb Struve in Berkeley, and under diplomatic protection, it was sent to the United States.[73]

It remains unclear exactly when Oksman passed the manuscript of *Requiem* on to Kathryn, but it reached California no later than mid-May, as becomes clear from Kathryn's letter to Struve on May 14, 1963. By this time, Kathryn "had in all 3 meetings with XYZ," as she and Struve referred to Oksman for conspiracy purposes: "By now you have doubtless received the photograph and the A[nna] A[khmatova] poems."[74] In her letter Kathryn also informed Struve that *Requiem* was circulating in Moscow in "copies evidently made in the *Новый мир* [*Novyi mir*] office," and that while no one could tell whether Akhmatova wanted it to be published abroad, Oksman decided to leave the decision "entirely to [Struve's] discretion and judgment," guided by the fact that "meanwhile the poems would be preserved."[75]

On June 5, 1963, Kathryn and her daughter Robin boarded a night train from Moscow for Leningrad, where they planned to spend a day sightseeing before continuing back to the United States via Helsinki and Stockholm; Lewis had to stay in Moscow a few more days. That eerie train ride and the rest of their journey was later described in detail by Robin Feuer Miller in her short memoir, as well as by Kathryn

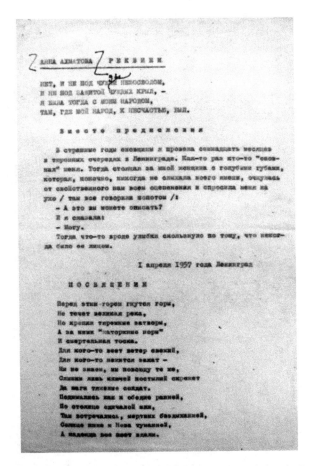

FIGURE 2.2.   The first page of the original typescript of *Requiem* smuggled out by Kathryn Feuer to the United States. Gleb Struve Collection, Hoover Institution Archives, Stanford University.

in several letters to Struve written immediately after the incident.[76] On the Soviet-Finnish border, the train from Leningrad to Helsinki was stopped. The mother and daughter were subjected to physical and psychological violence by the KGB. Kathryn's notebook with Moscow addresses, phone numbers, and records of her conversations with Oksman was confiscated. Later in August a search was conducted in Oksman's apartment: Struve's letters to him and clippings from émigré newspapers and journals were also confiscated. The investigation that followed exposed Oksman's contacts with Malia, through whom "he maintained illegal correspondence with the White émigré in the U.S., professor of Russian Language at the University of California, Gleb Struve."[77] At

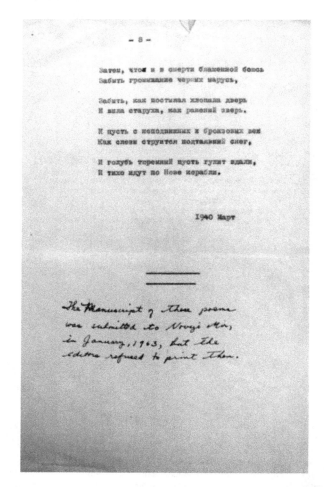

the end of the year, Oksman was expelled from the Writers' Union and forced to retire. His name was removed from the editorial board of the editions he had initiated.[78] Furthermore, the incident was linked to the so-called Berkeley plot, which the KGB tried to expose in order to cut short contraband traffic of manuscripts across Soviet state borders, including Oksman's own subversive article "On Informers and Traitors among Soviet Writers and Scholars" (referred to as the "Memorandum" in Struve's correspondence with both Feuer and Malia).[79] According to Marietta Chudakova, the persecution of Oksman could be related to the incident involving another American exchange scholar, albeit one not affiliated with Berkeley—the Yale historian Frederick Barghoorn. On October 29, 1963, Barghoorn was detained in Moscow outside the Hotel Metropol, charged with espionage, and jailed for sixteen days, until John F. Kennedy interfered in the affair, convincing Khrushchev to release Barghoorn, lest American wheat sales to Russia be jeopardized.[80] Meanwhile, the typescript of *Requiem* was already in California.

Throughout the summer of 1963, I kept "sitting" on it without sharing either the text itself or any information about it with practically anyone. But I realized that once "Requiem" began circulating, it would be typed and retyped over and over again and may spread around in deficient copies. . . . In September 1963, while in Munich, I raised the question of publishing it with G. A. Khomiakov, the head of the publishing house Tovarishchestvo zarubezhnykh pisatelei, but I had not given it out even to him what work exactly we were discussing. On October 21, 1963, G. A. Khomiakov received the typescript from me, and on November 27, "Requiem" was out. Thus, at least half a year had passed since I received it from Russia.[81]

A wartime émigré author who wrote under the penname Gennady Andreev,[82] Khomiakov was the head of the publishing house Tovarishchestvo zarubezhnykh pisatelei in Munich, which brought out *Requiem*, as well as the editor of the almanac *Mosty* (*Bridges*), where Struve had first suggested they publish this "material of utmost interest and value."[83] Much of Struve and Khomiakov's correspondence in October and November 1963 is devoted to the technical and financial aspects of the publication, which was funded by Struve out of pocket in the amount of approximately $250, with a print run of 1,200 copies, at a cost of $1.50 each for sales in the United States, 4 DM in Germany, and 5 Fr in France, with the agreement that should *Requiem* bring any profit, the funds would be used to finance further issues of Khomiakov's almanac *Mosty*, since "it would hardly be possible to send any money to the author."[84] Struve insisted that the author's name be kept secret as long as possible and that neither the printer nor the artist who worked on the book's cover should know it until necessary.[85] It was also discussed which portrait of Akhmatova to use: one of the color paintings by Yury Annenkov from 1921 or the earlier drawing by Savely Sorin from 1913, which Oksman had sent Struve together with the typescript of *Requiem* and which was eventually chosen, partly because it was less known, having never been reproduced.[86] Another important aspect of the negotiations was distribution. Once published, the book was sent out for review to both the émigré and Western newspapers and academic journals, and offered—wholesale or on commission—to Russian booksellers in Paris, London, New York, and Washington.[87] In the meantime, Khomiakov also approached the American Committee for Liberation from Bolshevism, a CIA organization founded in 1951 (originally under the name of the American Committee for Freedom for the Peoples of the USSR), one of whose projects was Radio Free Europe in Munich (first called Radio Liberation). Khomiakov hoped that the committee would buy a large number of copies of *Requiem* for distribution through its own channels, including those used to smuggle tamizdat back to the Soviet Union: "Should they take a large quantity, we will increase the print run," Khomiakov wrote to Struve on October 31.[88] However, the deal failed; the proposal was turned down in Washington on the grounds that Akhmatova's *Requiem* was already "quite well-known," that is, not worth the investment.[89] One of the committee's consultants was Boris Filippov, Struve's closest partner in other publishing projects, including Akhmatova's collected works, whom Khomiakov described as "a very peculiar personality" and actually suspected of standing behind the rejection.[90] Indeed, as he thanked Khomiakov for a copy of the newly released *Requiem*, Filippov mentioned that although he "loves Akhmatova very much" and considered her book "very valuable, interesting and extremely important," it was in his view "rather motley" [*pestrovataia*], so much so that it made him doubt "whether or not this or that part [of *Requiem*] had perhaps been distorted in the manuscript at your disposal: some lines are just too weak for a master like Akhmatova."[91]

Meanwhile, as Struve predicted, counterfeit copies of *Requiem* started reaching the West, threatening to outrun the Munich edition.[92] On October 21, 1963, acknowledging receipt of Akhmatova's original typescript from Struve, Khomiakov informed him that one such copy could have become available to Grynberg,[93] possibly via Sergei Rittenberg, professor of Russian literature in Stockholm, who had traveled to Russia more than once in the 1960s and met with Akhmatova.[94] Khomiakov assured Struve, however, that although he could not guarantee that Grynberg actually had the manuscript ("he was not clear about it"), it did not even matter: "We will outrun him anyway."[95] But once *Requiem* was out, it was Grynberg's turn to question the authenticity of the Munich edition. In his letter to Struve on December 21, 1963, not knowing who stood behind the publication, Grynberg complained that the Munich edition left him "unsatisfied," in particular, because his version had six additional poems that had been "omitted" by Khomiakov.[96] Besides, in his copy, Grynberg lamented, the epigraph came not before "In Place of a Foreword," but after it. Grynberg also confessed that when he had visited Khomiakov in Munich in September, "the manuscript of this work was already in my pocket"; he was bewildered as to where Khomiakov's version came from and why he had preferred it over Grynberg's in the first place. Finally, the editor of *Vozdushnye puti* added that he had apparently decided against publishing *Requiem* in his almanac even before he learned about the Munich edition, and that he was sure, along these lines, that Akhmatova was going to be "truly indignant that 'Requiem' had appeared in Western Germany, not to mention everything else."[97]

While Grynberg abstained from printing *Requiem* in his almanac,[98] another "stray" copy of *Requiem* did appear in Frankfurt in the émigré journal *Grani* a year or so later.[99] On December 24, 1964, in his letter to the editor of *Grani*, Natalia Tarasova, Struve highlighted the numerous discrepancies between her version and the Munich edition. One could, perhaps, take these discrepancies between the two versions for Akhmatova's own changes introduced to the text of *Requiem* at a later stage, but most of them were so out of tune that there was no doubt they were merely "errors or personal inventions of the scribe" [*otsebiatina perepischika*], as Struve rightly pointed out.[100] Tarasova, in turn, explained that she had faced a difficult choice,

> either to edit the manuscript based on your version, which I felt much more confident about . . ., or to print it as we received it from Russia. . . . I kept thinking, hesitating and weighing each option for a long time, and at last, so to say, I decided to print it as is, for the most basic reason: had I edited [the manuscript] based on your version, no one would believe that we, too, received *Requiem* from Russia, nor that it is being passed from hand to hand over there. Meanwhile, for us, the fact that Akhmatova's poems circulate in different copies is also important. . . . Each of us, you and I, have fulfilled our own respective functions: to register the Russian contemporaneity in all its fullness. That is how history will judge our editions of *Requiem*: yours as the classic example, the one in *Grani*—as "half-folklore."[101]

For Tarasova, *Requiem* was more a barometer of the sociopolitical climate in Russia than a work of art with its own unchangeable text, structure, and composition. Yet Struve's exasperation with seeing *Requiem* published in *Grani* stemmed not only from textual flaws but also from the journal's overt anti-Soviet orientation and its affiliation with the National Alliance of Russian Solidarists (NTS), the most ominous émigré organization in the eyes of the Soviet authorities. Not only was it rumored that the NTS was financed by the CIA, but it also had ties with the Nazi regime in the relatively recent past, in particular with General Vlasov's ill-famed Russian Liberation Army. Both Struve and Tarasova were perfectly aware that authors behind the Curtain whose collaboration with the NTS or contributions to one of its periodicals, authorized or not, were exposed were likely to face grave consequences. Indeed, while the Munich edition, despite Akhmatova's and her friends' apprehensions, seems to have been virtually ignored by the authorities, the publication of *Requiem* in *Grani* entailed an unpleasant conversation between the author and a Soviet literary official, who, in the poet's own words, "came and said: 'Anna Andreevna! What is this?' And showed me the issue of *Grani* where my *Requiem* was printed. On the last page, there was God knows what: instructions on how to smuggle manuscripts abroad, to whom to address them, some appeals."[102] The name of the visitor, ironically, was Daniil Granin, at the time the second secretary of the Leningrad branch of the Writers' Union (a year before, he had been involved in the persecution of Brodsky, although he tried to protect him later on). Based on Chukovskaia's diary entry, Granin's visit to Akhmatova took place no later than May 10, 1965,[103] a month before she was scheduled to depart for England to receive the honorary degree from Oxford (and, respectively, half a year after she traveled to Italy, where she was awarded another international literary prize, the Etna Taormina).[104] According to Peter Norman, who met Akhmatova in Leningrad in the summer of 1964 and welcomed her in London a year later, Granin (whose name Akhmatova chose not to disclose) had told her,

> "I know, I am quite sure, Anna Andreevna," he said, "that you are not going to commit anything anti-Soviet while there. But still, be careful." He had with him the journal *Grani*, where at the end of 1964 "Requiem" was printed. He said there were rumors that the publication was a result of Akhmatova's meetings with the journal editors back in Italy. Akhmatova fervently objected: "And

where, I wonder, do these rumors come from?" As if in passing and half in jest, the visitor said: "You are not going to stay in England, are you?" Akhmatova took his words as a warning.[105]

In London, Oxford, and Paris, where she stayed for several days not quite legally on her way back to Russia, Akhmatova met with old friends whom she had not seen for nearly half a century, as well as others, including the "shark of capitalism," Roman Grynberg. Many of them, including Georgy Adamovich, Yury Annenkov, Boris Anrep, and Nikita Struve, wrote memoirs and shared their impressions of Akhmatova with each other in personal correspondence.[106] Hopes were high that later that year Akhmatova would receive the Nobel Prize (instead, it was awarded to Mikhail Sholokhov) and take another trip to Paris in the fall as part of an official delegation of Soviet poets, a trip she eventually refused. Among those who came to England to meet with Akhmatova was Gleb Struve. Like some of his fellow First-Wave émigrés, he had also last seen Akhmatova nearly half a century earlier, before his departure from Russia in 1919. Struve's several meetings with her in England resulted in the final, authorized redaction of *Requiem*, which was included, along with a photograph of Akhmatova taken in London, in the first volume of her collected works published in the United States the same year. The poem was also published as a revised separate edition in 1969.[107] In England Struve was finally able to offer Akhmatova a honorarium for the first Munich edition of *Requiem*. Akhmatova's brief sojourn in England and France in June 1965 became an event of paramount importance in the life of the Russian literary diaspora, where passions for *Requiem* had already been raging for a year and a half since its first publication.

Akhmatova and the Russian Emigration: *Requiem*'s Epigraph

Нет, и не под чуждым небосводом, И не под защитой чуждых крыл—	[No, not under foreign skies, Nor under the protection of foreign wings—
Я была тогда с моим народом, Там, где мой народ, к несчастью, был.	I was then with my people, There, where my people, unfortunately, were.]
	1961

The above stanza of *Requiem*'s epigraph was adopted from Akhmatova's other poem "No, we didn't suffer together in vain . . ." ("Tak ne zria my vmeste bedovali . . ."), written a year before the cycle took shape and was first written down. The idea belonged to Lev Kopelev, who visited Akhmatova at Glen's apartment in Moscow in early December 1962, when she recited that poem to him and, upon hearing his suggestion, "immediately agreed."[108] It was not uncommon for Akhmatova to adjust "her poems to her epigraphs rather than the epigraphs to the poems."[109] The "youngest" poem in the cycle, the epigraph serves as a coda to Akhmatova's uneasy relationship with Russian emigration, which dated back to the year 1917 and was as old as the emigration itself. A text by definition "external" to the rest of the poem and "deliberately emphasized by the author,"[110] the epigraph threw down a challenge to the identity of those who had, under different circumstances, found themselves "under foreign skies," much as *Requiem* itself delivered a blow to Stalinism and served as a monument to its victims.

Akhmatova's ties with the Russian emigration, severed as they were until the Thaw era, fully reflect the void that came between the "two Russias" in the wake of the Revolution: one that the émigrés "carried away" into exile, and the other that Akhmatova refused to abandon. Since 1917 she had written a number of poems that influenced the reception of *Requiem* abroad half a century later. Her uncompromising position vis-à-vis emigration is for the first time declared "indifferently and calmly" in her 1917 poem dedicated to Boris Anrep, who "left for London on the first train after the Kerensky revolution":[111]

Мне голос был. Он звал утешно,

Он говорил: "Иди сюда,
Оставь свой край глухой и грешный.

Оставь Россию навсегда."
. . .

Но равнодушно и спокойно
Руками я замкнула слух,
Чтоб этой речью недостойной
Не осквернился скорбный дух.

I heard a voice—oh it was soothing!—
that cried: "Come here,
leave your wild and sinful country,
leave Russia forever!"
. . .

But indifferently and calmly
I blocked my ears, like a child,
not to be tempted by dirty talk,
not, in my mourning, to be defiled.[112]

Addressed to her romantic friend on his departure from Russia, Akhmatova's poem is as personal as it is civic: Anrep's voice is "depersonalized" as the collective call of those who left to those who stayed, a call that is proclaimed not only unacceptable, but utterly ignominious ("dirty talk"). This poem was among Akhmatova's texts that allowed Soviet critics during the Thaw to "promote" her to official status at home, although in gosizdat editions it appeared invariably without the first two stanzas, which invoke the nation's "suicidal anguish" and "German guests" during World War I. These unpublishable stanzas also compare the city on the Neva, engulfed by the revolutions, to a "drunken prostitute" who does not know "who would take her next":

Когда в тоске самоубийства	When in suicidal anguish
Народ гостей немецких ждал,	The nation awaited its German guests
И дух суровый византийства	And the stern spirit of Byzantium
От русской Церкви отлетал,	Had deserted the Russian Church;
Когда приневская столица,	When the capital by the Neva
Забыв величие свое,	Had forgotten its majesty
Как опьяневшая блудница,	And like a drunken prostitute
Не знала, кто берет ее,—	Did not know who would take it next.[113]

Five years later the same motif recurs in Akhmatova's poem "I am not with those who have abandoned their land . . ." ("Ne s temi ia, kto brosil zemliu . . .," 1922) written a year after the execution of her husband Nikolai Gumilev, at the end of the civil war, when it was clear that in the decades to follow, Russian literature would remain split into two different fields: one at home, the other abroad. In this poem, promoted as an invective against emigration by some Soviet critics,[114] Akhmatova's decision to stay and her condemnation of those who left sound even more proud and uncompromising. The "voice" that tempted her to abandon Russia forever in her earlier poem to Anrep here grows into "vulgar flattery" [*grubaia lest'*], while the émigrés are referred to as those who have forsaken their land "for the enemies to tear it apart" [*kto brosil zemliu / na rasterzanie vragam*]. It is those who left that deserve pity "like a prisoner, like the sick" [*Kak zakliuchennyi, kak bol'noi*]; it is *their* bread of exile that "smells like wormwood" [*polyn'iu pakhnet khleb chuzhoi*] and *their* path that is "dark" [*temna tvoia doroga, strannik*].[115] More importantly, in this poem Akhmatova declares her categorical refusal not only to listen to the émigrés' "vulgar flattery" but also to share with them her songs" [*Im pesen ia svoikh ne dam*],[116] not knowing, of course, that *Requiem* and her other works yet to be written would be first published abroad long before they would see the light of day in Russia.

Twenty years later, in Tashkent, Akhmatova wrote her famous poem "Courage" ("Muzhestvo"), which does not address emigration directly but contains a promise to "preserve Russian speech" and save "the great Russian word" [*I my sokhranim tebia, russkaia rech', / Velikoe russkoe slovo*].[117] Responding to Mandelshtam's "Preserve My Speech . . ." ("Sokhrani moiu rech' navsegda . . .") of 1931, which she believed was dedicated to her, Akhmatova translates it into another historical context: "Russian speech" [*russkaia rech'*] here rhymes with "falling from bullets" [*pod puliami lech'*], suggesting that death itself is the price to pay for one's native tongue, while the "Russian word" [*russkoe slovo*] is linked with "being left without a home" [*ostat'sia bez krova*], whereby language is, so to speak, deterritorialized. The somber meaning of these unsophisticated rhymes in Akhmatova's poem (dated February 23, 1942, the Day of the Red Army), had a profound resonance not only among readers at home, who saw it published in *Pravda* (on March 8, 1942, International Women's Day), but also among her émigré audience abroad.

Soviet critics had reason to claim that the war endowed Akhmatova's poetry, only recently branded "pessimist" and "decadent," with true civic value and made it ring out as the voice of the entire Soviet people. In May 1959, the head of the Soviet Writers' Union, Aleksei Surkov, requested Khrushchev's permission to celebrate Akhmatova's seventieth birthday in the official Soviet press, claiming that "party criticism has not gone unnoticed" and that she had since not only been positively "reformed" but also written "a series of new lyrical poems on civic themes that speak to the fact that she has successfully overcome her pessimistic attitudes of 1946."[118] In an attempt to create "a recipe for rehabilitation . . ., much as the monks of the early Church created the official lives of the saints,"[119] Surkov argued that these poems "are devoted to the heroism of the people during the war" and "praise the joy of . . . Soviet childhood and the people's struggle for peace."[120] Promoting "the old and talented Russian poetess" to official status, therefore, should have "a very positive resonance" both locally and internationally, especially given that "the reactionary pack of the whole world" was still raising their "revolting brouhaha" about Pasternak and his *Doctor Zhivago* (1: 169). It was not only from Pasternak but also Tsvetaeva and Mandelshtam, whose works had been published in tamizdat,[121] that Akhmatova was distinguished. According to another Soviet critic, Akhmatova, unlike Tsvetaeva, "was aware of the strong link between her own fate and that of her country," which was precisely what allowed her to withstand the temptation of emigration and the ordeal of war, as well as become a true patriot and write a poem like "Courage."[122] As for Mandelshtam, it was implied that Akhmatova, unlike her fellow Acmeist, managed to overcome the illusions of the past without giving in to "the ghost of the bourgeois civilization of the West."[123] Little did it matter that neither Tsvetaeva nor Mandelshtam lived to the end of the war.

Unsurprisingly, the same poems on civic themes evoked suspicion and even hostility abroad. Trying their best to represent Akhmatova as a martyr herself and a defender of Stalin's victims, some émigré critics refused to acknowledge the price she had to pay in the desperate hope to save her son, arrested for the third time in 1949. Akhmatova's ode to Stalin, "Song of Peace" ("Slava miru"), published in Ogonek in 1950, was meant "to convince the public (especially those abroad) that Akhmatova was alive, well, and loyal," while the poem itself, therefore, was "in no way ... regarded as her own," as Brodsky argued years later.[124] But the reaction of the émigré literary community was quite different. In his 1951 monograph *Soviet Russian Literature* Struve simply doubted the authorship of these poems,[125] while Vladimir Markov, an expert on Futurism and the avant-garde, in his introduction to a 1952 anthology of Russian poetry behind the Iron Curtain, went so far as to claim that "after long years of oblivion, misfortunes and losses, Akhmatova has turned from a silent symbol of the rejection of Soviet literature into a fact not only of this literature, but also of its politics." While her cycle "Slava Miru" "sounds like a defendant's speech at a Moscow trial," Markov wrote, it was also possible that she "never wrote these poems."[126] Indeed, looking at these poems from afar, it was hard to believe that in one of them, written on the occasion of Stalin's seventieth anniversary ("December 21, 1949"), Akhmatova could actually praise him as "a friend" and "a teacher" who "twice saved Leningrad" and "each of us" from death. In another poem dated the same month ("I Vozhd' orlinymi ochami . . ."), one hears the unanimous voice of gratitude of the Soviet people to Stalin: "And the Leader hears the voice / of the grateful people: / 'We have come / to say that freedom, / peace and greatness of the world / are there, where Stalin is!' [*I blagodarnogo naroda / Vozhd' slyshit golos: / "My prishli / Skazat',—gde Stalin, tam svogoda, / Mir i velichie zemli!"*].[127] At the height of postwar repressions, by some standards even more merciless than the Terror of the 1930s, the publication of these poems in *Ogonek* under Akhmatova's name drove the Russian diaspora into shock, prompting one émigré critic in particular to mourn the moral "defeat" of Akhmatova. "Can we regard these poems as Akhmatova's fruit of creation? No. . . . We can now be sure that the Russian poetess Anna Akhmatova is no more," the critic concluded. "There is now yet another slave of Stalin in Soviet literature. Will her talent survive long under such circumstances? And will her honest heart be able to endure it? We cannot blame Akhmatova. We have to understand and pity her and bow to her tortured soul and enslaved talent."[128] This article was published in England in September 1951, when communication across the Curtain was still virtually impossible. Akhmatova's harrowing lines about "groveling at the hangman's feet" [*kidalas' v nogi palachu*] from *Requiem*'s prologue,[129] although written in 1939, were not yet available abroad. In Russia, however, "Slava Miru" was read by the narrow circle of Akhmatova's initiated readers in a context informed by their firsthand familiarity with the reality that dictated the poem: "Can it be that, crawling on her knees before Stalin, Akhmatova is still taking revenge on him on the sly . . . through the sheer mediocrity of these poems?" wrote Aleksandr Gladkov upon reading these poems while still in the camps.[130] But when the émigré poet and critic Yury Terapiano remembered Akhmatova's "Slava Miru" as late as 1965, he still found it necessary to alert Struve that should he plan on including the cycle in the first volume of Akhmatova's collected works, it would be necessary to offer "a commentary for the future; otherwise some 'literary historian' may say, 'Although Akhmatova was an internal émigré, Stalin's powerful personality attracted her.' "[131]

Misreading Akhmatova's poems on civic themes had to do not only with the aesthetic formation and literary tastes of the émigrés, who still viewed her from afar as a poet of the Silver Age, both aesthetically and historically. It can also be explained by the biographical circumstances of many of those who found themselves abroad in the 1940s. Long before *Requiem* appeared as a separate edition in Munich, some of its poems had first been printed in pro-Nazi Russian-language newspapers on the occupied territories of the Soviet Union and elsewhere in Europe (in Riga and Pskov, as well as Berlin and Paris). On December 4, 1963, Filippov informed Khomiakov that while one poem from *Requiem*, "The Sentence" ("Prigovor") had previously appeared in the USSR,[132] two other poems—"They took you away at daybreak . . ." ("Uvodili tebia na rassvete . . .") and "The silent Don flows silently . . ." ("Tikho l'etsia tikhii Don . . ."), that is, parts 1 and 2—"were published under the German occupation in the Russian press of Riga and in Berlin."[133] On January 16, 1964, in his letter to Struve, Filippov specified that the second poem ("Tikho l'etsia tikhii Don . . .") had been printed "in an article by N. Anin . . ., a lieutenant in the ROA [Russian Liberation Army], Davidenkov, son of the famous surgeon."[134] A biology student at Leningrad State University, Nikolai Davidenkov (1916–1950) was arrested in 1938 together with Lev Gumilev and other members of the so-called Leningrad student terrorist organization and convicted of state crimes, but he was soon acquitted and released from prison. On August 14, 1939, upon hearing from Akhmatova that her son was being transferred from Leningrad to the distant camps, Davidenkov helped gather warm clothes for him, and early next morning, joined by Chukovskaia, held the line for Akhmatova by the gates of the Kresty Prison.[135] It was there that Akhmatova spent "seventeen months" and once heard "a woman with blue lips" whisper to her the solemn question, to which *Requiem* became an answer: " 'Can you describe this?' And I said, 'Yes, I can.' " [*"A eto vy mozhete opisat?" I ia skazala: "Mogu"*].[136] Davidenkov was among Akhmatova's closest friends who knew *Requiem* by heart before it was finally entrusted to paper; he may have heard parts of it from Akhmatova before his arrest or between his release from prison and conscription to the army in the summer of 1941. Soon after the outbreak of the war, Davidenkov was taken prisoner by the Germans, and after a while publications signed with his pen name, N. Anin, began to appear in the Russian collaborationist newspapers. On August 21, 1943, one such newspaper in Nazi-occupied Paris ran his article "Leningrad Nights" ("Leningradskie nochi"), in which he refuted the popular myth about Akhmatova's "keeping silent" during the Great Terror. To prove his point, Davidenkov-Anin cited "Tikho l'etsia tikhii Don . . .": "Those who did not want to, did not keep silent. Anna Akhmatova was not silent either. It was during these past few years that she has given Russia these splendid and inspiring verses."[137] The poem from the future *Requiem* was, evidently, reproduced by Davidenkov from memory, with minor discrepancies in punctuation and with the fifth and the sixth lines reversed. Davidenkov's article, however, ended as follows: "One can only wish . . . that, looking back at our lost youth, we would see the heroic efforts of separate individuals as they carry the holy of holiest Russian culture through the black night of the Jewish yoke [*zhidovskoe igo*] into the broad daylight of tomorrow."[138]

Exposing Davidenkov's identity, nowhere does Filippov reveal, however, that he also quoted a stanza from Akhmatova's *Requiem* ("The Sentence") as an epigraph to his own article in another collaborationist newspaper, *Za Rodinu*, published under Nazi occupation in Pskov two weeks after Davidenkov's. This article, titled "How Akhmatova Was Published" ("Kak napechatali Akhmatovu"), was signed with Filippov's real name, Boris Filistinsky, and dwelt on Akhmatova's prewar collection of poetry *Iz shesti knig* (1940), which appeared "in Soviet Russia with unheard-of swiftness" as a result of Stalin's personal commission; allegedly, the leader ordered the book published after he caught his daughter Svetlana read Akhmatova's early lyrics. Then "they again stopped publishing Akhmatova," Filippov continued, "and now, threatened by her son's fate in the hands of the NKVD, Akhmatova is again writing . . . overblown fake propaganda verses [*nadutye, fal'shivye agitki*]. . . . What wouldn't one do to save one's children! Foul, but understandable."[139] Filippov does not specify just what "propaganda verses" he had in mind, but there is little doubt that a poem like "Courage" could leave him indifferent during the years he spent as a Nazi collaborator. Twenty years after Filippov-Filistinsky moved from Germany to the United States and embarked on his career as a publisher and professor of Russian literature, the epigraph to *Requiem* could not but stir his memory of the wartime past.

Nor could the past let go of Vladimir Markov, professor of Russian at Monterey: like Filippov, he also used to write for Russian collaborationist newspapers in the 1940s. Having read *Requiem* soon after its first publication, he claimed that "in poems like these, one should have forsaken . . . one's personal grief and spoken instead of the Russian grief only."[140] Paraphrasing almost verbatim what Solzhenitsyn had once told Akhmatova upon hearing *Requiem*, Markov articulated the reluctance of some émigré critics to come to terms with the fact that what distinguished *Requiem* from other accounts of Stalin's terror, whether fictional or documentary, was precisely the "balance between the lyric and the epic."[141] Three years earlier, when he read Akhmatova's "Poem without a Hero," Markov found it "merely interesting," but in *Requiem*, as he wrote to Struve, Akhmatova "simply failed to pull off the topic" [*prosto ne podniala temu*]. Some of its individual poems were "not bad" [*popadaiutsia i neplokhie*], but they "added nothing to her reputation," which for Markov rested exclusively on Akhmatova's poetry written before the Revolution. "She could have still produced wonderful works in exile (like Georgy Ivanov, whom she despises)," Markov suggested, had she also emigrated, or at least stopped regarding her refusal to emigrate as "a moral victory."[142] Complaining to Struve of being "troubled" by *Requiem*'s epilogue, where Akhmatova "does not forget about a monument to herself,"[143] half a year later Markov concluded that for him, she "simply plopped down from a pedestal" [*prosto shlepnulas's p'edestala*].[144] It was not until 2006 that a monument to Akhmatova was erected in St. Petersburg on the opposite bank of the Neva from the Kresty Prison, where "under that red blind prison-wall" [*pod krasnoiu oslepsheiu stenoiu*] she stood "for three hundred hours / And where they never, never opened the doors for me" [*zdes', gde stoiala ia trista chasov / I gde dlia menia ne otkryli zasov*],[145] as she wrote in March 1940. The monument in the epilogue to *Requiem* is, of course, neither a monument to herself alone, nor even to those whose names it was meant to rescue from oblivion. It is also a monument to the world literary tradition—from Horace's ode "Exegi monumentum" to Pushkin's "Monument" ("Ia pamiatnik sebe vozdvig nerukotvornyi ...," 1836)—that continues the topos of the Roman classic in the historical context of nineteenth-century Russia with a similar formal simplicity employed a century later by Akhmatova.

Another poem from *Requiem*, according to Filippov, was "printed in Riga or Rezhitsa [Rēzekne], also during the war—'Uvodili tebia na rassvete ....'"[146] Whether or not it was actually published in one of the local pro-Nazi newspapers remains unknown, but this poem did appear long before *Requiem* in the New York émigré newspaper *Novoe russkoe slovo*: it was quoted—evidently from memory and with significant textual discrepancies—by the émigré critic Viacheslav Zavalishin, a graduate of the history and philology department of Leningrad State University, where Akhmatova's son had studied until his expulsion in December 1935. During the war Zavalishin, like Filippov, stayed in Nazi-occupied Pskov and Riga and also wrote for the local collaborationist press. In his 1952 article on Akhmatova, Zavalishin writes that not only did he study together with Lev Gumilev in Leningrad but he also visited Akhmatova several times and "helped her send parcels for her son to the concentration camp in Krasnoyarsk (the last time I took one of these parcels to the post office was in the spring of 1941)."[147]

However far from reality Zavalishin's account may be, the number of people who knew Akhmatova's *Requiem* (or parts of it) by heart was evidently more than eleven, as the poet naively believed.

As for the older generation of Russian émigrés, most of whom spent the war years in France (some, like Adamovich, joined the French army), their reaction to *Requiem*'s epigraph was not entirely favorable either. In the Paris-based Russian émigré newspaper *Russkaia mysl'*, Arkady Slizskoi, a former participant of the White movement, remarked bitterly that "those who are fated to die away from their motherland usually ask to throw a handful of their native earth into their graves, which may seem like excessive sentimentality to the 'tearless people'" [*bessleznym liudiam*].[148] Slizskoi invoked Akhmatova's poem "Native Land" ("Rodnaia zemlia," 1961), which appeared—instead of *Requiem*—in the January 1963 issue of *Novyi mir*, with the epigraph "recycled" from her earlier 1922 poem "I am not with those who have abandoned their land . . ." ("Ne s temi ia, kto brosil zemliu . . .").[149] A poetic rejoinder to Akhmatova's "Native Land" was soon published in *Novoe russkoe slovo* in New York, authored by Gizella Lakhman, the "Akhmatova of the Russian emigration," as Yury Leving referred to her.[150] In her sonnet dated March 17, 1963, Lakhman enters a polemical dialogue with Akhmatova, putting some of her lines in quotation marks and directly responding, negating, or adjusting them *to her* idea of "native land" and that of her fellow émigrés:

"О ней стихи навзрыд не сочиняем"	"We do not write of her, heart-wrung, in verses,"
И в наших снах ее благословляем,	And in our dreams we sing her praises,
Но в ладанках не носим на груди.	But we don't press it to our chest as an amulet.
Зачем? Она у нас—в сердцах, Недосягаемый и драгоценный прах—	What for? It is in our hearts, The precious ash out of our reach,
Тот, что не ждет нас впереди, Когда в чужую землю ляжем,	One that does not await us When we lie down in the foreign earth,
Что нам не мачеха и не родная мать.	Which is neither our stepmother, nor a mother.

(А ваших слов о "Купле и продаже,"   (As for your words about
                                    "Buying and selling,"
признаться, не могу понять.)   I confess I don't understand
                                    them.)

Болея и сгибаясь под тяжелой ношей,   Sick and bent under our
                                    heavy burden,
Мы помним хруст в зубах ее песка,   We taste against our teeth the
                                    grit of her sand,
И грязь и снег на маленьких   The mud and snow clinging
калошах . . .   to our little galoshes . . .
Но мать отвергла нас и ныне далека.   But our mother rejected us
                                    and now she is far away.

А мы, рожденные и вскормленные ею,   Yet we, nurtured and raised
                                    by her,
Мы смеем звать ее, как вы,—своею.   Dare, like you, to call her
                                    our own.[151]

Although Lakhman's response to Akhmatova appeared before she could read *Requiem* in the Munich edition, it was symptomatic of the reception of *Requiem* in tamizdat only months later. Some went so far as to question the authenticity of *Requiem*, arguably not only because of its epigraph's message but because the poem as a whole failed to live up to their expectations of Akhmatova as a Silver Age poet and master of versification. Suspecting that most poems in *Requiem* were "fake" [*podlog*], in her letter to Markov on March 12, 1965, Irina Odoevtseva, one of the "matriarchs" of Russian poetry in exile, confessed that for her, like for Markov, "Akhmatova ended in 1922. Everything else," she continued, including *Requiem*, "could just as well not have been written at all" [*Ostal'nogo moglo by i ne byt'*].[152] Akhmatova's former friend and addressee of some of her earlier lyrics, Arthur Lourié allegedly also called *Requiem* a "forgery," having only recently composed a libretto for "Poem without a Hero," which he dedicated to Olga Glebova-Sudeikina.[153] Much like his ideological opponents in Soviet Russia, Roman Gul', the editor of *Novyi zhurnal*, agreed that in *Requiem* Akhmatova's voice ceased to be "chamber-like" and now resounded as the voice of "all Russia" [*vserossiiskii*].[154] But "while Akhmatova's conscious choice of the motherland, not of freedom, which she made in 1917, should be regarded as heroic," Gul' argued that "no less conscious and perhaps even more heroic" was the choice made by Zinaida Gippius, who emigrated to France with her husband Dmitry Merezhkovsky in 1920.[155] Gippius and Merezhkovsky were terrified by the Revolution, seeing it as the advent of the Antichrist, but much to his wife's dismay, Merezhkovsky later supported Hitler, whom he was rumored to have once compared to "the new Joan of Arc" on the radio, seeing him as the "lesser evil" compared to Stalin.[156] It was perhaps for that reason that Gul', himself a staunch anticommunist, did not mention Merezhkovsky in his review of *Requiem* and spoke only of Gippius and her "choice of freedom." "At the same time as Akhmatova, Gippius chose to break with the motherland in the name of freedom. . . . I suppose it is not good that Akhmatova, in her own time, wrote rather haughtily about those who left. . . . The fact that life away from the motherland is tragically difficult to all should not have become the subject of haughty [*vysokomernye*] versification."[157]

Adamovich, who met with Akhmatova in Paris a year and a half after *Requiem* was published, also spoke of the imperative to regard both choices as equally legitimate, but he specified that "Russia is not a geographical and certainly not a political notion," and in this sense, "for the past forty-five years, emigration has been an integral part of Russia." Without arguing with Akhmatova over the uneasy question that could not have an answer in principle, Adamovich nevertheless concluded, "It was not because we opted for 'the protection of foreign wings' that we have lived our lives and, of course, will die away from home."[158] Indeed, as long as the idea of home was reduced to geography and ideology, all attempts to reconcile the message of *Requiem*'s epigraph with its émigré audience appeared futile. The solution, as Adamovich implied, lay elsewhere, outside the geographical and even historical setting of *Requiem*, perhaps even beyond Akhmatova's own biography as its author.

It was not until after Akhmatova's death that Alexander Schmemann, a priest of the Russian Orthodox Church Abroad, in his speech at the memorial service for Akhmatova in New York on March 13, 1966, suggested an interpretation of *Requiem* that finally pointed to a possible reconciliation. Instead of fanning the old flames of ideological disputes between the diaspora and the metropolia, Schmemann insisted that *Requiem* was "devoid of any 'ideology'" and suggested that one look at it instead through the prism of gender.

An ideological approach to motherland is a masculine approach, and that is, essentially, how motherland has always been treated in Russian poetry. . . . Such an ideological approach is capable not only of justifying one's departure, but also of making it morally necessary and unavoidable, because going away—*for the sake* of the motherland, in the name of it—is a manifestation of one's loyalty to it. But the point is that there was no such option for Akhmatova, since she does not "relate" to Russia but, so to speak, herself *is* Russia, much like the mother does not "relate" to the family but herself *is* the family. . . . Akhmatova was such a mother and wife, one of the millions of such mothers, who *could not* leave. . . . And this is why, I repeat, Akhmatova's relationship with Russia is not "ideological"; hers is . . . a voice not *about* Russia, but of Russia itself, its air, its truth, its light.[159]

Schmemann highlighted one important dimension of the political identity of the Russian diaspora that had been rarely spoken of in the categories of gender: like a soldier on the frontlines, the emigration had traditionally seen itself on a mission to "save" its motherland from the Soviet oppressor within. Such self-representation, as Schmemann argued, was inherently masculine. Ironically, it mirrored the conventions of gender in Soviet literature, epitomized, for instance, in Konstantin Simonov's iconic war poem "Wait for Me" ("Zhdi menia") of 1941: while the men fought the enemy away from home, the women kept faithfully waiting for their husbands and sons to come back home safe. The émigrés' ties with their motherland, however, had been severed forever, whereby the ancient myth of a homecoming was hardly applicable to their reality. Having taken shape in the early 1920s, when exile still seemed to some to be only temporary, throughout the rest of the Soviet century, the hope of going back could no longer be entertained (except by a handful of returnees in the mid-1930s and after the war).[160] Instead, the homecoming myth, as old as Homer's *Odyssey*, was bound to take on a life of its own, confined and readjusted to the identity and rituals of the émigré community. Little as it had to do with reality, it continued, nevertheless, to offer exiles a meaningful narrative and justification for their departure.

As the story of the first publication and reception of Akhmatova's *Requiem* abroad demonstrates, the Russian emigration went on carrying out its political mission through literary means. By smuggling contraband manuscripts out of Russia and publishing them elsewhere, it rescued them from oblivion and desecration at home. Once published, tamizdat editions could even repatriate—to offset, so to say, the émigrés' inability to do so physically. This roundtrip journey of clandestine Russian literature from the USSR covered not only geographical space but also historical time, as can be inferred, for example, from Chukovskaia's thoughts on December 28, 1963, when Akhmatova showed her the Munich edition of *Requiem*:

> My hands grew cold, and my heart sank to my knees. *Requiem* is published! It is no longer a typescript but a book.... Immediately in front of my eyes appeared the Fountain House, the old armchair by the stove, the mess, her uncombed hair on the rumpled pillow, a spark of flame in the ashtray, the burnt edges of a curling scrap of paper. Ash. 1938. And now, her words rose from the ashes and turned into the most simple, mundane, ordinary object: a book! There are millions or perhaps even billions of books in the world, and here another is added. One more book—as simple as that. "The Ashes of Claes." . . . As for us, there is enough embarrassment that a great work like *Requiem* has resounded in the West earlier than at home. "Munich."[161]

Requiem, as Jean-Philippe Jaccard put it, was a product of *"goszakaz"* (state commission) in that it was "commissioned" to Akhmatova by the multitude of women of the years of Terror. Their plea was metonymically articulated by one old woman "with blue lips" who "identified" Akhmatova in one of the endless lines by the Leningrad prisons and asked her in a whisper whether she could "describe it."[162] That woman became "the Muse of *Requiem*," much as *Requiem* itself became an answer to this innermost question, which called it into being. Her figure "is suggestive of Virgil's appearance in *The Divine Comedy* . . ., as well as Dante's conversations with the spirits of Hell,"[163] making *Requiem* not only a statement on the historical reality of Stalin's Russia but also a text inscribed to world mythology and literary tradition, including the age-old myth of exile invoked in the poem's epigraph, which émigré critics reduced to the specifics of Soviet history and their own biographies. Akhmatova's female voice, alternating in *Requiem* between the grammatical categories of person and number ("I"/"we"/"she"), by the same token, belongs not only to the poem's author, as it was ubiquitously maintained, but also to a series of both historical and mythological female characters outside Soviet history, such as the seventeenth-century wives of *strel'tsy* (*streletskie zhenki*) wailing "under the Kremlin walls," or the biblical ones, including Mary Magdalene and the Mother of God, both of whom appear together in *Requiem*'s "Crucifixion" ("Raspiatie"). It is both surprising and symptomatic, along these lines, that hardly any émigré critic, not even Schmemann, dwelt on the religious orchestration of *Requiem* and its numerous biblical allegories.

It is in this context that *Requiem*'s epigraph, too, may be read not only literally but also metaphorically. In keeping with the tendency of prison narratives as a genre to invert commonly accepted notions by rendering metaphors literal and vice versa, the epigraph, which was written last but comes first in the cycle, straightforward and categorical as it may sound on the surface, reverses the notions of home and abroad. Home is referred to as "there," *tam* ("there, where my people, unfortunately, were"), introducing a measure of ambiguity to the geographical and linguistic realities of Soviet history and blurring the line between the "Soviet" and the "émigré" branches of Russian literature. Irreducible to a mere condemnation of exile, the epigraph of *Requiem* anticipated the story of its first publication abroad, in tamizdat.

CHAPTER 3

Lydia Chukovskaia's *Sofia Petrovna* and *Going Under*

Fictionalizing Stalin's Purges

Named by Akhmatova as her *Requiem*'s "sister" and singled out as the most important work on Stalinism next to that poem and Solzhenitsyn's *Ivan Denisovich*,[1] Chukovskaia's *Sofia Petrovna* is the only known work of fiction that deals with the Great Terror not in hindsight but simultaneously with the events described. "To this day," Chukovskaia wrote in 1974, "I know of no volume of prose about 1937 written in *this* country and at *that* time."[2] Unlike *Requiem*, however, *Sofia Petrovna* survived the years of Terror, the siege of Leningrad, postwar repressions, and Stalin himself, not just in the memory of the author's closest friends, but as a physical manuscript. "What you did was a feat," Akhmatova once told Chukovskaia. "All of us were thinking about it, we wrote poems and committed them to our memory, or wrote them down on paper for a split second and burned them right away, but you wrote it!"[3] Chukovskaia, for her part, recalled that writing *Sofia Petrovna* felt "no more heroic than breathing or washing my face" and that "*not* to write would have been more difficult and frightening." Writing gave her a way to understand "the reason for the unconsciousness and blindness of the society," which she had given "the most ordinary name": Sofia Petrovna. The blindness and unconsciousness of Chukovskaia's titular heroine, metonymically, "stood for the blindness of millions."[4] A decade later, Sofia Petrovna was partly "atoned for" in Chukovskaia's second novella *Going Under* (*Spusk pod vodu*), whose female protagonist, a Soviet author and translator, revisits the year 1937 and verbalizes her past experiences in a manuscript she is secretly writing.

That conversation between Akhmatova and Chukovskaia took place on November 4, 1962, two weeks before the long-awaited publication of Solzhenitsyn's *Ivan Denisovich* in *Novyi mir*. *Sofia Petrovna* had embarked on its own journey to publication at home a year before, together with Solzhenitsyn's manuscript, but unlike *Ivan Denisovich*, it failed to see the light in Russia. Chukovskaia's efforts to have *Sofia Petrovna* published at home were, in some sense, even more relentless than those of Akhmatova to publish *Requiem*. Yet the stories of their manuscripts' release from the drawer, clandestine circulation at home, and first publications abroad are in many ways parallel and equally symptomatic of the historical, political, and literary paradigms of the Thaw. Kept secret for over twenty years, Chukovskaia's manuscript went public in the wake of the Twenty-second Congress of the Party. After being rejected by several Soviet periodicals and a publishing house, it circulated in samizdat and was eventually leaked abroad, where it was brought out in two different versions, under different titles, in Paris and New York in 1966.[5] Like *Requiem*, *Sofia Petrovna* had to wait two more decades to be published in Russia during perestroika.[6]

Tracing the history of *Sofia Petrovna* from its inception and first attempts at publication at home during the Thaw, this chapter discusses the journey of Chukovskaia's manuscript abroad, its first publication and reception in tamizdat, and the political and aesthetic reasons for its rejection in gosizdat vis-à-vis its reception abroad. Situating *Sofia Petrovna* in the context of Chukovskaia's later novella, *Going Under*, the second part of the chapter addresses those aspects of both works that go beyond the author's incontestable historical accomplishment—daring " 'to name the torture chamber' in its presence."[7] Because of the immediate proximity of Chukovskaia's fiction to the historical events described, *Sofia Petrovna* was read primarily "as history rather than fiction,"[8] while *Going Under* was often read as an autobiography, rather than a creative amplification of the earlier work. This chapter argues, however, that the two works, set and written ten years apart, are "indexical" to each other and may be read as a cycle or diptych without being reduced to the respective historical contexts that inform their subject matter: the Great Terror of the 1930s and Stalin's persecution of the Soviet intelligentsia and Jewry in the late 1940s. Moreover, the historical import of Chukovskaia's fiction brings home mainstream Soviet literary paradigms from the Thaw to the Brezhnev era, including socialist realism, which she effectively undermines and departs from. As a result, both *Sofia Petrovna* and *Going Under* were forced out elsewhere, beyond the confines of the Soviet literary jurisdiction. Thus, a parallel reading of the reception of *Sofia Petrovna* and *Going Under* on opposite sides of the Soviet state borders puts gosizdat and tamizdat in the relationship of mutual complementarity, rather than binary opposition.

Sofia Petrovna: Attempts to Publish at Home

In 1962, in her preface to *Sofia Petrovna*, Chukovskaia emphasized that she had written it "twenty-two years ago, in Leningrad, in the winter of 1939–1940," without much hope "that the school exercise book containing the clean copy of it would escape destruction and be preserved."[9] The novella's first draft was completed at the Writers' House in Detskoe Selo in December 1939. "Today is a happy, or an unhappy, day for me," Chukovskaia wrote to her father Kornei Chukovsky that month. "I have completed a short novella I began writing two months ago. It is only a draft, of course. Now I am going to start polishing it."[10] On February 4, 1940, she read her newly completed work, referred to in code, to Akhmatova: "Today is a big day for me. I read my historical research on Mikhailov to Anna Andreevna."[11] But until the late 1950s, *Sofia Petrovna* was known to only nine people:

> At about the same time I read *Sofia Petrovna* to Anna Andreevna, I also read it to some of my friends. I invited eight people to my place, but the ninth one turned up uninvited, almost against my will. No, he was not a traitor, and he did not run to the Big House to inform on me. But he did talk too much. He told someone the interesting piece of news, and that someone told someone else, and by the end of 1940, this news in a distorted form became known *over there* "through grapevine"; *there*, they found out I was hiding some "document about '37"—that is how the interrogator who questioned my close and not-so-close ones referred to *Sofia Petrovna*.[12]

Writing this from the distance of more than quarter century, Chukovskaia found it hard to understand "why I wasn't arrested and shot as soon as they found out about my novella," a mystery that Akhmatova interpreted sarcastically: "You are like a glass that rolled under the

bench during an explosion in a china shop."[13] Unable to keep at home
the "thick school exercise book with pages numbered by Lyusha" (Chukovskaia's nine-year-old daughter), she placed it "in reliable hands."[14]
In May 1941 Chukovskaia had to flee Leningrad for Moscow. This was
her second flight from Leningrad since the arrest of her husband, Matvei Bronshtein, in August 1937.[15] While the "ninth" member of Chukovskaia's audience in 1940 remains unknown, the friend who saved
the only copy of *Sofia Petrovna* was her former classmate at the Institute
of Art History, Isidor Glikin. Found unfit for the army as the result of
a prewar illness, Glikin stayed in the besieged Leningrad, where he died
of starvation on January 22, 1942. It was he whom Chukovskaia viewed
as a hero: "To keep [the manuscript] safe—that was heroism [*podvig*].
And to walk from one part of the city to the other on the eve of dying from hunger . . . just to pass my notebook on to his sister, that
was heroism too."[16] The news of Glikin's death reached Chukovskaia
during her evacuation in Tashkent. It was not until June 1944, when
Chukovskaia was able to return to Leningrad, that she reunited with
her manuscript at Glikin's sister's apartment. "With a strange feeling
of alienation I was leafing through these pages . . . about another, prewar death: 1937–1940. . . . In 1944, it seemed to me that *that* war was
over."[17] There was, however, another war to be fought twenty years later:
to publish *Sofia Petrovna* at home.

Kept secret as the only available copy until the Thaw, the manuscript of *Sofia Petrovna*, like many others, emerged from the drawer in
the aftermath of the Twenty-second Party Congress in October 1961,
although after Khrushchev's "secret speech" of 1956, Chukovskaia
could no longer resist the temptation to share her clandestine work
with new readers.[18] In November 1961 *Sofia Petrovna* was submitted to
Novyi mir via Anna Berzer, who passed it on to Tvardovsky the following
month together with the manuscript of Solzhenitsyn's *Ivan Denisovich*.
The adventures of *Sofia Petrovna* and *Ivan Denisovich* in gosizdat, thus,
have the same starting point, despite their "age difference" of twenty
years and Chukovskaia's skepticism about seeing her work published in
Tvardovsky's journal. "Of course, they are not going to publish it," she
remarked on November 6, 1961, before handing the manuscript over to
Berzer. "The conception is wrong. And besides, Tvardovsky cannot stand
me."[19] Still, the next mention of *Sofia Petrovna* in Chukovskaia's diary,
on January 1, 1962, is both elated and metaphorical: "The blizzard died
out. Quiet half-darkness around quiet buildings. Narrow paths gleam
between pink snowdrifts everywhere. On my way to the tram stop,

I remembered: 'I have forgotten to tell Anna Andreevna about 'Sofia.''"[20] Evidently, it was not only the "blizzard" but the entire era of Stalinism that had "died out" for Chukovskaia that New Year's evening, and while the "snowdrifts" were still high, the "narrow paths" between them no longer made the Soviet literary landscape impassable. On her way from the hospital, where she had visited Akhmatova after her third heart attack, Chukovskaia felt inspired with hope—not only for *Sofia Petrovna* and Akhmatova's *Requiem* and "Poem without a Hero," but for the future in general. Akhmatova, too, "seemed invigorated, at times even cheerful. No wonder! Since we last saw each other, so many events have happened, and all of them happy: the twenty-second congress, Stalin removed from the Mausoleum."[21] On that first day of January 1962, "spring" was in the air.

Five days later, however, Chukovskaia received a rejection from *Novyi mir* and by the end of the month became familiar with Tvardovsky's internal review of her manuscript.[22] The review stated that Sofia Petrovna "does not feel the background of all-people's life" [*ne chuvstvuet fona obshchenarodnoi zhizni*], that the text on such a "spicy" topic "is boring to read," that no character "invokes compassion" [*nikogo ne zhalko*], and that the author has failed to portray her personages as "live people," having reduced them to "mere conventional literary designations" [*vsego lish uslovnye literaturnye oboznacheniia*]. "There is no need," Tvardovsky concluded, "to go further in discussing the ideological and artistic failure of the work. The author is not a beginner in need of literary advice but an experienced writer and editor, who, as I see it, took up a project that is none of her business" [*mnogoopytnyi literator i redaktor, tol'ko vziavshiisia, po-moemu, ne za svoe delo*].[23] Another internal review of *Sofia Petrovna* written the same month by Tvardovsky's deputy, Aleksandr Dementiev, asserted that although the work is faithful in its portrayal of the year 1937, "the author's attitude to the Soviet regime is unclear."[24] Intuition did not fail Chukovskaia when she refused to believe that *Sofia Petrovna* could win Tvardovsky's approval, especially over such potent male competition as *Ivan Denisovich*. Although both works belonged to the same genre, they stood too far apart from each other ideologically and aesthetically, motivating Tvardovsky's preference for Solzhenitsyn's "positive hero" over Chukovskaia's not-so-heroic mad mother. In fact, the more similar the two works may have seemed on the surface, the deeper were the irreconcilable differences between them. Unlike Solzhenitsyn, Chukovskaia failed to address the plight of "the people" (*narod*) during collectivization but focused instead on the persecution of the intelligentsia during the Great Terror, which for Tvardovsky was secondary not only historically but also ethically. In her conversation with Akhmatova soon after the publication of *Ivan Denisovich*, Chukovskaia may have pretended that Tvardovsky did not like her *Sofia Petrovna* "aesthetically." But she realized that "one ought to give a *muzhik* to Tvardovsky [*Tvardovskomu muzhika podavai*], whereas Sofia Petrovna is a city-dweller, half-intelligentsia. He is not interested in this. What interests him is the village. 'Requiem' is no village either, said Anna Andreevna."[25] Neither *Requiem* nor *Sofia Petrovna* was, strictly speaking, a firsthand account of the camps, which also disqualified them from publication in Tvardovsky's journal. Rather, as Leona Toker defined them, *Sofia Petrovna* and *Requiem* were "narratives by non-witnesses," in which the camps and the prisons represent the Orwellian "*Room 101*, where imagination fears to tread." In contrast to the detailed interiors of Ivan Denisovich's camp, the settings of *Sofia Petrovna* and *Requiem* were limited to "the liminal spaces familiar to the authors," that is, the lines of women *outside* prison.[26]

In September and October 1962, Chukovskaia submitted *Sofia Petrovna* to three other periodicals (*Sibirskie ogni*, *Moskva*, and *Znamia*), as well as to the publishing house Sovetskii pisatel'. For a while the chances to see *Sofia Petrovna* in print seemed good. Indeed, days after the publication of *Ivan Denisovich* in *Novyi mir*, *Sofia Petrovna* was accepted and scheduled for publication in *Sibirskie ogni*, whose editors at the time were eager to serve Khrushchev's cause of unmasking "infractions of Socialist legality" (*narusheniia sotsialisticheskoi zakonnosti*) under Stalin. But on December 13, two weeks after Khrushchev's appearance at the Manezh Exhibition of Moscow Artists, the journal sent Chukovskaia an edited version of *Sofia Petrovna* with the request not to make any further changes. This meant, in Chukovskaia's words, that "the editors have 'set the manuscript straight' on their own, . . . and any attempt on the author's part to restore the original text at this point would be regarded as 'new changes' no longer acceptable at the printing stage."[27] *Sibirskie ogni* also proposed a new title, "Odna iz tysiach" ("One of the Thousands").[28] Although the changes were mainly stylistic rather than ideological, Chukovskaia restored the original text and sent the new typescript back to Novosibirsk, where the journal was published, with the demand to print it as is or not at all. "I should have flown to Novosibirsk myself," Chukovskaia later remarked, but "there were rumors that Lavrentiev, the editor of *Sibirskie ogni*, was on his way to Moscow."[29]

Viktor Lavrentiev arrived in Moscow on December 17, 1962, to take part in the meeting of Party leaders with Soviet writers and artists. Chukovskaia decided to seek him out after hearing from a friend in Novosibirsk that *Sofia Petrovna*, in Lavrentiev's words, "lacked the background of all-people's life" [*ne khvataet fona obshchenarodnoi zhizni*], a phrase that sounded all too familiar from Tvardovsky's review earlier that year.[30] Her meeting with Lavrentiev at the Moskva Hotel took place on December 20, three days after Khrushchev's proclamation at the meeting with the Soviet intelligentsia that it was time to draw a line between works of art that are truly "life-affirming" and those that are "pessimistic" and "slanderous."

> I listened to Lavrentiev for twenty minutes without interrupting. . . . My female protagonist must be enthusiastic about this background [of all people's life], only then would her son's downfall "occupy," as he put it, "the right place in our life—the place of fatal haphazardness, an error." It was very hard for me to listen to him without interrupting, but I held myself back. An error! Then I spoke. I said there were millions of those like Kolya; . . . that I conceived of Sofia Petrovna as a negative heroine. . . . "She is not likeable [*nesimpatichna*]," Lavrentiev said. "Of course," I replied. "She is poisoned by lies in the newspapers and on the radio, and for this reason she is unable to see the all-people's background. But it is not her fault. It is the fault of those who deceived her." Lavrentiev understood that our debate had gone too far and, without answering, suggested that I withdraw the preface and the date underneath. "But it is precisely this date that points to the documentary nature of my novella!" I said. "If there is any value to it at all, it is the date when the work was written." "It doesn't matter when it was written," Lavrentiev replied didactically. "What matters is that it be truthful. Think of the background of all-people's life."[31]

"I said goodbye and left," Chukovskaia concludes her account. "It was clear they were not going to publish *Sofia Petrovna* no matter what."[32] Indeed, the next month, she received Lavrentiev's formal rejection, which stated that, after rereading the manuscript, he decided that "*Sofia Petrovna*, in its current form, cannot be published." Lavrentiev also cited Khrushchev's message to the Soviet writers and artists that merely to describe the horrors of Stalinism was no longer sufficient; it was also necessary to raise readers' faith in the fairness and humanity of Soviet society.[33]

A week before meeting Lavrentiev, Chukovskaia received a rejection from Boris Evgeniev, the editor in chief of *Moskva*, although a junior editor of the journal had found *Sofia Petrovna* not only suitable for publication, but even "more powerful than Solzhenitsyn,"[34] a phrase Chukovskaia reports hearing "ten times a day" at the time.[35] The pattern was becoming clear: after initially producing a favorable impression on junior editors, *Sofia Petrovna* was repeatedly blocked at the higher levels, where fluctuations in the political climate had more immediate resonance, especially after December 17, 1962. Even earlier, however, a week before Khrushchev's "pogrom" at the Manezh, *Sofia Petrovna* was rejected by the journal *Znamia*. On November 23, 1962, its lifetime editor, Vadim Kozhevnikov, explained his reasons to Chukovskaia on the phone: "There are two other works on the same topic in our office. But they are more advantageous than yours ideologically and artistically."[36] Chukovskaia was not told or chose not to mention the other two manuscripts that Kozhevnikov had in mind, but it was clear that *Sofia Petrovna* could hardly compete with such "advantageous" characters as Ivan Denisovich, who set the limit of the admissible in the Soviet press during the warmest months of the Thaw. Not that Solzhenitsyn himself had any chance to publish *Ivan Denisovich* in Kozhevnikov's hardline *Znamia*: that required an editor like Tvardovsky and Khrushchev's personal approval.[37] But it was the triumph of Solzhenitsyn's peasant protagonist that inadvertently precluded other works on Stalinism, including those of Chukovskaia and Akhmatova, from being published in Russia around the same time. Still, Solzhenitsyn's breakthrough even seemed to atone for the shared failure to see *Requiem* and *Sofia Petrovna* in print at home. On December 2, 1962, Chukovskaia admitted that things "were not so bad after all, since *One Day in the Life of Ivan Denisovich* managed to break through and, with God's help, so will 'Requiem.'"[38]

By mid-December 1962 *Sofia Petrovna* had been rejected by all four journals (first *Novyi mir*, then *Znamia* and *Moskva*, and finally *Sibirskie ogni*). The only hope left for publication was Sovetskii pisatel'. By the time Chukovskaia met with Lavrentiev, she already knew that the publishing house had accepted her manuscript. On December 21, 1962, she reported that "the other day" she had received a phone call from Elia Moroz, an editor at Sovetskii pisatel', who announced the news and invited her to stop by and sign the contract. It was clear, however, that a book edition would take longer for publication than a periodical, making Chukovskaia anxious it might be too late, that "the loophole will close any minute [and] Solzhenitsyn's mighty breach will soon be patched up." Compared to Akhmatova and Chukovskaia's relative optimism only weeks earlier, by the end of 1962, their hopes had begun to evaporate. Only a year since the Twenty-second Party Congress, Akhmatova went so far as to compare what now seemed to be a return to Stalinism to the repeated arrests of the late 1940s and early 1950s (the so-called *povtornichestvo*). "And what about us?" Chukovskaia wrote down Akhmatova's words on December 21, 1962. "How can we tolerate praise for Stalin again, after his horrific resolutions have been made public?"[39]

Nevertheless, not only had the contract with Sovetskii pisatel' been signed, but early the next year an advance payment of 60 percent of the future honorarium was issued to Chukovskaia. Illustrations, cover design, and the frontispiece for *Sofia Petrovna* were also ready by March 1963. On February 22, 1963, however, Chukovskaia still had doubts. "It all seems real. And yet, there will be no book."[40] The storm broke two weeks later, on March 7–8, at the next meeting of Party leaders with the intelligentsia. Khrushchev's "yelling, cursing and faultfinding were just the form," Chukovskaia explained, while "the real meaning of that meeting was the refusal to expose Stalin. I understood that my 'Sofia Petrovna' is done for." Indeed, on March 11, 1963, when she was invited to look at the artwork for her book, the artist "spoke with me as if nothing [had] happened," but one of the publishing house's higher-ups, Lev Levin, confessed that the plans for *Sofia Petrovna* would now have to be reconsidered, whether or not the manuscript had been accepted. "You waited 25 years. Wait a couple of more months," Levin told Chukovskaia. "In a couple of months, things should become clearer."[41] The plans were indeed reconsidered when Chukovskaia's manuscript was passed on to Ivan Kozlov, a critic who specialized in books on the Great Patriotic War. Chukovskaia met with Kozlov on May 20, 1963:

> His first phrase: "I don't think we will publish your novella." He explained why. "It is all true, completely true, I worked at the time at the 'Molodaia gvardiia' publishing house myself, and everything was exactly as you have described. But this kind of truth does not reinforce the Soviet regime." Me: "But is it the truth?"—"I have told you already: it is the truth, but it does not reinforce people's faith in the Soviet regime." Me: "So it means, millions of people perished, but to remember them is forbidden?"—"No, why? Perhaps in fifteen years or so your novella will be published. But not

earlier." Me: "Actually, perhaps earlier. I am an optimist."—"I do not share your optimism." Me: "Why not? After all, when I was writing it, I had no hope anyone would ever read it, but now you and I are sitting here and discussing it freely, and dozens of people have read it as a manuscript."[42]

The last opportunity to see *Sofia Petrovna* published at home thus failed. "It is no longer about those who were killed, but about our own memory," Chukovskaia summarized her conversation with Kozlov to Akhmatova. "It is the killing of memory."[43] But two years later, on April 24, 1965, Chukovskaia won a lawsuit against Sovetskii pisatel' and received the remaining 40 percent of the honorarium for her manuscript, which the publishing house refused to print. The transcript of the court hearing, later published abroad, reflects the dynamic of the changing directives of the Party passed to the Soviet publishing houses and journals in 1962–1964. The lawsuit brought Chukovskaia more than financial gain. It enabled her to declare in public that "considering the novella good today, before finding it ideologically skewed [*ideiinyi perekos*] tomorrow," was in fact not much different from "what took place in 1937."[44] What Chukovskaia did not mention in the courtroom, however, was that apart from the changing political climate, *Sofia Petrovna* had few, if any, chances to be published in Russia even in 1961, when it was first submitted for publication along with Solzhenitsyn's novella; unlike her younger male contender *Ivan Denisovich*, she lacked the protective socialist-realist armor to pave her way into gosizdat. The concomitant question of Sofia Petrovna and her author's gender, vis-à-vis the *muzhiks* who decided her fate, was clearly not subject to legal scrutiny either.

Sofia Petrovna and (Socialist) Realism

The extent to which *Sofia Petrovna* enacted the socialist-realist conventions while in fact undermining and deviating from them was a question Chukovskaia pondered as soon as she finished writing the book: in a letter to her father on February 12, 1940, she called *Sofia Petrovna* "a novella in the spirit of socialist realism."[45] Neither a model nor a direct disavowal of socialist realism, *Sofia Petrovna*, according to Holmgren, is instead a "gamut of nineteenth-century radical fiction and its socialist realist offspring."[46] Nikolai Chernyshevsky's novel *What Is to Be Done?* (*Chto delat'?*), written during the author's incarceration at the Peter and

Paul Fortress, is one of Chukovskaia's many subtexts: not entirely un-like Chernyshevsky's female protagonist Vera Pavlovna, emancipated after the "death" of her husband (who in fact did not die but left for America), Chukovskaia's titular character, if only in the beginning, is "a woman 'different' from herself, but representative of her society and times—a woman, who until the (natural) death of her husband, had contended with the traditional roles of wife and mother and is then drawn into public life."[47] Sofia Petrovna's emancipation, however, is un-done by the arrest of her son, which turns her short-lived social climb into a fall: not only is she excluded from the public sphere as a result, but she also steadily loses her mind. Hence, rather than continuing the traditions of nineteenth-century radical fiction in an entirely different historical setting, Chukovskaia articulates the void between the clas-sical and the Soviet periods. One parallel between the works of Cher-nyshevsky and Chukovskaia is striking: although *What Is to Be Done?* was first serialized in Russia in Nikolai Nekrasov's progressive journal *Sovremennik* in 1863, it soon fell out of favor with the tsarist authorities and, like *Sofia Petrovna* a century later, for the next forty years could only be published abroad until the ban on the novel was lifted in the wake of the Revolution of 1905, which paved the way for the first book edition at home the following year.[48]

While traveling in America in 1906, Maxim Gorky wrote his novel *Mother (Mat')*, which was destined to become a model for socialist-realist writing throughout the Soviet era, and which, as Sibelan Forrester has argued, Chukovskaia's *Sofia Petrovna* "polemically rewrites."[49] It is not the two widowed mothers in the two works, however, but their fatherless sons who embody the typical traits of socialist-realist positive heroes, while "each mother . . . refuses to believe anything bad of her son,"[50] in-heriting their sons' values. After Sofia Petrovna's son Kolya is arrested in Sverdlovsk, having only recently been praised as a shock worker on the pages of *Pravda*, it is her faith in his innocence that forces her out of society. Both stories, as Forrester has observed, "end with upsetting and ambiguous scenes," causing readers to disagree about whether Nilovna at the end of *Mother* is arrested or killed, "just as they question what it means that Sofia Petrovna burns her son's letter" at the end of Chu-kovskaia's novella.[51] And yet, the differences between the endings are as significant as the parallels: unlike Nilovna, who is beaten (arrested, or killed) by the tsarist gendarmes for refusing to denounce her son or hide his political proclamations from prison, Sofia Petrovna, afflicted by self-delusion, destroys her son's letter, severing her ties not only with him but also with the idea of a mother in socialist realism, according to Gorky. As is often the case with socialist-realist mythology, Gorky's *Mother*, although atheist in spirit, is a version of the biblical story of the Mother of God and her Son, while Chukovskaia's Sofia Petrovna is far from being portrayed as a saint or a martyr in the religious sense. It was for religious blasphemy, among other things, that Gorky's novel was banned in tsarist Russia. Not until the Bolsheviks came to power in 1917 could it be published in Russia under the new regime. Chukovskaia's *Sofia Petrovna* had to wait much longer to be published at home, when the very regime that retrieved Gorky's *Mother* started falling apart during perestroika.

Complicating *Sofia Petrovna*'s relationship with socialist realism is its closer stance to the classical Russian literary tradition, including the "Petersburg text" of the nineteenth century, which Chukovskaia reinvents in the Soviet (Leningrad) context. Not entirely unlike Dostoevsky's Titular Councilor Goliadkin, who is gradually replaced by his doppelganger in *The Double* (1846), Sofia Petrovna "cannot be sure exactly what is going on in this society, though something is definitely wrong";[52] she is ultimately annihilated by the nightmarish phantasmagoria of Stalin's purges she is unable to comprehend. Needless to say, the mental affliction of characters like Goliadkin, immersed in the mirage-like atmosphere of nineteenth-century Petersburg, did not sit well with the socialist-realist mandate for a positive hero in pursuit of a purpose in life. Chukovskaia herself points out Sofia Petrovna's innate relation to yet another classical literary character, Gogol's Akaky Akakievich. Responding to a Soviet critic's admonition that "certain authors depict our people as if they were Akaky Akakieviches," Chukovskaia recalled that during her conversation with Lavrentiev in December 1962, when she still hoped to publish her novella in *Sibirskie ogni*, she referred to Sofia Petrovna as an "Akaky Akakievich in a skirt."[53] Indeed, a century after Gogol's "The Overcoat" (1842), Sofia Petrovna functions as the female Soviet offspring of Akaky Akakievich, the forefather of all proverbial "little men" of Russian literature, whose knack for neat copying she shares as a typist at the Leningrad branch of the state publishing house. She seems as unaware of what goes on in her society as Akaky Akakievich in the bureaucracy-ridden Petersburg under Nicholas I, where he is employed by one of the state departments that Gogol famously refuses to name ("In the department of . . . but it would be better not to say in which department.")[54] Like her classical predecessor who is unable to produce a meaningful text of his own but enjoys and excels in copying texts written by others, Sofia Petrovna, too, "loved going to the office" despite the shivering cold, "and although Soviet stories and novels seemed boring to her . . ., she couldn't help being flattered."[55] One might go so far as to compare Sofia Petrovna's losing her son to the state, whose power she praised and perpetuated, to Akaky Akakievich's being robbed of his new overcoat in the middle of an empty square in nineteenth-century Petersburg. This turning point in the plot of "The Overcoat," which reads not only as an unfortunate accident but also as a political allegory, is compositionally parallel to the arrest of Sofia Petrovna's son, Kolya. For Akaky Akakievich, the new overcoat meant not only physical warmth but also personal happiness. For Sofia Petrovna, Kolya was more than her only child—he was her main point of reference in public and moral concerns. Across almost a century of Russian history and literature, their losses mark the two characters' downfalls. The disappearance of Sofia Petrovna's son and her own withdrawal from the outside world befits Gogol's conclusion: "And Petersburg was left without Akaky Akakievich, as if he had never been there."[56] But while Akaky Akakievich comes back to St. Petersburg as a phantom to take revenge on his state-employed torturers, giving "The Overcoat" a fantastic twist, Chukovskaia stays true to historical reality, refraining from supernatural wonders. Rather than the fictional character, as Gogol would have it, it is the manuscript of Sofia Petrovna that finds itself elsewhere, and once published abroad, comes back home two decades later to deliver a blow not only to Stalinism, but also to Soviet censorship and the literary establishment that had rejected it in 1960s.

Sofia Petrovna Abroad

Chukovskaia knew that Sofia Petrovna had leaked abroad before she filed her lawsuit against Sovetskii pisatel', although by the time the court hearing took place on April 24, 1965, the novella had not yet appeared in tamizdat. On April 9, 1964, she informed Akhmatova that Yury Annenkov, whom Chukovskaia had known since childhood but not been in touch with since his emigration in 1924, had sent her a note that Sofia Petrovna was about to appear in Paris. The news was conveyed to Akhmatova in a way reminiscent of the "sad and beautiful ritual" of the 1930s, when Akhmatova would hastily write down parts of her Requiem for Chukovskaia to read and memorize before just as hurriedly burning the scraps of paper over an ashtray. "I took a piece of paper from the desk and wrote my news for Anna Andreevna. . . . Will there be a scandal? Or will they deign not to notice? . . . Anna Andreevna read it, returned the note to me, then, glancing up at the ceiling, shrugged with a sigh, and I threw the paper out into the toilet."[57]

In 1965, in a letter to Chukovskaia's father, Annenkov asked on behalf of the Parisian publisher if they had received the sample copy of *Sofia Petrovna*: "The publisher would very much like to hear your opinion. . . . Lyda's book is superb and deeply moving."[58] The modest repertoire of the publishing house, Five Continents (Cinq Continents), included the Russian classics and reprints of some earlier Soviet editions (e.g., Mayakovsky's *The Bedbug* and Zoshchenko's *Stories about Lenin*), as well as a volume of Gumilev's selected poetry. Annenkov did not specify just how Chukovskaia's manuscript had ended up in the West, nor did he offer any details about the obscure publisher, whose innocent profile, however, was not as dangerous as, for example, that of the much older and larger Paris-based tamizdat venture YMCA-Press. Annenkov's role in the affair was not specified either. But for the Chukovskys, who used to know Annenkov as an artist and personal friend before his departure from Russia, it was not difficult to recognize that the cover design and illustrations in the sample copy of *Sofia Petrovna* were actually his own.[59]

However, it was hardly a book that Chukovskaia could approve of and authorize. Instead of *Sofia Petrovna*, it was titled *Povest' o skorbnoi materi* (*The Tale of a Dolorous Mother*), while the name of the titular character had been changed to "Olga Petrovna." Other characters' names were also modified (e.g., investigator Ershov was renamed Rudnev), not to mention other, smaller discrepancies. A professional editor herself, Chukovskaia knew firsthand what a plain typo, let alone deliberate manipulation of the original text, could entail in the Soviet context. As an example, Chukovskaia's protagonist (renamed "Olga" in the Parisian edition) stands up to defend her younger colleague at the publishing house against accusations of counterrevolutionary activity for as little as letting a typo slip into the text of an article she had typeset: "Ret Army" (*Krysnaia armiia*) instead of "Red Army" (*Krasnaia armiia*). "Certainly, it was dreadful, dreadful, what she wrote," says Sofia Petrovna. "But everyone can make mistakes in his work, isn't that true? She wrote not *Red* [красная] but *Ret* [крысная] simply because on the typewriter— as every typist knows—the letter 't' [ы] is not far from the letter 'd' [а]. Comrade Timofeyev said she wrote *Rat* [крысиная], but she didn't, she wrote *Ret* [крысная], which is not quite the same thing. . . This was simply an accident."[60] For Chukovskaia, who refused to comply with the changes imposed by the Soviet editors at home, those introduced into her text abroad must have been equally unacceptable.

Whether or not the changes in the sample copy from Paris were also "simply an accident," at the end of 1966, when the book was finally out, it had yet another title: *Opustelyi dom* (*The Deserted House*). The reasons for this change were quite transparent: the title alluded to the seventh part of Akhmatova's *Requiem* ("The Sentence"), dated June 22, 1939: "I have long foreseen this / Bright day and deserted house" [*Ia davno predchustvovala etot / Svetlyi den' i opustelyi dom*].[61] It would be naïve, however, to view the new title merely as a tribute to Akhmatova, whose *Requiem* had gained unconditional fame abroad since its first publication in Munich in 1963; the change in title was, no doubt, also meant to help raise the sales of Chukovskaia's book. As for the protagonist's first name, one could assume it was replicated from one of the stray manuscripts of Chukovskaia's work making the rounds in samizdat. But when three years later the Dutch critic Kees Verheul asked the Parisian publisher about the reasons for this otherwise inexplicable modification, the answer he received was most unusual—as it happens, just when the book was already typeset and ready to be printed, the Moscow Mossovet Theater was on a tour in Paris with a stage adaptation of Dostoevsky's *Uncle's Dream* (1859), one of whose characters—Sofia Petrovna Farpukhina, the colonel's wife (played by Serafima Birman)—is an alcoholic, "a spiteful and malignant gossip."[62] It was "to avoid undesirable associations," as the publisher explained to Verheul, that "we decided to change Sofia Petrovna to Olga Petrovna." He added that the title was altered "for purely practical reasons," since the protagonist's "meaningless" name could not help promote a book by an author "completely unknown to the Western reader."[63]

In his letter to the *Times Literary Supplement*, written in response to Alexander Werth's first English-language review of *Opustelyi dom*,[64] Gleb Struve, the publisher of Akhmatova's *Requiem*, confirmed that *Sofia Petrovna* was going to be brought out in Paris as *Povest' o skorbnoi materi*, and that he had even seen a sample copy under that title in the summer of 1965.[65] It had been shown to him by Annenkov, most likely when they met in Paris during or soon after Akhmatova's visit to Europe in June 1965.[66] The decision to change the title from *Povest' o skorbnoi materi* to *Opustelyi dom* must have been made in Paris around that time. "I do not know why the name of the heroine was changed in the Cinq Continents edition from Sofya Petrovna to Olga Petrovna," Struve added, "but I happen to know that it was *Sofya Petrovna* in the version about which some American visitors to Moscow had heard as early as 1962."[67] Struve's American acquaintances in Moscow must have referred to the authentic manuscript of *Sofia Petrovna*, which found its way abroad through different channels only later.

The reason the Paris edition of *Opustelyi dom* was delayed until the end of 1966 could have to do with Chukovskaia's refusal to authorize the sample copy received from Annenkov.[68] But the delay is also explained by the arrest and trial of Andrei Sinyavsky and Yuly Daniel in Moscow in February 1966, when the two writers were sentenced, respectively, to seven and five years of hard labor for publishing their "slanderous" works in tamizdat. In his letter to the editor of the émigré newspaper *Russkaia mysl'*, where one of Chukovskaia's open letters in defense of Sinyavsky and Daniel was printed on November 29, 1966,[69] the publisher Five Continents explained that, although the book was "supposed to be released for sale after the holiday fever" (that is, by the fall of 1965), he had decided to postpone it "despite the considerable funds invested," so as not to involve Chukovskaia in the same "crime" as Sinyavsky and Daniel. "True, in our edition we clearly indicated that we were releasing the book without the author's knowledge," the publisher wrote, "but as the Soviet people themselves put it, it is sometimes very difficult to prove 'you are not a goof' [*chto ty ne verbliud*]."[70] The publisher's real purpose for writing his letter to *Russkaia mysl'*, however, was to dispel "the wrong impression that 'Five Continents' published Lydia Chukovskaia's novella after it had come out under the title 'Sofia Petrovna' in the New York *Novyi zhurnal*." Indeed, it was not until *Sofia Petrovna* was published in its authentic form and under the correct title in *Novyi zhurnal* in New York in the spring and fall issues of 1966 that the Parisian edition of *Opustelyi dom* was taken off the back burner.

Unlike the Parisian publisher, a Soviet sympathizer until the trial of Sinyavsky and Daniel,[71] the editor of *Novyi zhurnal*, Roman Gul', a First-Wave émigré and former participant of the White movement, had a different opinion about the potential impact of tamizdat publications on the authors in Russia. He believed that printing contraband manuscripts from the USSR in the West could in fact help protect their authors against the authorities at home, rather than put them under greater threat. Hence, months after the Sinyavsky-Daniel trial on February 10–14, 1966, the first part of *Sofia Petrovna* appeared in *Novyi zhurnal* with a note that the manuscript had been received "from the Soviet Union via an intermediary" and was being printed "without the author's knowledge or consent."[72] This publication of *Sofia Petrovna* may also have been unauthorized, but it was based on the authentic manuscript. By the end of the year, when the two issues of *Novyi zhurnal* reached the author in Moscow, she wrote in her diary: "I am happy: I am seeing 'Sofia.' I am holding it in my hands. Not 'The [Deserted] House' but 'Sofia.' "[73]

FIGURE 3.1.   Lydia Chukovskaia. *Opustelyi dom*. Cover design by Yury Annenkov. Paris: Cinq Continents, 1965.

Новый
Журнал

84

THE NEW
REVIEW

FIGURE 3.2.   Cover of the New York émigré journal *Novyi zhurnal* 83 (1966), where the first part of
Sofia Petrovna was serialized.

Ideologically, the approaches of Chukovskaia's first two publishers were as different as the versions of *Sofia Petrovna* they published. While the Parisian publisher's preface to *Opustelyi dom* referred to Chukovskaia as "a Soviet author and Soviet patriot,"[74] something more conservative émigrés such as Gul' would consider simply an insult, Struve placed *Sofia Petrovna* among "émigré books by non-émigré Russian authors," as he defined tamizdat, emphasizing its anti-Soviet agenda.[75] Nevertheless, it was the Parisian edition of *Opustelyi dom*, not *Sofia Petrovna*, that became the source text for translations into foreign languages. As a result, the non-Russian reader was introduced to Chukovskaia's work under the wrong title.[76] Alexander Werth, a British journalist and husband of the English translator of *Sofia Petrovna*, challenged Struve's definition of Chukovskaia's novella as an "émigré book by a non-émigré Russian writer," arguing that "it is surely not for somebody living in Berkeley, California, to stick on such labels which come dangerously close to the Stalinist-type term of abuse, 'internal émigré.' . . . Her book is profoundly Russian and pro-Russian; it is *not* anti-Soviet; if it is anti-anything, it is only anti-Stalin and anti-*Yezhovshchina*."[77] Werth also assured Struve that he knew "all about the two versions of Lydia Chukovskaya's *The Deserted House* and about the reasons why the publication of the Paris version was delayed from 1965 to 1967."[78]

While Chukovskaia knew that her novella was going to be brought out in Paris, there is no evidence that she was aware of the parallel publication of *Sofia Petrovna* in New York. The news came on May 31, 1966, from Chukovskaia's father, who had learned about it from a letter from the United States a day earlier. Chukovsky assumed it was while the manuscript of *Sofia Petrovna* was being held at one of the Soviet periodicals or at Sovetskii pisatel' that "some wheeler-dealer secretly made a copy and sent it abroad."[79] Chukovsky's American correspondent was no one other than Roman Grynberg, the first publisher of Akhmatova's "Poem without a Hero" and other manuscripts from the USSR, such as Frida Vigdorova's transcript of Joseph Brodsky's trial and Brodsky's poetry. The epistolary exchange between Chukovsky and Grynberg went on for three years, from 1964 to 1967, and was one of the greatest mystifications in tamizdat history: Grynberg corresponded with Chukovsky in English in the guise of "Sonya Gordon," a young woman of Russian descent with a passion for literature. Chukovsky kept his epistolary affair with the mysterious "Sonya" secret even from his daughter and never found out who "Sonya" really was.[80] On May 21, 1966, informing Chukovsky that the first part of *Sofia Petrovna* had appeared in *Novyi zhurnal*, "Sonya" added that "this story about the events of 1937" had produced a lasting impression on her. On July 15, 1966, Chukovsky replied that his daughter "would like to know who took it from the editorial office of Sovetskii pisatel'," but he never received any answer.[81] On this note, the trace of *Sofia Petrovna* in Chukovsky and "Sonya Gordon's" correspondence broke off. But the manuscript's adventures abroad continued.

Unaware that a book edition of the novella had already been prepared but not yet released in Paris, on October 4, 1966, Gul' offered the typeset of *Sofia Petrova* to Boris Filippov, head of Inter-Language Literary Associates, in exchange for "200 copies free of charge," should Filippov decide to print it as a book under the auspices of his publishing house. "This way we would save a few hundred dollars, which is not insignificant for our budget, and you will have a good book for both foreign and Soviet readers."[82] Having initially agreed, Filippov promised to "pass on the novella along with my (very positive, of course) evaluation to my main benefactor's adviser Mr. E[dward] Kline," a New York entrepreneur who supported Russian tamizdat publishers then and throughout the 1980s.[83] However, when it became clear that there was already a book edition of the same work in Paris, soon to be released, Gul"s offer was declined. It follows from Filippov's answer to Gul' on October 27, 1966, that Chukovskaia was in fact against publishing her novella in Paris, and Filippov did not want to violate her will. Besides, another book edition of the same work, which had, moreover, just been made available on the pages of *Novyi zhurnal*, was not financially lucrative. Filippov's main reason for turning down Gul"s proposal, however, was not financial but political: in the wake of the trial of Sinyavsky and Daniel, whose "slanderous" works were published abroad in Russian primarily if not exclusively by Inter-Language Literary Associates, with Filippov's introductions, his name and the name of his publishing house were anathema in the Soviet Union.[84] The following year, after a scandal in the American press that exposed its reliance on CIA funding, Filippov's publishing house ceased to exist.[85] For the next two decades, *Sofia Petrovna* was bound to exist abroad under the title *The Deserted House* both in Russian and in foreign-language translations, leaving Chukovskaia with mixed feelings:

> I am grateful to Samizdat, to the foreign publishers and translators. . . . No random search . . . can now destroy my testimony. Certainly it was wrong to give my novella a different title (*The*

Deserted House instead of the name of the heroine); . . . But for all that, I'm still grateful. However, despite my gratitude, I'm not consoled. There's only one thing I want, just one thing I'm waiting for: to see my book published in the Soviet Union. In my own country. In Sofia Petrovna's country.[86]

Before this dream could finally come true in 1988, *Sofia Petrovna* was first read abroad, where its reception was largely determined by the aesthetic and ideological agendas of the Russian diaspora and the Western literary and academic community.

The West Reads *Sofia Petrovna*

It was the Parisian edition of *Opustelyi dom*, rather than the authentic version of *Sofia Petrovna* from *Novyi zhurnal*, that was considered the "original" and translated into foreign languages, having drawn most scholarly and critical attention. Yet because the Parisian edition was delayed, the first responses to *Sofia Petrovna* abroad were based on its first New York publication. It was first mentioned by Grigory Aronson in his review of the spring 1966 issue of *Novyi zhurnal* (number 83) in *Novoe russkoe slovo*, but while Aronson went no further than merely referring to *Sofia Petrovna* as a "simple, artless, and realist story,"[87] Yury Terapiano, a month later, pointed out its "truthfulness" and inherent connection to Akhmatova's *Requiem*, although Chukovskaia "could not have been aware of it," as the émigré critic naively assumed.[88] After reading the rest of *Sofia Petrovna* in the next issue of *Novyi zhurnal*, Terapiano, unsurprisingly, concluded that the main value of Chukovskaia's work lay in its immediate "proximity to the years of the Terror."[89] Another émigré critic, Yury Bolshukhin, lamented that "there is little artistic merit in it, which, of course, should in no way diminish its historical or psychological value."[90] Citing Akhmatova's *Requiem*, Bolshukhin defined *Sofia Petrovna* as "a mournful testimony about being 'there, where my people, unfortunately, were.'" Discussing the works of Akhmatova and Chukovskaia, neither critic named any of their specific intertexts and dwelt only on their shared historical subject matter and setting. The intertextual relationship between *Requiem* and *Sofia Petrovna*, however, worked two ways: completed in 1939–1940, *Sofia Petrovna*, although first published three years after *Requiem*, was "older" than some parts of Akhmatova's poem. For example, the "woman with blue lips," who had "identified" Akhmatova in a prison line and whispered the innermost question, "Can you describe this?" ("Instead of a Preface," 1957), came into *Requiem* from Chukovskaia's novella, where one morning the elderly secretary tells Sofia Petrovna "voicelessly, moving only her lips," that the director of their publishing house has been arrested. "Her lips were blue."[91] Such details escaped most Western critics, who rightly placed *Sofia Petrovna* in the context of *Requiem* but followed Chukovskaia's admonition that her work's main "claim to the reader's attention" lay in its proximity to the reality described.[92] It was not until 1988, when *Sofia Petrovna* could finally see the light of day in Russia during a new era, that "the woman with blue lips" in Akhmatova's *Requiem* was identified as "one of the countless Sofia Petrovnas."[93]

Reviewing the Parisian edition of *Opustelyi dom* in the *Times Literary Supplement*, Alexander Werth came close to seeing *Requiem* and *Sofia Petrovna* in a creative flux, rather than merely as a historical and biographical coincidence: Chukovskaia's novella is "almost a prose version of that famous poem on the Stalin terror, in which Akhmatova's own son suffered, like thousands of others, the same fate as Chukovskaia's Kolya."[94] (Chukovskaia, of course, did not have a son, though her fictional character did.) However, Werth's conclusion that "Akhmatova herself went through the same agony as Olga Petrovna" went against Chukovskaia's portrayal of Sofia Petrovna as the embodiment of the blindness and unconsciousness of society under Stalin. True, Akhmatova burned her *Requiem* when it was too dangerous to keep it, but it was hardly possible, after all, to imagine her burning her son's letters from prison, as Sofia Petrovna does. This difference, one would think, should have precluded *Sofia Petrovna* from being read (auto)biographically, and yet another British reviewer claimed that Chukovskaia's book was precisely "tragically autobiographical."[95]

It was also claimed that before it appeared abroad, Chukovskaia hoped to see *Sofia Petrovna* published in Russia as a result of "Khrushchev's authorization of the publication of Alexander Solzhenitsyn's 'One Day in the Life of Ivan Denisovich,' "[96] while in fact Chukovskaia had submitted her manuscript to *Novyi mir* one year earlier, after the Twenty-second Party Congress, that is, not after but simultaneously with Solzhenitsyn. Whereas it was clear that the reason *Sofia Petrovna* "remains unpublished in the Soviet Union" had to do with the fact that it is "strong medicine. There is nothing in it to 'fill the hearts of Soviet people with pride in their country,' "[97] the Parisian publisher of *Opustelyi dom* nevertheless asserted in his anonymous preface that much of what Tvardovsky had written apropos *Ivan Denisovich* in *Novyi mir* "fully applies" to *Sofia Petrovna*.[98]

Apart from the references to *Requiem* and the inevitable parallels with *Ivan Denisovich*, two other works that were smuggled out from the USSR and published abroad around the same time help to establish the reception context for *Sofia Petrovna* in the West: Eugenia Ginzburg's memoir *Journey into the Whirlwind* (*Krutoi Marshrut*) and *Twenty Letters to a Friend* (*Dvadtsat' pisem k drugu*) by Stalin's daughter, Svetlana Allilueva.[99] Like *Ivan Denisovich*, both Ginzburg's and Allilueva's manuscripts were younger than *Sofia Petrovna* by two decades and belonged to a different genre. It was the modified title of Chukovskaia's novella that invited a parallel with Allilueva's autobiography. "Even the title, *The Deserted House*," wrote Saul Maloff, "hauntingly echoes the most unforgettable lines in Stalin's daughter's book, when, recalling the unaccountable disappearance from the family's usually crowded villa of beloved relatives, Svetlana cries, as if she were still a mystified child: 'Where have they all gone? Why is the house empty?'"[100] Born in 1926, Svetlana was "eleven at the time," and the episode described must have taken place in 1937—the historical setting of *Sofia Petrovna*.[101] By then, Chukovskaia's Sofia Petrovna was already a widow and her son Kolya a student. Nevertheless, she is portrayed as "a woman so uncomplicated as to be nearly childlike," whereas the novella itself "strikes immediately and maintains throughout the quality of folk tale, of a children's fable."[102] In contrast to the "deserted house" of Allilueva's childhood (*"Pochemu obezliudel nash dom?"*), Sofia Petrovna's room in her communal apartment in Leningrad is never described as "empty" (*opustelyi*) in Chukovskaia's original. Instead, it is the mailbox where she hopes to find a letter from her son that remains "empty": "Empty. Empty as could be. Sofia Petrovna stared for a moment at its yellow side—as if hoping her stare could call forth a letter from the box"; "Empty. No letter. Her heart sank, as it always did when she saw the box empty."[103] Besides, the word "empty," or rather its root (*pust*), is uttered by Sofia Petrovna in a state of delusion, as she tries to convince herself and others that Kolya has been set free (*vypustili*); in this context, it is repeated nineteen times, suggesting that it is the protagonist's consciousness, rather than her "house," that has been "emptied" by the purges.

Ginzburg's memoir, according to the émigré critic Nikolai Belov, "brings to mind Lydia Chukovskaia's book *Opustelyi dom* published earlier in Paris" because "both are mothers, [although] while Olga Petrovna suffers only from her love for her son, the suffering of Evgenia

Semenovna starts with her faith in the political idea and only then extends to herself, her children, her family, her whole life." "Both heroines, one fictional, the other real," Belov continues, "react to the events of the Stalinist era in the same way. Both the ignorant Olga Petrovna and the self-aware Evgenia Semenovna, with a higher education degree, are equally naïve in their denial that the cruel reality of Stalinism is actually taking place."[104] While "in both books the protagonists are loyal, uncompromisingly devoted Soviet citizens,"[105] the differences between the two works are, of course, just as obvious. Harrison Salisbury points out that while Chukovskaia "tells the story from the viewpoint of one who is left behind, Mrs. Ginzburg [does so] as one who was caught up in the very maelstrom of the terror."[106] Helen Muchnic's choice to review the two works together was explained by the fact that "the document," i.e., Ginzburg's memoir, "seems a nightmare fantasy," while "the novelette," i.e., Chukovskaia's fiction, reads like "a document"; moreover, while "Eugenia Ginzburg's is a tale of heroic survival, Lydia Chukovskaya's is one of heart-rending loss."[107]

It was not only Chukovskaia's novella and Ginzburg's memoir that were ascribed wholesale to the "genre" of "purge literature," but also other narratives about Stalinism and the gulag, including Solzhenitsyn's *Ivan Denisovich*, Shalamov's *Kolyma Tales* (*Kolymskie rasskazy*), General Alexander Gorbatov's *Years of My Life* (*Gody i voiny*), and even *Sandstorm* (*Smerch*) by Galina Serebriakova, the author of novels about Karl Marx and a staunch anti-liberal party functionary after her two stretches in the gulag.[108] Clearly, the term "purge literature" could refer, at best, to the subject matter of these otherwise heterogeneous texts, but not to their formal organization.[109] The definition was questioned, however, by some academics, who lamented that tamizdat "publishers and critics alike tend to lump each new arrival under some tired rubric, such as 'purge literature' or 'prison camp exposé,' with the result that little consideration is given to literary quality or individual talent."[110] Among Chukovskaia's talents, Thompson Bradley of Swarthmore College singled out her "power of understatement" and style, "simple and spare with a limited, plain vocabulary" that is "in perfect accord" with Sofia Petrovna's psychology.[111] Herman Ermolaev from Princeton also noted the "clear, idiomatic, but impersonal language" of the novella, whose "author was obviously not concerned with verbal wizardry."[112] As an exception to the general trend, Ermolaev underscored *Sofia Petrovna*'s singularity "in not being autobiographical," in addition to "dealing with the impact of the purges outside prisons and camps and in having been written as early as 1939–1940 under the fresh impressions."[113]

And yet, as Robert Granat complained in the *New Leader*, "It is still extremely difficult to evaluate any literary work coming out of the Soviet Union 'normally': on its own intrinsic merits, apart from the political overtones." Referring to *Sofia Petrovna* as "an important book, but not an important novel," Granat, like many others, also assumed that Chukovskaia hoped to publish her work in Russia only after being "heartened by the appearance of Aleksandr Solzhenitsyn's *One Day in the Life of Ivan Denisovich*," whose "positive hero" of a peasant background, favored in socialist realism over Chukovskaia's female character, lurks behind her blind faith in the Soviet regime matched only by "the religious piety of the old time Russian peasant." *Sofia Petrovna*, or rather its English translation, *The Deserted House*, as Granat confessed, "engaged, even moved [me], in the sense that one can be affected by a good honest piece of journalism or a terrible case history conscientiously documented," but it "had little impact at that urgent personal level a real work of art can reach." Pondering the question of why the book "failed to move me deeply," Granat falls into the same trap as others, reading *Sofia Petrovna* as an autobiography. As a result, rather than Sofia Petrovna's "vision of truth," it is Chukovskaia's that he calls "nearsighted." Whether or not the critic knew of Chukovskaia's quickly deteriorating eyesight in 1968, he admitted that "perhaps her sight is clearer now. In 1940, she gave no indication of seeing the real tragedy in her story," which is allegedly why "more sophisticated readers can feel pity but no real identification." For this "identification" to take place, and for Chukovskaia to have written a great novel and not just "a courageous contribution to our knowledge about the effect of Stalin's purges on the ordinary Soviet citizen," Chukovskaia, it was proclaimed, "would have had to know better."[114]

A new era had to dawn in order to change the reception of Chukovskaia's fiction. In 1988, reviewing the first publication of *Sofia Petrovna* in Russia, Maria Muravnik wrote in the same New York émigré newspaper, "Chukovskaia writes neither about herself, nor on her own behalf. It was more important for her to offer an alienated document, where her personal tragedy is only vaguely implied, but the tragedy of the society comes to the foreground instead. That society consists not of the farsighted and experienced ones, but of those like Sofia Petrovna."[115] In tamizdat criticism of the 1960s, the fact that the author was not the same as her character, no matter how autobiographical the novella was, remained overshadowed by the nearly ubiquitous tendency to read contraband literature from the USSR as factual evidence rather than as works of art. Such a reception may have been decried, as in Granat's review, but it remained inescapable nevertheless. As if in anticipation of the responses to *Sofia Petrovna* abroad, in her second novella, *Going Under* (1949–1957), Chukovskaia went on to explore the uneasy relationship between the author and the protagonist, historical truth and its allegorical orchestration, as well as other dichotomies in works of fiction inspired by, but not limited to, the firsthand experiences of their authors.

Going Under and Abroad

Chukovskaia's *Going Under* is both a chronological continuation of *Sofia Petrovna* and an amplification of its subject matter, characters, and setting, making it possible to read the two works as a cycle. Like *Sofia Petrovna*, this novella was also written in immediate proximity to the events described, specifically, in February and March 1949, at the height of Stalin's postwar terror against so-called rootless cosmopolitans, or Soviet Jewry, and the intelligentsia at large.[116] Like the manuscript of *Sofia Petrovna*, *Going Under* also "existed for many years as a single copy I did not risk keeping home. After the Twentieth Congress, I retyped it in four copies and ventured showing it to my friends."[117] Chukovskaia's first work of fiction was largely completed during her stay at the writers' residence in Detskoe Selo in December 1939; *Going Under* is set ten years later in Maleevka, another resort for Soviet writers outside Moscow, fictionalized as Litvinovka.[118] Thus, the place where Chukovskaia wrote *Sofia Petrovna* and the fictional setting of *Going Under* reflect one another and situate the two works between reality and fiction. Both manuscripts traveled abroad approximately twenty-five years after they were written. *Going Under* was published in New York in 1972, six years after *Sofia Petrovna*. Both were first published in Russia in 1988.

Going Under, too, is centered on a female protagonist—Nina Sergeevna, who has lost her husband in the Great Terror. But while *Sofia Petrovna* is a third-person account of the titular character's gradual descent into madness, *Going Under* is made up of diary entries narrated in the first person, whose author, working on a translation project during her stay in Litvinovka, undertakes nightly "plunges" (*spusk*) into the haunted space of her memory as she tries to make sense of the incomprehensible reality of the 1930s and commit it to paper. Her "going under" results in a manuscript that, once complete, is "published" as an inserted novella in one of the diary entries. In the course of the ten years since Chukovskaia wrote *Sofia Petrovna*, the heroine of *Going Under* has grown from an uncomprehending typist employed at a Soviet publishing house, unable to understand what has happened to her, her son, and society at large, into a cognizant writer, whose "going under" in a sense foreshadows underground Russian literature in the years to follow.[119] The forlorn yet self-conscious Nina Sergeevna comes to redeem the blindness and credulity of her predecessor, Sofia Petrovna.

While *Sofia Petrovna* poses uncomfortably as a work of socialist realism, *Going Under* wears no such mask. Instead of Sofia Petrovna's attempted ascent to the ranks of socialist-realist positive heroines, aborted overnight by the arrest of her son, the true positive hero, *Going Under* plunges the reader headlong into the depths of Nina Sergeevna's visions of the Great Terror and down the funnel of late Stalinism. The opening sentence of *Sofia Petrova* locks the death of her husband outside the plot, since the protagonist herself does not believe it could be the source of her and her son's later misfortunes: "After the death of her husband, Sofia Petrovna took a course in typing. She felt she simply had to acquire a profession."[120] Nina Sergeevna, conversely, keeps "going under" and down the memory of her executed husband whom she is unable to forget. (Both husbands were doctors.) In her first work of fiction Chukovskaia is preoccupied with the obliteration of memory (at the end of the novella, Sofia Petrovna burns her son's letter from prison); *Going Under* is about the preservation of memory in the act of writing and is, thereby, a commentary on Soviet literature. However, with roots deep in Soviet terrain, Chukovskaia's work could only shoot aboveground elsewhere, i.e., abroad.

Not unlike Chukovskaia's manuscript of *Sofia Petrovna*, the manuscript Nina Sergeevna is writing in *Going Under* is also meant as a monument to the victims of Stalinism, although unbuilt—unpublished—in Chukovskaia's home country until decades later. Yet while in the early 1960s Chukovskaia believed *Sofia Petrovna* could actually be published in Russia—not only because the Thaw years seemed ripe for it, but also because Sofia Petrovna was equipped with some of the pseudo socialist-realist attributes, albeit far from sufficient—the downward trajectory of Nina Sergeevna in *Going Under* left no room for such hopes: unlike *Sofia Petrovna*, *Going Under*, to the best of our knowledge, was never submitted for publication at home until perestroika. And while the publication of

Sofia Petrovna in tamizdat in 1966 did not seem to directly incriminate Chukovskaia before the Soviet authorities, at least not for a while, the publication of *Going Under* in 1972 in New York earned her complete ostracism from the official literary field at home, making her name unmentionable even in publications about her father, the famous Soviet critic, translator, and children's author, who had died three years earlier, in 1969.[121] Chukovskaia's last appearance in the Soviet press was her monograph on Herzen's *My Past and Thoughts*, published in Moscow months after the trial of Sinyavsky and Daniel and the same year as *Sofia Petrovna* appeared in tamizdat.[122] Ironically, the monograph was devoted to the writer whose publishing efforts in Europe a century earlier served as a platform for his like-minded brethren in Russia to bypass tsarist censorship and print their words abroad.[123] In the wake of the persecution and show trials of Brodsky in 1964 and Sinyavsky and Daniel, in 1965–1966, Chukovskaia joined the Soviet dissident movement and spoke out against the suppression of political freedoms.[124] On January 9, 1974, she was unanimously expelled from the Soviet Writers' Union. Solzhenitsyn, whom she defended along with Andrei Sakharov in one of her most outspoken essays, "People's Wrath" ("Gnev naroda"), was banished from the country the following month. In addition to being silenced at home, Chukovskaia's ties with foreigners and Russian dissidents in the West were closely watched.[125]

Completed in 1957, *Going Under* found its way to the West at least ten years later and was published in March 1972. The manuscript was sent via the diplomatic pouch to England, where it was received by Peter Norman, a British Slavist and "the most beautiful Englishman," as Akhmatova once called him,[126] whom Chukovskaia first met in Peredelkino in 1959 but became friends with later, after Akhmatova's death.[127] After visiting Chukovskaia in 1967, Norman recalled that "a large envelope arrived from Austria to Golders Green. On behalf of Lydia Korneevna, a diplomat sent me the manuscript of her book *Going Under*, with the request to help get it published and translated into English," whereupon Norman "forwarded the manuscript to the U.S., and Chekhov Publishing House brought out *Going Under* in Russian."[128] The publication of *Going Under*, according to Norman, was thus authorized, although the choice of publisher for the Russian edition may not have been discussed with the author directly.

The consequences soon became apparent. On October 8, 1972, Chukovskaia learned that the publication in gosizdat of her memoirs about her father had been suspended. Her conversation with Yury

Лидия Чуковская

СПУСК ПОД ВОДУ

ИЗДАТЕЛЬСТВО ИМЕНИ ЧЕХОВА

FIGURE 3.3. Lydia Chukovskaia. *Spusk pod vodu*. New York: Izdatel'stvo imeni Chekhova, 1972.

Strekhnin, then secretary of the Moscow Organization of Soviet Writers, was "nothing but a model interrogation, despite his politeness."[129] It brought to mind Chukovskaia's confrontation with Lavrentiev, the editor of *Sibirskie ogni*, ten years earlier, when she still hoped to see *Sofia Petrovna* published in Russia. Strekhnin's "police questions" included, "How did *Going Under* end up in America? Did I show or offer it to anybody for publication here? Why is there nothing light in it? Why does it speak disrespectfully about the army . . .? Why does it say that antisemitism was imposed from above? Why is there nothing light in it, but only the worst of the worst?" As seems to have been especially common that year, Strekhnin suggested that Chukovskaia place an "indignant letter" in *Literaturnaia gazeta*, in other words, a renunciation of her tamizdat publication. "Don't you understand that your book is being used by the enemy?"[130] Chukovskaia replied that while she did not know how her work ended up in the West, she was glad that it had. "At least it is not going to vanish." And instead of renouncing its publication abroad, she asked on what basis Chekhov Publishing House was referred to as an "enemy."[131]

The English translation of *Going Under* was out by midsummer 1972, four months after the Russian edition.[132] The translator was identified as "Peter M. Weston," but the translation had in fact been made by Norman. "I was apprehensive at the time to use my own name, and so the translator was camouflaged under the pseudonym P. Winster [sic!]. I had to be cautious, because I still wanted to go to the Soviet Union more than once, and I remembered how the Soviet consulate in London had already denied me a visa previously."[133] Norman's precautions, however, proved in vain; he was not issued a visa to Russia for the next twenty years. Still, he made sure that Chukovskaia received both the Russian and English editions, although "for a long time she did not know that P. Winster was actually me."[134] The next time Norman was able to travel to Moscow and meet with Chukovskaia was 1988, the same year that both her novellas were published in Russia in one volume.[135]

Long before then, however, *Going Under* was first read by Western audiences. Symptomatically, Mikhail Koriakov, a columnist for *Novoe russkoe slovo*, traced the novella back to Akhmatova's *Requiem*, which since its first publication in Munich in 1963, had served as the ultimate point of reference for other women's writings from the USSR on the subject of Stalinism. The manuscript Nina Sergeevna is secretly writing in Litvinovka was interpreted by Koriakov as her—and

Chukovskaia's—"answer" to the same question once whispered by "a woman with blue lips" to Akhmatova in the prison line back in Leningrad in the 1930s: "Can you describe this?" In *Requiem*, Akhmatova answered affirmatively. "Lydia Chukovskaia could give the same answer: the story about the prison line is included in her work as an inserted novella."[136] The "inserted novella" was indeed what Akhmatova liked most of all about *Going Under* when she first read it in April 1958.[137] Yet praising Chukovskaia for her descriptions of the Russian countryside, which reminded the émigré critic of his own visit to Tolstoy's Yasnaya Poliana, Koriakov claimed that no reader would be able to skip these "pages about nature . . . so beautifully written, so well woven into the fabric of the novella that it seems the work is indeed 'about nature.' "[138] True, Chukovskaia quoted Tolstoy in the epigraph to *Going Under*: "The integrity of a man is evident from his attitude to the word."[139] But it was hardly the idyllic landscape of Yasnaya Poliana that motivated her choice of the epigraph; rather, it was Tolstoy's "attitude to the word." As for the original Russian title, *Spusk pod vodu* (literally, "going under water"), Koriakov, from the opposite shore of the Atlantic, wrote about Russia as "a gigantic ocean": "I think that no matter how much waste, filth and rot floats on the surface, there is still some mysterious glow deep down in its depths," the depths that Nina Sergeevna hopes to reach as she keeps "going under."[140]

Whether because one's debut work is usually viewed more favorably or because *Going Under*, although written earlier, came out abroad when revelations about Stalinism from the USSR no longer produced such a sensation in the West as they had in the 1960s, the English translation of Chukovskaia's second novella was not received well by Anglophone critics.[141] It was concluded that *Sofia Petrovna* (or rather, *The Deserted House*, as it was known in English) "was a better book than *Going Under*, which is written in the first person and reads less like a novel than a chapter of autobiography." While *The Deserted House* was "beautifully translated by Aline Werth," *Going Under* was "clumsily translated and supplied with a few unhelpful notes, and also carelessly printed."[142] Helpful or not, in this review Chukovskaia is referred to as Kornei Chukovsky's "adopted daughter," while her text "depends closely on atmosphere and tone of a Chekhovian kind."[143] One classic, Tolstoy (in Koriakov's review), is easily replaced by another, Chekhov, with only Dostoevsky perhaps still missing from the Western pantheon of Russian literature to make the picture complete.[144] Little did it matter that both Chukovskaia's works were inextricably rooted in Soviet reality, rather than in the classical

period, not to mention that her second novella was written as a response, if not a "sequel," to her first.

The American writer Anatole Broyard, on the other hand, went so
far as to entirely dismiss *Going Under* as "a matter of literary politics,"
a work that was "dull, stodgy, amateurish and almost wholly bereft of
ideas."[145] Confessing that he had not read Chukovskaia's first book,
Broyard makes clear that he was not familiar with the style of state-
sponsored campaigns against writers in Russia either; otherwise his
review would not have echoed almost verbatim the notorious invective
against Pasternak from 1958 ("I have not read Pasternak, but . . .").[146]
"I have not read 'The Deserted House,'" Broyard wrote, and yet, "it cannot have been a good book. If it had been, some trace of its competence
would have shown itself in this one. What we have here is an example of
literary politics: the praising of a novel for its 'message,' its 'honesty,' its
'courage,' as if these were esthetic criteria."[147] Understandably allergic
to the premise that "if you are a freedom fighter, all is forgiven," Broyard claimed that Chukovskaia "sounds as if she has been brainwashed
[and] totally ignorant of the advances modern fiction has made—in
fact, she writes as if she were trying to reconstruct a theory of the novel
out of the most antiquated and sentimental English models." Invoking
the near-impenetrable wall between writers in Russia and their peers
abroad throughout the Soviet period, Broyard is not entirely wrong
to assume that "perhaps that is all she is allowed to read of Western
literature," that the "inadvertent poverty of the author's style is more
poignant evidence of alienation than her story of political repression."
But Broyard's own vision of Soviet literature was, evidently, just as limited. True, it was hard to make out from Brooklyn and Greenwich Village, where he had made his career,[148] that *Going Under* was set not "in
the Russian-controlled sector of Finland," but outside Moscow, where
Nina Sergeevna and other Soviet writers are enjoying "a luxurious free
vacation conferred by a grateful government," and it was certainly even
harder to grasp just "how these writers qualify for this sort of V.I.P.
treatment if they are not more securely established."[149] Unlike Koriakov
and other Russian émigré critics, who cherished Chukovskaia's work
for its "pages about nature,"[150] Broyard dismisses the protagonist's
"communing with nature" as "a pathetic fallacy," and Chukovskaia's
"recurring weather report" as "the only 'technical' trick in the author's
repertory."[151]

Having completely misread *Going Under*, Broyard was right in one
thing—for all its political message, it was a work about Soviet literature

and writers. Its publication abroad in 1972 took place when tamizdat and the Russian diaspora were gradually rejuvenated by new arrivals from the USSR, who were bringing with them not only new manuscripts but also a more intimate familiarity with Soviet history, literature, and even geography than the older generation of émigrés could afford, having left Russia in the 1920s (the First Wave) or during the war (the Second Wave). Unlike Broyard, who assumed that *Going Under* was set "in the Russian-controlled sector of Finland," or Koriakov, who looked at his native Russia from a distance as a "gigantic ocean," Andrei Klenov (born Aron Kupershtok), a Soviet-Jewish poet and novelist who emigrated to Israel and then to New York in 1973, was the first to point out that the setting of *Going Under* was Maleevka. As a member of the Soviet Writers' Union before emigration, Klenov had "often stayed" in Maleevka. In February 1949, he recalled, "I arrived before breakfast and immediately saw many good people in the cafeteria, including Mikhail Prishvin. . . . I sat at a free table, looked around, and soon realized that a tragedy had taken place . . .—the atmosphere in the cafeteria was depressing. Sure enough, I found out right away that one of the best Jewish poets, Samuil Galkin, a charming and handsome man, was arrested here that night."[152]

While Prishvin, one of Maleevka's old-timers, is absent from the plot of *Going Under* (except perhaps in the "pages about nature" that his celebrated portrayals of the Russian countryside may have inspired),[153] Samuil Galkin (Shmuel Halkin, 1897–1960) serves as the prototype for the Yiddish poet Veksler, one of the characters of *Going Under*, whom Nina Sergeevna, taking a stroll through Litvinovka, first sees through the window by his desk wearing military decorations. "He fought here," her companion, the prose writer Nikolai Bilibin explains. "They were driving the Germans out of Bykovo."[154] Later, Nina Sergeevna asks Veksler to recite his poetry to her in Yiddish (a language that, she remarks, "always seemed to me ugly"), then retell the same poems in his own words in Russian (a language that, Veksler admits, he does not know well), and finally read the poetic translations, which Veksler hopes soon to see published in *Novyi mir* and *Znamia*. Nina Sergeevna, a translator herself, finds the Russian translations of his Yiddish poems slated for publication in gosizdat inadequate to the original: "Oh, how ugly our language can be, how harshly words can be thrust into lines! How unwilling they may be to stand side by side! They seem to want to stick out in all directions!" One of Veksler's poems about the war in particular—

about the night of the commanding-officer, a communist, who had to send into battle at dawn the next morning eighteen-year-olds just arrived at the front [while] somewhere on another sector of the front another commanding-officer, just as advanced in years and a communist like himself—would send into battle his own eighteen-year-old son on the very same morning[155]

—may seem to have been modeled on Galkin's book of war poems published in Moscow in 1945 in Yiddish.[156] The book was brought out by the publishing house Der Emes, named after the eponymous Jewish newspaper founded in 1918 under the auspices of the Central Committee of the Communist Party. In Yiddish, "Emes" means "truth," a cognate for the title of the main Soviet newspaper, *Pravda*. Unlike the newspaper *Der Emes*, which was liquidated in 1939, the publishing house survived as an organ of non-Russian gosizdat throughout the late 1940s.

However, there is no such poem in Galkin's book. Instead, the poem Chukovskaia's heroine paraphrases is attributed to another Soviet-Jewish poet, Aron Kushnirov (1890–1949). Under the title "Father-Commander" ("Foter-Komandir"), it appeared in 1947 in the first issue of the Moscow Yiddish almanac *Heymland* (*Homeland*), edited by Kushnirov[157] and was published the same year in *Novyi mir*, where Chukovskaia read it, in a Russian translation by Ruvim Moran.[158] Like Veksler, who confides in Nina Sergeevna that his only eighteen-year-old son was killed on the frontline, Kushnirov, too, lost his son in the war. But unlike Galkin, who was arrested in Maleevka on February 26, 1949, Kushnirov was the only poet-member of the Jewish Anti-Fascist Committee (JAC), headed by Solomon Mikhoels, who was not purged by Stalin after the war. He died in Moscow in September 1949, half a year after the rest of the JAC poets were arrested (most of them executed three years later, on August 12, 1952, in the Lubyanka Prison).[159] Thus, in Chukovskaia's novella, it is Kushnirov's poem rather than Galkin's that Veksler recites to Nina Sergeevna, but it is Galkin, not Kushnirov, who serves as Veksler's historical prototype.

Appalled by the poem's Russian translation scheduled for publication in a Soviet journal, Nina Sergeevna speaks of the proverbial untranslatability of poetry, which stands for her own acute, if only intuitive, sensitivity to the clichés of socialist realism that Veksler's poem no doubt exhibits despite being written in a language other than Russian.

Ironically, one of Galkin's—although not Kushnirov's—Russian translators was Akhmatova, who valued his philosophical lyrics, as well as the
poet personally. This is why one of Akhmatova's earlier poems ("Khorosho zdes': i shelest, i khrust . . .," 1922) is quoted—of course, without
the attribution—amid Nina Sergeevna's ruminations on the nature of
poetry and translation as an antithesis to the upbeat Russian versions
of Veksler's verses about the war, no matter how genuine and sincere
they may have been in the original Yiddish and in the poet's consciousness. "Nothing makes it so apparent than the helplessness of a translation," Nina Sergeevna laments, "that verse is created not merely, indeed,
not so much from words, thoughts, meters, and images, but from the
weather, nervousness, from silence, separation. . . Not only from the
black lines of print, but also from the gaps between the lines, deep
pauses which govern the breathing—and the soul."[160] Two quatrains of
Akhmatova's poem "about winter" are quoted as an example of what
true poetry "grows from," echoing Akhmatova's own poetic credo.[161]

Increasingly disillusioned with Veksler and his patriotic poems,
which she is unable to appreciate in the original, Nina Sergeevna soon
starts to avoid him and is irritated by his unannounced visits that
sidetrack her from "going under" in her own clandestine manuscript.
Instead, she becomes irresistibly drawn to Bilibin, who has recently returned from the camps. It is his firsthand experience of the past, and
not Veksler's, that she is seeking in order to find out what happened to
her husband a decade ago, during the Great Terror. " 'I'm going to listen
to something he wouldn't say in your presence!' was what I wanted to
reply. 'I'm going to listen to news from over there, news from another
planet about Alyosha. What has it got to do with you?' "[162] It is indeed
Bilibin who, one day, explains to her that her husband's verdict—"ten
years without the right to correspondence"—in reality meant a death
sentence.

The past and the present collide for Nina Sergeevna when, toward
the end of her stay in Litvinovka and shortly before she completes
her manuscript about the Terror, the news breaks that the publishing house Der Emes has been shut down and its Jewish director and
editors arrested. The news is brought to Litvinovka by Petr Klokov, a
Soviet critic whose recent arrival vexes Nina Sergeevna as she has to
listen to his antisemitic insinuations, pontifications on literature, and
propaganda about "the unpatriotic activity of certain non-Russian nationalist groups,"[163] as well as his personal story about how as a twelve-
year-old boy he learned to shoot by tying a cat to a tree, "because when

it moved, jumped or ran it was difficult to hit."[164] Upon hearing the news of Der Emes, Veksler, who "knew the editors there very well," falls sick: "Pages of verses were strewn all over the place and his service jacket with its decoration hung shapeless and dejected on the back of a chair." Visiting him, Nina Sergeevna understands "that he was trying to make some positive sense of what was going on"; she "remembered trying too, once, to make it all comprehensible and acceptable" when a decade ago her husband was arrested. It was her firsthand experience of the past that allowed her to see beyond Veksler's instinctive attempt to reconcile what was happening in the present. "There, at the top, they see things more clearly," he tried to explain to her. "From Stalin's viewpoint one can see the whole world." Praising "the brilliance of Stalin's plan for the defense of Moscow" and deluding himself that "Stalin threw into the battle untrained men to give time for the reserves to be brought up,"[165] Veksler, whose only son was killed at the front at the age of eighteen, hides behind the protective shield of the war poem he has only recently recited to Nina Sergeevna (even though Stalin is not explicitly mentioned in it). Veksler's rapid and irreversible fall down the spiral of self-deception is reminiscent not only of Nina Sergeevna's own experience ten years earlier; even more so, it brings to mind the delusional protagonist of Chukovskaia's first novella, Sofia Petrovna. What also points to this parallel between the two works across a decade is that Sofia Petrovna is employed at a Leningrad publishing house, whose director and editors are arrested and disappear overnight in the 1930s, not entirely unlike the Jewish editors of Der Emes. The arrests at Sofia Petrovna's publishing house, in turn, are a reference to the story of Samuil Marshak's Leningrad branch of the State Children's Publishing House (Lendetgiz), where Chukovskaia worked until 1937, when it was purged and ultimately liquidated. Among those arrested at Lendetgiz was Chukovskaia's second husband, the physicist Matvei Bronshtein, who was shot on February 18, 1939. Not entirely unlike Nina Sergeevna, whose "going under" results in a manuscript about the years of Terror, Chukovskaia, apart from her two works of fiction, later wrote another book dedicated to her husband's memory. Its title—*Dash* (*Procherk*)—stands for the cross-out replacing the "cause of death" on Bronshtein's death certificate, which she managed to obtain eighteen years later, in 1957, the year she completed *Going Under*.[166]

Two days after the news of Der Emes shakes Litvinovka, Veksler himself is arrested at night. Nina Sergeevna learns about it from Bilibin in the morning at breakfast—much like Klenov, who reports having found out about the arrest of Samuil Galkin the morning he had arrived in Maleevka just in time for breakfast. Although the date of Galkin's arrest—February 26, 1949—is left out of Klenov's account, the length of Nina Sergeevna's stay in Litvinovka—twenty-six days—may be read as a reference to Galkin, Veksler's historical prototype. Yet unlike Veksler, whose trace disappears as *Going Under* soon comes to an end—and unlike those poets of the Jewish Anti-Fascist Committee who were shot on August 12, 1952—the poet, playwright, and translator Samuil Galkin survived and returned to Moscow in 1955, bringing with him new poems composed in prison and in the camps, which were published in several of his lifetime editions in Yiddish and Russian translation, both in Russia and abroad.[167]

Throughout her twenty-six days in Litvinovka, Nina Sergeevna keeps a diary of twenty-two entries, with four consecutive days when she wrote nothing.[168] On the fifteenth day, her secret manuscript is finally completed: "I had finished, finished! Finished my writing! . . . Here it lay in front of me, written, rewritten, finished. I turned over the pages and corrected the pagination. I would stick it into my diary. A single notebook was easier to hide than two."[169] What follows is Nina Sergeevna's ten-page "memoir" about the women of the Great Terror, narrated in the first person. In this text, which Chukovskaia "self-publishes" on behalf of her fictional character, making it a counterpoint to *Going Under* as a whole, Nina Sergeevna travels back in time ten years and finds herself next to Sofia Petrovna and other women in the interminable prison lines. But it is only now, ten years later, that she is finally able to put their shared experience into words. In this sense, Nina Sergeevna becomes a surrogate parent of sorts to Sofia Petrovna, whose naiveté fails her not just as a citizen but also as a mother.

One more striking parallel between Chukovskaia's two works of fiction is worth noting: both *Sofia Petrovna* and Nina Sergeevna's inserted novella in *Going Under* deal with the death of a child, whether a baby or adult, whether physical or allegorical. In the final scene of *Sofia Petrovna*, the titular mother, in her last fit of madness, burns her son's letter from prison: she "threw it to the floor and stamped on it" [*rastoptala nogoi*].[170] On the symbolic (and stylistic) level, the action she performs on her son's handwritten text, the only "manuscript" she has received from him since he disappeared, is the same as what is done to him physically in prison. Before burning the letter, Sofia Petrovna read her son's words: "Mama dear, Investigator Ershov beat me and trampled me" [*i toptal nogami*].[171] These marked tautologies in the original Russian text—*toptal nogami* and *rastoptala nogoi*—are not only reflected in each other, but render the two scenes excessive, suggesting not just a beating or burning the letter, but murder and death. Moreover, burning her son's letter from prison, Sofia Petrovna does precisely what Chukovskaia could not do to the manuscript of *Sofia Petrovna* when its physical existence was in itself the question of life and death: "It was dangerous to keep it in the drawer of my desk, but I couldn't bring myself to burn it. I regarded it not so much as a story as a piece of evidence, which it would be dishonorable to destroy."[172]

In *Going Under*, Nina Sergeevna describes the young Finnish mother of a four-month-old baby in the same prison line early one morning: "My attention was caught by the way she held her little girl, somehow oddly, on arms stretched out straight, and kept watching the tall door without blinking."[173] Upon leaving the prison building and seeing the Finnish woman again in the courtyard, Nina Sergeevna hears that the baby had died in her mother's hands "'already in there' . . . 'But I not want to lose my place in the queue of mothers, I want get information. I much loved my husband,'" the woman explains to her with a strong Finnish accent.[174] It is not only the biological (and ethical) norms that Chukovskaia questions in both texts, confronting the nightmarish phantasmagoria of the Great Terror, but also the linguistic ones: as the mothers are "orphaned" of their children, language, unable to catch up with reality, starts to disintegrate, causing tautology and excess, as in *Sofia Petrovna*, or corroding the Finnish woman's command of her non-native Russian, in *Going Under*.

Only ten years after the morning described does Nina Sergeevna come to realize that what had tormented her, Sofia Petrovna, and countless other women like them at the time was "the incomprehensibility and namelessness of what was taking place. . . . My head seemed to be spinning and my heart gradually growing heavier not from the sixteen hours spent on my feet but from fruitless efforts to grasp what had happened and give it a name."[175] Still unable to call it by its name, Nina Sergeevna attempts to do so in the process of writing. Her "going under," to the depths of her memory, brings a sense of fatigue and oblivion to the calendar: "How many days was it now since I hadn't kept my diary? Three? Five? I couldn't remember. I didn't know and didn't want to know. I tried to avoid knowing what today's date was. The days were already rolling down hill—towards my departure, the end, and I didn't want to count them."[176] Through oblivion to the present, she is able to bring back the past and relive it not just in her own memory and in solitude, but on paper, with the hope "to find brothers—if not now, then in the future."[177]

Nina Sergeevna is not the only one in Litvinovka who is working on a manuscript about the Great Terror. Bilibin too is writing his text about the past, which Nina Sergeevna longs to read. But when she finally does so, two days before leaving Litvinovka for Moscow, she feels betrayed and ashamed:

> I read it through. . . . I would never forget a single word. At first I recognized everything and rejoiced at it all. . . . Well, of course, he couldn't very well write about the camp for *Znamya*. . . .. But then why use those mountains, that forest, those people. . . .. When I had finished reading I closed the manuscript and sat at the desk for a long time, gazing at the neat folder. "Nikolai Bilibin" had been inscribed on it in distinct round letters. "Fedosya's Victory. A Tale." So this was what he had been writing from seven o'clock in the morning. This was why he had come here, to be quiet. This was the memorial he had raised to the memory of his friend. . . . Up till now I had often experienced grief in my life. But this was the first time that I felt shame.[178]

Like Veksler, the character of Bilibin, too, has a historical prototype. In émigré criticism, it was first named by Grigory Svirsky, a recent arrival from the Soviet Union. (Like Klenov, Svirsky was a World War II veteran and a member of the Writers' Union before his emigration to Israel and then to Canada in 1972.) The name of the writer who served as the model for Bilibin was Vasily Azhaev (1915–1968), author of the famous novel *Far from Moscow* (*Daleko ot Moskvy*), which Svirsky referred to as "a record of falsehood in the age of bloodthirsty falsifications."[179] From 1934 to 1937, Azhaev was a prisoner in the gulag, but his quasi-autobiographical novel, much like Bilibin's manuscript, rendered this firsthand experience in Stalin's camps barely recognizable. A less lacquered version of the novel, however, was first published in the journal *Dal'nii Vostok* in Khabarovsk, where Azhaev worked as an editor upon his release.[180] But in 1948 the novel was reworked for publication in *Novyi mir*, at the time headed by Konstantin Simonov.[181] In fact, it was Simonov and his crew who, according to Svirsky, introduced most of the changes to Azhaev's text on the author's behalf, so much so that the emaciated prisoners employed at the construction of an oil pipeline in the Far East were replaced by free workers, and the portrayal of the construction project itself became infused with the pathos of joyful enthusiasm for socialist labor; then head of the far-eastern camps, colonel Barabanov, evolved into a typical socialist-realist father figure, Batmanov, etc. In his foreword, Simonov wrote that it was solely out of irresistible inner need that Azhaev described gulag prisoners "as free people and Soviet citizens, who, under the inhuman conditions, contributed to our victory over fascism. And he did so quite consciously, in the hope that his novel would become a monument to their efforts, courage, and faithfulness to the motherland."[182] It is this kind of literature that Chukovskaia, through Nina Sergeevna's words, brands as the ultimate abuse of the written word, not just in the Tolstoyan sense, as the epigraph to *Going Under* suggests, but in the Orwellian one.[183]

In *Going Under*, the title of Azhaev's conformist novel is camouflaged as "Fedosya's Victory," while Simonov's *Novyi mir* becomes *Znamya*. As Anne Hartmann points out, "It is not only the author who is held accountable for writing a book that beats 'the record of falsehood in the age of bloodthirsty falsifications,'" as Svirsky put it, "but the literary community and the society, whose traumas Azhaev serviced, having fallen victim to those traumas himself."[184] While Chukovskaia must have been familiar with Azhaev's work before she began writing *Going Under* in 1949, the details about his career and his novel—namely, that it was rewritten by Simonov and his crew—may not have been widely known just yet. Still, in this context, *Going Under* is more than a work of fiction; it is also an uncompromising commentary on Soviet literature. By "going under," the protagonist was able to plunge "into the depths of the inner world of a Soviet writer intimidated and perverted by the regime,"[185] and although his character was modeled on Azhaev, Bilibin may be interpreted more generally as "a cumulative image of all the unfortunate writers who have betrayed their friends,"[186] afraid as they were in the late 1940s of receiving a second term in the gulag.[187]

When Bilibin comes back to pick up his manuscript, Nina Sergeevna calls him a "coward," a "false witness," and a "liar."[188] But on the eve of her departure from Litvinovka, she repents her judgment of the sick old man's lies.

> "Forgive me!" I wanted to say. "I didn't have the right to judge you; least of all I, for no dogs ever threw themselves on me and I've never seen the wooden tag on the leg of a dead man. . . . Forgive me! You wouldn't wish to go back there: to felling trees, to the mines. Go back for a second time! The story you wrote is your weak shield, your unreliable wall. . . . Forgive me! You've already

had one heart attack—illness is expensive and you need your earnings. And how else can you earn money as a sick man? Only by writing. Writing lies like a hack. . . . Forgive me! I didn't have the right to demand the truth from you. I'm healthy and yet I keep silent. I was never beaten at night in the investigator's room. And when they beat you I kept silent. What right have I then to judge you now? Forgive me my cursed cruelty, forgive me!"[189]

However, at that moment Bilibin was already "walking out" of her life forever, "slowly and uncertainly, his legs bearing his big body—the broad shoulders and large head—unsteadily."[190] Nina Sergeevna did not let Bilibin hear her inner cry. Chukovskaia, for her part, never invoked Azhaev directly by name in any of her writings, having confined him and his conformist novel to the world of fiction.[191]

The deeper Nina Sergeevna "plunges" into her own memory and her country's past, the fewer chances there are for her secret manuscript—and, for that matter, Chukovskaia's novella—to emerge from these depths aboveground at home. "Why, then, bother to go under?" Nina Sergeevna asks herself early on. "For even if my spoils were turned into a manuscript—into paper and ink—they would never be turned into a book. In any event not before my death. Why then did I descend?" As it happened with clandestine texts such as hers at the time, forced out of the official literary field into the underground (or "underwater") at home, they were bound to resurface abroad in tamizdat. In this sense the title of Chukovskaia's *Going Under* implied going elsewhere, as well as into the future, however near or far. Answering her own question, Nina Sergeevna saw both destinations as the ultimate terminus of her manuscript: "I wanted to find brothers—if not now, then in the future. . . . I had been writing a book to find brothers, even if only there in the unknown distance."[192] While the "future" meant those times when Chukovskaia's fiction could finally be published in Russia, the "unknown distance" may be understood geographically. The "brothers" Nina Sergeevna was looking for but failed to find in Litvinovka identified themselves elsewhere, across the ocean. When *Going Under* resurfaced on their shore, one of them, conflating Chukovskaia and her fictional character and thus blurring the line between fiction and history, assured the author that "her plunges were not in vain; that her memory became a book, if only outside her motherland, through the efforts of the brothers she was looking for."[193]

One wonders, however, why "brothers" and not "sisters," if Nina Sergeevna's manuscript (for which she even pondered the title "Daughter") describes "the undersociety of women in the prison lines"?[194] In her portrayal of this "undersociety," Nina Sergeevna stands next to her tongue-tied and grief-stricken "sisters," but in Litvinovka she finds herself surrounded by male writers, be they Russian or Jewish, war veterans like Veksler or former gulag prisoners like Bilibin. Her nonconformity is thus marked not only as a literary but also as a gender phenomenon.[195] Indeed, Nina Sergeevna is "the only writer in the sanatorium who explicitly protests official lies and voices her own independent opinions," but her role is nevertheless reduced to that of "a listener and a seeker of hidden 'truth'" carried and passed on to her by men, in whose midst she appears as "a shining anomaly."[196]

While *Going Under* is not, strictly speaking, a prison narrative, the manuscript that Nina Sergeevna secretly writes and "self-publishes" in her diary fits the tradition of gulag narratives as a genre in which the conventional meanings of words are inverted (as when mothers are "orphaned" by the death of their children). It is in this context, epitomized in Orwell's dystopia *1984* where newspeak is the only official "language" allowed in print, that the "truths" or "true meanings" of the historical past bestowed upon Nina Sergeevna by her fellow male writers at the end of the day also appear inverted: Veksler's poems, or rather their Russian translations, as well as his fatal self-deception on the eve of arrest, upend the reality he had witnessed on the frontlines of World War II; the promised revelations about the gulag in Bilibin's manuscript turn out to be the opposite of what Nina Sergeevna hoped to read; her husband's official verdict—"ten years without the right to correspondence"—is but a euphemism for the death sentence. On the scale of gender, the "brothers" she longs to find as a result of her "going under," accordingly, may also imply the reverse—the women, or "sisters," of the Great Terror who shared the firsthand experiences of Nina Sergeevna and Chukovskaia.

Going Under is written by a "widow writing about a widow writing about her loss."[197] But it is also a work of literature about literature deemed "un-literature," as Orwell would have it, in its native geography and jurisdiction. As such, apart from Orwell's famous dystopia set in 1984 but published in 1949, the year of the historical setting of *Going Under*, Chukovskaia's fiction, despite its historical authenticity, brings to mind another British author, whose seemingly apolitical nineteenth-century classic favored worldwide by children as much as by adults depicts the adventures of one female character, although much younger than Nina Sergeevna, who famously falls through a rabbit hole underground: "'I wonder if I shall fall right THROUGH the earth! How funny it'll seem to come out among the people that walk with their heads downward! The Antipathies, I think—. . . but I shall have to ask them what the name of the country is, you know.'"[198] Lewis Carroll's Victorian fantasy *Alice's Adventures in Wonderland* (draft title: *Alice's Adventures Under Ground*), built on absurdist play with language and overturning other life concepts, in an uncanny way translates Nina Sergeevna's "going under" into the story of the first publications of Chukovskaia's fiction in the tamizdat "wonderland," where both *Sofia Petrovna* and *Going Under* were bound to resurface after being rejected or never submitted for publication at home. The "empowerment" of Alice via her magic fall down and under the symbolic passageway through the ground, resulting in physical displacement and bodily disproportion, is akin to nearly as miraculous a transformation of Chukovskaia's manuscripts into books abroad. Having defied the physical laws of gravity, it is there, in the magical underground, that Alice discovers the "brotherhood" of anthropomorphic creatures, whose society and system of justice she challenges and upsets but whom she considers more interesting than the reality above ground: "Alice, in her final adventure in Wonderland, becomes increasingly bold during the trial to determine who stole the tarts of the Queen of Hearts. . . . As Alice comes into herself, chaos becomes the order of the day, and one senses that Wonderland's system of justice will never be quite the same."[199] Alice's adventures, however, turn out to be but a dream: having rebelled, wreaked havoc, grown back to her true size, and acquired personhood in the wonderland, Alice wakes up on her sister's knees exactly where she had left off, just in time for tea. Chukovskaia's *Sofia Petrovna* and *Going Under* return home from "wonderland" at the height of perestroika, just in time for a new historical era to make tamizdat a thing of the past.

CHAPTER 4

Varlam Shalamov's *Kolyma Tales*

The Gulag in Search of a Genre

The story of the first publication abroad of Shalamov's *Kolyma Tales* (*Kolymskie rasskazy*) begins where it might be expected to end: months after the Moscow trial of Sinyavsky and Daniel on February 10–14, 1966, Shalamov's manuscript was smuggled out of the country and serialized for the next ten years in the Russian émigré quarterly *Novyi zhurnal* (*The New Review*) in New York, following the publication of Chukovskaia's *Sofia Petrovna* in the same journal's two previous issues. This chapter traces the itinerary of the first manuscript of Shalamov's *Kolyma Tales* from Moscow to New York, based on archival findings, and analyzes its reception abroad, in particular vis-à-vis Solzhenitsyn's *Ivan Denisovich*, which seems to have overshadowed most other texts on the gulag since its momentous publication in Russia in 1962. In contrast to Solzhenitsyn's pioneering work on the topic published in gosizdat, it was the formal(ist) orchestration of the topic in Shalamov's "new prose," defined by the author as neither memoirs, nor short stories, nor even literature as such, but as "prose suffered through like a document" [*proza, vystradannaia kak document*],[1] that remained virtually inaccessible to the Russian émigré community of the old generation, who lacked sufficient familiarity with the Soviet vernacular, let alone a firsthand experience of the gulag, where much of this language and Soviet culture had been tempered. With *Kolyma Tales* as a case study, this chapter revisits the traditional dichotomy between official and underground fields of Russian literature in the late 1960s and 1970s, with tamizdat as their common denominator.

The decade that had passed since Shalamov's first manuscript traveled abroad in 1966 until *Kolyma Tales* first appeared as a book in London in 1978[2] encompassed the end of the Thaw, the birth of the dissident movement, and the rise of political samizdat in Russia. Abroad, it came between two distinct generations of Russian émigré writers, critics, and publishers, exposing the stylistic and ideological controversies between them, fueled by the profound differences in their linguistic and sociocultural backgrounds. It was also then that the ideological agendas of the Soviet literary establishment on the one hand and that of the transnational network of tamizdat on the other were perhaps most directly opposed to each other, sometimes resembling a mirror symmetry, as the publication history and reception of Shalamov's *Kolyma Tales* at home and abroad demonstrates.

Since his return to the mainland from Kolyma, Shalamov was known in Russia as a minor poet, but not as a prose writer; with five collections of poetry published at home during his lifetime, he managed to publish only one short story in gosizdat.[3] Abroad, Shalamov's reputation was the opposite. His poems left tamizdat publishers largely indifferent (partly because they were published in Russia), but *Kolyma Tales*, perhaps the most merciless account of the gulag ever committed to paper, became a sensation, although not a literary one. Shalamov's deliberately "imperfect" writing, meant to reflect the disintegration of the language and the body of Kolyma prisoners, was taken for insufficient literary mastery—so much so that *Kolyma Tales* was even edited for publication in tamizdat to make the stories fit the expectations of local readers. More importantly, regardless of geography, it was the ultimate impossibility of translating gulag experience in its extreme into any language, even one's native tongue that compromised the reception of *Kolyma Tales* both at home and abroad until much later, when the very futility of such an attempt was finally understood as the only available means to describe Kolyma.

Kolyma Tales in Novyi zhurnal (1966–1976)

Kolyma Tales first saw the light of day in *Novyi zhurnal*, a journal founded in New York in 1942 by Mark Aldanov and Mikhail Tsetlin as a transatlantic extension of the old Russian émigré periodical *Sovremennye zapiski* (*Contemporary Notes*), which was active in Paris before the war. From 1966 the editor in chief of *Novyi zhurnal* was Roman Gul', a prose writer and memoirist of the First Wave of the Russian emigration, who had moved to New York from France in 1950. It was under Gul"s leadership that *Novyi zhurnal* entered the "third stage" of its history, which, in the editor's words, began during the Thaw, "when individual voices of writers and readers from the Soviet Union started reaching us here."[4] Among those voices was Shalamov's *Kolyma Tales*. In December 1966 his first four short stories appeared in *Novyi zhurnal* with the editor's preamble: "We received the manuscript of these short stories from the USSR through an intermediary. Their author is V.T. Shalamov, a poet and prose writer, who spent approximately 20 years in concentration camps. We are printing *Kolyma Tales* without the author's knowledge or consent. For this, we extend V.T. Shalamov our apologies. But we consider it our civic duty to publish *Kolyma Tales* as a human document of exceptional value."[5] Although the standard disclaimer "without the author's knowledge or consent" had been used by tamizdat publishers for years, in 1966, in the wake of Sinyavsky and Daniel's trial, declaring the author's noninvolvement with his publications abroad was especially important. But it also made it impossible to say just how the manuscript of *Kolyma Tales* was smuggled out of Russia and ended up in New York. Years later, after Shalamov's death, Gul' recalled:

> The greatest gift to *Novyi zhurnal* was Varlam Shalamov's voluminous manuscript—*Kolyma Tales*. Here is how it happened. A renowned American professor of Slavic Studies telephoned me and said that he had been to Moscow and had brought back a large manuscript for *Novyi zhurnal*. I thanked him, and the following day the professor delivered the manuscript of *Kolyma Tales* to my apartment. It was a very large manuscript, about 600 pages. Handing it to me, the professor said that the author had met with him in person and asked him to take his manuscript for publication in *Novyi zhurnal*. The professor asked: "Aren't you afraid of publishing it in the West?" To which Shalamov replied: "We are tired of being afraid. . . ." This is how the publication of Varlam Shalamov's *Kolyma Tales* began in *Novyi zhurnal*, from issue to issue. We published Shalamov for more than ten years and were the first to introduce the West to this wonderful writer, who chose the dreadful and merciless hell of Kolyma as his topic. After Shalamov's short stories had almost entirely been printed in *Novyi zhurnal*,

I granted the rights to publish them as a book to the late Stypulkowski, head of Overseas Publications in London, who came to visit me. In London, *Kolyma Tales* came out as a book.[6]

Indeed, beginning in 1966 *Novyi zhurnal* published Shalamov more or less regularly for ten years, although some of his short stories appeared in other émigré journals as early as the following year.[7] It is also true that *Kolyma Tales* first appeared as a book in London in 1978, two years after Gul' ceased publishing them in *Novyi zhurnal*. The book was brought out by Overseas Publications Interchange (OPI), a publishing house founded by Andrzej Stypulkowski in 1964 under the auspices of Polonia Book Fund. However, as the editor of the volume, Mikhail Geller, specified in his preface, he compiled it "as accurately—given the absence of the author—as possible from a manuscript that circulated in samizdat," i.e., not from the one Gul' had at his disposal in New York.[8] Finally, the total of forty-nine short stories serialized in *Novyi zhurnal* in the course of ten years could hardly exhaust the "large manuscript, about 600 pages," as Gul described it, which included over a hundred texts from Shalamov's four cycles.[9]

The professor of Slavic Studies who delivered Shalamov's manuscript to Gul' was Clarence Brown, a Princeton specialist on Osip Mandelshtam, who had since the early 1960s collaborated with two other Russian-American publishers, Gleb Struve and Boris Filippov, on the first edition of Mandelshtam's complete works.[10] As an American exchange scholar, Brown had traveled to Russia several times and was a frequent guest at the apartment of the poet's widow, Nadezhda Mandelshtam, where he had met Shalamov "some three or four times every week, he being almost as regular a frequenter of Nadezhda Mandelstam's kitchen as I was."[11] Shalamov must have passed the manuscript of *Kolyma Tales* on to Brown no later than May 24, 1966, which is when, according to Brown's Moscow journals, they last saw each other.[12] In the words of Shalamov's friend and literary executor, Irina Sirotinskaia, who had met him earlier that spring, this was the first and only attempt to transfer the manuscript of *Kolyma Tales* abroad that Shalamov himself authorized.[13] While it is no longer possible to determine what exactly was said, by 1966 *Kolyma Tales* had crystallized into separate cycles, making it unlikely that Shalamov wished to see his short stories published abroad separately, in a disjointed form; "He hoped," according to Sirotinskaia, "that *Kolyma Tales* would appear as a book, and that it would bring some kind of a blow, a resonance."

The manuscript must have been shipped from Moscow to the United States by diplomatic pouch and reached Princeton no later than September 12, 1966, when Brown informed Gul', "I recently returned from the Soviet Union, as you may know, but as you certainly do not know, I also brought with me a manuscript that may prove to be of an explosive significance. I should like to show it to you. . . . I think that you would be interested in the Russian text."[14] Assuming Shalamov had not asked Brown to deliver the manuscript of *Kolyma Tales* directly to *Novyi zhurnal* (or any other émigré periodical, for that matter) but hoped that it would come out as a book, why was it not offered to a book publisher instead? True, half a year after the trial of Sinyavsky and Daniel, it was no longer possible to offer *Kolyma Tales*, for example, to Filippov, whose publishing house Inter-Language Literary Associates had become an anathema in Russia for having published Tertz and Arzhak (aka Sinyavsky and Daniel).[15] In 1966 there were not many alternatives. Max Hayward's Chekhov Publishing House in New York, Carl and Ellendea Proffers' Ardis in Ann Arbor, Karel van het Reve and Peter Reddaway's Alexander Herzen Foundation in Amsterdam, among other tamizdat publishing venues of the new generation, did not take shape until a few years later. Still, why did the "explosive" effect of *Kolyma Tales*, as Brown put it, have to be postponed?

One of the reasons was that Shalamov's name was virtually unknown abroad and did not mean much to Gul', who later confessed that by 1966 he had only "read some of his poetry but was not impressed."[16] Nevertheless, the news of the manuscript could not leave Gul' indifferent, and on September 15, 1966, he replied to Brown: "Of course, I would VERY MUCH like to publish this material in *Novyi zhurnal*. As it happens, I have just started submitting materials for No. 85 (December). . . . I am ready to meet with you—whenever you want, in whichever way is convenient."[17] They must have met within the next two weeks. On September 29, 1966, Gul' notified Brown that he was returning the manuscript, indicating which of Shalamov's short stories he was going to publish first, and offered his general opinion on *Kolyma Tales*:

> I am sending you the manuscript of *Kolyma Tales* by registered mail. I have not yet read all of it. In the next (December) issue of *Novyi zhurnal*, I will publish several short stories: "The Parcel," "Pushover," "Field Rations," "Maxim," and possibly "Cherry Brandy," although there is much unfulfilled in this story, but it is, clearly, written on the death of Mandelshtam. There are texts

that are completely bad, such as "The Green Prosecutor." There are those that require literary refinement, such as "The Cross" (it could be a very good short story, but it is badly written). In short, thank you very much for familiarizing me with this manuscript. . . . The fact of the matter is that they are very monotonous and heavy in their themes. However, I consider the manuscript to be valuable. It should be turned into a small book—approximately 150–200 pages (no reader would be able to cope with more).[18]

As it happens, Gul's take on "Cherry Brandy," in particular, had to do not only with his rather sour impression of Shalamov's prose but also with his dislike of Mandelshtam's poetry. More than a year earlier, Gul' had lamented to Brown, then the leading specialist on Mandelshtam, "Of course, objectively, I very much value Mandelshtam's Muse, as well as that of Khodasevich. But I cannot say that I am particularly fond of this Muse; it is not 'my' Muse. . . . Behind Mandelshtam's poetry I do not see a PERSON, a poet as a human being, a personality. It is as if his poems (many great ones!) have been created by *no one*."[19] This helps explain why the first selection of *Kolyma Tales* in *Novyi zhurnal* did not include "Cherry Brandy," a meditation on Mandelshtam's death in the transit camp outside Vladivostok. Instead, the selection opened with the other text of Shalamov's Mandelshtam cycle, "Sententsiia" ("Maxim"), written later and dedicated to the poet's widow. Answering Gul"s letter of September 29, 1966, Brown warned him that "Cherry Brandy" was "an *imagined* account of the death of Osip Mandelstam, as the author himself explained to me" and that it could not, therefore, be treated as documentary evidence of the poet's death, no matter how important such evidence may have been at the time when not even his widow knew its exact date, place, or cause: "I hope," Brown wrote to Gul', "that you somehow make this clear in an editorial note—that it is *fiction*."[20] But when "Cherry Brandy" did finally appear in *Novyi zhurnal* two years later, in 1968 (issue no. 91), it was abridged and edited in such a way that it read precisely like a documentary account of the last days of the poet. Preoccupied with the factographic rather than the aesthetic aspects of Shalamov's text, Gul' supplied an epigraph from Mandelshtam's poem that informs its title but is absent from Shalamov's original: "I'll tell you bluntly / One last time: / It's only maddening cherry brandy, / Angel mine" [*Ia skazhu tebe s poslednei priamotoi: / Vse lish' bredni, sherri-brendi, angel moi!*].[21] However, key passages on the nature of poetry and inspiration, which, according to Shalamov, Mandelshtam came to grasp only on the threshold of death, were left out. The last sentence, which renders the poet's death as an allegory for his posthumous legacy—"Therefore he died earlier than the date of his death, quite an important detail for his future biographers"—was also discarded.[22]

Gul' was not the only émigré critic of his generation who was frustrated with "Cherry Brandy." Even after Gul's "improvements" in *Novyi zhurnal*, the short story outraged Yury Terapiano, who accused Shalamov of treating Mandelshtam's death frivolously: "Especially now, when what actually happened to Mandelshtam in the transit camp is known only by hearsay, his death should not have been turned into a work of literature."[23] "Cherry Brandy," Terapiano lamented, "touches us in a rather unpleasant way" [*nas neskol'ko nepriiatno zadevaet*], while the dying poet's thoughts on having written "bad prose" in the past and having "had no pupils," as Shalamov wrote, raised the question "What gives Shalamov the right to make Mandelshtam speak of his prose in such a way, and what makes him think that Mandelshtam has not influenced contemporary poets?" Sharing Gul's reading of "Cherry Brandy" merely as a source of information on life in the camps, Terapiano underscored that "the most important thing in [*Kolyma Tales*] for us has been their truthfulness, although as far as the form is concerned, Shalamov is also a talented storyteller." Unaware that, after Gul's edits, the short stories he read in *Novyi zhurnal* were no longer exactly Shalamov's, it was not the author Terapiano praised as "a talented storyteller," but rather the editor of the journal under review.

Shalamov's Mandelshtam Cycle (A Digression)

Although they appeared in reverse order in *Novyi zhurnal*, "Cherry Brandy" (1958) and "Sententsiia" (1965) form a cycle, not only because the former is devoted to the poet and the latter to his widow.[24] Both texts begin with a clinical description of the same physical condition that situates their respective protagonists between life and death. But while the poet's apathy in "Cherry Brandy" results in physical death, the anger of the first-person narrator in "Sententsiia" serves as a starting point in his inner journey in the opposite direction. One might go so far as to say that the dying poet in the former text and the first-person narrator of the latter are, essentially, one and the same "character" undergoing the same cycle, albeit in reverse. In both short stories, the different stages of this cycle are punctuated linguistically.

Despite its clinical precision and claim to biographical authenticity, "Cherry Brandy" is less about physical death than about immortality: the dying poet "believed in immortality, in real human immortality. He had often thought there were simply no biological reasons why man shouldn't live forever. . . . Or at least until he was tired of life. And he hadn't tired of life at all. Even now, in this transit barracks."[25] Immortality is thus conceived of as a liminal state, marked linguistically (grammatically) in the short story's opening sentence: "The poet was dying" (as opposed, for instance, to "They had all died," the first sentence of Shalamov's short story "A Funeral Speech," where real-life characters, who had indeed died in Kolyma, are referred to by their real names).[26] "Cherry Brandy," in other words, focuses on the process of dying rather than on death itself, which is "postponed" at the end of the story, as if in response to the grammatical tension of the opening sentence: "By evening [the poet] was dead. But they wrote him off two days later," so that "his enterprising neighbors managed to get a dead man's bread for two days; when it was distributed, the dead man's hand rose up like a puppet's. Therefore he died earlier than the date of his death, quite an important detail for his future biographers."[27] As a "biographer" of Mandelshtam, Shalamov recounts his life as a poet but extends it beyond the last day of his life as a human. The last days of the poet are portrayed as his life's cumulative sum total, while his physical oscillation between life and death comprises the essence of poetic inspiration. Much like the transit barrack itself, where the poet died, inspiration is also localized: "This transit camp was the antechamber to horror, but it wasn't horror itself. On the contrary, there was a living spirit of freedom here, and everyone could sense that. The camps were yet to come, the prisons were in the past. This was ['a world in transit'], and the poet understood that."[28]

The poet's thoughts grow as basic as his emaciated body, allowing him to zoom in on death as a clinical phenomenon, rather than an object of poetic description. "What was wonderful was that now he didn't have to hurry, that he could think slowly. And he thought at leisure of the great monotony of deathbed movements, something that doctors had understood and described long before artists and poets." As the dying poet keeps thinking of art as a form of immortality, he recalls the lines from Fedor Tiutchev's poem "Cicero" (1829): "Blessed is he who visits this world / In its most fateful moments" [*Blazhen, kto posetil sei mir / V ego minuty rokovye*].[29] Because "Cherry Brandy" is centered on the disintegration of language in the face of death, the reference to Tiutchev has a special significance as it brings to mind Tiutchev's other poem, "Silentium!" (1830), with its famous dictum "A thought, once spoken, is a lie" [*Mysl' izrechennaia est' lozh'*], which inspired Mandelshtam's own poem of the same title eighty years after Tiutchev. Mandelshtam's "Silentium" (1910), addressing the same problem of the inexpressibility of the world in a spoken word, defines the divine, prelinguistic source of poetry as a "prime muteness" [*pervonachal'naia nemota*], as if to claim that in the beginning there was not the Word, but silence: "Let my lips acquire / The prime muteness, / Like a crystal note, / That is innately pure!" [*Da obretut moi usta / Pervonachal'nuiu nemotu, / Kak ristallicheskuiu notu, / Chto ot rozhdeniia chista!*].[30] It is not until the last day of his life that Mandelshtam, in Shalamov's "Cherry Brandy," "acquired the prime muteness" that earns him poetic immortality. Granting the poet divine silence, death offers him the initial, preverbal state, one that is a priori truer, more adequate to the surrounding world, including Kolyma. Death in "Cherry Brandy" is thus reinvented as a supralinguistic experience—not as the loss of voice but, on the contrary, as the poet's attainment of the true voice of poetry, a voice that remains inevitably split in an act of speech.[31]

The age-old motif of the inexpressible dates back to the tradition of apophatic theology, but Shalamov's theodicy of language in his Mandelshtam cycle is radically different, not only from this theological tradition but also from the poetry of Russian Romanticism epitomized, for example, in Vasily Zhukovsky's "The Inexpressible" ("Nevyrazimoe,") of 1819, where human language is deemed incapable of expressing the divine nature.[32] It is for this reason that Shalamov is preoccupied with the last days of Mandelshtam and his physical death, rather than with his previous life as a poet, when verbal language was still available to him: "His entire past life was literature, books, fairy tales, dreams, and only this present day was real life."[33] Shalamov, who rejected literary embellishment and proclaimed the "new prose" as the only adequate method of writing about Kolyma, carries on the Acmeist principle of clarity and translates it, through Mandelshtam, into a different historical setting, where human language fails to register the inhuman experience of the gulag, including the transit camp where Mandelshtam had died and where Shalamov himself had been a year before on his way to Kolyma.[34] Shalamov heard about Mandelshtam's death in 1944 from doctor Nina Savoeva, who retold the story she had herself heard in Vladivostok while awaiting a ship to Kolyma, where she had decided to come as a free worker. Savoeva's story included the detail about Mandelshtam's campmates' receiving his food ration for two days after his death, which Shalamov included in "Cherry Brandy."[35]

Unlike Theodor Adorno, who claimed that "to write poetry after Auschwitz is barbaric,"[36] Shalamov reaffirms the triumph of language over death itself in the second short story of his Mandelshtam cycle, "Sententsiia." Unlike "Cherry Brandy," "Sententsiia" is written in the first person, but it begins exactly where "Cherry Brandy" left off: "People were arising, one after the other, out of nonexistence" [*Liudi voznikali iz nebytiia*].[37] It affirms Mandelshtam's belief in immortality by reviving the poetic word after his physical death in the earlier story of the cycle.[38] While "Cherry Brandy" dealt entirely with the liminal state between life and death followed only by "prime muteness," "Sententsiia" presents a range of feelings and emotions, probing their hierarchy and dynamics. In this hierarchy, anger (*zloba*) is "the last human feeling to go," the only one left after all other feelings have abandoned the first-person narrator: "What did I retain until the very end? [Anger.] By hanging on to this [anger], I counted on dying. But death, which had very recently been so near, began to recede little by little. It wasn't life that displaced death but a half-conscious state, an existence that couldn't be formulated or even called life."[39] Having reached nearly the same state as the dying poet in "Cherry Brandy," the narrator of "Sententsiia" moves in the opposite direction—not toward death but away from it. Each step in his "outbound" inner journey toward physical and spiritual rebirth is punctuated by a specific feeling: after anger comes indifference; after indifference, the ability to keep track of his surroundings and less need for sleep; then, the surprising awareness of his body; then, fearlessness, followed again by fear; then, envy, pity, and mercy, first for animals and only then for humans. The only feeling that has not returned to him is love. But the last feeling that does come back to the narrator is for the spoken word—the same feeling that had abandoned the poet in "Cherry Brandy."

To articulate the successive stages of this process, Shalamov deconstructs traditional laws of signification and linguistic conventions, challenging the relationship between words and the phenomena, objects, or qualities they denote. Water, in "Sententsiia," is suitable for drinking not because it is boiled but because it is hot: "Kolyma had taught us all to identify drinking water only by temperature. We could tell hot and cold apart, but not boiled and unboiled."[40] After years without books or newspapers, the narrator's lexicon has been reduced to a couple of dozen words, just enough to fulfil the most basic needs of communication: "My language, my coarse miner's language, was as impoverished as the feelings that still survived around my bones. . . . I was happy not to have to search for other words. I didn't know if they even existed."[41] This long period of numbness, when language had almost completely atrophied in the prisoner's consciousness, is suddenly interrupted when

> my brain—right here, I clearly remember, under the right temple bone—gave birth to a word that was utterly unsuitable for the taiga, a word that neither I nor my comrades could understand. I got up on my bunk and yelled out this word to the heavens, to infinity: "[Sententsiia! Sententsiia!]"
> And then I burst into loud laughter.
> ["Sententsiia!"] I roared straight into the northern sky, the double dawn; I roared it without yet understanding the meaning of the word that had been born within me. If this was a word that had returned, that had been found again, so much the better, so much the better! A great joy filled all my being.[42]

Like a child just learning to speak, the narrator shouts out the foreign word *sententsiia* and believes in it as one can believe only in pure sound or music, devoid, as it were, of any semantic relationship to the material world. The value of this newly rediscovered sound is so absolute that it seems it can be applied to any object or phenomenon of the natural world that surrounds the narrator: "[Sententsiia]. That could be a new name for the little river that ran by our settlement, our posting: the Rio Rita. In what way was that a better name than [Sententsiia]?" In the next few days, more and more words come back to him, each arising "suddenly and separately . . ., on its own, not escorted by other familiar words," and each "came back to my tongue before it came back to my brain."[43] Finally, the narrator grasps both the lexical meaning and etymology of the word *sententsiia* that had returned to him first:

> There is something Roman, firm, Latin about the word ["sententsiia"]. . . . ["Sententsiia"] is a Roman word. It took me a week to understand what [sententsiia] meant. I whispered it, shouted it out, frightening and amusing my neighbors with it. I demanded a solution, an explanation, a translation from the world, from the heavens. . . . A week later I understood it, and quivered with fear and joy. With fear, because I was frightened of any return to a

world I had no way of returning to. Joy, because I could see life returning to me against my will.[44]

But why, of all words "utterly unsuitable for the taiga," whether foreign or Russian, does Shalamov choose the Latin *sententsiia* to articulate his narrator's gradual return from the world of the dead? The first reason has to do with the double meaning of the word itself in the Russian language: 1) a thought or opinion spoken out loud, and 2) a court verdict. As Valery Esipov has noted, the second meaning, now outdated, was popular in nineteenth- and early twentieth-century Russia and was, no doubt, familiar to Shalamov, a law student in Moscow in the 1920s. "First," Esipov explains, "the narrator-protagonist cannot remember the word's meaning. It is only 'a week later that he understood it—and quivered with fear and joy,' which speaks to the fact that he has remembered the word's *both* meanings . . ., one evoking fear, the other joy."[45] The second reason why Shalamov chooses *sententsiia* as the key word and title for his short story has to do with Mandelshtam. The Latin word *sententsiia* belongs to the same "dead" language, has the same number of syllables, and the initial letter as *Silentium*—the title of Mandelshtam's 1910 poem about divine silence defined as "prime muteness" and understood as an inalienable feature of the netherworld. Shalamov's "Sententsiia" thus derives linguistically and etymologically from Mandelshtam's poem and serves as an "extension" of the poet's life and biography. The death of the poet two days "earlier than the date of his death," in "Cherry Brandy," gives the narrator of "Sententsiia" just enough time to remember the word he had not so much forgotten as could no longer articulate. And while the poet's physical death in "Cherry Brandy" marks his transition to the nonverbal realm, where linguistic barriers cease to exist and where words are freed from their conventional referents, "Sententsiia," too, ends on a similar "nonverbal" note:

> Finally the day came when . . . a boss had arrived from Magadan. It was a clear, hot, dry day. There was a phonograph on the enormous larch stump by the entrance to the tent. It was playing something symphonic, the music drowning out the hiss of the needle. . . . The shellac disc revolved and hissed, even the stump was revolving, wound up for three hundred revolutions, like a taut spring wound up for three hundred years.[46]

As it happens, the return of the feeling for spoken language in "Sententsiia" was just a rehearsal. The narrator's true resurrection comes

only when he hears music—that primary "original," from which all poetry is but an imperfect "translation," as Mandelshtam had suggested
in the final stanza of his "Silentium": "Remain foam, Aphrodite, / And
word, return to music" [*Ostan'sia penoi, Afrodita, / I, slovo, v muzyku
vernis'*].[47] But when "Sententsiia" appeared in *Novyi zhurnal* as the first
of Shalamov's short stories to be published abroad, its last sentence,
which serves as a coda of sorts to Shalamov's composition, was also cut
off, like the last sentence of "Cherry Brandy." As a result, the text was
deprived of its scale of "three hundred years" and reduced to a mere
anecdote about the camps. Furthermore, without the last sentence, the
story ended instead with the image of the gulag boss from Magadan,
whose "facial expression suggested that he had composed this music
for us, for our remote posting in the backwoods of the taiga."[48] It is
the last sentence of "Sententsiia," according to Elena Mikhailik, that
"transports the narrator outside the camp context, into the outer world
where music, history, metaphors and alliteration still exist"; without it,
the short story itself is impossible, since "it is only here, at this boundary," that the narrator's inexpressible experience of Kolyma is finally
matched by the language required for this experience to be conveyed.
Until then, "the narrator, strictly speaking, is simply unable to nar-
rate, since his lexicon is too limited."[49] Inside the camp, such language
is only nascent, does not yet exist. Having stripped both short stories
of their final sentences, Gul' abbreviated the posthumous biography
of the poet in "Cherry Brandy" by two days and denied the narrator of
"Sententsiia" a reentry into the world of the living.

Kolyma Tales in *Novyi zhurnal* (Continued)

After Gul' returned the manuscript of *Kolyma Tales* to Brown on October 8, 1966,[50] it disappeared from their correspondence for the next five
years, until January 23, 1971, when Brown informed the editor of *Novyi
zhurnal* that a new anthology titled *Russia's Other Writers* had just been
published with two of Shalamov's short stories translated into English
by Martin Dewhirst.[51] "The editor of this anthology," Brown wrote,
"has at his disposal all *Kolyma Tales* . . . and, in the nearest future, is going to publish them all in English translation. V. T. Shalamov strongly
insists that his short stories should be published in the right order.
Scammell, the English translator, knows the order in which they ought
to be published."[52] Michael Scammell, the editor of the anthology (but

not the translator), had another manuscript of *Kolyma Tales*, which had been recently found in his home archive. According to Michael Brewer, this manuscript was smuggled to Prague in 1968 by Irina Kanevskaia-Khenkina,[53] who recalls visiting Shalamov in Moscow and taking back to Prague—where she and her husband lived until the Soviet invasion of Czechoslovakia—"a large, shabby Soviet-style fiber suitcase stuffed with manuscripts." From Prague, Kanevskaia telephoned "a Russian friend in Paris," who sent a student to get the suitcase, but "what happened next I cannot grasp to this day. Instead of publishing the short stories as a book, they sent them to America and started printing them piece by piece in a Russian journal, having thus delayed the reader's acquaintance with Shalamov for several—more than 10!—years."[54]

As it happens, Gul' had not one but two manuscripts of *Kolyma Tales*: one obtained from Brown in 1966, the other—likely via Kanevskaia—two or more years later. Indeed, in his letter to Struve on December 7, 1970, Gul' confessed that he had received "two different manuscripts via two channels."[55] But as he prepared them for publication in *Novyi zhurnal*, Gul' edited both, as he admitted on February 24, 1969, to Jerzy Giedroyc, the editor of the Polish émigré Instytut Literacki in Paris, who wanted to publish *Kolyma Tales* as a book in Polish translation. "I have two different manuscripts," Gul' wrote, "and both are in very bad Xerox copies. . . . But this is not the problem, after all. The problem is that I have edited Shalamov's short stories in *Novyi zhurnal*, sometimes rather heavily. WITHOUT being edited, they should not be published—they will not read well. To translate them straight from the manuscript is not a good idea either. I do not know how to go about it."[56] Although Gul' was ready to send him Shalamov's short stories free of charge, Giedroyc had to decline: "I very much regret that Shalamov's manuscript need[s] a serious adjustment. . . . I have, unfortunately, resign[ed] from the plan of publication in Polish, at least at present. It is possible that I shall return to this project later on."[57] As a result, no Polish edition was brought out at that time, and although *Kolyma Tales* was fated to appear in *Novyi zhurnal* for seven more years, on this note the epistolary exchange between Giedroyc and Gul' broke off. As for Gul' and Brown, their correspondence also ended on January 23, 1971, when Brown finally raised the issue that *Kolyma Tales* should be published in the proper order.

What prevented Gul' from publishing *Kolyma Tales* in the order in which they appeared in the manuscripts he received, and why five years later, after Shalamov's will had been explicitly communicated to him, did he decide to neglect it and went on publishing *Kolyma Tales* as if it was a disjointed assortment of documentary sketches of camp life without a unifying plot or overarching composition? In keeping with the author's design, all later editions of *Kolyma Tales*, including the first book edition brought out in London in 1978, open with the short sketch "Trampling the Snow" ("Po snegu"), whose seemingly artless plot reflects not only the composition of the first cycle but also Shalamov's entire oeuvre and, by extension, gulag narratives as a genre: each step of a prisoner marching in a column through the deep snow leaves an imprint as long as it does not overlap completely with the footprints of another prisoner marching ahead.

> If they had walked in single file, there would have been a barely passable narrow trail, a path, not a road: a series of holes that would be harder to walk over than virgin snow. The first man has the hardest job, and when he is completely exhausted, another man from this pioneer group of five steps forward. Of all the men following the trailblazer, even the smallest, the weakest must not just follow someone else's footprints but must walk a stretch of virgin snow himself. As for riding tractors or horses, that is the privilege of the [readers, not the writers].[58]

As Leona Toker has pointed out, the final sentence translates this ordinary scene of camp life into an allegory—"the snow becomes a blank page."[59] The allegory suggests a line of literary inheritance between different authors who have survived the gulag, whereby each of their texts is destined to leave a new trace in the readers' vision of the reality described, as long as it adds something new. In an extended sense, the entire tradition of Russian prison camp writing is thus conceived of as a file of prisoners beating a path through the snow. Every author in this literary procession is also bound to play the role of a reader—of those who came before him, of times and places he had not been to or witnessed firsthand. More specifically, "Trampling the Snow" points to the internal organization of *Kolyma Tales*, where "each short story stands in its right place," as Shalamov declared in his programmatic essay "On Prose" (1965).[60] Why did an entire decade have to pass before Shalamov's creative design could be heard, and what had to happen in the course of those years in Russia and abroad for *Kolyma Tales* to be first published and read as a book?

Shalamov's Letter to *Literaturnaia gazeta* (1972)

The publication of *Kolyma Tales* abroad is inseparable from the affair of *Doctor Zhivago*, Pasternak's forced rejection of the Nobel Prize, and his "notorious letters of remorse" in Soviet newspapers, which Shalamov claimed Pasternak "should not have written."[61] Almost ten years after the publication of *Doctor Zhivago* in Italy, Shalamov invoked Pasternak in his anonymous "Letter to an Old Friend" ("Pis'mo staromu drugu"), written in the wake of Sinyavsky and Daniel's trial, which, in Shalamov's words, "agitated the whole world much more deeply and broadly, more painfully and responsibly than the notorious affair of Pasternak. . . . The element of spiritual terror in Pasternak's case (I almost said: in Pasternak's trial) has grown here into terror of a physical sort."[62] In 1966 Shalamov could not yet fathom, of course, that "he was also fated to play the role of a live overturned Buddha,"[63] as Sirotinskaia, his friend and literary executor, put it later.

On February 15, 1972, Shalamov wrote his ill-fated letter to the editor of *Literaturnaia gazeta*, which began, "I became aware that the anti-Soviet petty journal *Posev*, printed in Russian in Western Germany, as well as the anti-Soviet émigré journal *Novyi zhurnal* in New York, have decided to take advantage of my good name as a Soviet author and citizen and are printing *Kolyma Tales* in their slanderous publications."[64] Shalamov claimed he "had never collaborated with . . . any foreign publications known for their shameful anti-Soviet activity" nor ever given them any manuscripts in the past and never would in the future. He complained of "the mean publishing method adopted by the editors of these foul-smelling petty journals [*zlovonnye zhurnal'chiki*]—one or two short stories per issue," which "aimed to create the impression that I was one of their regular contributors." Without mentioning the unauthorized book-length translations of *Kolyma Tales* into foreign languages that by that time had already appeared in Germany, South Africa, and France,[65] he assailed the Frankfurt-based émigré journal *Posev*, which published only two of his short stories in 1967 but, unlike *Novyi zhurnal*, was notorious for its affiliation with the National Alliance of Russian Solidarists (NTS), an émigré organization of the most odious reputation in the eyes of the Soviet authorities. "No Soviet writer will ever demean himself by publishing in this foul-smelling anti-Soviet leaflet" [*v etom zlovonnom antisovetskom listke*].[66] Protesting against being represented as an anti-Soviet writer and an internal émigré, Shalamov concluded his letter with a phrase that would cost him dearly both in Russia and abroad: "For a long time now, the problematics of *Kolyma Tales* has been removed by life" [*Problematika 'Kolymskikh rasskazov' davno sniata zhizn'iu*].[67]

The letter appeared in *Literaturnaia gazeta* soon after the first secretary of the Soviet Writers' Union, Georgy Markov, made Shalamov an unambiguous offer to have his fourth book of poetry, *Moskovskie Oblaka* (*Moscow Clouds*), published in Russia without delay in exchange for a public renunciation of the illegal publications of *Kolyma Tales* in tamizdat.[68] Frustrated by the way his texts were handled abroad and disillusioned with samizdat and the dissident movement at home,[69] Shalamov wanted to be read in Russia, if only as a poet. Indeed, according to Gladkov, who saw Shalamov five days after the letter came out, "his book of poetry had been blocked at Sovetskii pisatel', as well as a cycle of poems in *Literaturnaia gazeta*"; Shalamov, however, "regrets nothing and is in a lively spirit. He wants to become a member of the Union," which Gladkov explained by his "utter isolation from the literary environment . . . aggravated by his deafness, illnesses and poverty, etc."[70]

Contrary to some earlier assumptions that the letter was a forgery or a document that Shalamov was forced to sign,[71] there is little doubt it was genuine. In a note written the same month but not meant to go public, Shalamov explained, "It is ridiculous to assume someone can force me to sign anything. My statement, its language, its style belongs to me and no one else. . . . Had the question been about *The Times*, I would have found a different language, but there is no language other than swearing for *Posev*. . . . Everything is within the limits of language."[72] As Toker has convincingly argued, it is precisely the language of Shalamov's letter that does not allow its dismissal as a mere capitulation to the authorities. In particular, Shalamov's repeated use of *zlovonnye* ("foul-smelling"), his epithet for émigré journals, was meant to remind the reader of the typical invective of the 1920s, a period of ardent political debates between the ruling faction and the left opposition, which Shalamov belonged to and remembered firsthand. "To the readers of Shalamov's prose," Toker explains, "this word is strikingly 'alien' . . . smuggling the one and only public reference, by the actual title, to his 'Kolyma Tales' into the official Soviet media. The target audience of the letter is thus informed that such a work exists, a record is left, questions about accessibility are encouraged; the readers of the letter, who would know what the toponym Kolyma stands for, would hardly avoid asking "'Kolyma Tales'? Where?"[73] Invoking Shalamov's short story "A Piece of Flesh" ("Kusok miasa"), whose protagonist fakes acute appendicitis and sacrifices his flesh to avoid being sent off to one of the deadliest camps, where his chances to survive are too slim, Toker compares the epithet *zlovonnye* to a "'piece of meat' thrown to the hurdle audience of the letter (the newspaper editors, the censors) in order to distract its attention from what the letter really accomplishes."[74] The technique was, indeed, not uncommon among Soviet dissidents and intellectuals, "who wished to acquaint the readership with some 'unacceptable' theories" by "attacking such theories—while explaining them in detail in the process."[75] Of course, Shalamov's letter to *Literaturnaia gazeta* also stemmed from his inability to control the fate of his writings once they began circulating in samizdat and leaked abroad. The letter, Toker concludes, may thus be regarded as "an extension of his lack of control over his own fate as a prisoner in the camps."[76] But in 1972 Shalamov's public "repentance" could not but shock its readers both in Russia and abroad. Its subtexts remained eclipsed by the literal meaning of the text, and neither audience proved capable of reading it as a stylistically veiled message. It was the letter's final sentence that aroused the greatest indignation and was interpreted not only as Shalamov's renunciation of his own writings but also as a betrayal of the millions of victims of Kolyma.

A month after the letter appeared in *Literaturnaia gazeta*, an émigré newspaper in Paris ran an anonymous column by a recent arrival from the USSR titled "Undoing Kolyma?" ("Uprazdnenie Kolymy?"). The newspaper was then edited by Princess Zinaida Shakhovskaia, a poet and memoirist of the First Wave, who wrote in her introduction, "Two assumptions inevitably come to mind: either Shalamov has sold out [*ssuchilsia*], or he has always been 'one of theirs'—an informer [*stukach*]. A third [assumption] is also possible—that he was forced to write [the letter], although this version gives no credit to the author of *Kolyma Tales* either."[77] The anonymous author of the article was familiar with Shalamov through samizdat while still living in Russia. He mentioned the dissident Andrei Amalrik, who was still doing time in Kolyma despite Shalamov's claim that "the problematics of *Kolyma Tales* has been removed by life," and he raised the question of what it means to "sell out" (*ssuchit'sia*), addressing Shalamov directly: "Varlam Tikhonovich, everyone is responsible for what he is worth. As an old-timer of the camps, you too may be told: 'You have sold out!' [*Vy ssuchilis'*]." In Soviet criminal jargon, *ssuchit'sia* means to betray the code of honor (of professional thieves) and collaborate with the camp or prison authorities and the regime in general. But while Shalamov, as Toker has demonstrated, used the epithet *zlovonnye* as an oblique reference to the political rhetoric of the 1920s, Shakhovskaia, who had emigrated in 1920, and the anonymous author, who was familiar with the Soviet prison jargon firsthand, employed the verb *ssuchit'sia* against Shalamov directly and ascribed the epithet *zlovonnye* to the "rotten lexicon of the Zhdanov era."[78]

The March 1972 issue of *Novyi zhurnal* printed Shalamov as usual, but in addition to the routine disclaimer that the short story "The Lawyers' Conspiracy" ("Zagovor Iuristov") was being published "without the author's knowledge or consent," it also featured Gul''s deliberations about Shalamov's letter to *Literaturnaia gazeta*. Unlike Shakhovskaia, Gul' refused to believe the letter had been written by Shalamov. It was, he argued, "written in the language and style of the KGB and *Literaturnaia gazeta*, not in the language and style of V. Shalamov. . . . Instead of making up and printing such 'protests,' why doesn't *Literaturnaia gazeta* publish V. Shalamov's *Kolyma Tales* and other samizdat works? Then there would be no need to publish (or rather, republish) them here."[79] Despite his best intentions and his faith in Shalamov's morals, Gul' also took the text of the letter at its face value. Having emigrated from Russia in 1920, neither Gul' nor Shakhovskaia were sufficiently versed in the linguistic and political subtext of Shalamov's letter. Nevertheless, for a while it had set them apart. Responding to Shakhovskaia's attack on Shalamov, Gul' wrote in another émigré newspaper that twenty years in Kolyma is not the same as twenty years in Passy, Paris, and that publishing the anonymous invective against Shalamov in *Russkaia mysl'* discredited Shakhovskaia as its editor, adding nothing to the émigrés' understanding of the plight of writers in Russia.[80] Gul''s defense of Shalamov was echoed, for instance, by Gleb Struve: "Soviet repentances are, of course, a very sad thing, but one should not take them at their face value, nor invest too much meaning in them. . . . These letters of 'repentance' should not be silenced, but it is not worth jumping too fast to conclusions."[81] Struve was well familiar with the Soviet attacks on tamizdat and himself in particular since at least the late 1950s, but in 1972 he read Shalamov's letter to *Literaturnaia gazeta* in the immediate context of an article by the Soviet critic Aleksandr Dymshits published in *Literaturnaia Rossiia* (*Literary Russia*) only two weeks earlier, in which Struve was referred to, among others, as an "anti-Soviet slanderer." "Let the anti-Soviet slanderers keep their dirty hands off the writings of authors whose paths have not been easy, but whose best works belong to us by inheritance, not to gentlemen

Gleb and Nikita Struve, Boris Filippov, Ivask and other activists of the anti-science of 'Sovietology.' "[82] Although *Kolyma Tales* was not explicitly mentioned in Dymshits's article, it still spoke to the political climate in which Shalamov's letter was written and read at home and abroad. Later that year four other Soviet authors—Bulat Okudzhava, Anatoly Gladilin, and the Strugatsky brothers—published similar statements in *Literaturnaia gazeta* alone, likewise protesting the publications of their works abroad, whether or not authorized.[83]

In the dissident circles in Russia, the reaction to Shalamov's letter, and its last sentence in particular, produced a similar outcry. Petr Iakir, son of the famous army commander executed in 1937 and himself a longtime political prisoner, whose book of memoirs *A Childhood in Prison* (*Detstvo v tiur'me*) was published abroad the same year,[84] wrote his appeal "To the Honest Soviet Writer Varlam Shalamov" (dated February 29, 1972), in which he remarked that Shalamov's letter to *Literaturnaia gazeta* was indeed his "first and only prose piece published in our country."[85] Although unpublished, *Kolyma Tales*, according to Iakir, was still familiar to "tens of thousands" of samizdat readers in Russia, who "will forever value what you have accomplished and treat you with deepest gratitude and respect. The unrighteous, pathetic and talentless letter published in *Literaturnaia gazeta* under your name will change nothing in our attitude toward you. . . . Did you really think," Iakir wrote, "that we, your readers, were going to believe that a great writer like you could call himself thrice 'an honest Soviet writer and citizen' . . ., use the term 'anti-Soviet' six times, and several times such epithets as 'filthy,' 'slanderous,' 'foul-smelling' and 'base' to refer to the foreign journals that have published your *Kolyma Tales*?"[86] What Iakir regretted, however, was that in addition to gratitude and respect, Shalamov's readers would also feel pity for him from then on: "What a pity that a man who created *Kolyma Tales* . . . has been broken by time, or rather by timelessness." Iakir's "only reproach" to Shalamov had to do with the final phrase of his letter to *Literaturnaia gazeta*.

> Why did you sign the following statement: "The problematics of 'Kolyma Tales' has been removed by life . . .?" Are you really sure about it, dear Varlam Tikhonovich? . . . Think about it! Can you really, with one stroke of the pen, do away with, deem nonexistent all those who are now languishing there, where yourself and so many others had languished a while ago? Among today's martyrs, there must be many readers of your "Kolyma Tales," whom

your short stories have inspired for the noble and selfless struggle against evil.[87]

Later that year, in a footnote to *The Gulag Archipelago*, Solzhenitsyn proclaimed that Shalamov "has died": "The renunciation came out [in *Literaturnaia gazeta*] in a black frame, and so we all understood that Shalamov was dead."[88] The footnote was written in 1972, two years before Solzhenitsyn was banished from Russia, and no matter how much he may have disapproved of Shalamov, it is hard to imagine that an expert in Soviet publishing and literary politics, as Solzhenitsyn was, could have seriously taken polygraphy for the actual news of his fellow writer's death. Rather, it was Solzhenitsyn's literary rivalry with Shalamov that was at stake. In 1974, after the second volume of *The Gulag Archipelago* with the above footnote came out in Paris and Solzhenitsyn found himself in exile, Shalamov wrote, "I willingly accept your funeral joke about my death. With all solemnity and pride, I consider myself the first victim of the Cold War who has fallen by your hand. . . . To you and your friends, I did really die, although not when *Literaturnaia gazeta* published my letter, but much earlier." In his unsent letter Shalamov reminded Solzhenitsyn of what had actually set them apart long before the scandal in question. Their relationships and attempts to collaborate on the gulag topic were doomed to fail not only because Shalamov hoped "to say a word of [his] own in Russian prose," but mainly because he rejected Solzhenitsyn's literary method.[89]

Shalamov, Solzhenitsyn, and the End of the Novel

Although Shalamov pretended in his letter to *Literaturnaia gazeta* that he was not aware of the publications of *Kolyma Tales* in tamizdat until 1972, in fact he knew that his short stories were being published abroad since at least 1967.[90] He was also familiar with the first review of *Kolyma Tales* in the Russian émigré press and in September 1967 had even passed on his thanks to the reviewer, Georgy Adamovich, through an intermediary.[91] Adamovich's review was mainly devoted to Shalamov's third book of poetry, *Road and Fate* (*Doroga i sud'ba*), published in Moscow the same year, but it began with a discussion of *Kolyma Tales*, seven of which had appeared by then in *Novyi zhurnal*.

Hardly anyone who has read Varlam Shalamov's *Kolyma Tales* . . . would ever be able to forget them. In my view, they are more

frightening than *One Day in the Life of Ivan Denisovich*, which became famous worldwide, and had these short sketches appeared
not in an émigré but in a Soviet periodical, they would have probably produced a resonance and public discussion of no lesser
magnitude. . . . Hard labor in these short stories not only pursued
but fully accomplished its goal [*ne tol'ko sdelala, no i okonchatel'no
dodelala svoe delo*]—something that never takes place in Solzhenitsyn's novella.[92]

The seven short stories available to Adamovich at the time were
hardly enough for an in-depth analysis of Shalamov's prose vis-à-vis
Solzhenitsyn's. Nevertheless, Adamovich was the first, if not the only,
émigré critic of his generation whose reception of *Kolyma Tales* was not
overshadowed by Solzhenitsyn's celebrated novella. For the rest of the
First Wave of Russian emigration, including Gul', it was Solzhenitsyn,
not Shalamov, who personified nonconformist Russian literature and
stood as the stronghold of the anti-Soviet movement.

In 1963, soon after the breakthrough of *Ivan Denisovich* in the Soviet press, Gul' argued that its significance in Russia, where it served
Khrushchev's purpose of exposing the cult of personality, and in the
West, where readers "have known the truth about forced labor and concentration camps for several decades already," was far from being the
same. As a source of information on life in the camps, Solzhenitsyn's
novella, according to Gul', was even "extremely belated," and its main
value was "literary rather than political."[93] Conversely, it was the informational value of Shalamov's *Kolyma Tales* that preoccupied Gul'
from 1966 onward. If we look at the first selection of *Kolyma Tales* in
Novyi zhurnal (no. 85), it becomes clear that all four short stories are
written in the first person and in the simple past tense (unlike "Cherry
Brandy," where everything is defined by the grammatical tension of
the first sentence, i.e., "The poet was dying," as opposed to "died").
All four texts contain extended descriptions of the Kolyma landscape,
which for Shalamov was important functionally but which interested
Gul' ethnographically.[94] Shalamov's short story "Pushover" ("Kant")
could even be read as a miniature version of Solzhenitsyn's novella,
which describes one "unclouded day, almost a happy one"[95] in the life
of one ordinary prisoner: much like Ivan Denisovich, who is lucky to
have been transferred from the general camp to the "special" (political)
one, Shalamov's protagonist, who has narrowly escaped death in the
gold mines, is relieved to be appointed to an easier job. But while *Ivan*

Denisovich, as it seems on the surface, ends on an "almost" happy note, Shalamov's character returns to the zone only to find himself back at the general works again the next morning.

If we compare Gul's views on Shalamov in 1966 with the internal review of *Kolyma Tales* by the Soviet critic Anatoly Dremov, which resulted in *Novyi mir*'s rejection of the manuscript three years earlier, it is hard not to notice that the arguments of the émigré publisher and those of Dremov prove to be mirror opposites. Behind both Gul''s and Dremov's responses to *Kolyma Tales* lurks the image of Solzhenitsyn's positive hero, the peasant-cum-soldier Ivan Denisovich Shukhov, who "affirms the durability of a man who never loses his human traits, self-esteem and interest in physical labor even under the tragic, inhuman conditions of camp life."[96] The Soviet critic was not entirely wrong to say that *Kolyma Tales* "enter[s] into polemics with Solzhenitsyn's novella. Everything positive in it is demonstratively refuted. . . . While Solzhenitsyn tries to show that, no matter what, a human being can still avoid being turned into an animal, Shalamov focuses precisely on how people are turned into beasts by the cold, hunger, beatings and humiliations."[97] Publishing *Kolyma Tales* as a book in the Soviet Union, therefore, "would be a mistake"; it "cannot bring good to the people, since the naturalistic verisimilitude of the facts, which it no doubt contains, is not equal to the true and grand verity of life and art that the reader expects from any creative work."[98] In short, Dremov believed that *Kolyma Tales* was written by "a qualified and experienced writer" and thus required no further revisions in terms of style and composition, being flawed, instead, in its content and message.[99] Gul', on the contrary, considered *Kolyma Tales* to be too "monotonous and heavy," albeit valuable in its content; he noted that many of Shalamov's texts were poorly written and required more work.[100] Such diametrically opposite responses to the same text help explain why the "explosive" effect of *Kolyma Tales* that Brown had hoped Shalamov's manuscript would produce could only be realized more than ten years later—in Russia for ideological reasons, abroad for stylistic ones. It was Shalamov's "new prose," in which the traditions of Russian formalism and *literatura fakta* (literature of the fact) of the late 1920s were superimposed onto the author's eighteen-year-long camp experience, that proved to be the main obstacle for Gul' and most émigré critics of his generation, who could neither witness nor participate in the development of the new language and culture of the Soviet era. And while both Shalamov and Solzhenitsyn went far beyond the documentary genre in their gulag narratives, they did so along quite different paths.

In his first letter to Solzhenitsyn, written the night after he read *Ivan Denisovich* in November 1962, Shalamov admitted that everything in it was "perfect, everything makes sense" and that Solzhenitsyn's special success lay in his "deep and subtle depiction of Shukhov's peasant psychology." "The camp is seen from the perspective of a 'worker' [*rabotiaga*], . . . not a dying intellectual [*doplyvaiushchii intelligent*], but a peasant who has gone through a great ordeal, withstood that ordeal and is now telling about the past with humor."[101] However, two years later, Shalamov confronted Solzhenitsyn with a question that seemed to revoke his earlier admiration for the portrayal of Shukhov's peasant psychology. In his letter to Solzhenitsyn on November 15, 1964, Shalamov avoided referring to *Ivan Denisovich* directly but asked, "So who is the true hero? I believe that the duty of every honest reader is to heroicize specifically the humanistic intelligentsia, which has always and everywhere . . . accepted the hardest blow. Not only in the camps, but in the entire history of mankind."[102] Could Shalamov be drawing a parallel between Solzhenitsyn's concessions to gosizdat, including his choice of the peasant positive hero to speak on behalf of the gulag victims, and the protagonist of his own 1954 short story, "The Snake Charmer" ("Zaklinatel' zmei"), who imagines himself as an "enlightener" to the local thieves in an attempt to justify his consent to "pull novels" (*tiskat' rómany*) for their entertainment in the camp? "He would be exposing them to real literature; here, in the lower depths of life, he would be doing his job, his duty. Old habits blinded Platonov to the fact that he would only be fed, would get an extra soup for a job that was different, more dignified than carrying out the piss pot."[103] Could Solzhenitsyn, too, along these lines, have succumbed to the temptation of becoming "a snake charmer" to the literary authorities who decided whether or not his novel would "live" on the pages of a Soviet journal? Of course, the actual stakes of Shalamov's protagonist and Solzhenitsyn at the editorial office of *Novyi mir* were more difficult to compare: by agreeing to "pull novels" for the entertainment of the criminals, Shalamov's Platonov saves only his own life, though not for long, while Solzhenitsyn, by yielding to official demands and making *Ivan Denisovich* publishable, "saved" the entire gulag topic for Soviet readers. The difference was obvious to Shalamov when, in his first letter to Solzhenitsyn, he praised not only the literary aspects of *Ivan Denisovich* ("you managed to find an exceptionally powerful form"), but also its social value.[104] "For a meticulous reader, this novella is a revelation in every phrase. In our literature, it is the first . . . word on the topic that everyone talks yet no one has ever written anything about. . . . Your work is the long-awaited truth, without which our literature cannot move forward."[105]

Apart from the choice of the peasant protagonist, Shalamov also grew increasingly frustrated with the genre and method of Solzhenitsyn's novella. According to Shalamov's principles of "new prose," which he had fully formulated by the mid-1960s, it was vital that a writer who bears witness to the gulag remain faithful to the first draft, allowing even the most random slips of the tongue into the text. Unlike *Ivan Denisovich*, *Kolyma Tales*, according to Shalamov, is about martyrs without biographies "who have never been or become heroes" ("heroes" here also stands for "protagonists").[106] By contrast to the cyclical composition of Solzhenitsyn's novella, the characters of *Kolyma Tales* usually seem to be moving from point A to point B without much hope of return (as in the opening sketch "Trampling the Snow," which guides their movement). As for the author of "new prose," he is "neither a tourist nor an observer" but "an actual participant in the drama of life"— "Pluto rising from Hell, not Orpheus who descends into it."[107] Clearly, Shalamov's literary method, spelled out in his essay "On Prose" and sustained throughout *Kolyma Tales*, did not sit well not only with the mandates of socialist realism but also with the conventions of fiction in general and the novel in particular.

Long before *Kolyma Tales*, the death of the novel as a genre was proclaimed by Osip Mandelshtam in his 1922 eponymous essay ("Smert' romana"), which maintained that in the face of recent historical cataclysms, the role of a contemporary prose writer had been reduced to that of a chronicler, while the novel itself had gone back to its origins, such as *The Tale of Igor's Campaign*.[108] The novel, according to Mandelshtam, is inseparable from the role of the individual in history. But from the 1920s onward, "people without biographies," as Shalamov described his characters, could no longer sustain the viability of the novel, as twentieth-century history all but shattered one's individual biography. Decades after Mandelshtam, Shalamov proclaimed the novel to have died together with the millions of prisoners in Kolyma. Perhaps the novel, according to Shalamov, is even buried in the same grave. Yet Shalamov's disillusionment with the novel—and humanistic literature on the whole—stemmed not only from his experience in the deadliest camps of the gulag, but also from the neo-formalist ideas on literature and society that were in the air in the late 1920s, when he began his career as a writer and journalist.[109] Shalamov's "new prose," thus, equals his firsthand experience in Kolyma multiplied by his literary background. The revolutionary debates on literature and journalism of the late 1920s had been "frozen," or conserved in Shalamov until he reformulated them in *Kolyma Tales* in the late 1950s and 1960s.

A crusade on the novel as a genre that had exhausted itself in the new historical reality continued in 1929 by the New LEF group (Sergei Tretiakov, Viktor Shklovsky, Osip Brik, and Nikolai Chuzhak, among others), who sought to expose the "creative deadmen" of classical literature, the *belles lettres* as "opium for the people," and the "shamanism of literary priests."[110] Their manifestos, brought together under one cover as *Literatura fakta* (*Literature of the Fact*), came out after Shalamov's first arrest on February 19, 1929, but throughout the previous year Shalamov had frequented Tretiakov's literary workshops on Malaia Bronnaia and was familiar with the teachings of the "factists" (*faktoviki*), including their disavowal of fiction (*vymysel*), plot (*siuzhetnost'*), and the emphasis on the psychology of the protagonist set forth in the traditional novel. Instead, the factists proposed to "shift the focus from human feelings and emotions to the organization of the society."[111] In particular, Chuzhak's claim that "new literature" (cf. Shalamov's "new prose") does not tolerate "a writer who is divorced from the subject s/he writes about"[112] may stand behind Shalamov's rejection of the "touristic" approach to literature and his definition of a writer as "a participant in the drama of life."[113] However, in their attempt to do away with the traditional plot, the advocates for *literatura fakta* faced the inevitable question, What should be used instead to connect the disjointed pieces of writing? ("Without a plot, a work of prose falls apart like a poem without rhymes.") Chuzhak's solution was to look for "natural plots" (*natural'naia siuzhetnost'*) abundant in life itself, which was proclaimed, in turn, "not such a bad inventor" (*neplokhaia vydumshchitsa*). And when "natural plots" were either absent or scarce, it was up to the author's talent to find and use them in his or her writing, which constituted the essence of art—"the art of seeing, on the one hand, and rendering it, on the other."[114] The monotonous, gray, utterly uneventful reality of the camps, where the only "natural plot" was to survive, became for Shalamov an opportunity to test this ambitious principle of the new revolutionary aesthetics against the reality from which it derived. Of course, the radical doctrine of *literatura fakta* was motivated not only by aesthetics but also by a political agenda, formulated just around the time when the new revolutionary reality mutated into one of the cruelest systems of annihilation of the human body and spirit the world has ever known. The deaths of millions in the gulag, still in its early stages, thus overlapped with the proclaimed extinction of the novel as a genre.

Tretiakov's manifesto "The Biography of the Object" ("Biografiia veshchi") compares the composition of a new work of literature to a production line, along which units of raw material move in order to be turned, at the end of the line, into "useful products." The figure of the protagonist, whose psychology and emotions are part and parcel of a traditional novel, is reduced in the process to an "object," devoid of feelings or agency of his or her own, animated instead by the society.

> People's individual and distinctive characteristics are no longer relevant here. The tics and epilepsies of the individual go unperceived. Instead, social neuroses and the professional diseases of a given group are foregrounded. . . . Thus: not the individual person moving through a system of objects, but the object proceeding through the system of people—for literature this is the methodological device that seems to us more progressive than those of classical belles lettres.[115]

Could this radical postulate of *literatura fakta* inform Shalamov's *Kolyma Tales* in general and the compositional allegory of the opening sketch, "Trampling the Snow," in particular? Instead of describing a character with a clearly outlined biographical past and articulated emotions in the present, Shalamov's "Trampling the Snow," essentially, *is* such a "conveyor belt," where the "units of raw material," portrayed as humans, are reduced to "objects." It is their "biography" that Shalamov commits to record in *Kolyma Tales*. In his other essay, "The New Leo Tolstoy" ("Novyi Lev Tolstoi"), Tretiakov proclaimed the newspaper to be "the bible of our days" and the novel to be a genre redundant and obsolete. In reading a newspaper, he claimed, "we, basically, turn a new page of that wonderful novel that our contemporaneity represents. The characters of this novel, its writers and readers, are ourselves."[116] In "Trampling the Snow," Shalamov redistributes the roles of writers and readers as he portrays the file of nameless prisoners marching through virgin snow, as if their footsteps were covering the blank page of such a newspaper.

Similarly, in "The Snake Charmer," whose protagonist dies before he can write down his story, thus "inviting" the frame narrator to step in and retell it to the hypothetical future reader, Shalamov shows what is left of a traditional novel in the gulag: it is reduced from *román* to a *róman* and exists in a distorted, barely recognizable form only as cheap entertainment for the thieves. In 1962 what particularly bewildered Shalamov about Solzhenitsyn's novella, groundbreaking as it was in its content but conventional in its genre, was the infamous cat that walked around in the medical barracks of Ivan Denisovich's camp and was not eaten by starving prisoners. "A cat!" Shalamov wrote in his first letter to Solzhenitsyn. "Where is this wonderful camp? If only I could spend a year there in my own time."[117] In Kolyma, as Shalamov remembered it, a live cat was impossible. Nor could the novel remain a *román*, but only a *róman*.

The First Book Edition of *Kolyma Tales* (1978)

The first book edition of *Kolyma Tales*, brought out in London in 1978, marked a new era in tamizdat publishing as it was gradually rejuvenated by new arrivals from the USSR, whose carry-on baggage included not only new manuscripts but also a more intimate, firsthand familiarity with Soviet language and culture, something that the older generations of émigrés lacked, having left Russia soon after the Revolution or during World War II. In 1973 Shalamov's first publisher, Roman Gul', expressed a hope that "there will certainly come a day when . . . works by Soviet writers, who managed to remain free in spite of everything, will blend with those by the free Russian writers in emigration. And then Russian literature will no longer have to 'ride on two horses' [*odvukon'*]."[118] By 1973 the day Gul' had written about in the future tense had to some extent arrived, and his hopes for the reunification of free Russian literature at home and abroad sounded somewhat belated. Not only new authors but also younger critics and publishers had already found themselves in the West to take over tamizdat as a literary practice and political institution for the years to follow. It was also then, in the 1970s, that the question of "one or two Russian Literatures," first raised by the First Wave in the 1920s and valid for half a century, was finally reformulated; the new answer was "one," not "two." What came to the foreground was no longer the geographical-cum-ideological division of Russian writers into émigré and Soviet ones, but the linguistic and stylistic differences between mainstream and nonconformist Russian culture on either side of the curtain, a distinction that prompted Sinyavsky in the early 1980s to describe his "disagreements with the Soviet government" as "basically aesthetic."[119] However, as becomes clear

FIGURE 4.1. Varlam Shalamov. *Kolymskie rasskazy*. Edited, with an introduction by Mikhail Geller. London: Overseas Publications Interchange, 1978. Cover of the first book edition of *Kolyma Tales* in Russian.

from the reception of Shalamov's first book edition across two generations of émigré critics, the disagreements between them were far from
purely aesthetic. They also influenced the publication and reception of
Shalamov's early editions in English and other languages.[120]

Compiled by Mikhail Geller, an historian and political prisoner before his emigration to Warsaw in 1957 and on to Paris in 1968, Shalamov's first book came out with a drawing by Boris Sveshnikov, which
looked like a portrait of the author, in the upper left corner of the green
cover and the dust jacket.[121] In his preface Geller referred to the manner in which *Kolyma Tales* had been previously published in tamizdat
as "perhaps the greatest blow to the writer"—not an understatement,
in light of Shalamov's camp experience. Such a publishing method, according to Geller, was akin to "a Rembrandt painting, discovered in an
attic, cut into small pieces, and displayed as a pile of scraps. In these disjointed pieces, one might still recognize a great work of art: here is an
eye, here is an arm. But there would be no painting."[122] Speaking of the
book-length translations of *Kolyma Tales* into foreign languages, some
of which had appeared as early as 1967, Geller decried the fact that not
only was the author's name misspelled on the covers of both the German and the French editions as "Schalanow" and "Chalanov," respectively, and that both editions were arbitrarily titled (*Article 58*), but also
that in the French volume, the stories had actually been translated from
the German.[123] "Still, there was no Russian book," Geller lamented.[124]

When the book was finally out, it was the old émigrés' turn to
settle scores with Shalamov's new publisher and brand the edition
as "a weighty cobblestone" [*uvesistyi bulyzhnik*] and an "extremely
unfortunate" publication as a whole.[125] This first review published
in the old émigré newspaper *Russkaia mysl'* in Paris belonged to Gennady Andreev, aka Khomiakov, a wartime émigré, author, and tamizdat publisher, who had printed Akhmatova's *Requiem* in 1963. Indeed,
the book's bulky format of 896 pages complicated the task of sending
it back to the Soviet Union and thus undermined the political mission
of tamizdat, which treated contraband manuscripts from the USSR,
especially those on the gulag, as weapons in the Cold War: "We have
always considered the publication of Russian books abroad, whose
main reader is in Russia, from the perspective of sending those books
back behind the 'iron curtain,'" Andreev admitted. It was a mission
that tamizdat publishers of the old generation considered superior to
the aesthetic merits of Russian literature, even after the curtain began
to rust.

Still, it was not only the physical properties of the edition under review that frustrated Andreev. "Perhaps the author wanted the book to include everything he had ever written about Kolyma, which is exactly what the publisher did." As a result, the book, according to Andreev, included "records [*zapisi*] that tell little about the camps and tend to have neither artistic nor educational value," as well as "straightforward repetitions," as in the short story "Major Pugachev's Last Battle" ("Poslednii boi maiora Pugacheva"), which the reviewer found to be "included entirely in the stretched-out sketch 'The Green Prosecutor,' where characters are only given different names. Why such duplication? To make the book bigger?" Invoking Shalamov's letter to *Literaturnaia gazeta*, Andreev mentioned Solzhenitsyn's condemnation of it and blamed the author of *Kolyma Tales* for writing "unkindly, without a shadow of gratitude" about those who had helped him survive in Kolyma.[126] Like Solzhenitsyn, Andreev questioned Shalamov's belief that "the camps are a negative experience for a human being—from the first to the last hour. No human should know or even hear about it. No one becomes better or stronger after the camps. The camps are a negative experience . . . that corrupts everyone."[127] Shalamov's categorical rejection of the very idea that the camps could bear a positive effect on the prisoners ran against the life-affirming pathos of his fellow gulag survivor Solzhenitsyn. In fact, it stands closer to Primo Levi's observation about Auschwitz, where only "the worst survived, the selfish, the violent, the insensitive, the collaborators of the 'gray zone,' the spies. It was not a certain rule . . ., but it was nevertheless a rule."[128] Besides, it was "not always clear" to Andreev "that the events in [Shalamov's] short stories are actually taking place under the Soviet rule."[129] Little did he know that the year the first manuscript of *Kolyma Tales* was smuggled out abroad and serialized in New York, Shalamov had noted in his diary: "I am writing about the camps no more than Saint-Exupéry wrote about the sky or Melville about the sea."[130] But while the readers of Saint-Exupéry and Melville, as Mikhailik remarked, knew about the sky and the sea and could tell one apart from the other even without having ever seen either, Shalamov was "in a much more precarious position," since "the question of what the camps and the camp experience stood for . . . was still open."[131]

As it happens, before Geller, it was Andreev-Khomiakov who first collected Shalamov's short stories published in *Novyi zhurnal* and elsewhere in émigré periodicals for the London edition. After moving from Germany to New York in 1967, in 1975–1977 Khomiakov helped Gul'

edit *Novyi zhurnal*. It was then, "after Shalamov's short stories had almost entirely been printed in *Novyi zhurnal*," as Gul' recalled years later,
that Andrzej Stypulkowski, the founder of OPI, visited him in New York
and obtained the rights to publish *Kolyma Tales* as a book (to what extent the rights actually belonged to Gul' is a different question).[132] On
August 19, 1977, in a letter to Yury Ivask, Khomiakov wrote that in
the spring he collected "all" of Shalamov's short stories, "200 pages or
so," and wrote a preface for the future edition. "I have sent them to the
publisher (the book will be printed in London because of how cheap
the sterling is now). They should have already sent back the proofs,
but there is a delay."[133] Khomiakov did not know that in the meantime
another, more comprehensive manuscript had reached Geller in Paris,
making his work on the volume, as well as his preface, redundant. (This
manuscript was sent to Paris from Moscow by Ilya Ehrenburg's former
secretary Natalia Stoliarova no earlier than November 1977.)[134] "Where
did they even manage to get them from?" Khomiakov wondered in his
letter to Ivask on November 24, 1978, after the book was already out.
"I would be interested to see it myself but do not have a copy yet."[135]
Indeed, it was only a short while before he reviewed it for *Russkaia mysl'*
(on April 19, 1979) that Khomiakov finally saw the edition he thought
he was putting together.

His unpublished preface, however, held among Geller's papers in
Paris, is different from the frustrated review in *Russkaia mysl'*, not only
in length but also in tone, shedding light on Khomiakov's own biography before the war. "I may well be the first one here," Khomiakov
wrote, "who read these short stories not piece by piece but all at once,
almost in one sitting."[136] He lamented the nuisance of having to com-
pile the book without being able to consult the author. "No doubt,
he has his own conception of it and would probably arrange his short
stories differently, according to his own long thought-through plan."
But, to the editor's disadvantage, "the author lives in the Soviet Union,
on the other side of the globe, and one cannot even send him a letter."
As Khomiakov's preface makes clear, the book was going to open with
the short story "How It Began" ("Kak eto nachalos'"), whose title deceptively promises a historical account of the Kolyma camps (unlike,
for that matter, "Trampling the Snow," which offers instead a compositional allegory for *Kolyma Tales* and, by extension, gulag narratives
as a genre). "How It Began," however, is not a piece of mere historical evidence either, as its first paragraph ends with a phrase left deliberately unfinished: "How did it begin? On what winter day did the

wind change and everything become frightening? In autumn we were still work-" [*osen'iu my eshcho rabo* . . .]. [137] As the truncated syntax of the sentence suggests, history suffers irreparable damage in Kolyma, where time itself acquires another dimension. Therefore, the historical subject matter of *Kolyma Tales* alone is misleading in establishing the order in which the short stories should follow. Still, for Khomiakov, *Kolyma Tales* were only "eyewitness accounts" written "in the traditional Russian realist manner, without pretentiousness or attempts at unnecessary modernism."[138]

"It is a small world," Khomiakov interjected in his unpublished preface, and "the world of the concentration camps, a multimillion one, is probably not so large either." Author of two books of memoirs and fiction about his own experiences in the gulag in 1927–1935,[139] Khomiakov recognized several "names and people" in *Kolyma Tales*. Those included the infamous NKVD official Rodion Vas'kov, whose name was imprinted onto the memory of nearly every Kolyma prisoner: the prison in Magadan was called Vas'kov House in the vernacular.[140] Khomiakov "often saw" Vas'kov in the early 1930s in Syktyvkar, where he "was working for the camp administration"; for a while, he even lived next to Vas'kov "in a large room rented from a local teacher," until Vas'kov's secretary "told me to look for another apartment or go back to live in the camp," since the camp boss "did not like the idea that a prisoner like me could peek through his window and see how he lived."[141] It was also there, in Syktyvkar, that Khomiakov met Pesniakevich, a character from Shalamov's short story "Artificial Limbs" ("Protezy"), where he is portrayed overseeing "the operation" of stripping prisoners of their prostheses before throwing them to the punishment block. In Syktyvkar, where Khomiakov worked at the camp's finance department and "was in charge of payments to the free workers and the guards," Pesniakevich was responsible for hunting down fugitives and rewarding free residents of the nearby villages for their cooperation. "Pesniakevich brought me his financial settlements, already approved by the head of the guards." Since 1929, when he was transferred from Solovki to Syktyvkar in the Komi Republic to "open northern camps," Khomiakov, as his unpublished preface to Shalamov's book makes clear, had been a "trusty," or *pridurok*, in the camp jargon, holding privileged jobs and working for the gulag administration, if only as a prisoner, until his release in 1935.[142] These circumstances of Khomiakov's biography help explain his uneasy relationship with *Kolyma Tales* forty years later.

Two other reviews of the first edition of *Kolyma Tales* were authored by critics of the younger generation, Violetta Iverni and Andrei Sinyavsky, both of whom emigrated to Paris in 1973. As if in response to Khomiakov's earlier review in *Russkaia mysl'*, Iverni also dwelt on the incongruous "weighty volume of 890 pages." "This is not how books are made," she wrote. "If it is a collection of miniatures, the volume itself shouldn't be large either." But unlike Khomiakov, Iverni emphasized that "in this book, violations of literary rules only confirm the authenticity of what is described." Because the edition was based on a samizdat manuscript the author could not control, "it is completely impossible to know what exactly should be viewed as mistakes resulting from retyping, and what should be attributed to the author's outright disdain for the laws of writing." The stylistic and even grammatical "flaws" of *Kolyma Tales* listed by Iverni, such as repetitions of the same word two or three times in one phrase; alternations of short, clear sentences with the long and convoluted ones, whereby time markers change places and what had occurred earlier turns out to have taken place later; irregularity of the short stories' rhythm (*neritmichnost'*) and the uneven distribution of the subject matter; compositional asymmetry; incompleteness—all such "infringements" on literary conventions may equally result from the manuscript's having been passed from one typewriter to another, or from the author's profound neglect of literary conventions. "Indeed," Iverni concluded, "if the society's moral laws, which one is accustomed to respect or at least regard as somehow immutable, prove to be so fragile and unviable, what can be said about the laws of literature, which, in inhuman conditions, become but a meaningless, ridiculous, and incredibly expensive toy in the hands of the lucky ones who were allowed to live?"[143]

Imperfect as Shalamov's first book was, it was only after *Kolyma Tales* were brought together under one cover that it became clear why his prose had often been regarded as flawed. Referring to the serialized method of publishing *Kolyma Tales* as "castration," Iverni argued that Shalamov's characters neither care whether or not they are understood by the reader, nor do they hope to add anything to the readers' worldviews. They "do not look into the eyes of their interlocutors. They look into their own memory and retell what they had seen on the other side of consciousness," where there is no chronology or continuity. "Time has no continuity in Kolyma. . . . It had stopped and been frozen there. . . . Time had the qualities of light and darkness, replacing each other, but it had lost its main feature: flow." This is why, according to Iverni, Shalamov's characters "change their names and surnames; act interchangeably as protagonists, listeners, or mere observers; tell the same story several times; die in front of our eyes before turning up again at their first interrogation, then appear as free men who have returned to normal life and—without any transition—are plunged again back into hell."[144] Such near-fantastical metamorphoses, utterly inappropriate from the realist perspective, suggest the metaphor of a "conveyor belt" to the reviewer: Shalamov's characters are pulled "into its process, into its cycle, into its motion, . . . into its work, simply *work*."[145] Iverni does not cite Tretiakov's "The Biography of the Object," or for that matter "Trampling the Snow," the opening text of *Kolyma Tales*, but her metaphor is nevertheless driven by the compositional singularity of Shalamov's short stories in the book under review, in which "Trampling the Snow" serves as an "epigraph" for the rest of the short stories to follow in its footsteps.

Walking down the trail of *Kolyma Tales* to the end is not an easy task for the reader, as Sinyavsky pointed out in his review. "In *Kolyma Tales*, the reader is identified not with the author . . . (who 'knows everything' and 'takes the reader along'), but with the prisoner." Like the prisoners, Shalamov's readers are "locked" in the space of his texts and are forced "to pull a log or a wheelbarrow with stones" as they move along. Shalamov, according to Sinyavsky, is an "antipode" to "the rest of the literature about the camps," perhaps most notably to Solzhenitsyn, because "he does not leave us a way out."[146] But for Sinyavsky, herein lies Shalamov's claim to authenticity. Comparing his short stories to logs of wood (*balany*) from the deadliest tree-felling sites of the gulag ("Shalamov's short stories are measured in cubic meters of forest"), Sinyavsky tells a chilling camp legend about how, soon after the war, the prisoners tried to reveal to the world what Stalin's hard labor stood for; unable to cope with the impossible work quotas and desperate to avoid them at any cost, they would chop off their wrists and fingers and pack them inside cords of timber exported to England. The Englishmen got the message and stopped their otherwise lucrative trade with Stalin. "Of course," Sinyavsky adds, "it is in part only folklore, but the legend is still making rounds in the camps and passed from one generation of prisoners to another as an undeniable fact. . . . A fairytale. A dream. The eternal dream of the doomed about some higher justice." When Sinyavsky heard this legend in the late 1960s in Mordovia, where he served his own sentence for publishing in tamizdat, he thought of Shalamov. Of all gulag authors, Sinyavsky reckoned, Shalamov would be the least likely to fall for such a hopeful scenario. "It is not his writings per se," Sinyavsky specified, "but rather their fate, the fate of the author, Varlam Shalamov, that brings to mind this camp legend."[147]

Like the prisoners' limbs packaged in cords of timber to be shipped to England, the manuscript of *Kolyma Tales* was also meant to inform its recipients across the Atlantic of what the author, albeit no longer a prisoner, had gone through and registered in his prose as adequately as language permitted. The failure of language to communicate the Kolyma experience was part of the message. However, unlike the recipients of the eerie cargo in the camp legend, the message that Shalamov's manuscript carried was largely lost on his first tamizdat publisher, who cut the final sentences of both "Sententsiia" and "Cherry Brandy," turning the short stories into stumps. Without its "taut spring wound up for three hundred years," "Sententsiia"—a text meant to end with "something symphonic"[148]—produced little music. Ten years later, introducing the readers to *Kolyma Tales* as a book, Geller specified that the "symphony" they were going to hear was not a traditional, realist harmony. "The reality in which the characters of *Kolyma Tales* are working and dying is like a nightmare, a monstrous dream."[149] To place Shalamov's nightmarish phantasmagoria in context, Geller cited Zamiatin, who wrote in 1922 that today, when "the Apocalypse can be published as our daily newspaper," art that responds to contemporary reality can only be "fantastic."[150] But while Zamiatin's dystopia *We* (1921), read at the time as science fiction, was set in the hypothetical distant future, Shalamov's *Kolyma Tales* were "written" by the historical reality of the still recent past, which was far more "fantastic" than one could ever imagine.

In 1966, in his "Letter to an Old Friend," addressed to an imaginary contemporary with a gulag experience similar to his own ("Both you and I know the times of Stalin"), Shalamov wrote about two younger writers on trial, who used the fantastic as a solution to socialist realism: "I believe your experience and mine rule out the genre of the grotesque and the fantastic. But neither Sinyavsky nor Daniel saw the rivers of blood we had seen. Of course, they may both use the fantastic and the grotesque."[151] The historical experience Shalamov and his hypothetical addressee shared was "not the grotesque, nor science fiction."[152] And yet, the extraterrestrial character from Sinyavsky-Tertz's fantastic short story "Pkhentz" was more "real" for Shalamov than the infamous cat from Solzhenitsyn's *Ivan Denisovich*. More "real," perhaps, than Ivan Denisovich himself. Not only because Solzhenitsyn had seen only tributaries of the "rivers of blood" that Shalamov described, while Sinyavsky had not seen any at all. Rather, it was because Pkhentz was an alien, while Solzhenitsyn's protagonist, the cat, and the novella itself were "domestic." Shalamov's "translation" of gulag reality into literature took a different path: instead of domesticating Kolyma, it was based on foreignization at the expense of the target language of the reader, wherever that reader was.

Epilogue
The Tamizdat Project of Abram Tertz

Tamizdat did not end in 1966, when the Soviet critic Andrei Sinyavsky and the translator Yuly Daniel were put on trial for publishing their fiction abroad under the pen names Abram Tertz and Nikolai Arzhak. On the contrary, as a literary practice and political institution of the late-Soviet era, tamizdat may have begun in earnest only then—thanks to the unprecedented political resonance of the trial worldwide, but perhaps more importantly, because of the two writers' creative strategy, which was fulfilled as a result of the trial and finally recognized both in Russia and in the West as a literary, rather than political, affair. Their trial may have temporarily complicated the task of sending, receiving, and publishing contraband manuscripts from the Soviet Union, but it introduced a new dynamic to the relationships between Russian literature at home and abroad, for the first time since the 1920s shifting the emphasis from ideology to style and endowing geography with a creative function.

Sinyavsky and Daniel were arrested in Moscow on September 15, 1965, two weeks before another "tamizdat author," Joseph Brodsky, was released from internal exile.[1] There are reasons to believe that Brodsky's release and Sinyavsky and Daniel's arrests were coordinated. However, while the unauthorized publication of Brodsky's first book of poetry in tamizdat earlier that spring was but an immediate outcome of his trial in Leningrad (moreover, despite his friends' apprehensions, the book did not prevent the poet from being set free ahead of time),[2] in the case of Sinyavsky and Daniel, the cause-and-effect relationship between publishing abroad and persecution at home was the reverse. The difference was especially telling given that Brodsky's first book and the Russian editions of Tertz and Arzhak had the same publisher: Boris Filippov's Inter-Language Literary Associates.[3] Still, it was the trial of Sinyavsky and Daniel on February 10–14, 1966, not Brodsky's trial two years earlier, that marked a new era for tamizdat, although the change, of course, did not take place overnight.

In the early years of tamizdat, geographical borders, not without reason, were perceived as utterly impassable. The tamizdat project of

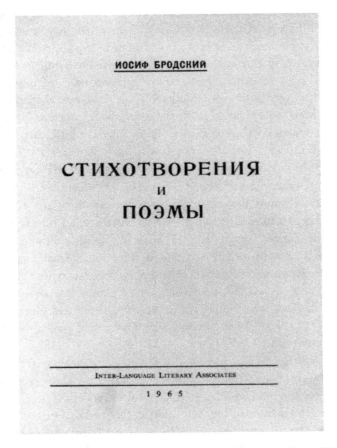

FIGURE 5.1. Iosif Brodsky. *Stikhotvoreniia i poemy*. Afterword by Georgy Stukov [Gleb Struve]. Washington, DC: Inter-Language Literary Associates, 1965.

Tertz and Arzhak revealed that geography could, in fact, be transgressed not only by manuscripts but also by authors, so long as they did so in the guise of alternative identities. In this sense, the affair of Sinyavsky and Daniel heralded what from the early 1970s onward would become known as the Third Wave of the Russian literary emigration, when the authors of manuscripts previously published abroad were allowed (or forced) to follow in their footsteps, as happened with Sinyavsky himself in 1973, soon after he had served his sentence for publishing abroad as Abram Tertz. Until the early 1970s tamizdat had been a product of the geographic discontinuity between authors in Russia and their runaway manuscripts, but when this gap began shrinking, the ecosystem of tamizdat was also bound to change. Having emerged from the largely imagined expanse of the Soviet Union, including its camps, and acquired physical features in the eyes of the older generation of tamizdat publishers and critics, some of the new arrivals, such as Sinyavsky, themselves became publishers in emigration.[4] Their arrival meant rivalry and was not always welcomed by émigrés of the old generation, who routinely suspected the newcomers of being Soviet spies, double agents, and saboteurs.[5] Their ideological backgrounds and aesthetic tastes clashed with those of the younger emigres since the two generations were products of essentially different "Russias" and "Russian literatures"—so much so that when Tertz's *Strolls with Pushkin* (*Progulki s Pushkinym*), written while he was still a prisoner in Mordovia, first appeared abroad soon after Sinyavsky's emigration, it caused such a major uproar among émigré critics of the old school (most notably Roman Gul') that Michel Aucouturier referred to it as "the second trial of Abram Tertz."[6] Whether aesthetic or ideological, the polemics now unfolded not only across Soviet state borders, i.e., between the Russian emigration and the Soviet literary establishment, but within the same field, transforming tamizdat forever—or at least until perestroika, when publishing Russian literature elsewhere became history. It was Tertz, not Sinyavsky, who had paved the way for this transformation.

So far as the concept of truth, understood as the foundation of socialist realism, was confined to a specific geography and governed by a particular state jurisdiction, truth remained territorial. On the opposite side of the Curtain, truth remained just as peculiar to the identity, ideology, and aesthetic tastes of the Russian literary diaspora and Western audiences. Contingent upon border crossing and deterritorialization, the mission of tamizdat in its early years was to unearth the truth about life behind bars—understood more broadly than just life in the camps, although the gulag was no doubt the hottest topic of tamizdat throughout the Cold War era. This mission mirrored the quest for truth in Soviet Russia, where art was put at the service of the "truthful, historically concrete representation of reality," as socialist realism was originally defined. The tamizdat project of Tertz and Arzhak revealed an alternative way to deterritorialize truth and authenticate it through border crossing: fantastic realism.

Tertz's programmatic essay "On Socialist Realism" ("Chto takoe sotsialisticheskii realism?"), the first work he wrote in 1956 for publication abroad, offers a "solution" to the titular method of socialist realism prescribed to Soviet artists and writers. Rather than rejecting the socialist-realist commandments directly, Tertz probes the doctrine proclaimed as the holy scripture of Soviet art by declaring his own credo as a fantastic realist: "I put my hope in a phantasmagoric art . . . in which the grotesque will replace realistic descriptions of ordinary life."[7] Smuggled abroad in 1957, the same year that Pasternak's *Doctor Zhivago* was first published in Italy, Tertz's essay, along with his debut fantastic-realist novel *The Trial Begins* (*Sud idet*), stood next to Pasternak's historical epic as the earliest tamizdat. Unlike Akhmatova, Chukovskaia, Shalamov, and other authors whose works were published abroad without their knowledge or consent, Tertz, along with his friend and fellow fantastic-realist writer Nikolai Arzhak, not only authorized but also artfully orchestrated their contraband publications. Geography itself was made an integral part of their tandem project, as was the use of pen names and alternative identities that served as a vehicle for deterritorialization. The sense of the boundary their texts had to cross on their way out to the reader was built into the creative strategy of Tertz and Arzhak as a transgression and even a crime, as Catharine Nepomnyashchy argues in her seminal study of Tertz's poetics.[8] One might go so far as to say that after Tertz and Arzhak's identities were exposed, the show trial of Andrei Sinyavsky and Yuly Daniel became the ultimate realization of their project. Perhaps it was even their biggest success.

The method of fantastic realism proposed in Tertz's essay, as well as the extraterritorial publication of the essay itself, challenged the very concept of "truth," including the truth of authorship, by shifting its geographical context. Transplanted onto the foreign ground, truth revealed a potential to transform into its mirror opposite: the grotesque and phantasmagoria. And yet, Tertz's revolt against the socialist-realist mandate for the "truthful, historically concrete representation of reality" at home only fueled the émigrés' quest for truth, no matter how grotesque and phantasmagoric Tertz's texts were designed. No sooner did Tertz and Arzhak's fantastic-realist writings make landfall on the other shore, the question immediately arose as to who their authors were *in reality*, a mystery hardly any tamizdat critic could resist pondering.[9] Some assumed it was all a forgery and that the real author was in fact a fellow émigré whose identity and whereabouts remained unknown: he could be living in Israel, or he may have written it all from around the corner, say, in New York or in West Germany. Some doubted that the author of the anonymous essay "On Socialist Realism" was the same as the author of the novel *The Trial Begins*, published under Tertz's pen name. Others, disagreeing with both assumptions, rightly argued that the two texts "could only be written by a man who not only knows Soviet literature well, but knows it from the inside. . . . No émigré could ever manage that."[10]

The hunt for the true author of Tertz and Arzhak's writings abroad was mirrored at home, in Soviet criticism, long before the investigation and the trial. In 1962 Boris Riurikov, former editor of *Literaturnaia gazeta*, assumed that the author of Tertz's "On Socialist Realism" was Peter Demetz, an émigré professor of comparative literature at Yale.[11] A year or so later, when the tamizdat publications of Tertz and Arzhak came under the radar of the KGB, the investigation briefly entertained the idea that Tertz was Yulian Oksman, a Soviet literary scholar who had indeed helped smuggle out some clandestine texts, including Akhmatova's *Requiem* and his own work but who had no relation to Tertz or Arzhak.[12] Whoever the suspects on either side of the Curtain were, the mystification of Tertz and Arzhak remained in effect for nearly ten years, a period long enough for their works to enter the Russian literary canon. Having strategically placed themselves between two jurisdictions, Tertz and Arzhak avoided belonging to either. The very concept of authorship was thus estranged, if not altogether recalled, from the sacred marriage of the text and the author, divorcing one from the other. As it happened, the question of the true author could not have an answer in principle, since the authors were fictional rather than real. And so long as the authors' identities were covered in mystery, how "truthful" could the representation of reality in such texts be, wherever their readers were geographically?

Meant as an invective against the West and a signal to other Soviet authors to avoid tamizdat at all costs, Sinyavsky and Daniel's trial served the opposite propagandistic function in the West. A week after the trial, the American publisher of Tertz and Arzhak, Boris Filippov, lashed out against his political opponents in Moscow in his "letter to the editor of *Literaturnaia gazeta*" on behalf of the Russian émigré community (the letter, of course, was never published in the Soviet newspaper).[13] It was written particularly in response to the notorious articles "Turncoats" ("Perevertyshi") by Dmitry Eremin and "Heirs of Smerdiakov" ("Nasledniki Smerdiakova") by Zoya Kedrina, who quoted Filippov's introductions to Tertz and Arzhak's culpable editions.[14] What makes Filippov's letter remarkable is that, while opposing Eremin and Kedrina ideologically, it employs essentially the same style. Whereas Eremin brands Tertz and Arzhak's publications as "anti-Soviet libels" (*antisovetskie paskvili*), Filippov writes that such "libels" (*paskvili*) are the articles of Eremin and Kedrina. While Tertz is referred to by Eremin as "the so-called man of letters" (*tak nazyvaemyi literator*), for Filippov, it is the trial of Sinyavsky and Daniel that is a "so-called Soviet trial" (*tak nazyvaemyi sovetskii sud*). While the "internal émigrés" Tertz and Arzhak "have sheltered themselves in their rotten pathetic little world" (*zamknulis' v svoem prognivshem mirke*), it is not their writings but literature that is "socially and ideologically upright" (*klassovo i partiino vyderzhannaia*) that, in Filippov's words, "always smells of rot" (*vsegda otdaet tukhliatinoi*). Whereas for Eremin Sinyavsky and Daniel are "renegades employed by the most unbridled and rampant enemies of Communism" (*otshchepentsy, postupivshie na sluzhbu k samym ogoltelym, samym raznuzdannym vragam kommunizma*), it is Eremin and Kedrina whom Filippov assails as "rampant, dogmatic, and orthodox" (*ogoltelye dogmatiki-ortodoksy*), and so on. The evocative title of Eremin's article "Perevertyshi" (that is, "Shifters") renders the metaphor both literal and literary: translated into the discourse of ideological confrontation between the Soviet literary establishment (gosizdat) and its anti-Soviet counterpart (tamizdat), it reveals a striking stylistic semblance. Filippov's letter to *Literaturnaia gazeta*, like Sinyavsky and Daniel's trial itself, marked the end of the old era and the beginning of a new one, when, as Sinyavsky put it, his disagreements with the Soviet government were "basically stylistic," rather than ideological or political.[15]

As a literary practice and political institution, tamizdat in general, and the project of Tertz and Arzhak in particular, reinstated the role of the publisher as an active participant in the creative process, complicating the traditional idea of literature as texts written by writers and read by readers. For better or worse, tamizdat made "no less an important figure than a writer"[16] other "agents of cultural production," to use

Pierre Bourdieu's term, including not only publishers, but also smugglers of contraband manuscripts from the USSR and those who smuggled them back in printed form. As a contraband operation, the project of Tertz and Arzhak was, of course, confidential, so much so that those involved should perhaps be regarded as the two writers' "coauthors," or "accomplices." One of them was the daughter of a French diplomat of Polish descent stationed in Moscow, Helene Peltier, whom Sinyavsky met at Moscow State University as early as 1947. Pressed by the KGB to start a relationship with her to spy on her father, Sinyavsky turned this classical plot of the Cold War into a literary affair and made it serve a creative function.[17] In December 1956 he asked Peltier to smuggle his first two works out of Russia and have them published abroad, preferably by a press as unengaged in politics as possible. In this role Peltier facilitated the separation of the newborn author Abram Tertz from the Soviet critic Sinyavsky (as well as that of Arzhak from the Soviet translator Yuly Daniel). But when Sinyavsky and Tertz, as well as Daniel and Arzhak, were forcefully "reunited" at the trial, it was much to the detriment of the former, but without particular harm to the latter, who in fact only triumphed as their physical authors' literary incarnations. While Sinyavsky and Daniel were sentenced, respectively, to seven and five years of hard labor in Mordovia, Tertz and Arzhak continued to be published abroad, undermining the conventional idea of authorship as an inseverable tie between physical authors and their texts.[18] (Possessive pronouns are not of much help here, since texts may apparently have authors other than their own.) The platform for this near-magical bifurcation was geography, immutable and inescapable as it seemed.

Olga Matich has described Tertz's creative strategy as "textual embodiment": "This was Sinyavsky's metaphor for the fragmentation and illegal journey of his alternate literary body as shaped by a Gogolian metaphor, representing the *embodiment* of his spatial turn or publishing in forbidden space. Textually, in other words, he possessed two bodies, public and private (secret), that is, publishable and unpublishable in panoptic gosizdat."[19] But while his "publishable" body, that which was known in gosizdat as Sinyavsky, did not require an intermediary, his "unpublishable" one—or rather, that which was "publishable" only abroad—was utterly powerless without the participation of an "accomplice." As the Soviet authorities on one hand and tamizdat critics on the other were trying to solve the equation and find out the truth about Tertz and Arzhak, it was the geographical Other who, to a point, rendered the equation unsolvable. (The other "coauthor" of

Tertz and Arzhak was Jerzy Giedroyc, editor of the Polish émigré journal *Kultura* and head of the publishing house Instytut Literacki in Paris,
who received their manuscripts through Peltier and handled their publications abroad, including translation into foreign languages as well as
the Russian editions brought out by Filippov in the United States.) The
trial of Sinyavsky and Daniel exposed, along those lines, what Michel
Foucault ascribed to the middle ages, when "the major target of penal
repression" was still the body, before corporal punishment was replaced
"by a punishment that acts in depth on the heart, the thoughts, the
will, the inclinations," targeting the "bodiless reality" of the prisoner.[20]
Indeed, it was the punishable "bodies" of Sinyavsky and Daniel, rather
than the "bodiless reality" of Tertz and Arzhak, upon which the punishment could be inflicted. Unlike the physical bodies of Sinyavsky and
Daniel, the writings of Tertz and Arzhak remained unbound by Soviet
laws, since they never belonged to any particular jurisdiction or ideology, Soviet or not, in the first place.

Arguably, much the same could be said of nearly all tamizdat, since
as a literary practice and political institution it had always relied on
the geographic breach between texts and their authors. What makes
the project of Tertz and Arzhak especially poignant, however, is that it
targeted both the literary establishment at home, where art was put at
the service of truth, and abroad, where truth may have had the opposite
ideological value but still prevailed over the literary merits of texts in
which it was to be found. The new method of fantastic realism, coined
as a solution to socialist realism and sustained throughout Tertz and
Arzhak's fiction, effectively challenged the ongoing pursuit of truth as
the alleged superior purpose of literature on both sides of the Curtain.

Tertz's short story "Pkhentz" (1957) puts the postulates of fantastic
realism into practice, casting "the text as a 'criminal' body in order to
explore the origins of art's alterity."[21] Set in post-Stalinist Russia but
devoid of any specific historical markers, it is a first-person narrative,
or undated "notes," written "in a local dialect" by an alien, whose space-
ship had crash-landed in Siberia thirty-two years earlier. ("The influence
of an alien *milieu*," the narrator laments, "is felt in every sentence.")[22]
The length of the alien's stay on earth is nearing the age of Christ, while
dating back to Sinyavsky's year of birth (1925). "Pkhentz" may be the
alien's name, or the only word of his native tongue he still remembers,
or both. It may also stand for the name of his native planet. But it
is also, unmistakably, a euphonic reference to Tertz, Sinyavsky's pen

ABRAM TERC

OPOWIEŚCI
FANTASTYCZNE

INSTYTUT LITERACKI

PARYŻ 1961

АБРАМ ТЕРЦ

ФАНТАСТИЧЕСКИЕ
ПОВЕСТИ

INSTYTUT ⚓ LITERACKI
PARYŻ   1 9 6 1

FIGURE 5.3.   Abram Tertz. *Fantasticheskie povesti*. Paris: Instytut Literacki, 1961.

name. For thirty-two years, however, Pkhentz has successfully passed himself for Andrei Kazimirovich Sushinsky without ever being exposed, sharing not only his terrestrial first name and the Polish origins of his patronymic with Andrei Donatovich Sinyavsky, but also part of his last name (Sinyavsky versus Sushinsky), the other part likely inherited from Pushkin.[23] The conflation of Sinyavsky and Pushkin's last names earns Pkhentz not only an honorable literary lineage but also a sign of physical alterity and vulnerability: "Sushinsky" suggests "dryness" (*susha*), a threat to his survival as a vegetative, cactus-like creature, whose life sustenance is water—not drunk, but poured over his body. Living in a communal apartment in Moscow, he can only enjoy his "meal" once a day late at night, after his neighbors have fallen asleep and stop lining

FIGURE 5.4. Nikolai Arzhak. *Govorit Moskva. Povesti i rasskazy.* With an introduction and an afterword by Boris Filippov. Cover design by Nikolai Safonov [Serge Hollerbach]. [Washington DC]:
Inter-Language Literary Associates, 1966.

up for the shared bathroom. But when it rains outside, it is a good day
for Pkhentz, despite the suspicious looks of the passers-by.[24] Camouflaged by his adopted earthly identity and Soviet-style outfit, Pkhentz's
body is all but human: he has four hands, two of which he keeps on the
surface, while the other two must remain tightly tied underneath his
clothes at all times in public, imitating a hunch. The extra eyes on the
back of his head and the temple, as well as on his hands and feet, have
grown weak without daylight, always covered by the rough clothes, the
shoes, and the wig ("the friction of my right shoe had cost me the sight
of one eye back in 1934").[25] When Pkhentz's neighbor Veronika, despite
her best intentions, decides to treat him to dinner, he "emptied [his]

plate into a sheet of newspaper," pondering, "What about preparing a man to the same recipe? Take an engineer or writer, stuff him with his own brains, place a violet in one braised nostril, and dish him up to his colleagues for dinner."[26] Compared to the "agony of a fish jerked out of water on a hook," Pkhentz goes on, revealing just how familiar he has become with human history and culture, "the torments of Christ, Jan Hus, and Stenka Razin are a bagatelle. . . . They at least knew what it was all for."[27]

Sexuality is also absent from Pkhentz in the sense it is present in and among humans. When Veronika offers herself to him after the dinner prelude, it is much to his utter dismay: "It was—I repeat—horrible. . . . A pair of white breasts dangled in front. At first I took them for secondary arms, amputated above the elbow. But each of them terminated in a round nipple like a push button." Instead of arousing desire, the female human body frightens and repels Pkhentz—not because he is chaste, nor even because a Soviet anatomy book he had once come across "has nothing to say on the subject, or says it so vaguely and cursorily that no one can guess what it truly means," but because, as an alien, he is queer:

> So now, overcoming my confusion, I decided to take advantage of the opportunity, to take a look at the place mentioned in the anatomy textbook as the site of that genital apparatus which shoots out ready-made infants like a catapult. . . . Only it didn't look female to me, but more like an old man's face, unshaven and baring his teeth. A hungry, angry man dwelt there between her legs. He probably snored at night, and relieved his boredom with foul language.[28]

To translate Pkhentz's sexual encounter into the literary context, the Soviet anatomy book may be understood as socialist realism and Veronika's body as one of its "bestsellers," which the alien can neither admire nor even comprehend.[29] Far from a "positive hero in pursuit of a Purpose," as Tertz summarizes one of the socialist-realist premises in his essay, Pkhentz is neither positive nor negative. Nor does he pursue any purpose other than to survive by watering himself in secret from his neighbors.[30] Instead, although an alien, Pkhentz is a Soviet-era progeny of Akaky Akakievich, much as all Russian literature, including Tertz and Arzhak's fantastic realism, is but a continuation of Gogol's "The Overcoat." Literally outlandish, Pkhentz, like his nineteenth-century ancestor, has to make do with his "humble job as a book-keeper" at a Soviet state institution, although by the time he finishes writing his notes, he is sixty-one and already retired. At the end of the short story, Pkhentz joins Gogol's petty clerk, famously incapable of producing a text of his own, by confessing that he has, too, "even forgotten how to think as I used to, let alone read or write." The disintegration of his identity is orchestrated through the loss of his native language and a near-complete assimilation to humans, a transformation he still recognizes as fatal: "Lord, oh Lord! I seem to be turning into a man!"[31] "Infected" by the purposelessness of Gogol's proverbial "little man" (*malen'kii chelovek*), Pkhentz, lying sick in his room, realizes that "the only way I can preserve what is left of me" is "to die without causing a sensation,"[32] bringing to mind the deplorable demise of Akaky Akakievich, whose unremarkable life left no trace in the fictional world he inhabited ("and Petersburg was left without Akaky Akakievich, as if he had never been there")[33] but became ineffaceable from Russian literary tradition ever since. Not unlike Gogol's character, Pkhentz even mentions that the past winter he "didn't spend anything on a fur coat, nor on trams or trolleybuses," despite the cold he could hardly endure. His equivalent of the new overcoat is a "seat-reservation to Irkutsk."[34] As he prepares to go back to Siberia and on to the outer space where he had come from, Pkhentz longs to find the sacred hole in the ground where thirty-two years earlier his earthly journey began—craving, as Freud would have it, to return to the womb.

For all its fantastic import, "Pkhentz" may also be read as a historical and even political allegory. The extraterrestrial character's thirty-two-year-long stretch on earth and in Soviet Russia, framed by his crash in Siberia on the one end and his imagined escape through the same hole in the ground on the other, renders Pkhentz a prisoner. Geographically, freedom and captivity, in Pkhentz's case, have changed places: Moscow, where he lives and works as a bookkeeper, *is* his prison, whereas Siberia is his anteroom to freedom. Given that the short story was written in 1957, the year Pkhentz landed on earth thirty-two years previously is the year of Stalin's gradual consolidation of power (1925), whereas the text's setting in the late 1950s is the dawn of Khrushchev's Thaw, de-Stalinization, and rehabilitation of political prisoners. (The first Sputnik was also launched into outer space in 1957, perhaps with Pkhentz as a passenger on his imaginary way back home.)

Yet the short story is too ambiguous—or simply fantastic—to end on a positive note. With its last paragraphs written entirely in the future tense, it does not deprive Pkhentz of hope, but it inspires no confidence in the happy outcome of his contemplated escape (as if there can be any confidence in fantastic realism): "I'll sit down in the hole, untie myself and wait. Not a single human thought will I think, not a single word of alien speech will I utter." Although the mere thought of escape brings Pkhentz relief, the escape itself remains only imagined rather than actually accomplished. Furthermore, Pkhentz has planned to end his life on earth in self-immolation: "When the first frosts begin and I see that time is ripe—just one match will be enough. There will be nothing left of me."[35] With the short story framed as his personal diary in the "local dialect," it is not only himself Pkhentz plans to set on fire, but his notes, or manuscript, too: "My lot will never read them or hear anything about me."[36] In other words, Pkhentz has plotted the same symbolic act that numerous other Russian literary characters and their authors had (or had not) already performed before him.[37] What is left of Pkhentz is a series of exclamations in the Pkhentz language, with the addition of words from German ("GUTENABEND!") and French ("BONJOUR!"), as well as the onomatopoeic "MIAOW, MIAOW!" Pkhentz's burning himself in his thirty-third year, Nepomnyashchy argues, "echoes the Crucifixion," or rather an auto-da-fé of the Inquisition. What we are reading, then, is "the very same text that the narrator says he will burn," in other words, "a text that ostensibly has been destroyed."[38] However, having proclaimed his own physical destruction, "Pkhentz" survived as a manuscript "in the local dialect," imperfect and inadequate as it may be to its extraterrestrial author's earthly experience. And while Pkhentz's escape from captivity, much as his fantastic existence, remains uncertain, the manuscript of Abram Tertz becomes all the more real and material: it was smuggled out of the country and published in tamizdat just as Sinyavsky, its physical author, was sent in the opposite direction, to a labor camp in Mordovia.

The opposite interpretation of "Pkhentz" as an allegory for prison experience is also possible: the alien's inability to fit the society of mankind, although described in fantastic terms, resembles the inability of former prisoners to reunite with life outside upon their release from the camps. As a "contemporary" of the gulag returnees around 1957, Pkhentz carries with him the inexpressible knowledge of the otherworld he had witnessed, which proves just as unsuitable for freedom as his extraterrestrial body and language are unsuitable for life among humans. (The word "Pkhentz" itself, in this sense, is synonymous with Shalamov's "Sententsiia," the "foreign" word "utterly unsuitable for the taiga, a word that neither I nor my comrades could understand.")[39] Ever since Dostoevsky defined it as "a world apart, unlike everything else, with laws of its own, its own dress, its own manners and customs,"[40] prison—"another planet"—has become but a natural environment for Pkhentz, confined as he is to life on earth for thirty-two years. Hence his desperate longing to find and identify with other "returnees." "How long since you left?" [*Vy davno ottuda?*] Pkhentz asks the hunchback Leopold Sergeevich, whom he meets at the laundry and mistakes for a fellow "alien," or a queer, like himself. "I recognized you at first sight. You and I come from the same place. We're relatives, so to speak. PKHENTZ! PKHENTZ!" But when the word, meant to establish a common identity through shared experience, falls on deaf ears, Pkhentz goes into denial: "He had entered too fully into his part, gone native, become human, over-adjusted to his surroundings, surrendered to alien influences. He had forgotten his former name, betrayed his distant homeland."[41] In this possible reading of "Pkhentz," the hunchback's indifference stands, among other things, for the betrayal of the gulag survivors' brotherhood. The encounter brings disillusionment; not only does Leopold Sergeevich turn out to be just an ordinary human heterosexual and Soviet citizen, hunchback or not, but he also nearly turns Pkhentz in to the authorities. It is then, after his failed attempt to find others like him, that Pkhentz falls sick and contemplates setting himself and his notes on fire as a way to break away from the prison that human freedom has turned out to be.

I have chosen "Pkhentz" to conclude my study of the formative years of tamizdat because it is also a story about displacement and exile. The alien's ruminations on living away from home and trying in vain to preserve his native language and identity in a foreign environment must have sounded strangely familiar, if not altogether autobiographical, to the older generation of émigré publishers when the short story reached them abroad—after approximately as many years in exile as Pkhentz had spent on earth. In the course of that time, much like the first Russian emigration, Pkhentz has grown to take pride in his otherness: "If I hadn't been living in exile for thirty-two years I should probably never dream of admiring my exterior. But here I am the only example of that lost harmony and beauty which I call my homeland. What is there for me to do on this earth except delight in my person?"[42] His narcissism mirrors the émigrés' pride in preserving and guarding their native language, literature, and culture from being defiled at home after the Revolution. Pkhentz's nostalgia and desperate longing to go back, along the same lines, reflects the émigrés' hope to return to

Russia in the indefinite future, except that the Russia they fled from in the 1920s has in the meantime grown nearly as "fantastic" as the alien's native planet while he has been gone.[43] Whether or not they were ready to admit it, for the old generation of the Russian emigration, Pkhentz was sorely recognizable.

His inability to return on the one hand or to turn into a human on the other make Pkhentz a ghost, adding a gothic touch to the short story. Pkhentz's imagined "repatriation" remains unfulfilled because, while stranded on earth, he has grown irreparably estranged from his native environment. As a ghost he is no longer recognizable by other "aliens" like him. For them, he is simply invisible. Having lived for thirty-two years in between and internalized his own liminality, he is nevertheless ever drawn back, like a ghost. It is precisely this magical faculty that enables Pkhentz to be simultaneously a former prisoner "unseen" by those who lack the experience he had been through, still a prisoner unable to adjust to life in captivity after the "crash," and an émigré who finds himself elsewhere geographically due to one tragic "accident" in Russian history.[44]

Paraphrasing Viktor Shklovsky's revolutionary 1917 study of *ostranenie*, or alienation, in "Art as a Device," Zinovy Zinik, an émigré of the Third Wave, suggests in his essay "Emigration as a Literary Device" that "the prison, an uninhabited island, and interaction with ghosts in the next world are equally suitable metaphors for the émigré experience, the life of a stranger and an outcast in a foreign country."[45] An émigré, according to Zinik, is a ghost whose motherland has become fictional rather than real, but who still needs it, if only to justify his existence elsewhere, since otherwise there would be nowhere to return—and a ghost always longs to return. For the old generation of Russian émigrés, the Russia they longed to return to had become a utopia. However, this Russia of the indefinite future was, paradoxically, reconstructed from the historical past, which was, after all, what served as the object of their nostalgia. It was a utopia of the future in the past, as Zinik has evocatively defined it in his other essay "The Gothic Horror Novel of Emigration."[46] Pkhentz's Russia, however, was never his motherland. In fact, it was nearly as foreign to him as Paris, Berlin, and New York to Russian émigrés of the old generation. It took an alien not only "to defamiliarize the Soviet present," as Elio Borenstein has put it, but also to "alienate" the historical experience of the Russian emigration.[47]

Still, insofar as emigration is conceived of as a virtual death, Pkhentz's life did not end in 1957, when he thought he would set himself and his notes on fire and vanish in the vast expanse of Siberia. Like Akaky Akakievich, who did not "really" die as a petty clerk in St. Petersburg but returned from the otherworld as a phantom to take revenge and reclaim his place in Russian literature posthumously, Pkhentz, too, having announced his own destruction, has survived as a manuscript and come back after all. He returned at the height of perestroika, when Tertz's short story was for the first time published in Russia in 1989—thirty-two years after Pkhentz's imagined escape.[48] Pkhentz was gone for exactly as long as he had lived in "exile" in Soviet Russia as an alien. As a work of fantastic realism, "Pkhentz" proved to be as much about the past as about the future, however unimaginable at the time.

Even less plausibly, no sooner did "Pkhentz" (re)appear in Russia in print, not only state censorship but geography itself ceased being an obstacle for unorthodox characters like him, fantastic or not, to find their way to the reader. Paranormal as it may have seemed at the time even to the fantastic-realist author of "Pkhentz," the internet soon became a reality and an epilogue of sorts to tamizdat, the Cold War, and the Soviet era. It delivered a greater blow to censorship—and by extension to tamizdat as a practice and institution—than any political change was ever capable of. Or so it seemed for a while . . .

Putin's war in Ukraine and the crackdown on the liberal opposition and the freedom of speech in Russia since at least 2014 seem to have brought the Cold War and tamizdat back to reality. Independent Russian media are being shut down, or they yet again operate from abroad, or use foreign servers to host their websites. Journalists and opposition leaders are being locked up and physically annihilated. Hundreds of thousands, if not millions, of Russians have left the country in the past eight years, especially since the full-scale invasion of Ukraine on February 24, 2022. They are fleeing political persecution or find it morally, ideologically, or economically impossible to stay put, constituting yet another "wave" of Russian emigration. Many authors who have stayed again publish abroad, often anonymously or under pennames,[49] while readers in Russia use VPNs to circumvent state censorship or to hide their identities and IP addresses. If tamizdat as a literary practice and political institution is bound to return, it will no doubt be of a different nature compared to the Soviet, pre-internet era. But since the late 1980s it is clearly more instructive than ever to look back at old patterns in order to understand new ones, however different the world has become in the last thirty years.

NOTES

Acknowledgments

1. Joseph Brodsky, "In Memory of Carl Proffer," Joseph Brodsky Papers, Gen Mss 613, Box 123, Folder 2772, Beinecke Rare Book and Manuscript Library, Yale University; Iosif Brodsky, "Pamiati Karla Proffera," trans. Olga Voronina, *Zvezda*, no. 4 (2005): 122–25.

2. Lysander Jaffe, " 'Writing as a Stranger': Two Translations of Shalamov's 'The Snake Charmer,' " https://shalamov.ru/en/research/207/.

3. The program, abstracts, participants' bios, and video recordings of the conference are available at https://www.reechunter.com/tamizdat-conference.html.

4. Yasha Klots, ed., *Tamizdat: Publishing Russian Literature across Borders*, special issue of *Wiener Slawistischer Almanach* Band 86 (Berlin: Peter Lang, 2021).

5. *Tamizdat Project: Contraband Russian Literature Across Borders*, http://tamizdatproject.org/en.

Introduction

1. Viktor Shklovsky, *Zoo, or Letters Not about Love*, trans. Richard Sheldon (Champaign, IL: Dalkey Archives, 2012), 95. The original word for "plates" (*listy*) has a meaning that, in typical Shklovsky fashion, translates the metaphor into the literary context: "pages" (e.g., of a book or a manuscript).

2. Glazkov's last appearance in the underground took place in 1959, when he contributed five poems to the first issue of Aleksandr Ginzburg's samizdat journal *Sintaksis*. *Sintaksis* was first published abroad in *Grani* 58 (1965): 95–193. On Glazkov, see, for example, Lev Losev, "Krestnyi otets samizdata," in his *Meandr. Memuarnaia proza* (Moscow: Novoe izdatel'stvo, 2010), 289–92.

3. Dimitry Pospielovsky, "From Gosizdat to Samizdat and Tamizdat," *Canadian Slavonic Papers* 20, no. 1 (March 1978): 44–45. In contrast to Pospielovsky's dated approach, see Friederike Kind-Kovács and Jessie Labov, "Samizdat and Tamizdat. Entangled Phenomena?" In *Samizdat, Tamizdat, and Beyond: Transnational Media during and after Socialism*, ed. Friederike Kind-Kovács and Jessie Labov (New York: Berghahn, 2013), 1–23.

4. On Solzhenitsyn and tamizdat, see chapter 1. Dudintsev's and Bulgakov's novels also came out abroad soon after they appeared in gosizdat. *Not by Bread Alone*, first printed in *Novyi mir* in 1956 (nos. 8–10) and then as a separate book in 1957, was reprinted the same year by two émigré publishers (Munich: Tsentral'noe ob'edinenie politicheskikh emigrantov iz SSSR, 1957; New York:

Novoe russkoe slovo, 1957). *The Master and Margarita*, first serialized in a censored form in the Soviet journal *Moskva* (no. 11, 1966; no. 1, 1967), appeared as a separate edition the following year (Paris: YMCA-Press, 1967).

5. Gleb Struve, *Russian Literature under Lenin and Stalin, 1917–1953* (Norman: University of Oklahoma Press, 1971), viii; Struve's emphasis. Pospielovsky's broad definition of tamizdat, along these lines, includes works "written by Russian émigrés" (Pospielovsky, "From Gosizdat," 44).

6. Friederike Kind-Kovács, *Written Here, Published There. How Underground Literature Crossed the Iron Curtain* (Budapest: Central European University Press, 2014), 9.

7. Anna Akhmatova, *Rekviem* (Munich: Tovarishchestvo zarubezhnykh pisatelei, 1963), 7.

8. Lydia Chukovskaia, *Zapiski ob Anne Akhmatovoi*, 3 vols. (Moscow: Soglasie, 1997), 3: 131.

9. See, for example, Ann Komaromi, "Ardis Facsimile and Reprint Editions: Giving Back Russian Literature," in *Samizdat, Tamizdat and Beyond: Transnational Media during and after Socialism*, ed. Friederike Kind-Kovács and Jessie Labov (New York: Berghahn, 2013), 27–50.

10. Other means of precaution included signing the publisher's prefaces, introductions and afterwords with a pseudonym. See Manfred Shruba and Oleg Korostelev, eds., *Psevdonimy russkogo zarubezh'ia. Materialy i issledovaniia* (Moscow: Novoe literaturnoe obozrenie, 2016).

11. Ann Komaromi suggests, for example, that socially conditioned binaries of official versus dissident literary spheres "may still be useful . . . to cordon off an autonomous space of unofficial culture with fluid boundaries and dynamic distinctions," "The Unofficial Field of Late Soviet Culture," *Slavic Review* 66, no. 4 (Winter 2007): 606.

12. Pierre Bourdieu, *The Field of Cultural Production* (New York: Columbia University Press, 1994).

13. Irina Paperno, *Stories of the Soviet Experience: Memoirs, Diaries, Dreams* (Ithaca, NY: Cornell University Press, 2009), 97.

14. Tamara Petkevich recalls once meeting a group of old Bolsheviks, arrested in 1937 and rehabilitated in 1956, who "had been invited to the representative offices of the Party, where they were told: 'A special room has been allotted to you at the Lenin Public Library, where you can sit and write your memoirs about your revolutionary activity, and about the camps too'. . . . They were glad that the state itself was encouraging them to tell their stories." "Their worldviews," Petkevich adds bitterly, "were motivated by the politicized, yet essentially biological, thrust for thoughtless existence" (Tamara Petkevich, *Memoir of a Gulag Actress*, trans. Yasha Klots and Ross Ufberg (DeKalb, IL: Northern Illinois University Press, 2010), 452–53).

15. Chukovskaia, *Zapiski*, 2: 190.

16. Paperno, *Soviet Experience*, 101–2.

17. Paperno, 106.

18. Mikhail Bulgakov, *The Master and Margarita*, trans. Richard Pevear and Larissa Volokhonsky (New York: Penguin, 1997), 287.

19. Aleksandr Solzhenitsyn, "Odin den' Ivana Denisovicha," *Novyi mir*, no. 11 (1962): 8–74.

20. See, for example, Yale Richmond, *Cultural Exchange and the Cold War: Raising the Iron Curtain* (University Park: Pennsylvania State University Press, 2003).

21. Carl R. Proffer, *The Widows of Russia and Other Writings* (Ann Arbor, MI: Ardis, 1987), 19–20.

22. Proffer, 20–21. Despite her fears, the first book of Nadezhda Mandelshtam's memoirs was smuggled out by Clarence Brown and published in New York in 1970 by Izdatel'stvo imeni Chekhova, followed by two more book editions in Paris, in 1972 and posthumously in 1987 (both by YMCA-Press).

23. Chukovskaia, *Zapiski*, 2: 179.

24. Paperno, *Soviet Experience*, 114.

25. Aleksandr Genis, "Tret'ia volna: primerka svobody," *Zvezda*, no. 5 (2010): 206. Genis's metaphor, however, appears more applicable to his own generation of the Third Wave of Russian emigration in the 1970–1980s; in the early 1960s the relationship between Russia and abroad resembled, rather, a mirror symmetry.

26. Iosif Brodsky, *Stikhotvoreniia i poemy*, with a foreword by Georgy Stukov (Washington, DC: Inter-Language Literary Associates, 1965).

27. Leona Toker, *Return from the Archipelago. Narratives of Gulag Survivors* (Bloomington: Indiana University Press, 2000), 91–93.

28. Michel Foucault, "Of Other Spaces: Utopias and Heterotopias," *Heterotopia and the City: Public Space in a Postcivil Society*, ed. Michiel Dehaene and Lieven de Cauter (London: Routledge, 2008), 14.

29. Olga Matich, "*Tamizdat*: The Spatial Turn, Textual Embodiment, My Personal Stories," in *Tamizdat: Publishing Russian Literature across Borders*, ed. Yasha Klots, special issue of *Wiener Slawistischer Almanach* 86 (Berlin: Peter Lang, 2021), 29; emphasis in the original.

30. Michel Foucault, *Discipline and Punish. The Birth of Prison*, trans. Alan Sheridan (New York: Vintage, 1979), 249.

31. Hans Robert Jauss, *Toward an Aesthetic of Reception*, trans. Timothy Bahti, with an introduction by Paul de Man (Minneapolis: University of Minnesota Press, 1982), 21, 19.

32. On the history of the first publications of *Doctor Zhivago*, which I have chosen to refer to only in passing as it has already been dealt with elsewhere, see Lazar Fleishman, *Vstrecha russkoi emigratsii s "Doktorom Zhivago": Boris Pasternak i "kholodnaia voina"* (Stanford, CA: Stanford Slavic Series, 2009); Ivan Tolstoi, *Otmytyi roman Pasternaka: "Doktor Zhivago" mezhdu KGB i TsRU* (Moscow: Vremia, 2009); Ivan Tolstoi, *"Doktor Zhivago": novye fakty i nakhodki v Nobelevskom arkhive* (Prague: Human Rights Publishers, 2010); Peter Finn and Petra Couvée, *The Zhivago Affair: The Kremlin, the CIA, and the Battle over a Forbidden Book* (New York: Vintage, 2015); Paolo Mancosu, *Zhivago's Secret Journey: from Typescript to Book* (Stanford, CA: Hoover Institution Press, 2016); Paolo Mancosu, *Kontrabandisty, buntari, piraty: perepetii istorii izdaniia "Doktora Zhivago"* (Moscow: Azbukovnik, 2017).

33. Andrew Wachtel and Ilya Vinitsky, *Russian Literature* (Cambridge, MA: Polity, 2009), 28–29. Centuries later, Avvakum's *Life* was reclaimed, first by

poets and scholars of the early Soviet period, then by nonconformist authors of the post-Stalin era, as the ultimate prototype of their own writings. Ironically, the revival of interest in Avvakum after the Revolution coincided with the rise of Soviet atheism. For example, Nikolai Kliuev's poem "Lenin" (1918) portrays Avvakum as a defender of the working class and Lenin's ideological forerunner. It was clearly not the religious but the aesthetic aspects of Avvakum's text that resonated in the 1920s with some of the formalists, e.g., in Vladimir Vinogradov, "O zadachakh stilistiki: nabliudeniia za stilem 'Zhitiia Protopopa Avvakuma,'" in *Russkaia rech': sbornik statei*, ed. Lev Scherba (Petrograd: Foneticheskii institut prakticheskogo izucheniia iazykov, 1923), 195–273. At the time, Vinogradov was affiliated with the OPOYAZ. Decades later Avvakum is invoked, for instance, in Varlam Shalamov's "Avvakum in Pustozersk" (1955)— "one of [his] most important" and "especially dear" poems, according to the author's own remark, Varlam Shalamov, *Sobranie sochinenii v 7 tomakh* (Moscow: Terra, 2013), 3: 458. In this poem Shalamov speaks through the words of the seventeenth-century religious martyr while translating them into the language of his own historical reality, addressing the reader in the first-person plural and thus grammatically blurring the line between his own and Avvakum's fates. According to Josefina Lundblad-Janjić, the poem's thirty-seven stanzas point to the year 1937, whereby Shalamov calls for an allegorical reading of his poem. "Avvakum in Pustozersk" was published in Shalamov's second collection of poetry *Doroga i sud'ba* (Moscow: Sovetskii pisatel', 1967) in a heavily censored and abridged form: the number of stanzas was reduced from 37 to 26, Josefina Lundblad-Janjić, "Poetry and Politics: An Allegorical Reading of Varlam Shalamov's Poem 'Avvakum v Pustozerske," https://shalamov.ru/research/239/.

34. Andrei Ranchin and Nikita Sapov, eds., *Stikhi ne dlia dam: russkaia netsenzurnaia poeziia vtoroi poloviny XIX* veka (Moscow: Ladomir, 1994), 47. No book by Longinov that would be brought out in Karlsruhe or elsewhere abroad, however, has been located. In 1871–1874, Longinov was head of the Central Administration for Publishing Affairs, a branch of the Ministry for Internal Affairs of the Russian empire, instituted in 1865 and active throughout the tsarist period until 1917.

35. Alexander Herzen, *A Herzen Reader*, ed. and trans., with an introduction by Kathleen Parthe, and a critical essay by Robert Harris (Evanston, IL: Northwestern University Press, 2012), 28–30. In June 1853, before *Kolokol*, Herzen's Free Russian Press published *Iuriev Den'* (*St. George's Day*), a brochure that called for the abolition of serfdom. Other notable periodicals brought out by the press were *Poliarnaia zvezda* (*Polar Star*, 1855–1868), an almanac whose title invoked the eponymous publication of the Decembrists from 1823–1825, with portraits of the five executed rebels in St. Petersburg twenty-nine years earlier reproduced on the cover; and *Golosa iz Rossii* (*Voices from Russia*; 1856–1860), which printed articles on social and political issues including, apart from Herzen's own, writings by Boris Chicherin, Konstantin Kavelin, Nikolai Melgunov, Nikolai Ogarev, Valerian Panaev, Konstantin Pobedonostsev, as well as anonymous authors. Separate editions of Herzen's press included, in 1858, Aleksandr Radishchev's *Puteshestvie iz Peterburga v Moskvu* (*Journey from Petersburg to*

Moscow), which despite its numerous editorial flaws, remained the only edition available in Russia for the rest of the century.

36. On August 25, 1968, the slogan "For our freedom and yours" was picked up by seven Soviet dissidents who walked onto Red Square to protest the Soviet invasion of Czechoslovakia. See Natalia Gorbanevskaia, *Polden': delo o demonstratsii 25 avgusta 1968 goda na Krasnoi ploshchadi* (Moscow: Novoe izdatel'stvo, 2007). Gorbanevskaia's firsthand account was published abroad while she was confined at the Serbsky Institute for forced psychiatric treatment (Frankfurt: Possev, 1970).

37. Herzen, *Herzen Reader*, 29.

38. Martin Malia, *Alexander Herzen and the Birth of Russian Socialism, 1812–1855* (Cambridge, MA: Harvard University Press, 1961), 394. Malia's biography of Herzen, however, does not go beyond 1855 and barely touches on his publishing mission in Europe. It is symbolic that only a year after his book on Herzen was out, Malia traveled as an exchange scholar to the USSR, where he met Chukovskaia (also a Herzen scholar) and Akhmatova, whose *Requiem* he helped smuggle out (see chapter 2).

39. Herzen was able to finance his activity thanks to James Mayer de Rothschild, a German banker and founder of the French branch of the Rothschild family, who used his personal influence on Nicholas I to help Herzen cash out familial property confiscated from him in absentia by the tsarist authorities after Herzen refused to return to Russia from exile. Thus the socialist cause that Herzen fought for was assisted, ironically, by one of the world's leading capitalists (see Herzen's own account in his *My Past and Thoughts: The Memoirs of Alexander Herzen*, trans. Constance Garnett, with an introduction by Isaiah Berlin (Berkeley: University of California Press, 1982), 405; see also Derek Offord, "Alexander Herzen and James de Rothschild," *Rothschild Archive* (April 2005–March 2006): 39–47.

40. Lazar Fleishman, "Iz arkhiva Guverovskogo instituta. Pis'ma Iu. G. Oksmana k G. P. Struve," *Stanford Slavic Studies* 1 (1987): 49; quoted in Gleb Struve, "Russia Abroad," *Russian Review* 35, no. 1 (January 1976): 95–96.

41. For information on this short-lived samizdat periodical, see Ann Komaromi's *Project for the Study of Dissidence and Samizdat*, https://samizdat.library.utoronto.ca/content/kolokol.

42. Anatoly Marchenko, *My Testimony*, trans. Michael Scammell (New York: Dutton, 1969), 103. Writing his memoir in 1967, between his first and second arrests, Marchenko did not know it was destined to come out in tamizdat in two years' time and become the earliest known firsthand account of Soviet hard-labor camps after Stalin.

43. Paperno, *Soviet Experience*, 10.

44. Paperno, 11. See also Jay Bergman, "Soviet Dissidents on the Russian Intelligentsia, 1956–1985: The Search for a Usable Past," *Russian Review* 51, no. 1 (January 1992): 16–35.

45. Paperno, *Soviet Experience*, 11.

46. It seems the uncanny cyclicity of history itself dictated the following to Chukovskaia on December 29, 1962: "I quietly said [to Akhmatova] I was

reading Herzen, every free minute I had, taking [him] along on my tram rides and trolleys. I said . . . it was time to study Herzen's words as words of poetry. . . . But mainly, that Herzen is, of course, extremely relevant in our times; . . . In 1962, I am constantly drawn to what Herzen was writing, recalling and thinking about in 1862-1863. After all, the year 1963 is drawing close upon us. A hundred years ago, the times in Russia were in some ways similar to ours, namely in their ambiguity; it was hard to predict what will turn where. After the great liberation of the peasants in '61—the atrocities in Poland. And all these staged fires, unnecessary exiles, unnecessary executions! What we have now, after the great liberation of prisoners, is Hungary, blood, and Stalinism that seems to be mobilizing again. . . . What's next—go figure. . . . I am reading and rereading, in sequence and at random, what he had written in 1862-1863. . . . The main motif is that Russia had awakened and one must not let it fall back asleep, one must not let the era of Alexander II turn back into the era of Nicholas I" (Chukovskaia, Zapiski, 2: 576-77). At the time, Chukovskaia was writing her monograph 'Byloe i dumy' Gertsena (Moscow: Khudozhestvennaia literatura, 1966).

47. Belinkov was elected editor in chief of Novyi kolokol at a conference of Russian émigrés in London in 1970, but he died the same year. The almanac was completed two years later by his widow, Natalie Belinkov, Novyi kolokol. Literaturno-publitsisticheskii sbornik (London, 1972).

48. Struve, "Russia Abroad," 96. In Russia, Belinkov was Oksman's student and younger colleague. Struve's response to Novyi kolokol comes from his review of another tamizdat periodical: the journal Kontinent founded in Paris in 1974 by Vladimir Maksimov as the main journal of the Third Wave and a bridge between the Russian and East European diasporas and Western intellectuals.

49. Novyi kolokol, 6.

50. Struve, "Russia Abroad," 98.

51. Andrei Sinyavsky, "Dissent as a Personal Experience," trans. Maria-Regina Kecht, Dissent 31, no. 2 (Spring 1984): 154.

52. Catalog of Alexander Herzen Foundation (March 1972), International Institute of Social History. Despite the foundation's initial agenda to publish manuscripts "of literary or documentary value," its titles consisted mainly of memoirs, nonfiction, and political samizdat, with the exception of Andrei Amalrik's P'esy (Plays, 1970) and Yuli Daniel's Stikhi iz nevoli (Poems from Prison, 1971).

53. Catalog of Alexander Herzen Foundation.

54. On Soviet copyright, including the USSR's ascension to the Universal Copyright Convention in 1973, see, for example, Michael A. Newcity, Copyright Law in the Soviet Union (New York: Praeger, 1978); Mark Boguslavsky, The USSR and International Copyright Protection, trans. Yury Shirokov (Moscow: Progress Publishers, 1979); Jon A. Baumgarten, U.S.-U.S.S.R. Copyright Relations under the Universal Copyright Convention (New York: Practicing Law Institute, 1973); Serge L. Levitsky, Copyright, Defamation, and Privacy in Soviet Civil Law (Alphen aan den Rijn: Sijthoff & Noordhoff, 1979); D. A. Loeber, "VAAP: The Soviet Copyright Agency," University of Illinois Law Forum 2 (1979): 401-52.

55. On the history of the publication of *Resurrection*, see Nikolai Gudzy, "Istoriia pisaniia i pechataniia 'Voskreseniia,'" in Lev Tolstoi, *Polnoe sobranie sochinenii v 90 tomakh* (Moscow: Khudozhestvennaia literatura, 1935), 33: 329–422.

56. In 1899 the Dukhobors were allowed to emigrate and settled mainly in Canada.

57. In the wake of the First Russian Revolution, on October 30, 1905, Nicolas II signed the "October Manifesto" (a precursor to the first Russian Constitution adopted the following year), which guaranteed, among other things, freedom of speech and assembly and thus revoked political censorship. However, days after the coup of 1917, the newly established Council of People's Commissars (Sovnarkom) issued its "Decree on Publishing," which branded all bourgeois publications illegal and reinstituted censorship in the Soviet state.

58. Evgeny Zamiatin, *Litsa* (Washington, DC: Inter-Language Literary Associates, 1967), 188–90. First published in *Dom iskusstv* 1 (1921): 43–45, one of the last independent journals in Petrograd.

59. Boris Volin [Iosif Fradkin], "Nedopustimye iavleniia," *Literaturnaia gazeta*, August 26, 1929.

60. In 1921 Zamiatin sent the manuscript of his newly written novel by regular mail to Zinovy Grzhebin, a Berlin-based publisher with branches in Moscow and Petrograd, who in turn passed it on to American publishers for an English translation. *We* first came out in Gregory Zilboorg's allegedly authorized English translation: Eugene Zamiatin, *We*, trans. Gregory Zilboorg (New York: Dutton, 1924); then in Czech: Jevgenij Ivanovič Zamjatin, *My*, trans. Václav Koenig (Prague: Štorch-Marien, 1927); and in French: Evgenij Ivanovič Zamâtin, *Nous autres*, trans. B. Cauvet-Duhamel (Paris: Gallimard, 1929). A separate Russian edition did not appear, however, until decades later: Evgeny Zamiatin, *My* (New York: Izdatel'stvo imeni Chekhova, 1952). While allowing translations into foreign languages, Zamiatin never authorized the original publication of *We* abroad during his lifetime, at least not officially. On the history of the first publications and translations of *We* into foreign languages, see J. Curtis, "Istoriia izdaniia romana 'My', perevody i publikatsii," in *"My": Tekst i materialy k tvorcheskoi istroii romana*, ed. M. Yu. Liubimova and J. Curtis (St. Petersburg: Mir, 2011), 499–534; see also her biography of Zamiatin, *The Englishman from Lebedian': A Life of Evgeny Zamiatin* (Boston: Academic Studies Press, 2013), as well as Boris Andronikashvili-Pilniak, "Dva izgoia, dva muchenika: Boris Pil'niak i Evgeny Zamiatin," *Znamia*, no. 9 (1994): 123–53; Aleksandr Galushkin, "Delo Pil'niaka i Zamiatina. Predvaritel'nye itogi rassledovaniia," in *Novoe o Zamiatine*, ed. Leonid Geller (Moscow: MIK, 1997), 89–148.

61. Mark Slonim, "Predislovie (ko vtoromu izdaniiu)," in *"My": Tekst i materialy k tvorcheskoi istroii romana*, ed. M. Yu. Liubimova and J. Curtis (St. Petersburg: Mir, 2011), 313.

62. Volin, "Nedopustimye iavleniia."

63. Vladimir Mayakovsky, "Nashe otnoshenie," *Literaturnaia gazeta*, September 2, 1929.

64. See also the notorious comment of Anatoly Safonov, twice laureate of the Stalin Prize for Literature and Art, at the meeting of writers in Moscow on October 31, 1958: "I have not read Pasternak either then or now. . . . There can be no two opinions about Pasternak. He did not want to be a Soviet man, a Soviet writer—then off he goes from our country! (Applause)" (quoted in *Novyi zhurnal* 83 (1966): 185–227).

65. Evgeny Zamiatin, "Pis'mo v redaktsiiu 'Literaturnoi gazety,'" *Literaturnaia gazeta*, October 7, 1929. The letter was accompanied by the editor's commentary, which branded *We* as "an outrageous parody of Communism," although the novel had been written nine years earlier.

66. Zygmunt Bauman, *Retrotopia* (Cambridge: Polity, 2017).

67. Three months earlier, on September 4, 1965, an event of comparable significance took place in Kyiv: the premiere screening of Sergei Paradjanov's *Shadows of Forgotten Ancestors*, with public speeches delivered by Ukrainian dissidents Ivan Dziuba, Viacheslav Chornovil, and Vasyl Stus.

68. Aleksandr Ginzburg, ed., *Belaia kniga po delu A. Sinyavskogo i Iu. Danielia* (Frankfurt: Possev, 1967).

69. The official representative of the *Chronicle* abroad was Pavel Litvinov, who emigrated in 1974 after serving time in internal exile. The bulletin was published in New York by Valery Chalidze's Khronika Press. See Pavel Litvinov, "Political and Human Rights Tamizdat," in *Tamizdat: Publishing Russian Literature across Borders*, ed. Yasha Klots, special issue of *Wiener Slawistischer Almanach* 86 (Berlin: Peter Lang, 2021), 329–35.

70. Benjamin Nathans, "Talking Fish: On Soviet Dissident Memoirs," *Journal of Modern History* 87 (September 2015): 581.

71. By pointing out that until the fall of the USSR, dissident memoirs "could only be published outside the country in which their narrative takes place," Nathans, "Talking Fish," 581, effectively complicates Tzvetan Todorov's dictum that "genres communicate indirectly with the society where they are operative through their institutionalization," Tzvetan Todorov, *Genres in Discourse*, trans. Catherine Potter (New York: Cambridge University Press, 2001), 19.

72. Aleksandr Solzhenitsyn, *The Nobel Lecture on Literature*, trans. Thomas P. Whitney (New York: Harper & Row, 1972), 33.

73. That said, while the CIA supported tamizdat financially, it could hardly play the key role in the choice of manuscripts for publication or the editing process, for which task it employed Russian émigrés. On the CIA involvement in cultural politics and tamizdat in particular, see, for example, Alfred A. Reisch, *Hot Books in the Cold War: The CIA-Funded Secret Western Book Distribution Program behind the Iron Curtain* (Budapest: Central European University Press, 2014).

74. Ardis was rivaled, in this regard, only by the Herzen Foundation in Amsterdam, which specialized in dissident literature, as well as the Chekhov Publishing Corporation founded in New York in 1970 by Max Hayward and Edward Kline (not to be confused with the old émigré Chekhov Publishing House, or Izdatel'stvo imeni Chekhova, active in New York in 1952–1956). On the history of the latter, see Pavel Tribunsky, "Fond Forda, fond 'Svobodnaia

Rossiia' / Vostochno-evropeiskii fond i sozdanie 'Izdatel'stva imeni Chek-hova,'" in *Ezhegodnik Doma russkogo zarubezh'ia imeni Aleksandra Solzhenitsyna* (Moscow: Dom russkogo zarubezh'ia, 2014), 577–600; and Pavel Tribunsky, "Likvidatsiia 'Izdatel'stva imeni Chekhova,' Khristianskii soiuz molodykh liu-dei i 'Tovarishchestvo ob'edinennykh izdatelei,'" in *Ezhegodnik Doma russkogo zarubezh'ia imeni Aleksandra Solzhenitsyna* (Moscow: Dom russkogo zarubezh'ia, 2015), 646–715.

75. Joseph Brodsky, "In Memory of Carl Proffer," Joseph Brodsky Papers, Gen Mss 613, Box 123, Folder 2772, Beinecke Rare Book and Manuscript Library, Yale University; Iosif Brodsky, "Pamiati," 122–25.

76. Pospielovsky, "From Gosizdat," 52.

77. Ellendea Proffer Teasley, *Brodsky among Us: A Memoir* (Boston: Academic Studies Press, 2017), xvi. Carl Proffer, the author of *Keys to Lolita* (1968), cor-responded with Vladimir and Vera Nabokov from 1966 to 1977, including the months he and his wife spent in the Soviet Union in 1969. See Galina Glusha-nok and Stanislav Shvabrin, "Perepiska Nabokovykh s Profferami," trans., with a commentary by Nina Zhutovskaia, *Zvezda*, no. 7 (2005): 123–71; see also Aleksandr Dolinin, "Karl Proffer i Vladimir Nabokov: k istorii dialoga," *Novoe literaturnoe obozrenie*, no. 1 (2014): 145–52.

78. Proffer Teasley, *Brodsky among Us*, xvi.

79. Lev Loseff, *Joseph Brodsky: A Literary Life*, trans. Jane Ann Miller (New Haven, CT: Yale University Press, 2011), 176.

80. Brodsky, "In Memory of Carl Proffer."

81. Proffer Teasley, *Brodsky among Us,* xi.

82. For example, in a letter to his fellow émigré critic and poet Yury Ivask on May 20, 1972, Struve wrote: "You are asking about Ardis. I do not like Proffer, and I don't think he likes me either. . . . His wife I liked even less. . . . Both are impudently self-confident. . . . I wonder where he got the money? As for Filippov and myself, we cannot get any to keep our [publishing] business going" (George Ivask Papers, Box 6, Folder 28, Amherst Center for Russian Culture). Proffer, in turn, later noted that "the only comprehensive edition" of Mandelshtam's works prepared by Struve and Filippov in the early 1960s "has been published in the West with the help of CIA money" (Proffer, *Widows of Russia,* 26).

83. Third-wave publishing houses in the 1970–1980s included Maria Roza-nova and Andrei Sinyavsky's Sintaksis and a journal of the same name (Fon-tenay-aux-Roses, France), Igor Efimov's Hermitage (Ann Arbor, MI, and Tenafly, NJ), Aleksandr Sumerkin's Russica (New York), Valery Chalidze's Khronika Press (New York), Grigory Poliak's Silver Age Publishing (New York), to name but a few. On *Novyi amerikanets*, see Sergei Dovlatov, *Rech' bez povoda . . . Ili kolonki redaktora* (Moscow: Makhaon, 2006).

84. For example, next to Solzhenitsyn's works, YMCA-Press published the first edition of Venedikt Erofeev's *Moskva-Petushki* in 1977 after it appeared in Israel two years earlier in the émigré journal *Ami* 3 (1975): 95–165.

85. Olga Mayorova, preface to "Ann Arbor v russkoi literature," *Novoe liter-aturnoe obozrenie*, no. 1 (2014): 130–37.

86. Proffer Teasley, *Brodsky among Us,* xx.

87. Mark Lipovetsky, "A Monument to Russian Modernism: The Ardis Vision of Contemporary Russian Literature," in *Tamizdat: Publishing Russian Literature across Borders*, ed. Yasha Klots, special issue of *Wiener Slawistischer Almanach* 86 (Berlin: Peter Lang, 2021), 205. Although the final word in Ardis's repertoire belonged to Carl, the decisions were usually made in consultation with other editors and friends of the Proffers, some of whom lived in Ann Arbor upon emigrating to the United States (Joseph Brodsky, Lev Loseff, Masha Slonim, Aleksei Tsvetkov, Igor Efimov, among others). On the other hand, as Lipovetsky remarks, Ardis's decision not to proceed with the publication of Vasily Grossman's *Zhizn' i sud'ba* (*Life and Fate*) means that the Proffers' editorial preferences were not always directly in line with recommendations from the Moscow and Leningrad circles. In this case, the decision was mediated by Vladimir Maksimov, the editor of the Third-Wave *Kontinent* in Paris, who published only separate chapters of Grossman's novel in his journal, namely, no. 4 (1975): 179–216; no. 5 (1975): 7–39; no. 6 (1976): 151–71; no. 7 (1976): 95–112; no. 8 (1976): 111–33. According to Benedikt Sarnov, Maksimov gave the Proffers a rather sour evaluation of it. Benedikt Sarnov, "Kak eto bylo. K istorii publikatsii romana V. Grossmana 'Zhizn' i sud'ba," *Voprosy literatury*, no. 6 (2012): 9–47. *Zhizn' i sud'ba* first came out in tamizdat years later (Lausanne: L'Age d'Homme, 1980).

88. Proffer Teasley, *Brodsky among Us*, xx–xxi.

89. Serguei Oushakine, "The Terrifying Mimicry of Samizdat," *Public Culture* 13, no. 2 (Spring 2001): 196.

90. Quoted in Sophie Pinkham, "*Zdesizdat* and Discursive Rebellion: The *Metropol* Affair," *Ulbandus Review* 17 (2016): 130. Pinkham quotes a similar statement about *Metropol* made by no one other than Yury Andropov, then head of the KGB: "Dissident literature is Soviet literature with a minus sign: if in Soviet literature the secretary of the regional committee is a good person, then in anti-Soviet literature he is bad. Types trade places, but the consciousness is the same, with the same dogmatism and conservative taste," Pinkham, 130.

91. Pinkham, 130–31.

92. Vasily Aksenov, "The Metropol Affair," *Wilson Quarterly* 6, no. 5 (1982): 156.

93. Pinkham, "*Zdesizdat*," 132.

94. *Metropol'. Literaturnyi al'manakh* (Ann Arbor, MI: Ardis, 1979); *Metropol: Literary Almanac*, trans. Kevin Klose (New York: Norton, 1982).

95. See, for example, Helen Muchnic, "From Russia with Candor," review of *Metropol*, *New York Times*, February 27, 1983.

96. Quoted in Pinkham, "*Zdesizdat*," 140. Reviews of *Metropol* in *Russkaia mysl'* were not all negative. See, for example, Vladimir Maksimov, "Metropol' ili metropol'," review of *Metropol*, *Russkaia mysl'*, May 17, 1979.

97. Pinkham, "*Zdesizdat*," 145.

98. Brodsky, "In Memory of Carl Proffer."

99. Sinyavsky, "Dissent," 153.

100. Brodsky, "In Memory of Carl Proffer."

101. Brodsky.
102. Maria Rozanova, "Na raznykh iazykakh," in *Odna ili dve russkikh literatury?* ed. Georges Nivat (Geneva: Edition L'Age d'Homme, 1981), 207.
103. Olga Matich and Michael Heim, eds., *The Third Wave: Russian Literature in Emigration* (Ann Arbor, MI: Ardis, 1982), 82. The conference served as the main setting of Dovlatov's last novel *Filial* (*The Outpost*), whose title suggests a metonymical (i.e., mutually complementary, rather than exclusive) relationship between Russia and abroad. See also Olga Matich, *Zapiski russkoi amerikanki. Semeinye khroniki i sluchainye vstrechi* (Moscow: Novoe literaturnoe obozrenie, 2016), 323–36.
104. Zinovy Zinik, *Emigratsiia kak literaturnyi priem* (Moscow: Novoe literaturnoe obozrenie, 2011), 256.
105. Robert Darnton, *Censors at Work: How States Shaped Literature* (New York: Norton, 2014), 13.
106. Darnton.

1. Aleksandr Solzhenitsyn's *One Day in the Life of Ivan Denisovich* at Home and Abroad

1. Aleksandr Solzhenitsyn, *One Day in the Life of Ivan Denisovich*, trans. H.T. Willetts, with an introduction by Katherine Shonk (New York: Farrar, Straus & Giroux, 2005), 182.
2. Written in April 1962, Chukovsky's internal review of Solzhenitsyn's manuscript proclaimed that "a very strong, original and mature writer has entered literature" (Kornei Chukovsky, "Literaturnoe chudo," in his *Sobranie sochinenii v 15 tomakh* (Moscow: Agentstvo FTM, 2012), 10: 661–62).
3. Aleksandr Solzhenitsyn, *Publitsistika v 3 tomakh* (Yaroslavl': Verkhniaia Volga, 1997), 3: 25. A few lines down, Solzhenitsyn admits that the publication became possible thanks to "Tvardovsky and Khrushchev, as well as the historical moment—everything must have come together."
4. Apart from *Doctor Zhivago*, important exceptions include, among others, Akhmatova's "Poema bez geroia" ("Poem without a Hero"), first published in New York in 1960 and 1961 (*Vozdushnye puti* 1 (1960); 6–42; *Vozdushnye puti* 2 (1961): 111–53), Aleksandr Esenin-Vol'pin's book of poetry *A Leaf of Spring* (New York: Praeger, 1961), and Mikhail Naritsa's novella *Nespetaia pesnia* (*The Song Unsung*), published under the penname M. Narymov first in *Grani* 48 (1960): 5–113, and then as a separate edition (Frankfurt: Possev, 1964).
5. Aleksandr Solzhenitsyn, *Bodalsia telenok s dubom. Ocherki literaturnoi zhizni* (Moscow: Soglasie, 1996), 21–22. This and some other passages are missing from the first Russian edition of Solzhenitsyn's memoir (Paris: YMCA-Press, 1975), as well as from its English translation, Alexander Solzhenitsyn, *The Oak and the Calf: Sketches on Literary Life in the Soviet Union*, trans. Harry Willetts (New York: Harper & Row, 1979).
6. Solzhenitsyn, *Bodalsia telenok*, 36.
7. "On some ghostly, gelid plane," as Richard Tempest has noted, Solzhenitsyn's Ivan Denisovich and the countless other "shivering zeks join a

procession of other ragged figures . . . dragging themselves through the ice and snow like furtive Akaky Akakievich in Gogol's 'The Overcoat,'" Richard Tempest, *Overwriting Chaos: Aleksandr Solzhenitsyn's Fictive Worlds* (Boston: Academic Studies Press, 2019), 74.

8. Vladimir Voinovich, *Portret na fone mifa* (Moscow: Eksmo, 2002), 18-20.

9. Cf., "For no particular reason, I simply took *Shch-854* and copied it out in a 'lightened' version, leaving out the roughest episodes and expressions of opinion," Solzhenitsyn, *Oak and Calf*, 13. As he liberated his texts from "all that my fellow countrymen could hardly be expected to accept at once," Solzhenitsyn discovered "that a piece only gained, that its effect was heightened, as the harsher tones were softened," *Oak and Calf*, 11. In 1963, Solzhenitsyn repeated the procedure with his novel *In the First Circle*, whose original "heavier" ("atomic") version of ninety-six chapters was "watered down" to eighty-seven chapters, with major adjustments to the plot. Neither version, however, could be published in Russia. The "atomic" version of the novel first appeared in tamizdat five years later: Aleksandr Solzhenitsyn, *V kruge pervom* (New York: Harper & Row, 1968). For a comparative analysis of the novel's versions, see, for example, George Nivat, *Soljenitsyne* (Paris: Seuil, 1980), 211-28; Lev Loseff, *On the Beneficence of Censorship: Aesopian Language in Modern Russian Literature* (Munich: Otto Sanger, 1984), 143-67. Olga Carlisle's memoir *Solzhenitsyn and the Secret Circle* (London: Routledge & K. Paul, 1978) discusses its publication abroad.

10. Quoted in Michael Scammell, *Solzhenitsyn: A Biography* (New York: W. W. Norton, 1984), 413. Cf. Vissarion Belinsky's definition of Pushkin's *Eugene Onegin* as "a picture of the Russian society in a specific era that is poetically true to reality" and "a highly national work" [*v vysshei stepeni narodnoe proizvedenie*], Vissarion Belinsky, *Polnoe sobranie sochinenii v 13 tomakh* (Moscow: Izdatel'stvo AN SSSR, 1953-1959), 7: 445, 503.

11. Solzhenitsyn, *Oak and Calf*, 20-21. See, for example, Alexis Klimoff, "The Sober Eye: Ivan Denisovich and the Peasant Perspective," in *One Day in the Life of Ivan Denisovich: A Critical Companion*, ed. Alexis Klimoff (Evanston, IL: Northwestern University Press, 1997), 3-31.

12. Quoted in Scammell, *Solzhenitsyn*, 414.

13. Scammell, *Solzhenitsyn*, 417.

14. Solzhenitsyn, *Oak and Calf*, 18-19.

15. "They suggested that I make my short story 'weightier' by calling it a 'tale' [*povest'*]; right then, a tale it is. Then Tvardovsky said, in a manner that precluded argument, that the tale could never be published with a title like *Shch-854*. . . . Suggestions were tossed back and forth over the table, with Kopelev joining in, and our collective creative effort produced *One Day in the Life of Ivan Denisovich*," Solzhenitsyn, *Oak and Calf*, 24-25. The original title was evidently not only too cryptic but also too risky, as it invoked Zamiatin's dystopian novel *We*, banned in the Soviet Union: citizens of Zamiatin's One State, much like political prisoners in Stalin's camps, are identified by a letter and number instead of names. Solzhenitsyn's own number at the Ekibastuz camp was Shch-262, as can be seen on his photograph in camp uniform in 1953 (the

photograph is said to be staged). On July 23, 1962, Solzhenitsyn took part in another editorial meeting at *Novyi mir*, where he fought further changes suggested by members of the board but conceded to others. For example, the letter "kh" in certain "unprintable" words had to be replaced by "f," whereby the neologism *smekhuechki* became *smefuechki*, the phrase *"Khuimetsia!—podnimetsia!"* was softened to *"Fuimetsia!,"* and *maslitse da khuiaslitse* changed to *maslitse da fuiaslitse*, Solzhenitsyn, "Odin den' Ivana Denisovicha," *Novyi mir*, no. 11 (1962): 24, 12, 41.

16. Aleksandr Tvardovsky, *Novomirskii dnevnik. 1961–1966* (Moscow: PRO-ZAiK, 2009), 123. Solzhenitsyn lamented, however, that Tvardovsky "held up publication for eleven months," causing "an improper delay" that precluded his novel *In the First Circle* from being published in Russia while it was allegedly still possible: "I had a clear, a vivid picture of my work published in *Pravda* (circulation a tidy five million). I could almost see it with my eyes open. . . . Without Tvardovsky's assistance, any number of Twenty-second Congresses would not have helped. At the same time, how can I refrain from saying now that Tvardovsky let slip a golden opportunity. . . . Literature could have accelerated history. It failed to do so." Solzhenitsyn, *Oak and Calf*, 32–33.

17. Aleksandr Solzhenitsyn, *"Odin den' Ivana Denisovicha," Roman-Gazeta* 277, no. 1 (1963); Aleksandr Solzhenitsyn, *Odin den' Ivana Denisovicha* (Moscow: Sovetskii pisatel', 1963).

18. As recalled, for example, in Tomas Venclova, *Pogranich'e* (St. Petersburg: Izdatel'stvo Ivana Limbakha, 2015), 49.

19. Ernst Neizvestnyi, "Moi dialog s Khrushchevym," *Vremia i my* 41 (May 1979): 176. See also Nina Moleva, *Manezh. God 1962* (Moscow: Sovetskii pisatel', 1989), and Elii Beliutin, "Khrushchev v Manezhe," *Druzhba narodov*, no. 1 (1990): 139–42.

20. Quoted in Vladimir Tol'ts, "Dekabr' 1962. Manezh. 50 let spustia," *Radio Svoboda*, December 1, 2012, https://www.svoboda.org/a/24786334.html.

21. Solzhenitsyn, *Bodalsia telenok*, 62.

22. Toker, *Return*, 190.

23. Scammell, *Solzhenitsyn*, 383. Shukhov became the named "brother of Vasily Terkin" even before the novella was published, Chukovsky, "Literaturnoe chudo," 661. Cf., in turn, Solzhenitsyn's praise of Tvardovsky's *Vasily Terkin*, which he read "long ago, at the front." "Tvardovsky had succeeded in writing something timeless, courageous and unsullied, helped by a rare sense of proportion, all his own, or perhaps by a sensitive tact not uncommon among peasants. . . . Though he was not free to tell the whole truth about the war, Tvardovsky nevertheless always stopped just one millimeter short of falsehood, and nowhere did he ever overstep the one-millimeter mark. The result was a miracle," Solzhenitsyn, *Oak and Calf*, 14.

24. Aleksandr Tvardovsky, "Vasily Terkin na tom svete," *Izvestiia*, August 18, 1963; several days later, in *Novyi mir*, no. 8 (1963): 3–42, followed by a separate book edition the same year. An unauthorized version was published without the author's name earlier that year in the Munich-based almanac *Mosty* 10 (1963): 129–44. The editorial note stated that the manuscript was received by

the Polish Literary Institute (Instytut Literacki) in Paris from Moscow, where it circulated in handwritten form and was ascribed, "perhaps erroneously," to Tvardovsky (129). In his letter to Gleb Struve on December 20, 1962, the editor of *Mosty*, Gennady Khomiakov (aka Andreev), reported, "I received 'Vasily Terkin in the Other World' about ten days ago from Paris and squeezed it right away into the tenth issue. The work is far from a masterpiece, but worth printing, although I think it is a forgery, or rather, an imitation," Gleb Struve Collection, box 94, folder 11, Hoover Institution Archives, Stanford University. In 1953 a post–World War II defector and correspondent for Radio Free Europe, Vladimir Zhabinsky (aka S. Iurasov), published an "adaptation" of Tvardovsky's poem, *Vasily Terkin after the War*, S. Iurasov, *Vasily Terkin posle voiny* (New York: Izdatel'stvo imeni Chekhova, 1953) that "could evoke nothing but abomination," Aleksandr Tvardovsky, "Kak byl napisan Vasily Terkin (otvet chitateliam)," in *Sobranie sochinenii v 6 tomakh* (Moscow: Khudozhestvennaia literatura, 1980), 5: 141.

25. Tvardovsky, *Sobranie sochinenii*, 3: 256.

26. T. Chugunov, "Kto on? O 'druge detstva' Tvardovskogo," *Novyi zhurnal* 86 (1967): 78–93.

27. Solzhenitsyn, *Ivan Denisovich*, 13.

28. Eugenia Ginzburg, *Journey into the Whirlwind*, trans. Paul Stevenson and Max Hayward (New York: Harcourt, Brace & World, 1967), 3.

29. Denis Kozlov, *The Readers of Novyi Mir. Coming to Terms with the Stalinist Past* (Cambridge, MA: Harvard University Press, 2013), 164.

30. Kozlov, *The Readers of Novyi Mir*, 135, 158–59. Cf.: "There was always something wrong with the other manuscripts: either the picture was not authentic enough, muddled by fictionalization and clichéd literariness, or the author's vision was not sufficiently broad and the text did not live up to the demand of being history" (158–59).

31. Toker, *Return*, 192.

32. Toker.

33. Tvardovsky, *Novomirskii dnevnik*, 243.

34. Soon after the publication Dudintsev was criticized for vilifying Soviet society. Months after it appeared in *Novyi mir*, nos. 8–10 (1956): 31–118, 37–118, 21–98, the novel was published abroad twice in Russian (Munich: Tsentral'noe ob'edinenie politicheskikh emigrantov iz SSSR, 1957; New York: Novoe russkoe slovo, 1957) and foreign-language translations (*Not by Bread Alone*, trans. Edith Bone (New York: Dutton, 1957)).

35. In 1963 Shelest's short story was adapted to the screen under the title *If You Are Right* (*Esli ty prav*), dir. Yury Egorov. A film adaptation of Kaverin's novella, dir. Vladimir Motyl', on the other hand, remained unrealized: after the overthrow of Khrushchev in 1964, it did not pass censorship.

36. Solzhenitsyn, *Ivan Denisovich*, 70.

37. Mikhail Sholokhov, *Fierce and Gentle Warriors*, trans. Miriam Morton (New York: Doubleday, 1967), 98–99.

38. Grossman, *Zhizn' i sud'ba*. On the history of the first publication of Grossman's novel, see Semyon Lipkin, *Stalingrad Vasiliia Grossmana* (Ann Arbor:

Ardis, 1986); Sarnov, "Kak eto bylo;" Yury Bit-Iunan and David Feldman, "Intriga i sud'ba Vasiliia Grossmana," *Voprosy literatury*, no. 6 (2010): 153–82, as well as Bit-Iunan's and Feldman's two monographs, *Vasily Grossman: Literaturnaia biografiia v istoriko-politicheskom kontekste* (Moscow: Neolit, 2016) and *Vasily Grossman v zerkale literaturnykh intrig* (Moscow: Forum, 2016).

39. Anatoly Kuznetsov, "Baby Yar," *Iunost'*, nos. 8–10 (1966): 6–42, 15–46, 23–51, followed by a separate edition the next year (Moscow: Molodaia gvardiia, 1967). The uncensored version of Kuznetsov's *Baby Yar* appeared in tamizdat after the author defected to the West in 1969 (Frankfurt: Possev, 1970).

40. Lydia Ginzburg, "Zapiski blokadnogo cheloveka," *Neva*, no. 1 (1984): 84–108.

41. Emily van Buskirk and Andrei Zorin, eds., *Lydia Ginzburg's Alternative Literary Identities: A Collection of Articles and New Translations* (Vienna: Peter Lang, 2012), 14.

42. Lydia Ginzburg, *Prokhodiashchie kharaktery. Proza voennykh let. Zapiski blokadnogo cheloveka*, ed. Emily van Buskirk and Andrei Zorin (Moscow: Novoe izdatel'stvo, 2011), 546–47. The chapter was to describe one day in the life of one apartment building at 18 Mokhovaia Street in Leningrad.

43. Ginzburg, 453.

44. Ginzburg, 277–78.

45. Ginzburg, 314.

46. See also, "Automatization eats away at things, at clothes, at furniture, at our wives, and at our fear of war. . . . And so, in order to return sensation to our limbs, in order to make us feel objects, to make a stone feel stony, man has been given the tool of art. . . . By 'enstranging' objects and complicating form, the device of art makes perception long and 'laborious,'" Viktor Shklovsky, *Theory of Prose*, trans. Benjamin Sher, with an introduction by Gerald L. Bruns (Elmwood Park, IL: Dalkey Archive, 1991), 5–6.

47. Solzhenitsyn, *Ivan Denisovich*, 100–112. This famous scene of laying bricks in the work zone is foreshadowed by Shukhov's washing floors for the camp warders in the morning: "Now that Shukhov had a job to do, his body seemed to have stopped aching" (11). "There are," however, "two ends to a stick, and there's more than one way of working. If it's for human beings—make sure and do it properly. If it's for the big man—just make it look good" (14). The scenes of washing floors for the camp authorities in the morning and laying bricks for the future power station in the afternoon are those "two ends to a stick," or two different "ways of working."

48. Emily van Buskirk, "Lichnyi i istoricheskii opyt v blokadnoi proze Lidii Ginzburg," in Lydia Ginzburg, *Prokhodiashchie kharaktery*, 515.

49. In Solzhenitsyn's novella this line is drawn as early as in the morning of the day described, when, hoping to get a work exemption from Kolya Vdovushkin, a former literature student now holding a privileged job in the camp's infirmary, Shukhov noticed that Kolya was busy "writing lines of exactly the same length, leaving a margin and starting each one with a capital letter exactly below the beginning of the last," "nothing that Shukhov would have comprehended," although he realized "this wasn't work but something

on the side" (Solzhenitsyn, *Ivan Denisovich*, 20–23). This scene, too, places Ivan Denisovich and Kolya on opposite sides of the boundary between "the people" and the intelligentsia: "Can a man who's warm understand one who's freezing?" Solzhenitsyn, 24. It anticipates the conversation about Eisenstein, art and censorship between Tsezar, another *intelligent* in the camp, and prisoner Kh-123. Overhearing the conversation during the midday break, Shukhov "felt awkward interrupting this educated conversation, but he couldn't just go on standing there" Solzhenitsyn, 85.

    50. Lydia Ginzburg, *Prokhodiashchie kharaktery*, 453.

    51. In his review of the manuscript that helped publication, Chukovsky, unlike Ginzburg, praised Solzhenitsyn's use of free indirect discourse: "Although [Ivan Denisovich] is described in the third person, the entire short story is written in HIS language, which is full of humor, vivid and accurate. The author does not boast linguistic quirks . . ., does not make separate juicy words stand out (as does the tasteless Leskov); his speech is not a stylization but a live, organic speech free like a breath. Splendid national [*narodnaia*] speech mixed with camp argot. It is only by having mastered such language that one could touch on the subject matter that informs this short story." Chukovsky, "Literaturnoe chudo," 661; emphasis in the original.

    52. Lydia Ginzburg, *Prokhodiashchie kharaktery*, 556.

    53. Natalya Reshetovskaia, *Sanya: My Life with Aleksandr Solzhenitsyn*, trans. Elena Ivanoff (New York: Bobbs-Merrill, 1975), 211–12. Although this memoir by Solzhenitsyn's first wife infuriated the author (Solzhenitsyn, *Bodalsia telenok*, 329–30, 554) and caused a scandal in the émigré press (see, for example, Ekaterina Breitbart's review of *Sanya* in *Grani* 100 (1976): 505–11), this date—albeit with no connection to the Writers' Congress—is quoted in Solzhenitsyn's critical biographies (e.g., in Scammell, *Solzhenitsyn*, 382). See also, Liudmila Saraskina, *Aleksandr Solzhenitsyn* (Moscow: Molodaia Gvardiia, 2008), 457, "Was that day in late spring . . ., when on May 18, 1959, he began writing 'One Day of One Zek,' a random one in Solzhenitsyn's life? Was it by chance that the idea from ten years ago . . . came back to his memory? This could be anything but a coincidence."

    54. Nikita Khrushchev, *Sluzhenie narodu—vysokoe prizvanie sovetskikh pisatelei* (Moscow: Gosudarstvennoe izdatel'stvo politicheskoi literatury, 1959), 8.

    55. Quoted in Victor Terras, *Belinskij and Russian Literary Criticism* (Madison: University of Wisconsin Press, 1974), 3.

    56. Kozlov, *Readers*, 2.

    57. Abram Tertz, *The Trial Begins: On Socialist Realism*, trans. Max Hayward and George Dennis, with an introduction by Czesław Miłosz (Berkeley: University of California Press, 1982), 168.

    58. Solzhenitsyn, *Ivan Denisovich*, 181.

    59. Chukovsky, "Literaturnoe chudo," 661; emphasis in the original.

    60. Solzhenitsyn, *Ivan Denisovich*, 179.

    61. The food Tsezar gives Shukhov at the end of the day "rhymes" with an earlier episode in the morning, when he lets Shukhov have a drag off his cigarette.

62. Solzhenitsyn, *Ivan Denisovich*, 10–11, 73.

63. Solzhenitsyn, 132. While the camp itself is referred to as "home," Shukhov's campmates, by extension, are like a "family," which may be read as a reduced version of the "Great Family," a myth that "gives the socialist realist novel its backbone, or overarching structure," Katerina Clark, "Socialist Realism *with* Shores: The Conventions for the Positive Hero," in *Socialist Realism without Shores*, ed. Thomas Lahusen and Evgeny Dobrenko (Durham, NC: Duke University Press, 1997), 30.

64. Solzhenitsyn, *Ivan Denisovich*, 144.

65. Solzhenitsyn, 151, 161.

66. Solzhenitsyn, 181.

67. Aleksandr Solzhenitsyn, "Matrenin dvor," *Novyi mir*, no. 1 (1963): 42–63. The other short story by Solzhenitsyn published in the same issue was "An Incident at Krechetovka Station" ("Sluchai na stantsii Krechetovka").

68. Aleksandr Solzhenitsyn, *Stories and Prose Poems*, trans. Michael Glenny (New York: Farrar, Straus & Giroux, 2014), 52. As was the case with *One Day in the Life of Ivan Denisovich*, the title "Matrena's House" was also suggested by Tvardovsky. Solzhenitsyn's original title used the folk saying "No village stands without a righteous person" ("Ne stoit selo bez pravednika"), which informs the text's parable-like ending.

69. Aleksandr Solzhenitsyn, *V kruge pervom* (Paris: YMCA-Press, 1969), 465–66. Although Spiridon is ten years older than Ivan Denisovich, the novel was written earlier but kept secret due to its heavier political content. Cf. Shalamov's comment on Spiridon in his unsent letter to Solzhenitsyn: "Spiridon is a weak character, especially considering the topic of squealers and informers. There were especially many informers among the peasants. A peasant yard keeper is certainly a squealer and cannot be otherwise. As a symbolic image of people's suffering, this character is unsuitable." Varlam Shalamov, *Sobranie sochinenii*, 6: 314.

70. "The whole figure of Platon in his French greatcoat tied with a rope, in a peaked cap and bast shoes, was round, his head was perfectly round, his back, chest, shoulders, even his arms, which he held as if always about to embrace something, were round; his pleasant smile and his large, brown, tender eyes were round," Leo Tolstoy, *War and Peace*, trans. Richard Pevear and Larissa Volokhonsky (New York: Vintage, 2008), 972. On Shukhov and Karataev, see, for example, Maria Shneerson, *Aleksandr Solzhenitsyn. Ocherki tvorchestva* (Frankfurt: Possev, 1984), 113–17. The fact that Ivan Denisovich "seems to have walked out straight from the works of classical Russian literature to live in our times" was listed among the novella's "publishable" qualities no censor would argue against (as it was claimed in yet another internal review of *Ivan Denisovich* by Mikhail Lifshits, quoted in P. E. Spivakovsky and T. V. Esina, *Ivanu Denisovichu polveka. Iubileinyi sbornik. 1962–2012* (Moscow: Russkii put', 2012), 26). As for Matrena, Ludmila Koehler has traced her genealogy, along with Solzhenitsyn's use of *skaz*, to Nikolai Leskov's *Malania, the Mutton-Head* (*Malan'ia—golova baran'ia*, 1888), whose protagonist "was so called because she was considered a fool, and a fool she was deemed because she was more

mindful of others than of herself" (Ludmila Koehler, "Alexander Solzhenitsyn and Russian Literary Tradition," *Russian Review* 26, no. 2 (April 1967): 177).

71. *Tolstoy's Short Fiction*, ed. and trans. by Michael R. Katz, 2nd ed. (New York: Norton, 2008), 287. Cf. Solzhenitsyn's comment: "Of course, I could have described my whole ten years there, I could have done the whole history of the camps that way, but it was sufficient to gather everything into one day, all the different fragments . . . and to describe just one day in the life of an average and in no way remarkable prisoner from morning till night" (quoted in Scammell, *Solzhenitsyn*, 382). Somewhat more obvious are parallels between the later works of Tolstoy and Solzhenitsyn, including the latter's *August 1914* (1971). See, for example, Viktor Frank, "Solzhenitsyn i Tolstoi," in his *Izbrannye stat'i*, ed. Leonid Shapiro (London: Overseas Publications Interchange, 1974), 127–34.

72. Tertz, *Trial Begins*, 199–201. Comparing socialist realism with previous mindsets, Clark goes further: "Socialist realism represents something of a return (with differences, of course) to an earlier stage in literary evolution, the age of parable. Essentially, the socialist realist 'novel' is grounded in something comparable to the medieval worldview," while its mandate for a positive hero makes it akin to "medieval hagiography" or even a folktale, "though the two have different ideological underpinnings" (Clark, "Socialist Realism, 27–28, 42).

73. Samuil Marshak, "Pravdivaia povest'," *Pravda*, January 30, 1964. Marshak concludes his review by expressing the hope that "as long as Ivan Denisovich is alive and healthy [*zhiv-zdorov*], he has no doubt been long rehabilitated and employed."

74. Chukovsky, "Literaturnoe chudo," 662.

75. V. Pallon, "Zdravstvuite, katvorang," *Izvestiia*, January 14, 1964. It is, of course, possible to assume that Burkovsky was forced to say what he said in the interview, perhaps in exchange for keeping his high-ranking position as the curator of the Cruiser Aurora Museum. It is also true that his interview in *Izvestiia* "made perfect propaganda for the Lenin Prize," for which Solzhenitsyn was nominated (Scammell, *Solzhenitsyn*, 482). See, however, Solzhenitsyn's account of "varnishing" Burkovsky's character: "The main thing Lebedev demanded was that I should remove all passages in which Captain Buynovsky was shown as a comic figure . . . and that I should put more emphasis on his Party membership (there must, after all, be a 'positive hero'!). This seemed to me the lightest of sacrifices. I removed the comedy, and all that was left could be seen as 'heroic.' . . . The protest Buynovsky made on work parade now looked a little overdone (I had intended it to be comic), but this did not perhaps mar the picture of the camp" (Solzhenitsyn, *Oak and Calf*, 39–40).

76. Solzhenitsyn, *Oak and Calf*, 8.

77. Lev Kopelev, "Pis'mo Solzhenitsynu," *Sintaksis* 37 (2001): 92. Kopelev wrote his response in Cologne between January 30 and February 5, 1985. Solzhenitsyn's letter, as much of his personal correspondence, is unavailable. Reshetovskaia recalls that Kopelev went as far as to brand *Ivan Denisovich* as "a typical production novel" (quoted in Scammell, *Solzhenitsyn*, 408). Far from

favorable was the reaction to *Ivan Denisovich* of Dmitry Panin, another fellow prisoner of Solzhenitsyn's at Marfino and then at Ekibastuz, the prototype for Dmitry Sologdin in *In the First Circle*. In his letter to Kopelev from Paris on May 5, 1981, Panin wrote: "As for the phony Ivan Denisovich—he is an invention, and a talentless one at that. Never had I met anyone like him in my entire 16-year term" (Lev Kopelev Papers, Fond 3, Center for East European Studies). See Panin's memoirs, *The Notebooks of Sologdin*, trans. John Moore (London: Harcourt Brace Jovanovich, 1976); first Russian edition: *Zapiski Sologdina* (Frankfurt: Posev, 1973), as well as his *Solzhenitsyn i deistvitel'nost'* (Paris, 1975) and *Lubyanka-Ekibastuz. Lagernye zapiski* (Moscow: Skify, 1991).

78. See, for example, Heinrich Böll, "Foreword to *Cancer Ward* by Aleksandr Solzhenitsyn (1968)," in his *Missing Persons and Other Essays*, trans. Leila Vennewitz (Evanston, IL: Northwestern University Press, 1994), 257–61; Georg Lukács, "Solzhenitsyn and the New Realism," *Socialist Register* (1965): 197–215. In his review of *The Gulag Archipelago*, Brodsky calls Solzhenitsyn "the genius of socialist realism," adding wryly that "Soviet rule has perhaps acquired its Homer in Solzhenitsyn," Joseph Brodsky, "Geography of Evil," *Partisan Review*, no. 4 (1977): 639.

79. Tempest, *Overwriting Chaos*, 534.

80. Tempest.

81. Quoted in Tempest.

82. Andrew Wachtel, "One Day—Fifty Years Later," *Slavic Review* 72, no. 1 (Spring 2013): 116.

83. Tertz, *Trial Begins*, 134.

84. Claude Levi-Strauss, *Structural Anthropology*, trans. Claire Jacobson and Brooke Grundfest Schoepf (New York: Basic Books, 1963), 229.

85. Clark has proposed another geometrical shape as the basic structure of a socialist-realist novel: the parabola. Linked as it were with the folkloric genre of a parable, it "requires a recurring structure that can be read off for different historical meanings" (Clark, "Socialist Realism," 28). See also Nico Israel, *Spirals: The Whirled Image in Twentieth-Century Literature and Art* (New York: Columbia University Press, 2015).

86. Thomas Lahusen, "Socialist Realism in Search of Its Shores," in *Socialist Realism without Shores*, ed. Thomas Lahusen and Evgeny Dobrenko (Durham, NC: Duke University Press, 1997), 13.

87. Solzhenitsyn, *Ivan Denisovich*, 3.

88. Incidentally, Solzhenitsyn's play *The Love Girl and the Innocent* (first draft, *Republic of Labor*, written in 1954) kicks off with a similar image to mark the beginning of the daily cycle in a different camp: "Behind the curtain one can hear the harsh sound of a crowbar against a metal rail," *The Love Girl and the Innocent*, trans. Nicholas Bethell and David Burg (New York: Bantam Books, 1969); no page cited. Although it describes not one but several days at the end of a calendar year and features a more heterogeneous setting, *In the First Circle*, whose "atomic" version Solzhenitsyn completed before *Ivan Denisovich*, features a similar exposition: "The filigreed hands [of the clock that hung on the wall in Innokenty Volodin's office] pointed to five minutes past four. The bronze of

the clock was lusterless in the dying light of a December day." *In the First Circle*, trans. H. T. Willetts (New York: Harper & Collins, 2009), 1.

89. Eduardas Mieželaitis, "Stikhi," *Novyi mir*, no. 11 (1962): 3; quoted in Wachtel, "One Day," 109.

90. Wachtel, "One Day."

91. Wachtel.

92. Mieželaitis, "Stikhi," 4.

93. Wachtel, "One Day," 110.

94. Mieželaitis, "Stikhi," 5.

95. Mieželaitis, 6.

96. Mieželaitis, 7.

97. Varlam Shalamov, *Kolymskie rasskazy*, edited with an introduction by Mikhail Geller (London: Overseas Publications Interchange, 1978).

98. See, for example, Nikolai Ulianov, "Zagadka Solzhenitsyna," *Novoe russkoe slovo*, August 1, 1971. This scandalous article provoked heated debates in émigré circles and was even rumored to have been commissioned by the KGB.

99. Aleksandr Semenov-Tian'-Shan'sky (Episkop), "Den' Ivana Denisovicha," *Vestnik RSKhD* 106 (April 1972): 357. On Solzhenitsyn's relationships with the Third Emigration, see his essay "Our Pluralists" (first published in *Vestnik RKhD* 139 (1983): 133–60), as well as his memoirs *Between Two Millstones. Book 1, Sketches of Exile. 1974–1978*, trans. Peter Constantine (Notre Dame, IN: University of Notre Dame Press, 2018).

100. Both Russian editions were brought out by Flegon Press in 1962 and 1963, the latter being a mere photostat of the *Novyi mir* publication (on Flegon and his legal confrontations with Solzhenitsyn, see Alexander Jacobson, "Pirate, Book Artist: An Introduction to Alec Flegon," *Wiener Slavistisches Jahrbuch* 8 (2020): 240–53. The first two translations into English were made, respectively, by Max Hayward and Ronald Hingley, with an introduction by Hayward and Leopold Labedz (New York: Praeger, 1963) and Ralph Parker, with an introduction by Marvin L. Kalb (New York: Dutton, 1963). "Solzhenitsyn's Russian tragedy is now being followed by an American comedy," Sidney Monas wrote about the two publishers "competing to present this book to the American public," "Ehrenburg's Life, Solzhenitsyn's Day," *Hudson Review* 16, no. 1 (Spring 1963), 121. "The appearance of his work in English," according to Robert Conquest, "was an enormously different phenomenon from the mere 'translation' of a 'writer' in the ordinary sense," "Solzhenitsyn in the British Media," in *Solzhenitsyn in Exile*, ed. John B. Dunlop, Richard S. Haugh, and Michael Nicholson (Stanford, CA: Hoover Institution Press, 1984), 4. A TV adaptation of *Ivan Denisovich* was produced the same year by NBC (dir. Daniel Petrie, starring John Abbot), followed by a Norwegian feature film in 1970 (dir. Caspar Wrede).

101. Fedor Abramov, "Vokrug da okolo," *Neva*, no. 1 (1963): 109–37; Fyodor Abramov, *One Day in the New Life*, trans. David Floyd (New York: Praeger, 1963). Soon after publishing Abramov's work in his journal, the editor of *Neva*, Sergei Voronin, was compelled to resign for lack of literary vigilance.

102. David Burg, "O rasskaze Solzhenitsyna 'Psy,' padenii Khrushcheva i sud'be Tvardovskogo," *Posev*, December 18, 1964. Vladimov's novel *Faithful Ruslan (Vernyi Ruslan)*, which portrays the closing of the camps and the onset of the Thaw from the perspective of a guard dog, began circulating anonymously in samizdat soon after the publication of *Ivan Denisovich*. It took a decade for the novel to appear in tamizdat: Georgy Vladimov, *Vernyi Ruslan. Istoriia karaul'noi sobaki* (Frankfurt: Possev, 1975).

103. Polly Jones, "The Thaw Goes International. Soviet Literature in Translation and Transit in the 1960s," in *The Socialist Sixties: Crossing Borders in the Second World*, ed. Anne E. Gorsuch and Diane P. Koenker (Bloomington: Indiana University Press, 2013), 121. "Ironically," Jones notes, "it was the Soviet authorities' refusal to join the international agreement on copyright that helped to 'internationalize' Soviet literature during this time, allowing multiple editions of the same text to coexist and often to fuel greater media interest," Jones, 124.

104. Evgeny Garanin, "Povest', posle kotoroi pisat' po-staromu nel'zia . . . Ob 'Odnom dne Ivana Denisovicha' A.I. Solzhenitsyna," *Posev*, December 23, 1962.

105. F. D. Reeve, "The House of the Living," *Kenyon Review*, no. 2 (Spring 1963): 357.

106. Roman Gul', "A. Solzhenitsyn, sotsrealizm i shkola Remizova," *Novyi zhurnal* 71 (1963): 60.

107. Arkady Slizskoi, "'Odin den'.' Povest' Solzhenitsyna," *Russkaia mysl'*, December 25, 1962.

108. Reeve, "House," 356–57.

109. Books cited especially often in this regard include *Russia in Chains (Rossiia v kontslagere)* by Ivan Solonevich (1934), *Conquerors of White Spots (Zavoevateli belykh piaten)* by Mikhail Rozanov (1951), *A Journey to the Land of the Zek (Puteshestvie v stranu ze-ka)* by Yuli Margolin (1952), *Prisons and Exiles (Tiur'my i ssylki)* by Ivanov-Razumnik (1953), *Eight Years in the Grip of the Lubyanka (Vosem' let vo vlasti Lubianki)* by Yury Tregubov (1957), *Difficult Roads (Trudnye dorogi)* by Gennady Andreev (1959). There had been even earlier publications on the gulag in the West, for example, *My Twenty-Six Prisons and My Escape from Solovki (Dvadtsat' shest' tiurem i pobeg s Solovkov)* by Yury Bezsonov (1928), *Ten Months in Bolshevik Prisons* by Irene Doubassoff (1926), and *An Island Hell: A Soviet Prison in the Far North* by S.A. Malsagoff (1926). As a result of the Sikorski Amnesty of 1941, when Stalin released Polish prisoners to fight Nazi Germany on his side under General Anders, Polish sources on the gulag began to appear in the West soon after the war. While Gustaw Herling's *A World Apart (Inny świat*, first published in Joseph Marek's English translation in 1951) stands out for its literary quality, it was preceded by Sylvester Mora and Peter Zwierniak's *La Justice Soviétique* (1945), David J. Dallin and Boris I. Nikolayevsky's study *Forced Labor in Soviet Russia* (1947), Joseph Czapski's *The Inhuman Land (Na nieludzkiej ziemi*, 1947), as well as the anthology *The Dark Side of the Moon* with a preface by T. S. Eliot (1946).

110. Leona Toker, *Gulag Literature and the Literature of Nazi Camps: An Intercontextual Reading* (Bloomington: Indiana University Press, 2019), 63.

111. Gleb Struve, "O povesti A. Solzhenitsyna," *Russkaia mysl'*, February 12, 1963. The general tendency to read even fictional accounts of the gulag as documentary prose is revealed in one of the earliest reviews of *Ivan Denisovich* in the émigré press, where the novella is called "memoirs [*vospominaniia*]," K. Gushchin, "Sobytie, o kotorom zagovorila vsia strana," *Posev*, December 14, 1962.

112. F. M. Dostoevsky, *Zapiski iz mertvago doma* (St. Petersburg: Tipografiia Eduarda Pratsa, 1862), with the censor's permission dated January 8, 1962. The novel was previously serialized for two years in the journals *Russkii mir* and *Vremia*.

113. Monas, "Ehrenburg's Life," 119.

114. Reeve, "House," 360.

115. Viacheslav Zavalishin, "Povest' o 'mertvykh domakh' i sovetskom krest'ianstve," *Grani* 54 (1963): 133–34. Nowhere does Zavalishin admit, however, that the Soviet biopic, *The House of the Dead, or the Prison of Peoples* (*Mertvyi dom, ili tiur'ma narodov*, dir. Vasily Fedorov) was commissioned to expose the vices of the tsarist regime, with Dostoevsky portrayed as a rebel and one of its victims. The film was produced in 1932, shortly before Dostoevsky was banned for the rest of the Stalin period.

116. The publication of Dostoevsky's works resumed during the first year of the Thaw: F. M. Dostoevsky, *Sobranie sochinenii v 10 tomakh* (Moscow: Gosudarstvennoe izdatel'stvo khudozhestvennoi literatury, 1956–1958).

117. Aleksandr Obolensky, "Alesha Dostoevskogo i Solzhenitsyna," *Russkaia mysl'*, September 7, 1972.

118. Tatiana Lopukhina-Rodzianko, *Dukhovnye osnovy tvorchestva Solzhenitsyna* (Frankfurt: Possev, 1974), 57.

119. Mihajlo Mihajlov, *Leto moskovskoe 1964. Mertvyi dom Dostoevskogo i Solzhenitsyna*, trans. Iaroslav Trushnovich (Frankfurt: Possev, 1967), 141.

120. Aleksandr Tvardovsky, foreword to "Odin' den' Ivana Denisovicha," by Aleksandr Solzhenitsyn, *Novyi mir*, no. 11 (1962): 8.

121. Mihajlov, *Leto moskovskoe 1964*, 143.

122. Mihajlov, 144.

123. Leonid Rzhevsky, *Prochtenie tvorcheskogo slova: literaturovedcheskie problemy i analizy* (New York: New York University Press, 1970), 252.

124. Fyodor Dostoevsky, *Memoirs from the House of the Dead*, trans. Jessie Coulson, with an introduction and notes by Ronald Hingley (Oxford: Oxford University Press, 2001), 24.

125. Rzhevsky, *Prochtenie tvorcheskogo slova*, 248.

126. Aleksandr Solzhenitsyn, *The Gulag Archipelago, 1918–1956: An Experiment in Literary Investigation*, trans. Thomas P. Whitney. 3 vols. (New York: Harper & Row, 1973), 2: 258–59.

127. "I do not think that *One Day* is a 'literary masterpiece' or a 'great work of art.' . . . The publication of this book was a political sensation, not a literary one," wrote Thomas F. Magner in his review in *Slavic and East European Journal* 7, no. 4 (Winter 1963): 418. He was echoed by David Stewart Hull: "*Ivan Denisovich* contains little . . . of stylistic interest to distinguish it from

the usual run of socialist-realist fiction," *Russian Review* 22, no. 3 (July 1963): 337. Irina Shapiro, on the other hand, maintained in her review that "Solzhenitsyn's style, skillfully interwoven as it is with the content, raises Ivan Denisovich's story high above the level of a mere ideological weapon, giving it flesh and blood," *Slavic Review* 22, no. 2 (June 1963): 377.

128. Georgy Adamovich, review of *Odin den' Ivana Denisovicha*, by Aleksandr Solzhenitsyn, *Russkaia mysl'*, January 3, 1963.

129. Georgy Adamovich, "Stikhi avtora 'Kolymskikh Rasskazov,' " *Russkaia mysl'*, August 24, 1967.

130. Gleb Struve, "O povesti Solzhenitsyna." See also his essay "After the Coffee-Break," *New Republic* 148 (February 2, 1963): 15–16. In his letter to Yury Ivask, Struve referred to Solzhenitsyn as "modesty incarnate" [*sama skromnost'*] and suggested that there is "something Chekhovian in him" (George Ivask Papers, Box 6, Folder 26. Amherst Center for Russian Culture).

131. Gul', "Solzhenitsyn," 58–59, 61.

132. Gul', 61.

133. The lineage between Remizov and Solzhenitsyn was questioned, for example, by Leonid Rzhevsky in "The New Idiom," in *Soviet Literature in the Sixties: An International Symposium*, ed. Max Hayward and Edward L. Crowley (New York: Praeger, 1964), 76. Ludmila Koehler argued that while "Remizov searched for his 'magic names' in old exorcism-charms, invocations, incantations, in the scribe-language of seventeenth-century Moscow, as well as in the popular speech of that period," "Solzhenitsyn's idiom is of a different nature entirely; it is a mixture of popular speech and Soviet slang," "Solzhenitsyn," 179.

134. Gul', "Solzhenitsyn," 65.

135. Gul', 69.

136. Gul', 74.

137. Garanin, "Povest'."

138. Grigory Baklanov, "Chtob eto nikogda ne povtorilos,' " *Literaturnaia gazeta*, November 22, 1962.

139. Garanin, "Povest'."

140. V. O. "Odin den' Ivana Denisovicha," *Chasovoi* 441 (February 1963): 15; emphasis in the original. The next issue of the periodical published a "letter to the editor" by a younger émigré, who complained that "the goal set forth by Solzhenitsyn's novella, designed as it were for the Party masses and foreign observers, has indeed been achieved. It is easy to get entangled in the nets of 'Ivan Denisovich' and Evgeny Evtushenko. . . Our émigré press has gotten itself trapped," "Syn ottsu," *Chasovoi* 442 (March 1963): 17.

141. See, e.g., "About the Past in the Name of the Future" ("O proshlom vo imia budushchego") by Konstantin Simonov; "So That It Never Repeats Itself" ("Chtob eto nikogda ne povtorilos' ") by Grigory Baklanov; "In the Name of Truth, In the Name of Life" ("Vo imia pravdy, vo imia zhizni") by Vladimir Ermilov; "Man Is Alive" ("Zhiv chelovek") by Aleksandr Dymshits; "The Grand Truth" ("Bol'shaia pravda") by Vladimir Ilyichev, to name only a few.

142. Vladimir Lakshin, "Ivan Denisovich, ego druz'ia i nedrugi," *Novyi mir*, no. 1 (1964): 245.

143. Toker, *Return*, 74.
144. Jones, "Thaw Goes International," 135.
145. Reeve, "House," 360, 357.
146. Quoted in Lahusen, "Socialist Realism," 5.
147. Wachtel, "One Day," 115–17.
148. From 1968 and until perestroika, all other writings by Solzhenitsyn could only be published abroad, where most of them, especially *The Gulag Archipelago*, became bestsellers. The stories of their first publications and reception in tamizdat deserve a separate study, which this book, regrettably, has no room to accommodate.

2. Anna Akhmatova's *Requiem* and the Thaw

1. A volume of Akhmatova's selected poetry was published by Chekhov Publishing House in New York in 1952, the first year of the press's operation: Anna Akhmatova, *Izbrannye stikhotvoreniia* (New York: Izdatel'stvo imeni Chekhova, 1952). This early tamizdat edition did not, however, include any of Akhmatova's unpublished poems and was based instead on her prewar volume *Iz shesti knig* (Leningrad: Sovetskii pisatel', 1940), with the addition of a few later texts published in the USSR during and after the war. In his annihilating review, Boris Filippov claimed that as a result of taking Soviet publications as their primary source, the editors of Chekhov Publishing House regrettably overlooked poems with religious themes, those dedicated to Nikolai Gumilev, or containing references to Soviet reality, many of which are first mentioned or extensively quoted by Filippov, Review of *Izbrannye stikhotvoreniia*, by Anna Akhmatova, *Novyi zhurnal* 32 (1953): 300–305. See Pavel Tribunsky, "'Izbrannye stikhotvoreniia' A.A. Akhmatovoi (1952): istoriia izdaniia," in *Izdatel'skoe delo rossiiskogo zarubezh'ia (XIX–XX vv.)*, ed. Pavel Tribunsky (Moscow: Russkii put', 2017), 321–28. In 1959 and 1960, Akhmatova's "Poem without a Hero" was published twice in two different versions in the New York almanac *Vozdushnye puti* 1 (1960): 5–42, and 2 (1961): 111–52.
2. Amanda Haight, *Anna Akhmatova: A Poetic Pilgrimage* (New York: Oxford University Press, 1976), 168.
3. Besides publications in Soviet periodicals, Akhmatova's lifetime editions in Russia included *Stikhotvoreniia* (1958), followed by *Stikhotvoreniia. 1909–1960* (Moscow: Khudozhestvennaia literatura, 1961) and *Beg vremeni. Stikhotvoreniia 1909–1965* (Moscow: Sovetskii pisatel', 1965).
4. See Franklin D. Reeve, *Robert Frost in Russia* (Boston: Little, Brown, 1964), 83–84. Akhmatova's meeting with Frost took place at the dacha of Professor Alekseev in Komarovo.
5. "Enough! Join in the Dancing! / But by what necromancy / Am I living and they dead?" [*Veselit'sia—tak veselit'sia!—/ Tol'ko kak zhe moglo sluchit'sia, / Chto odna ia iz nikh zhiva?*], Anna Akhmatova, *Requiem and Poem without a Hero*, trans. D.M. Thomas (Athens: Ohio University Press, 1978), 43; Anna Akhmatova, *Poema bez geroia* (Ann Arbor, MI: Ardis, 1978), 23.
6. Yury Trubetskoi, "Ob Anne Akhmatovoi," *Russkaia mysl'*, June 23, 1964. Trubetskoi (aka Yury Nolden), like many Second Wave émigrés, was a gulag

prisoner in the 1930s and then a Nazi collaborator. After the war he published two books of poetry in Paris (*Dvoinik* in 1954 and *Ternovnik* in 1962) and wrote for émigré periodicals.

7. Georgy Ivanov, *Peterburgskie zimy* (Paris: La Source, 1928), 66–67. According to Akhmatova, what Viacheslav Ivanov actually said when she first visited his "tower" in 1910 was, "What turgid romanticism!" [*Kakoi gustoi romantizm!*], which she took for "a rather questionable compliment," Anna Akhmatova, *Zapisnye knizhki Anny Akhmatovoi (1958–1966)*, ed. K. N. Suvorova, with an introduction by Emma Gershtein (Torino: Giulio Einaudi Editore, 1996), 80. See, for example, Akhmatova's letter to Alexis Rannit, Estonian poet, translator, and librarian at Yale: "I was pleased to learn that your opinion of Georgy Ivanov is the same as mine. . . . Consequently, having read your work, I will not yet again have to experience the kind of feeling described in the last chapter of Kafka's *The Trial*, when the protagonist is led through the brightly lit and quite well-maintained city of Prague only to be slaughtered at the end in a dark barn" (quoted in Chukovskaia, *Zapiski*, 2: 706). Another émigré whose memoirs enraged Akhmatova was Sergei Makovsky, the former editor of *Apollon*, where she published her early poetry. See his "Nikolai Gumilev po lichnym vospominaniiam," *Novyi zhurnal* 77 (1964): 157–89, and *Na Parnase Serebrianogo veka* (Munich: Tsentral'noe ob'edinenie politicheskikh emigrantov iz SSSR, 1962). Ironically, the same year as Akhmatova's *Requiem* appeared in Munich, Makovsky published his own collection of poetry under the same title: Sergei Makovsky, *Requiem* (Paris: Rifma, 1963). Finally, Akhmatova disagreed with the introduction to Gumilev's collected works authored by Gleb Struve, the future publisher of her *Requiem*. Gleb Struve, "N. S. Gumilev. Zhizn' i lichnost'," in *Nikolai Gumilev, Sobranie sochinenii v 4 tomakh*, ed. Gleb Struve and Boris Filippov (Washington DC: Victor Kamkin, 1962–1968), 1: vii–xliv.

8. Morhsen's letter to Struve on March 13, 1966. Gleb Struve Collection, box 108, folder 10, Hoover Institution Archives, Stanford University.

9. "I should like to call you all by name, / But they have lost the lists. . . . // I have woven from them a great shroud / Out of the poor words I overheard them speak" [*Khotelos' by vsekh poimenno nazvat', / Da otniali spisork, i negde uznat'. // Dlia nikh sotkala ia shirokii pokrov / Iz bednykh, u nikh zhe podslushannykh slov*]. Akhmatova, *Requiem and Poem without a Hero*, 31; Anna Akhmatova, *Requiem*. 2nd ed., revised by the author, with an afterword by Gleb Struve (Munich: Tovarishchestvo zarubezhnykh pisatelei, 1969), 20.

10. Georgy Adamovich, "Na poliakh 'Rekviema' Anny Akhmatovoi," *Mosty* 11 (1965): 210. Such a reading of *Requiem* was widespread not only among émigré critics, but also among western Slavists. See, e.g., Sam N. Driver, *Anna Akhmatova* (New York: Twayne 1972), 125: "An amazingly powerful statement which requires no elaboration or 'explanation.'"

11. Not only in *Requiem* but in her other poems too Akhmatova consistently imagines herself in their place, whether awaiting a verdict on the defendant's bench and wearing a camp uniform, as in "Imitation of Kafka" ("Podrazhanie Kafke") of 1960, or as their "double," in "Poem without a Hero: "And behind barbed wire / In the dense taiga's heart / —I don't know in what year / Transformed to a pile of camp-dust, an / Anecdote from the terrible fact— / My

double goes to interrogation" [*A za provolokoi koliuchei, / V samom serdtse taigi dremuchei— / Ia ne znaiu, kotoryi god— / Stavshii gorst'iu lagernoi pyli, / Stavshii skazkoi iz strashnoi byli, / Moi dvoinik na dopros idet*]. Akhmatova; *Requiem and Poem without a Hero*, 66; Akhmatova, *Poema bez geroia*, 58.

12. Grynberg co-edited (with V. L. Pastukhov) only the first three issues of *Opyty*. The remaining six were edited by Yury Ivask. On the history of *Opyty*, see Vladimir Khazan, "'My sluzhim ne partiiam, ne gosudarstvu, a cheloveku": iz istorii zhurnala 'Opyty' i al'manakha 'Vozdushnye puti,'" *Toronto Slavic Quarterly* 29 (2009), http://sites.utoronto.ca/tsq/29/hazan29.shtml; Oleg Korostelev, "Zhurnal 'Opyty' (New York, 1953–1958). Issledovaniia i materialy," *Literaturovedcheskii zhurnal* 17 (2003): 97–368.

13. Undated. Quoted in Roman Timenchik, *Poslednii poet: Anna Akhmatova v 60-e gody* (Moskva: Mosty kul'tury—Gesharim, 2014), 1: 143. The preface to the almanac's first issue reiterates that the title was chosen "to emphasize the illusory nature of obstacles set up in vain between us," *Vozdushnye puti* 1 (1960): 3.

14. Quoted in Timenchik, *Poslednii poet*, 1: 143.

15. *Vozdushnye puti* 1 (1960): 3. Only separate parts of "Poem without a Hero" had appeared previously in the Soviet Union, in *Leningrad*, no. 10–11 (1944), *Leningradskii al'manakh* (1945), *Antologiia russkoi sovetskoi poezii* (1957) and *Moskva*, no. 7 (1959).

16. Tatiana Dviniatina and Natalia Kraineva, "Acumiana P. N. Luknitskogo 1962 g. v fondakh IRLI i RNB," in *Ezhegodnik rukopisnogo otdela Pushkinskogo doma na 2011 god* (St. Petersburg: Pushkinskii dom, 2012), 762.

17. On the history of their relationships, see Rashit Iangirov, "Roman Grynberg i Roman Iakobson. Materialy k istorii vzaimootnoshenii," in *Roman Iakobson: Teksty, Dokumenty, Issledovaniia*, ed. Henryk Baran (Moscow: RGGU, 1999), 201–12. While Grynberg's friendship with Jakobson in emigration gradually withered, in 1940 Grynberg became a friend and correspondent of Vladimir and Vera Nabokov, as well as of Edmund Wilson. See Rashit Iangirov, "'Drebezzhan'e moikh rzhavykh strun . . .': iz perepiski Vladimira i Very Nabokovykh i Romana Grynberga (1940–1967)," in *In Memoriam: Istoricheskii sbornik pamiati A. I. Dobkina*, ed. Vladimir Aloi and Tatiana Pritykina (St. Petersburg: Feniks—Athenaeum, 2000), 345–97; and Rashit Iangirov, "Druz'ia, babochki i monstry: iz perepiski Vladimira i Very Nabokovykh s Romanom Grynbergom (1943–1967)," *Diaspora: novye materialy* 1 (2001): 477–556.

18. See Akhmatova's diary entries from December 1962 and August 15, 1964 (*Zapisnye knizhki*, 266–67, 480).

19. On Akhmatova and Isaiah Berlin, see, for example, György Dalos, *The Guest from the Future: Anna Akhmatova and Isaiah Berlin*, trans. Antony Wood (New York: Farrar, Straus & Giroux, 1999); and Isaiah Berlin, *Personal Impressions*, ed. Henry Hardy, with an introduction by Noel Annan, 2nd ed. (Princeton, NJ: Princeton University Press, 2001), 198–254. In the summer of 1956, three years before Moser, Berlin "was on a visit to Russia [and] telephoned to ask her if they could meet. Akhmatova refused, terrified that it might result in the re-arrest of her son. Their conversation and the present impossibility of meeting brought back vividly to Akhmatova their meeting in 1946. This time,

however, their only contact must be a 'non-meeting'" (Haight, *Akhmatova*, 168). Akhmatova believed that her meeting with Berlin in 1946, when she recited to him the early drafts of "Poem without a Hero," not only earned her the Zhdanov decree (*postanovlenie*) the same year but also nearly triggered the Cold War. See Akhmatova, *Requiem and Poem without a Hero*, 38; Akhmatova, *Poema bez geroia*, 15: "And behind it will come a man / Who won't become my husband, yet together / We shall deserve such things / That the twentieth century will stand agape" [*On ne stanet mne milym muzhem / No my s nim takoe zasluzhim, / Chto smutitsia dvadtsatyi vek*].

20. Grynberg's archive contains no correspondence with Moser (Vozdush-nye Puti Records, Library of Congress). Nor is Grynberg or his almanac mentioned in Moser's memoir "U Anny Akhmatovoi," *Grani* 73 (1969): 171–74.

21. *Vozdushnye puti* 2 (1961): 5. This issue also featured fifty-seven previously unpublished poems by Mandelshtam.

22. Evgeniia Klebanova [N. N-ko, pseud.], "Moi vstrechi s Annoi Akhmato-voi," *Novoe russkoe slovo*, March 13, 1966. The final redaction of "Poem without a Hero," however, was not completed until 1963, with further minor changes introduced as late as 1965. Three years after it first appeared in *Vozdushnye puti*, the poem was published in the Soviet almanac *Den' poezii 1963* in Moscow. See Chukovskaia, *Zapiski*, 3: 128; diary entry on December 20, 1963. Akhmatova received a copy of the Munich edition of *Requiem* five days later, Chukovskaia, 130–31.

23. Klebanova, "Moi vstrechi."

24. For details on Klebanova's meeting with Akhmatova, see Timenchik, *Po-slednii poet*, 1: 201–5. Since then, she occasionally corresponded with Akhmatova and is mentioned in the poet's notebooks (Akhmatova, *Zapisnye knizhki*, 96, 330, 312), as well as in Kornei Chukovsky's correspondence with Grynberg. See Leonid Rzhevsky, "Zagadochnaia korrespondentka Korneia Chukovsogo," *Novyi zhurnal* 123 (1976): 98–164.

25. Oleg Korostelev, "Perepiska G. V. Adamovicha s R. N. Grynbergom: 1953–1967," *Literaturovedcheskii zhurnal* 17 (2003): 159; emphasis in the original.

26. Moser, "U Anny Akhmatovoi," 172.

27. Moser, 173.

28. Chukovskaia, *Zapiski*, 2: 371; diary entry of February 20, 1960.

29. Roman Grynberg [Erge, pseud.], "Chitaia 'Poemu bez geroia,'" *Vozdu-shnye puti* 3 (1963): 295–300. We do not know Akhmatova's opinion of Gryn-berg's review, but in January 1962 she became familiar with an earlier review of her poem by Boris Filippov, "'Poema bez geroia' Akhmatovoi," *Vozdushnye puti* 2 (1961): 167–83, that left her generally satisfied, although she regretted that the initials "V.K." were mistakenly ascribed to Vasily Komarovsky instead of Vsevolod Kniazev, one of the poem's addressees. Chukovskaia, *Zapiski*, 2: 476).

30. Quoted in Timenchik, *Poslednii poet*, 2: 349.

31. Innokenty Basalaev, "Zapisi besed s Akhmatovoi (1961–1963)," ed. E. M. Tsarenkova, I. Kolosov, and N. Kraineva, *Minuvshee: Istoricheskii al'manakh* 23 (1998): 574. The playwright Aleksandr Gladkov met Akhmatova at the same hospital two weeks later and also heard her refer to Grynberg's postcard as "a letter from the shark of capitalism," although in Gladkov's diary entry on

December 20, 1961, Grynberg is mistakenly called "Filippov." Gladkov, *O poetakh, sovremennikakh i—nemnogo o sebe . . . (Iz dnevnikov i zapisnykh knizhek)*, ed. Mikhail Mikheev (Moscow: YASK, 2018), 111. That day Gladkov heard Akhmatova recite the epilogue of *Requiem* to him: "I told her that 'Requiem' must be written down. . . . She asked: 'You think it is possible?' 'Yes, yes, it is both possible and necessary to send it to all the publishing houses. . . . ' She smiled incredulously." Gladkov, 114–15.

32. Chukovskaia, *Zapiski*, 3: 294; diary entry of June 25, 1965. In addition to "Poem without a Hero," Grynberg published Akhmatova's memoirs about Amedeo Modigliani and Osip Mandelshtam, *Vozdushnye puti* 4 (1965): 15–43. On June 12, 1965, Struve reported to Filippov from England, "It was explained to Grynberg, who has produced a hideous impression on many people here, that Akhmatova is upset about not having received anything for the publication of her works in *V[ozdushnye] p[uti]*. First, he reacted by claiming that in this matter, the Soviet law is on his side (he told this to I. M. Berlin), then added (to V. S. Frank) that 'she is not living a bad life even without it' [*ei i bez togo khorosho zhivetsia*] (Frank was completely shocked . . .). Still, later Grynberg sent her a certain amount in an envelope (I don't know if she agreed to see him in person; it appears she did not), with a note that he publishes *V[ozdushnye] p[uti]* not for profit; she returned the money to him (apparently, a small amount), saying she does not take 'tips.'" Gleb Struve Collection, box 84, folder 3; quoted in Timenchik, *Poslednii poet*, 1: 439–40.

33. Korostelev, "Perepiska," 149–50.

34. Georgy Adamovich, "'Podarok Pasternaku'. Al'manakh 'Vozdushnye mosty'" [sic!], *Novoe russkoe slovo*, December 6, 1959.

35. Roman Timenchik and Vladimir Khazan, *Peterburg v poezii russkoi emigratsii (pervaia i vtoraia volna)*, with an introduction and commentary by the editors (St. Petersburg: Akademicheskii proekt, 2006), 89.

36. Joseph Brodsky, *Less Than One: Selected Essays* (New York: Farrar, Straus & Giroux, 1986), 91.

37. Georgy Adamovich, "Meetings with Anna Akhmatova," in *Anna Akhmatova and Her Circle*, ed. Konstantin Polivanov, trans. Patricia Beriozkina (Fayetteville: University of Arkansas Press, 1994), 71–72. Adamovich's memoir first appeared in *Vozdushnye puti* 5 (1967): 99–114.

38. Akhmatova, *Poema bez geroia*, 61; Akhmatova, *Requiem and Poem*, 68. These final lines of the poem were different in the earlier redaction available to Adamovich at the time he wrote his review. In the Soviet editions the ending was also different: "Young and loyal to her duty / Russia marched to save Moscow" [*Dolgu vernaia, molodaia / Shla Rossiia—spasat' Moskvu*] (quoted as a footnote in Akhmatova, *Poema bez geroia*, 61).

39. Adamovich, "Meetings with Akhmatova," 75. The article was written by the émigré poet Elena Grot and published when Akhmatova was already in Europe. Elena Grot, "Anna Akhmatova," *Novoe russkoe slovo*, June 6, 1965.

40. Adamovich, "Meetings with Akhmatova," 75–76. See, for example, Adamovich's letter to Mark Weinbaum, the editor of *Novoe russkoe slovo*, in Timenchik, *Poslednii poet*, 1: 459.

41. Akhmatova, *Poema bez geroia*, 60; Akhmatova, *Requiem and Poem*, 67.

42. Helen Muchnic, Review of *Vozdushnye puti* 1, *Russian Review* 20, no. 1 (January 1961): 87–88.

43. Muchnic, 88.

44. Chukovskaia, *Zapiski*, 2: 536; diary entry of October 30, 1962. According to Chukovskaia, the number of people who kept Akhmatova's *Requiem* alive in their memory varied from 7 to 11, Chukovskaia, 491. Apart from Chukovskaia herself, they were Boris Pasternak, Nikolai Davidenkov, Tamara Gabbe, Vladimir Garshin, Emma Gershtein, Nikolai Khardzhiev, Aleksandra Liubarskaia, as well as Sergei Rudakov, Mikhail Lozinsky, Nadezhda Mandelshtam, and Boris Tomashevsky, whose familiarity with *Requiem* is also likely. See Nina Popova and Tatiana Pozdniakova, *V tom dome bylo . . .* (St. Petersburg: Muzei Anny Akhmatovoi, 2019), 200–267.

45. Lydia Chukovskaya, *The Akhmatova Journals: 1938–1941*, trans. Milena Michalski and Sylva Rubashova, with poetry trans. Peter Norman (London: Harvill, 1994), 6.

46. Timenchik, *Poslednii poet*, 1: 283.

47. Akhmatova pronounced these words "slowly and clearly, almost syllable by syllable, as if announcing a verdict," Chukovskaia, *Zapiski*, 2: 512). Solzhenitsyn's manuscript was passed on to her by Lev Kopelev.

48. Chukovskaia, *Zapiski*, 2: 532–33. Upon hearing Akhmatova's story about meeting Solzhenitsyn, whom she referred to as a "light-bearer" (*svetonosets*), Chukovskaia concluded, "After all, we have lived not only to see the death of Stalin, but also to hear the voice of this z/k," Chukovskaia, 2:533.

49. Anna Akhmatova, *The World That Causes Death's Defeat: Poems of Memory*, ed. and trans., with an introduction, critical essays, and commentary by Nancy K. Anderson (New Haven, CT: Yale University Press, 2004), 124. After meeting Solzhenitsyn, Akhmatova told Kopelev, "Perhaps I am being subjective, but for me it is not poetry. I didn't want to upset him and only said, 'I think your strength is prose. You write wonderful prose. No need to get distracted.' Of course, he understood and, it seems, got offended." Lev Kopelev and Raisa Orlova, *My zhili v Moskve. 1956–1980* (Moscow: Kniga, 1990), 273.

50. Kopelev and Orlova, 273; modified English translation in Akhmatova, *The World*, 124. Later Solzhenitsyn "regretted" that at the time he was unable "to let Akhmatova read my secret works, even *In The First Circle*," suspecting her "for some reason of the same human weakness—inability to keep a secret. . . . She died without having read any of it." Solzhenitsyn, *Oak and Calf*, 239. It was not until Solzhenitsyn befriended Chukovskaia that he learned just how well Akhmatova could keep "secrets," her own *Requiem* included.

51. Akhmatova, *Zapisnye knizhki*, 452.

52. Nika Glen, "Vokrug starykh zapisei," in *Vospominaniia ob Anne Akhmatovoi*, ed. V. Ia. Vilenkin and V. A. Chernykh (Moscow: Sovetskii pisatel', 1991), 638.

53. Yulian Oksman, "Iz dnevnika, kotorogo ia ne vedu," in *Vospominaniia ob Anne Akhmatovoi*, 643. Slutsky's anti-Stalin poems "God" ("Bog") and "The

Master" ("Khoziain") appeared in *Literaturnaia gazeta* on November 21, 1962, days after the publication of *Ivan Denisovich*.

54. Chukovskaia, *Zapiski*, 2: 560–61. See Pushkin's "The Prophet" ("Prorok," 1826): "Rise, prophet, rise, and hear, and see, / And let my works be seen and heard / By all who turn aside from me, / And burn them with my fiery word." Alexander Pushkin, *The Bronze Horseman: Selected Poems of Alexander Pushkin*, trans., with an introduction by D. M. Thomas (New York: Viking, 1982), 57.

55. This selection of Akhmatova's poems included "Native Land" ("Rodnaia zemlia," 1961), "The Last Rose" ("Posledniaia roza," 1962) with an epigraph from Joseph Brodsky, "The Gold Gets Rusty and the Steel is Melting . . ." ("Rzhaveet zoloto, i istlevaet stal' . . .," 1945), "I Will Not Cry of My Own . . ." ("O svoem ia uzhe ne zaplachu . . .," 1962), and "A Tsarskoe Selo Ode" ("Tsarskosel'skaia oda," 1961): *Novyi mir* 1 (1963): 64–66. In his New Year's greetings to Akhmatova on December 27, 1962, Solzhenitsyn, who had seen the proofs of the *Novyi mir* issue, expressed satisfaction at seeing her poems next to his short stories "An Incident at Krechetovka Station" ("Sluchai na stantsii Krechetovka") and "Matrena's House" ("Matrenin dvor") (quoted in Timenchik, *Poslednii poet*, 1: 294).

56. Akhmatova, *Beg vremeni*. The book was supposed to include all three narrative poems: "Poem without a Hero," "Requiem," and "The Way of All the Earth" ("Putem vseia zemli"). "The Way of All the Earth" was indeed published in *Beg vremeni* with only minor concessions to censorship, while "Poem without a Hero" appeared without parts 2 and 3, which deal with the camps. As for *Requiem*, only two of its parts made it to the edition ("The Sentence" and "Crucifixion"), albeit "with no indication that they belonged to a larger whole, and the title of 'The Sentence' was removed, stripping it of its context," Akhmatova, *The World*, 129. Abroad, the hope that *Requiem* would be published in Russia lasted longer. For example, both Gul' and Adamovich still thought it would happen until as late as 1964 and 1965, respectively. As they claimed in their reviews of the Munich edition of *Requiem*, Akhmatova dealt with the period of Stalin's terror officially condemned by Khrushchev, which should have made the poem publishable, Roman Gul', " 'Rekviem' Anny Akhmatovoi," *Novyi zhurnal* 77 (1964): 290, much as it should have served the same sociopolitical function as Solzhenitsyn's *Ivan Denisovich*, Adamovich, "Na poliakh 'Rekviema,' " 208.

57. Natan Gotkhart, "Dvenadtsat' vstrech s Annoi Akhmatovoi," *Voprosy literatury*, no. 2 (1997): 286.

58. Georgy Glekin, "Vstrechi s Akhmatovoi (iz dnevnikovykh zapisei 1959–1966 godov)," *Voprosy literatury*, no. 2 (1997): 313.

59. Natalia Gorbanevskaia, "Ee golos," in *Akhmatovskii sbornik* 1, ed. Sergei Dediulin and Gabriel Superfin (Paris: Institute d'études slaves, 1989), 241. Gorbanevskaia adds that by then she had personally typed *Requiem* on her own typewriter "at least a hundred times." Her evidence thus contradicts Anatoly Naiman's claim that "*Requiem* began to circulate clandestinely at approximately the same time, in the same circles and in the same number of copies as Vigdorova's transcript of Brodsky's trial," Anatoly Nayman, *Remembering Anna*

Akhmatova, trans. Wendy Rosslyn, with an introduction by Joseph Brodsky (New York: Henry Holt, 1991), 135. Brodsky's trial in Leningrad took place in March 1964, not 1963. It is true, however, that "public opinion unconsciously made a link between these two things. . . . The transcript of the poet's trial sounded like poetry on the most profound themes of public concern; and *Requiem*, poetry on the most profound themes of public concerns, sounded like a transcript of the repressions, a kind of martyrology, a record of acts of self-sacrifice and martyrdom," Brodsky, 135.

60. Gleb Struve, "Kak byl vervye izdan 'Rekviem,'" afterword to *Rekviem*, by Anna Akhmatova, 2nd ed. (Munich: Tovarishchestvo zarubezhnykh pisatelei, 1969), 22–24.

61. It was Malia's second trip to Russia. In 1955 he was stationed in Moscow as an acquisition consultant for the Library of Congress; his meetings with Pasternak got him involved in the *Doctor Zhivago* affair. In a conversation with Timenchik, Malia recalled having first met Akhmatova at the apartment of Maria Petrovykh in April 1962, having then visited her in Komarovo in June, and again in Moscow at the apartment of Nika Glen in the fall of the same year, Timenchik, *Poslednii poet*, 2: 560. See also Chukovskaia's diary entry of June 5, 1962: "The conversation began with a question about Malia. Anna Andreevna saw him the day before. 'Do you think he is indeed intelligent [*sovsem umnyi*]?' she asked. 'Does he understand our life here?' Hm. It is generally difficult for me to have an opinion about foreigners, their level of intellect and *intelligentnost'*. Our life experiences and everything else are too different. Besides, how many of them have I met? Maybe one or two, not more. Malia is intelligent and tactful, he knows the Russian nineteenth century very well. His knowledge of Herzen, for example, is vaster than that of an average contemporary Russian *intelligent* who would have read *My Past and Thoughts* at best. . . . So, as far as the literary aspects of the nineteenth century are concerned, Malia is probably an expert, 'intelligent indeed.' But does he understand our life? I don't know. I talk to him openly, without being too cautious. But do I myself understand it? . . . What then should we ask of Malia?" Chukovskaia, *Zapiski*, 2: 504–5). On November 16, 1962, Chukovskaia recorded Akhmatova's words: "No wonder that Malia stays over for so long [*zasizhivaetsia*]. . . . After all, he is a friend of Sir Isaiah [Berlin], who had once stayed at my place for twelve hours or so in a row and earned me the [Zhdanov] decree" (2: 552). Malia was introduced to Isaiah Berlin as a student of Mikhail Karpovich at Harvard in the early 1950s.

62. Gleb Struve Collection, box 32, folder 14.

63. Anna Akhmatova, *Sochineniia v 3 tomakh*, ed. Gleb Struve and Boris Filippov ([Munich]: Inter-Language Literary Associates, 1965–1983).

64. In her diary entry of November 16, 1962, Chukovskaia recounts her conversation with Malia, who visited her, "extremely agitated," in the midst of the Cuban missile crisis in mid-October, when the world was on the verge of a nuclear war, Chukovskaia, *Zapiski*, 2: 553–54.

65. Gleb Struve Collection, box 32, folder 14; Cyrillic in the original.

66. Fleishman, "Iz arkhiva Guverovskogo instituta, 31. A month later, Oksman added, "Nor do I really believe that the complete works of Akhmatova (of

course, without 'Requiem') would be published, although she had given in to this possibility back in November. . . . The theme of the camps will no longer be allowed in our journals," Fleishman, 43.

67. Fleishman, 21, 31–32.

68. Struve, "Kak byl vervye izdan 'Rekviem'," 22–23.

69. Aleksei Adzhubei, "Ot okeana k okeanu," *Iunost'*, no. 2 (1956): 99.

70. Quoted in "Sovetskie zhurnalisty o G. P. Struve," *Russkaia mysl'*, January 19, 1956.

71. Gleb Struve Collection, box 32, folder 14; emphasis and Cyrillic in the original. Malia also informed Struve that in addition to *Requiem*, Akhmatova had written her memoir about Mandelshtam, which Oksman was trying to obtain; the memoir, however, was first published not by Struve, but by Grynberg in *Vozdushnye puti* 4 (1965): 23–43. Enclosed to Malia's epistle was a letter from Oksman addressed to "N. N." but clearly intended for Struve. It was about Mandelshtam, whom Oksman knew personally and whose volume of poetry prepared by Struve and Filippov (New York: Izdatel'stvo imeni Chekhova, 1955) he called "a true voice from the other world," Fleishman, "Iz arkhiva Guverovskogo instituta," 22. Throughout their epistolary exchange in the next three years, Oksman, in addition to Akhmatova's *Requiem*, supplied Struve with manuscripts of Mandelshtam and Elena Tager, as well biographical information on Vladimir Narbut. Struve, in turn, provided Oksman with tamizdat editions of Russian poets, clippings from émigré newspapers, as well as his own scholarship, e.g., his book *Russkaia literatura v izgnanii* (New York: Izdatel'stvo imeni Chekhova, 1956). Published during the first year of the Thaw, Struve's book had "never been checked out to anyone" from the special repositories of the Soviet libraries (the so-called *spetskhran*) but was "highly valued" by Oksman's friends and fellow Soviet scholars. See Oksman's letter to Struve on December 21, 1962, in Fleishman, "Iz arkhiva Guverovskogo instituta," 35.

72. See Kathryn Feuer's account of her first trip to Russia in 1956, "Russia's Young Intellectuals," *Encounter* (February 1957): 10–25.

73. Lewis S. Feuer, "Cultural Scholarly Exchange in the Soviet Union in 1963 and How the KGB Tried to Terrorize American Scholars and Suppress Truths," in *Tamizdat: Publishing Russian Literature across Borders*, ed. Yasha Klots, special issue of *Wiener Slawistischer Almanach* 86 (Berlin: Peter Lang, 2021), 301–2. Kathryn's former classmate from Columbia was Jack Matlock, cultural attaché at the American embassy in Moscow at the time. From 1987 to 1991, Matlock served as the US ambassador to Russia.

74. Gleb Struve Collection, box 28, folder 1. The photograph in question, enclosed in the typescript of *Requiem*, was a 1913 portrait of Akhmatova by Savely Sorin, which appeared on the title page of the Munich edition.

75. Gleb Struve Collections, box 28, folder 1; Cyrillic in the original.

76. Robin Feuer Miller, "Double Diaries and Layered Memories. Moscow, 1963," in *Tamizdat: Publishing Russian Literature across Borders*, ed. Yasha Klots, special issue of *Wiener Slawistischer Almanach* 86 (Berlin: Peter Lang, 2021), 311–20. See also Yasha Klots, "The Way Back. Kathryn Feuer's and Gleb Struve's Letters on Academic Exchange, Yulian Oksman and Crossing the Soviet-Finnish

Border (June 1963)," in *Across Borders: 20th Century Russian Literature and Russian-Jewish Cultural Contacts. Essays in Honor of Vladimir Khazan*, ed. Lazar Fleishman and Fedor Poljakov (Berlin: Peter Lang, 2018), 557–84.

77. KGB document quoted in Marietta Chudakova, "Po povodu vospominanii L. Feuera i R. Feuer-Miller," in *Tynianovskii sbornik: piatye Tynianovskie chtenia*, ed. Marietta Chudakova (Moscow: Imprint, 1994), 370.

78. In his last letter to Struve, in the summer of 1965, Oksman wrote that during the search of his apartment, the KGB showed him Kathryn's confiscated notebook. "The investigation lasted through early December of the same year, without any unpleasant consequences for me. There happened to be no materials serious enough to put me on trial." The letter ended, however, with the request "not to use anything I have said here in any way that can make my already quite unfavorable situation even worse." Fleishman, "Iz arkhiva Guverovskogo instituta," 68–69. In 1976 Kathryn Feuer edited a book of essays on Solzhenitsyn, which she dedicated to the memory of Oksman, who had died in 1970, *Solzhenitsyn: A Collection of Critical Essays*, ed. Kathryn Feuer (Englewood Cliffs, NJ: Prentice Hall, 1976).

79. The article exposed a number of Soviet officials in the cultural sphere who orchestrated the crackdown on the liberties of the Thaw. Smuggled out in the summer of 1962, it was published anonymously a year later, Yulian Oksman [N. N., pseud.], "Donoschiki i predateli sredi sovetskikh pisatelei i uchenykh," *Sotsialisticheskii vestnik* nos. 5–6 (May–June 1963): 74–76.

80. See Bruce Lambert, "Frederick Barghoorn, 90, Scholar Detained in Soviet Union in 1963," *New York Times*, November 26, 1991, as well as Barghoorn's own monograph, *The Soviet Cultural Offensive:. The Role of Cultural Diplomacy in Soviet Foreign Policy* (Princeton, NJ: Princeton University Press, 1960). The "pamphlet novella" by Soviet sci-fi author Roman Kim appears to be linked to the "Berkeley plot." "Kto ukral Punnakana?" ("Who Stole Punnakan?") was published in October 1963 in the journal *Oktiabr'*; Struve is invoked, along with other American Sovietologists, "disseminating rumors that underground literature is leaked from the Soviet Union to the U.S. via certain clandestine channels," *Octiabr'*, no. 10 (1963): 83. Kim's text was reprinted the following year in *V mire fantastiki i prikliuchenii*, ed. Evgeny Bradis and Vladimir Dmitrevsky (Leningrad: Lenizdat, 1964), 491–589. It was brought to Struve's attention by Malia in December 1963 (Gleb Struve Collection, box 32, folder 14).

81. Struve, "Kak byl vervye izdan 'Rekviem'," 23.

82. See, for example, his gulag memoirs, *Gor'kie vody* (Frankfurt: Possev, 1954) and *Trudnye dorogi* (Munich: Tovarishchestvo zarubezhnykh pisatelei, 1959).

83. Pavel Tribunsky and Vladimir Khazan, "'Tam nashi usiliia ne ostaiutsia tshchetnymi i prinimaiutsia s velichaishim vnimaniem' (piat' pisem iz perepiski redaktorov al'manakhov 'Mosty' i 'Vozdushnye puti')," in *Ezhegodnik Doma russkogo zarubezh'ia imeni Aleksandra Solzhenitsyna* (Moscow: Dom russkogo zarubezh'ia, 2018), 388. Struve's letter to Khomiakov is dated July 6, 1963; thus the question of publishing *Requiem* was first raised two months earlier, not in September, as Struve asserted in his afterword to the second

edition. See Struve's letter to Kathryn Feuer on July 28, 1963: "I came to the conclusion that it could really be published, provided all due precautions were taken, that is, if the poem was to be published without any comments or explanations, beyond mentioning that it was received and was being published without the author's knowledge. I thought of publishing it either in *Mosty* or as a separate booklet," quoted in Yakov Klots, "'Rekviem' Akhmatovoi v tamizdate: 56 pisem," *Colta.ru*, June 24, 2019, https://www.colta.ru/articles/literature/21637-rekviem-ahmatovoy-v-tamizdate-56-pisem; emphasis in the original. The discussion of whether *Requiem* might or might not be published just yet continued in Struve's correspondence with Feuer and Malia through September 1963.

84. Struve's unpublished letter to Khomiakov dated October 4, 1963. Gennady Khomiakov's Papers, Dom russkogo zarubezh'ia imeni Aleksandra Solzhenitsyna (Moscow). I thank Pavel Tribunsky for sharing a copy of this letter with me.

85. The only other two who knew that the poem belonged to Akhmatova were the historian, philosopher, critic, and cofounder of Tovarishchestvo zarubezhnykh pisatelei, Fedor Stepun, and the poet Dmitry Klenovsky. Struve met both in Munich after participating in a closed symposium on Soviet literature organized by Max Hayward in Tegernsee on September 1–6, 1963.

86. See Khomiakov's letter to Struve on October 28, 1963; Gleb Struve Collection, box 94, folder 11: "It is not easy with him [Annenkov]: before he answers, all deadlines will pass. . . . Perhaps we shouldn't hold off." See also Annenkov's account of painting Akhmatova in Petrograd before his departure from Russia in 1924 (Yury Annenkov, "Anna Akhmatova," *Vozrozhdenie* 129 [September 1962]: 41–52). A longtime member of Mir iskusstva, Annenkov met Akhmatova again only in June 1965. See his memoir "Anna Akhmatova," much of which is devoted to her stay in Paris on the way back to Russia from England, Yury Annenkov, *Dnevnik moikh vstrech. Tsikl tragedii* (Moscow: Khudozhestvennaia literatura, 1991), 1: 114–36.

87. Those included Mikhail Kaplan's Dom knigi and Les éditeurs réunis, at the time spearheaded by the editor of *Vestnik RSKhD* and director of YMCA-Press, Ivan Morozov, in Paris; Aleksei Struve, the brother of Gleb and father of Nikita Struve, also in Paris; Viktor Kamkin in Washington, DC, whose clientele, apart from the general public, included American universities; Nikolai Mart'ianov in New York, whose bookshop was affiliated with the newspaper *Novoe russkoe slovo*; in London, the sales of *Requiem* were largely handled by Viktor Frank, the son of the philosopher Semyon Frank and head of the local branch of Radio Free Europe's Russian service, who volunteered for the role (see his letters to Struve from November 29 and December 15, 1963, Gleb Struve Collection, box 85, folder 8).

88. Gleb Struve Collection, box 94, folder 11.

89. Quoted in Khomiakov's letter to Struve, November 18, 1963, Gleb Struve Collection, box 94, folder 11.

90. Khomiakov's letter to Struve, November 28, 1963, Gleb Struve Collection, box 94, folder 11. Filippov informed Struve of his involvement with

the American Committee as "a consultant in those matters" in 1962, when he "worked on a huge report about the penetration of serious local editions to the USSR," commissioned to him by "people who subsidize *Mosty* and other publications," Filippov's letter to Struve, August 24, 1963, quoted in Timenchik, *Poslednii poet*, 2: 563–64).

91. Filippov's letter to Khomiakov, December 4, 1963, Boris Filippov Papers, Gen Mss 334, Box 1, Folder 10, Beinecke Rare Book and Manuscript Library, Yale University. Cf. his letter to Struve of January 16, 1964: "The cycle is very strong, but some of its poems are so much below the artistic level of her [other writings] of the past 20 years that it immediately shows," Boris Filippov Papers, Gen Mss 334, Box 7, Folder 232.

92. One such copy, found among Struve's papers at the Hoover Institution Archives (box 71, folder 7), was delivered to him by his former student Paul Sjeklocha, aka Paul S. Cutter, who was employed in the early 1960s in Moscow by the US Information Agency and later the CIA. See Paul Sjeklocha and Igor Mead, *Unofficial Art in the Soviet Union* (Berkeley: University of California Press, 1967).

93. Gleb Struve Collection, box 94, folder 11.

94. In Russia Rittenberg visited his sister Tatiana German, second wife of the filmmaker Yury German. According to Timenchik, Rittenberg's biography is reflected in the storyline of the Swedish journalist in Aleksei German's 1988 film *Khrustalev, My Car!* (*Khrustalev, mashinu!*).

95. Gleb Struve Collection, box 94, folder 11.

96. See Grynberg's letter to Yury Ivask, January 13, 1964: "Khomiakov published an abridged cycle," George Ivask Papers, Box 3, Folder 38, Amherst Center for Russian Culture. Still unaware that the Munich edition was based on the manuscript that Struve had received from Oksman, Grynberg assumed, without naming his sources, that it had been smuggled out of Russia by Olga Andreeva-Carlisle.

97. Gleb Struve Collection, box 94, folder 11. The same concerns were expressed by Grynberg in his letter to Khomiakov on December 26, 1963, Pavel Tribunsky and Vladimir Khazan, "Tam nashi usiliia," 291–93. Having evaluated Grynberg's list of discrepancies between the two versions, Struve assumed that Grynberg's copy could actually be a later redaction, which Akhmatova might have expanded after submitting the earlier one to *Novyi mir* or that Grynberg's version was in fact the initial manuscript, not even intended for publication by Akhmatova, while "mine matched the one she had offered to *Novyi mir*." See Struve's letter to Khomiakov on December 23, 1963. I thank Pavel Tribunsky for familiarizing me with the letter.

98. Instead, in the fourth issue of *Vozdushnye puti* (1965), he published Akhmatova's memoirs about Mandelshtam and Modigliani, as well as a selection of Brodsky's poems and Frida Vigdorova's record of Brodsky's trial in Leningrad in March 1964.

99. Anna Akhmatova, "Rekviem," *Grani* 56 (October 1964): 11–19.

100. NTS Papers, Fond 98, Forschungsstelle Osteuropa, University of Bremen.

101. Gleb Struve Collection, box 34, folder 12; Tarasova's letter to Struve December 31, 1964.

102. Viktor Frank, *Izbrannye stat'i*, ed. Leonard Shapiro (London: Overseas Publications Interchange, 1974), 33.

103. Chukovskaia, *Zapiski*, 3: 281.

104. Having accepted the invitation from Giancarlo Vigorelli, head of the European Community of Writers (COMES), Akhmatova left for Italy on December 1, 1964. It was there, as she traveled through Rome on her way back to Russia, that she received the invitation to Oxford, according to an émigré newspaper ("A[khmatova] v Italii," *Russkaia mysl'*, January 9, 1965).

105. Irma Kudrova, *Russkie vstrechi Pitera Normana* (St. Petersburg: Zhurnal "Neva," 1999), 57. According to Akhmatova's step-granddaughter, Anna Kaminskaia, who accompanied her to England and France, not long before her departure Akhmatova was given a list of people she was supposed to avoid while abroad (quoted in Iu. Kovalenko, "A. A. vo Frantsii," *Nedelia*, June 15, 1989). In the words of Irina Ogorodnikova, who worked for the Foreign Commission of the Soviet Writers' Union and was in charge of Akhmatova's travel arrangements, as she was boarding the train in Moscow and taking cardiac medications, Akhmatova mentioned in passing: "Don't worry. I will never allow myself such a dirty trick [*gadost'*] as to die away from my motherland [*umeret' ne na rodine*]" (quoted in Timenchik, *Poslednii poet*, 1: 434).

106. In England, Akhmatova also met her nephew Andrew Gorenko, who spoke no Russian and whom she had never seen before. While "in England she had met again Salomea Halpern [Andronikova], Yury Annenkov (who came over from Paris), and friends of a later vintage such as Isaiah Berlin, in Paris she was to meet again many people whom she had known during her early married life and whom she had last seen when they were all young and beautiful. Now they came to see her one after the other, old, frail, deaf, incredibly changed: Olga Obolenskaia, Dmitri Bouchène, S.R. Ernst, . . . Georgy Adamovich and Boris Anrep [as well as] Joseph Czapski, whom she had not seen since Tashkent," Haight, *Akhmatova*, 191. See also Adamovich, "Meetings with Akhmatova," 62–77; Boris Anrep, "The Black Ring," in *Anna Akhmatova and Her Circle*, ed. Konstantin Polivanov, trans. Patricia Beriozkina (Fayetteville: University of Arkansas Press, 1994), 77–92; Viktor Frank, "Vstrechi s A. A. Akhmatovoi," in his *Izbrannye stat'i*, 32–36; Nikita Struve, "Vosem' chasov s Annoi Akhmatovoi," in Anna Akhmatova, *Sochineniia* (Munich: Inter-Language Literary Associates, 1968), 2: 325–46.

107. Akhmatova, *Sochineniia*, 2: 359–70; Anna Akhmatova. *Requiem*. 2nd ed., revised by the author, with an afterword by Gleb Struve (Munich: Tovarishchestvo zarubezhnykh pisatelei, 1969).

108. Glen, "Vokrug starykh zapisei," 638. The poem was written no later than June 1961, when Akhmatova read it, among others, to Chukovskaia and Glekin, who referred to it as "12 lines of truly civic lyrics," Georgy Glekin, *Chto mne dano . . . Ob Anne Akhmatovoi* (Moscow: Ekon-Inform, 2011), 210.

109. David Wells, "The Function of the Epigraph in Akhmatova's Poetry," in *Anna Akhmatova. 1889–1989. Papers from the Akhmatova Centennial Conference*,

ed. Sonia I. Ketchian (Oakland, CA: Berkeley Slavic Specialties, 1993), 267. Wells's survey of the epigraphs in Akhmatova's oeuvre does not address *Requiem*, although it does point out that while in the beginning of her creative career it was "considered poor taste . . . among members of Akhmatova's set to use epigraphs other than very sparingly and for very specific purposes," from the mid-1950s epigraphs became increasingly functional, appearing in 52 percent of Akhmatova's later lyrics, 268–69.

110. Wells, 266.

111. Anrep, "Black Ring," 83. "One day during the February revolution, he took off his officer's shoulder-straps and, risking his life, walked across the frozen river Neva to see her. He told her that he was leaving for England, and that it was 'the calm English civilization of reason, and not religious and political ravings' that he held dear. They said goodbye and he left for London," Nayman, *Remembering Anna Akhmatova*, 79. In the early 1960s Anrep and Akhmatova were able to exchange greetings through Struve, who corresponded with Anrep and asked Malia in Moscow to pass Anrep's greetings on to Akhmatova. On October 12, 1962, Malia reported to Struve that Akhmatova "was very pleased to receive them and is sending her own," Gleb Struve Collection, box 32, folder 14. Not long before his death in 1969, at Struve's suggestion, Anrep wrote down his memoir about Akhmatova and their meeting in Paris in June 1965 ("The Black Ring"), as well as his article "Nikolai Nedobrovo and Anna Akhmatova" (in *Anna Akhmatova and Her Circle*, 215–30). See also Anrep's poem "Remembrance" ("Pominanie") in memory of Akhmatova, in which he revisits their last meeting in Petrograd: "Blame me: I am a pathless wanderer, / And you ought to serve eternity, / Unable to live without your motherland. / Farewell, I know I am an apostate" [*Kori: ia bezdorozhnyi putnik, / Ty zh vechnosti dolzhna sluzhit', / Bez rodiny ne mozhesh' zhit'. / Proshchai, ia znaiu—ia otstupnik*], quoted in Lazar Fleishman, "Iz akhmatovskikh materialov v arkhive Guverovskogo instituta," in *Akhmatovskii Sbornik 1*, ed. Sergei Dediulin and Gabriel Superfin (Paris: Institute d'études slaves, 1989), 183.

112. Anna Akhmatova, *Sobranie sochinenii v 6 tomakh* (Moscow: Ellis Lak, 1998), 1: 316; *Poems of Anna Akhmatova*, ed. and trans., with an introduction by Stanley Kunitz and Max Hayward (Boston: Houghton Mifflin, 1973), 67.

113. Akhmatova, *Sobranie sochinenii*, 1: 316; English translation quoted in Haight, *Akhmatova*, 47.

114. For example, the poem "Mne golos byl . . ." was praised for its "national, rather than revolutionary, feeling" by N. Osinsky (aka Valerian Obolensky), a member of the left opposition executed in 1938, in his "Pobegi travy," *Pravda*, July 4, 1922. See also Evgeny Dobin, *Poeziia Anny Akhmatovoi* (Leningrad: Sovetskii pisatel', 1968), 99; Aleksei Pavlovsky, *Anna Akhmatova: ocherk tvorchestva* (Leningrad: Lenizdat, 1966), 62; Nikolai Bannikov, "Vysokii dar," afterword to Akhmatova, *Izbrannoe* (Moscow: Khudozhestvennaia literatura, 1974), 542. These texts, indeed, allowed Akhmatova scholars in the Soviet Union to demonize emigration. See Dmitry Bobyshev, "Akhmatova i emigratsiia," *Zvezda*, no. 2 (1991): 177–81.

115. Cf. the title of Ivan Bunin's cycle of short stories "Temnye allei" ("Dark Avenues,") 1937–1944, written in exile.

116. Akhmatova, *Sobranie sochinenii*, 1: 389.

117. *Pravda*, March 8, 1942.

118. Quoted in Timenchik, *Poslednii poet*, 1: 168.

119. Haight, *Akhmatova*, 173–74.

120. Quoted in Timenchik, *Poslednii poet*, 1: 168.

121. E.g., Osip Mandelshtam, *Sobranie sochinenii* (New York: Izdatel'stvo imeni Chekhova, 1955); Marina Tsvetaeva, *Proza*, with an introduction by Fedor Stepun (New York: Izdatel'stvo imeni Chekhova, 1953), and her *Lebedinyi Stan. Stikhi 1917–1921 gg.*, ed. Gleb Struve, with an introduction by Yury Ivask (Munich, 1957).

122. Elena Serebrovskaia, "Protiv nigilizma i vseiadnosti," *Zvezda*, no. 6 (1957): 201, quoted in Haight, *Akhmatova*, 172. Like Surkov, Serebrovskaia also implied that as a result of the Zhdanov campaign, Akhmatova had been set straight: "And it was not through anyone else's prompting but out of her own civic pride that she learned how to answer those unceremonious bourgeois guests who came to Leningrad in search of newspaper sensation shortly after the decree of the Central Committee about *Star* and *Leningrad*" (quoted in Haight, 172). See also Serebrovskaia's later article about Akhmatova, in which she insinuates that in February 1966 the poet's health was fatally aggravated not so much by the trial of Sinyavsky and Daniel itself ("two anti-Soviets who published their filth abroad and gradually saved up dollars in their Swiss bank accounts for selling their motherland") but by "the wife of one of these petty individuals," whose visit to "the good home of Anna Andreevna" and her plea to save her arrested husband was "like the bite of a viper," which Akhmatova's heart, "having just recovered from a dangerous illness," could not withstand, Elena Serebrovskaia, "Doch' svoei rodiny," *Zvezda*, no. 1 (1988): 178–83.

123. Aleksandr Kovalenkov, "Pis'mo staromu drugu," *Znamia*, no. 7 (1957): 165–73.

124. Brodsky, *Less Than One*, 48.

125. Gleb Struve, *Soviet Russian Literature, 1917–1950* (Norman: University of Oklahoma Press, 1951), 366.

126. Vladimir Markov, *Priglushennye golosa. Poeziia za zheleznym zanavesom* (New York: Izdatel'stvo imeni Chekhova, 1952), 12.

127. *Ogonek*, no. 14 (April 2, 1950): 20.

128. Lydia Nord, "Tragediia Anny Akhmatovoi," *Bulleten' russkogo obshchestva pomoshchi bezhentsam v Velikobritanii*, September 6, 1951; quoted in Timenchik, *Poslednii poet*, 2: 241–42. On Lydia Nord (aka Olga Olenich-Gnenenko, the cousin of Marshal Tukhachevsky's wife and a Nazi collaborator during the war), see Boris Ravdin and Gabriel Superfin, "Lydia Nord kak istochnik," in *Kul'tura russkoi diaspory: emigratsiia i memuary*, ed. S. Dotsenko (Tallinn: Tallinskii universitet, 2009), 199–204; Nikolai Bogomolov, "Lydia Nord i inzhenery dush," *Toronto Slavic Quarterly* 34 (2010): 203–17.

129. Akhmatova, *Requiem*. 2nd ed., 15; Akhmatova, *Requiem and Poem*, 27.

130. Gladkov, *O poetakh*, 107.

131. Terapiano's letter to Struve on February 12, 1966, Gleb Struve Collection, box 139, folder 16. "Slava Miru" was nevertheless included in the tamizdat

edition of Akhmatova's complete works, despite her request not to print it (Akhmatova, *Sochineniia*, 2: 147–54). On June 16, 1965, after he "spent 3 hours tête-à-tête with A.A.A." in London, Struve reported to Filippov, "She does not want us to include poems of 1950–51 from *Ogonek*. . . . We need to think how to explain this in the complete collection of her published poems (or simply leave it unexplained)?" Boris Filippov Papers, Gen Mss 334, Box 7, Folder 239, quoted in Ivan Tolstoi, "Upravliaia tamizdatom. Oksfordskii epizod Akhmatovoi," *Radio Free Europe*, March 5, 2016, https://www.svoboda.org/a/27590977.html.

132. Dated June 22, 1939, the poem was first published in *Zvezda*, no. 3–4 (1940): 75, and included in Akhmatova's *Izbrannoe* (Tashkent: Sovetskii pisatel', 1943), 105, and *Stikhotvoreniia*, 171, albeit without the title and incorrectly dated 1934 instead of 1935, ostensibly to hide the identity of the poem's addressee, Akhmatova's son. Lev Gumilev was arrested for the first time together with Nikolai Punin in 1935, although the poem deals with his second arrest on September 27, 1938. As for the title omitted in the Soviet publications ("The Sentence"), without it "the poem could read as a mere recollection of breaking up with a romantic friend . . ., although it is impossible to imagine such a 'sentimental' reading of the word [*prigovor*] at the time: had it been printed, it would have inevitably channeled the reader in the right direction," Jean-Philippe Jaccard, *Literatura kak takovaia. Ot Nabokova k Pushkinu* (Moscow: Novoe literaturnoe obozrenie, 2014), 375–76. One more poem from *Requiem* appeared in the Soviet Union before the Munich edition, "Already madness with her wing . . ." ("Uzhe bezumie krylom . . ."). Dated May 4, 1940, it was included in Akhmatova's Tashkent volume *Izbrannoe* (1943), with the fourth stanza, addressed to her son, censored out, but with the added title "K drugu" ("To a Friend"). It appears that Filippov either did not know about the Tashkent volume or had no access to it at the time.

133. Boris Filippov Papers, Gen Mss 334, Box 7, Folder 232.

134. Boris Filippov Papers, Gen Mss 334, Box 7, Folder 232, quoted in Timenchik, *Poslednii poet*, 2: 472.

135. Chukovskaia, *Zapiski*, 1: 42–43.

136. Akhmatova, *Requiem and Poem*, 23.

137. Nikolai Anin [Nikolai Davidenkov]. "Leningradskie nochi," *Parizhskii vestnik*, August 21, 1943.

138. Nina Berberova, who stayed in Paris under the Nazi occupation, recalls that in March 1944 "N. Davidenkov, a 'Vlasovist,' arrived. He's a friend of Akhmatova, studied at Leningrad University. He speaks long about Akhmatova and reads her verse, unknown to any of us: 'My husband in a grave, my son in prison. / Pray for me.' I could not hold back my tears and went out to the next room," Nina Berberova, *The Italics Are Mine*, trans. Philippe Radley (New York: Harcourt, Brace & World, 1969), 429. After the war Davidenkov was "interned and passed over to the Soviet side, sentenced to 10 years of hard labor, then given another sentence and shot," Boris Ravdin, "Pamiatka chitateliu gazety 'Parizhskii vestnik': 1942–1944," in *Vademecum. K 65-letiiu Lazaria Fleishmana*, ed. Anrei Ustinov (Moscow: Vodolei, 2010), 473–74. On Russian

collaborationist press in Latvia, see Boris Ravdin, *Na podmostkakh voiny. Russkaia kul'turnaia zhizn' Latvii vremen natsistskoi okkupatsii. 1941–1944* (Stanford, CA: Stanford University Press, 2005).

139. Boris Filistinsky [Boris Filippov, pseud.], "Kak napechatali Akhmatovu," *Za Rodinu*, September 2, 1943; reprinted in another collaborationist Russian-language newspaper in Belgrade: *Russkoe Delo*, September 26, 1943; quoted in Timenchik, *Poslednii poet*, 2: 565–66.

140. Markov's letter to Struve on December 21, 1963, Gleb Struve Collection, box 106, folder 3.

141. Akhmatova, *The World*, 181.

142. Markov's letter to Struve on December 21, 1963, Gleb Struve Collection, box 106, folder 3.

143. Markov's letter to Struve on December 21, 1963.

144. Markov's letter to Struve on May 14, 1964, Gleb Struve Collection, box 106, folder 3.

145. Akhmatova, *Requiem and Poem*, 31–32.

146. Filippov's letter to Struve on January 16, 1964, Boris Filippov Papers, Gen Mss 334, Box 7, Folder 232, quoted in Timenchik, *Poslednii poet*, 2: 472.

147. Viacheslav Zavalishin, "Anna Akhmatova," *Novoe russkoe slovo*, April 27, 1952.

148. *Russkaia mysl'*, March 12, 1963.

149. "And there are no more tearless people, / more proud and simpler ones than us in the world" [*I v mire net liudei bessleznei, / Nadmennee i proshche nas*], Akhmatova, *Sobranie sochinenii*, 1: 389. According to Wells, "Function of the Epigraph," 275, "Part of the reason . . . for Akhmatova's constant recyclization of her late lyrics lies in a tendency for the same themes to be restated in slightly different ways in different poems. Individual poems, indeed, tend to lose their independent existence." The reason, however, appears to be not only purely creative but also historical: the same themes require a new context and "readjustment" to the changing reality, while continuing to run like a thread through Akhmatova's long creative biography. *Requiem* and "Poem without a Hero" serve perhaps as the most vivid examples of such historically motivated recyclization.

150. Yury Leving, " 'Akhmatova' russkoi emigratsii—Gizella Lakhman," *Novoe literaturnoe obozrenie*, no. 5 (2006): 164–73. "There was hardly anyone else so often compared to Akhmatova in the émigré press," Leving writes, "and perhaps no other Russian-American poetess so consistently and zealously tried to live up to the role of carrying on the cause of her great Soviet contemporary, in exile." Yury Leving, "Zabytye imena russkoi emigratsii. Poet Gizella Lakhman," in *Russkie evrei v Amerike 2*, ed. Ernst Zaltsberg (Jerusalem: Russkoe evreistvo v zarubezh'e, 2007), 97. Zinaida Gippius and Irina Odoevtseva, two other Silver Age women poets far better known than Lakhman, competed for the status of an "Akhmatova in exile."

151. Gizella Lakhman, "Rodnaia zemlia. Otvet na stikhotvorenie Anny Akhmatovoi," *Novoe russkoe slovo*, April 7, 1963. I thank Betsy Hulick for translating Lakhman's poem into English and allowing me to use it.

152. "'. . . Ia ne imeiu otnosheniia k Serebrianomu veku . . .' Pis'ma Odo-evtsevoi V. F. Markovu," in *"Esli chudo voobsche vozmozhno za granitsei . . ." Epokha 1950-kh v perepiske russkikh literatorov-emigrantov*, ed.,with an introduction and commentary by Oleg Korostelev (Moscow: Russkii put', 2008), 780. "What a fool [*kakaia dura*], if I may say so," Struve commented on Odoevtseva in his let-ter to Filippov on January 30, 1964, Boris Filippov Papers, Gen Mss 334, Box 7, folder 232.

153. Lourié's reaction to *Requiem* was communicated to Struve by Clarence Brown, Lourié's colleague at Princeton, Gleb Struve Collection, box 26, folder 3. The libretto accompanied the publication of "Poem without a Hero" in *Voz-dushnye puti* 2 (1961): 153-66. A longtime companion of Glebova-Sudeikina before his departure from Russia in 1922, Lourié died in Princeton the same year as Akhmatova. See his "Olga Afanasievna Glebova-Sudeikina," in *Anna Akhmatova and Her Circle*, ed. Konstantin Polivanov (Fayetteville: University of Arkansas Press, 1994), 230-33.

154. Roman Gul', *Odvukon'. Sovetskaia i emigrantskaia literatura* (New York: Most, 1973), 268. Gul''s review, "Rekviem," was first published in *Novyi zhurnal* 77 (1964): 290-94.

155. Gul', *Odvukon'*, 270.

156. Allegedly, Merezhkovsky's speech on the radio was arranged by his secretary, Vladimir Zlobin, in secret from Gippius. Korostelev apologetically observes that "Merezhkovsky felt no particular admiration for fascism, let alone for the Führer himself, . . . [but] fascism was the only power capable of standing against bolshevism, that kingdom of Antichrist, in Merezhkovsky's words. . . . Forced to choose between Hitler and Stalin, the emigration was highly politicized during the war, and after the war ended, the winners would not forgive those who had clung to the defeated side or were at least suspected of it. All there was to Merezhkovsky's collaboration with Hitler was his ap-pearance on the radio not long before his death, which came on December 7, 1941." Oleg Korostelev, "Merezhkovsky v emigratsii," *Literaturovedcheskii zhur-nal* 15 (2001): 11.

157. Gul', *Odvukon'*, 269-71. In his letter to Gul' on October 12, 1964, Mark Weinbaum, the editor of *Novoe russkoe slovo*, agreed: "You have written very well both about her and about those who had gone into exile." Roman Gul' Papers, Box 10, Folder 233, Beinecke Rare Book and Manuscript Library, Yale University.

158. Adamovich, "Na poliakh 'Rekviema,'" 209-10.

159. Alexander Schmemann, "Anna Akhmatova," *Novyi zhurnal* 83 (1966): 87-89; emphasis in the original.

160. See, for example, Nina Krivosheina, *Chetyre treti nashei zhizni* (Moscow: Russkii Put', 2017), as well as the film *East/West* (1999, dir. Régis Wargnier), loosely based on her memoir.

161. Chukovskaia, *Zapiski*, 3: 130-31.

162. Akhmatova, *Requiem*, 6; Jaccard, *Literatura kak takovaia*, 371. *Requiem*, along these lines, should perhaps be more accurately referred to not as *goszakaz* (state commission), but as *sotszakaz* (social commission), as Anna Ljunggren

suggested in her article "Anna Akhmatova's *Requiem*: A Retrospective of the Love Lyric and Epos," in *Anna Akhmatova. 1889–1989, Papers from the Akhmatova Centennial Conference*, ed. Sonia I. Ketchian (Oakland, CA: Berkeley Slavic Specialties, 1993), 114.

163. Ljunggren, "Anna Akhmatova's *Requiem*," 117.

3. Lydia Chukovskaia's *Sofia Petrovna* and *Going Under*

1. Lydia Chukovskaia, "Posle kontsa. Iz 'akhmatovskogo' dnevnika," *Znamia*, no. 1 (2003): 161. On September 19, 1962, after Akhmatova and Chukovskaia read Solzhenitsyn's manuscript, Chukovskaia wrote down Akhmatova's words: "For me, there are three works: my 'Requiem,' your novella, and now—this 'z/k'," i.e., *Sch-854*, as *Ivan Denisovich* was first titled. Chukovskaia, *Zapiski*, 2: 512–13.

2. Lydia Chukovskaya, *Sofia Petrovna*, trans. Aline Werth (Evanston, IL: Northwestern University Press, 1994), 111. In her preface to *Sofia Petrovna* in 1962, Chukovskaia explained, "However great the merits of any future stories or accounts, they will all have been written at another period, separated from 1937 by decades; whereas my story was written with the impression of events still fresh in my mind. . . . Herein, I believe, lies its claim to the reader's attention" (2). Some of Chukovskaia's poems were also written in the mid-1930s. See Lydia Chukovskaia, *Po etu storonu smerti (iz dnevnika 1936–1976)* (Paris: YMCA-Press, 1978). See also chapter 7 in Annette Julius, *Lidija Čukovskaja: Leben und Werk* (Munich: Otto Sagner, 1995).

3. Chukovskaia, *Zapiski*, 2: 540. Similarly, in a letter to Chukovskaia on February 20, 1962, Leonid Panteleev referred to the writing of *Sofia Petrovna* during those years as a "feat" [*podvig*]. Leonid Panteleev and Lydia Chukovskaia, *L. Panteleev—L. Chukovskaia. Perepiska. 1929–1987*, with a foreword by Pavel Kriuchkov (Moscow: Novoe literaturnoe obozrenie, 2011), 194.

4. Chukovskaia, *Zapiski*, 2: 540.

5. Lydia Chukovskaia, *Opustelyi dom* (Paris: Cinq Continents, 1965); "Sofia Petrovna," *Novyi zhurnal* 83 (1965): 5–45, and 84 (1966): 5–46.

6. Lydia Chukovskaia, "Sofia Petrovna," *Neva*, no. 2 (1988): 51–93. *Requiem* appeared in the same journal half a year earlier. Akhmatova, "Rekviem," *Neva*, no. 6 (1987): 74–79.

7. Beth Holmgren, *Women's Works in Stalin's Time: On Lidiia Chukovskaia and Nadezhda Mandelshtam* (Bloomington: Indiana University Press, 1993), 44.

8. Such reception, as Holmgren points out at 44, accompanied *Sofia Petrovna* not only during the Thaw, but also during perestroika, after its long-awaited homecoming. As Forrester has also emphasized, "The sense of urgency during glasnost' of resurrecting information after decades of suppression, treating the book as a source of truth rather than art, helps to explain this interpretation." Sibelan Forrester, *"Mother* as Forebear: How Lidiia Chukovskaia's *Sof'ia Petrovna* Rewrites Maksim Gorkii's *Mat'*," in *American Contributions to the 14th International Congress of Slavists*, ed. David M. Bethea (Bloomington, IN: Slavica, 2008), 52.

9. Chukovskaya, *Sofia Petrovna*, 1. The preface was written in November 1962, when Sovetskii pisatel' planned to publish *Sofia Petrovna* as a book.

10. Kornei Chukovsky and Lydia Chukovskaia, *Kornei Chukovsky—Lydia Chukovskaia. Perepiska. 1912–1969*, ed. Zhozefina Khavkina and Elena Chukovskaia (Moscow: Novoe literaturnoe obozrenie, 2003), 255. Chukovsky had read *Sofia Petrovna* by the end of March 1940.

11. Chukovskaia, *Zapiski*, 1: 74. The idea of writing a work of fiction about the Great Terror first occurred to Chukovskaia in 1937, after she read Herzen's sketch "They Killed Him" ("Ubili") about the death of the poet Mikhail Mikhailov (1829–1865) in a Siberian prison. "But I never wrote about Mikhailov, I wrote *Sofia Petrovna* instead" (1: 74).

12. Chukovskaya, *Akhmatova Journals*, 180.

13. Chukovskaya, 180–81.

14. Chukovskaya, 18.

15. Bronshtein was shot on February 18, 1938. See Chukovskaia's memoir *Procherk* (Moscow: Vremia, 2009).

16. Chukovskaia, *Zapiski*, 2: 540–41. Glikin's name was first mentioned in this connection by Solzhenitsyn, who must have heard about him from Chukovskaia. Solzhenitsyn, *Gulag Archipelago*, 2: 641.

17. Chukovskaia, *Zapiski*, 2: 33; emphasis in the original.

18. On January 24, 1956, a month before the Twentieth Party Congress, Chukovskaia confessed to Akhmatova that she would "very much like Boris Leonidovich [Pasternak] to read my novella." Chukovskaia, *Zapiski*, 2: 182. There is no evidence that Pasternak ever read it.

19. Lydia Chukovskaia, "'Sofia Petrovna'—luchshaia moia kniga. Iz dnevnika," *Novyi mir*, no. 6 (2014): 141.

20. Chukovskaia, *Zapiski*, 2: 480.

21. Chukovskaia, 2: 474.

22. Tvardovsky's review was read to Chukovskaia by Berzer over the phone. A professional stenographer, Chukovskaia made a verbatim record of it.

23. Chukovskaia, *Zapiski*, 2: 769–70.

24. Quoted in Kozlov, *Readers*, 164.

25. Chukovskaia, *Zapiski*, 2: 574. Tvardovsky's contempt for Chukovskaia was also partly based on her privileged social and family background. On August 20, 1965, upon reading the memoirs of Nikolai Chukovsky, Tvardovsky referred to him as "the talentless son of a writer, who, much like his sister, became a writer out of genealogical circumstances [*po obstoiatel'stvam rozhdeniia*] and the environment—automatically." Tvardovsky, *Novomirskii dnevnik*, 1: 379.

26. Toker, *Return*, 222.

27. Chukovskaia, *Zapiski*, 2: 792.

28. Kornei Chukovsky, *Dnevnik. 1930–1969* (Moscow: Sovremennyi pisatel', 1994), 330–31; diary entry of December 16, 1962.

29. Chukovskaia, *Zapiski*, 2: 793.

30. Chukovskaia.

31. Chukovskaia, 2: 793–94.

32. Chukovskaia, 2: 794.

33. Chukovskaia, 3: 14.

34. Chukovskaia, 3: 793.

35. Lydia Chukovskaia, "Luchshaia moia kniga," 151.

36. Chukovskaia, *Zapiski*, 2: 556.

37. In the beginning of 1961, Kozhevnikov personally delivered a copy of Vasily Grossman's *Life and Fate* to the KGB after it was submitted to his journal. As a result, the novel was "arrested" and banned; all other copies except one, which was later smuggled out and published abroad, were confiscated from the author's archive. Solzhenitsyn recalls, however, that Grossman's manuscript was confiscated from the vault of Tvardovsky's *Novyi mir*. Solzhenitsyn, *Oak and Calf*, 101.

38. Chukovskaia, *Zapiski*, 2: 558–59.

39. Chukovskaia, 2: 571–72.

40. Chukovskaia, 3: 37.

41. Chukovskaia, 3: 348. See also Chukovskaia's diary entry on March 29, 1963: "Well, we have survived so many pogroms, and far more brutal ones. So we will survive one more. But 'Sofia' will no longer survive. 'Sofia.' She is on the threshold of death. Again." 3:38.

42. Chukovskaia, 3: 357.

43. Chukovskaia, 3: 52. Memory, according to Efim Etkind, is Chukovskaia's "favorite word," one that "appears more often than any other in her books and articles" and stands for the "triumph of truth over lies." (Efim Etkind, "Otets i doch'," *Vremia i my* 66 (May–June 1982): 177–78.

44. "Sudebnyi protsess Lidii Chukovskoi protiv izdatel'stva 'Sovetskii pisatel','" *Politicheskii dnevnik. 1964–1970* (Amsterdam: Alexander Herzen Foundation, 1972), 55.

45. Chukovsky and Chukovskaia, *Perepiska*, 259.

46. Holmgren, *Women's Works*, 192.

47. Holmgren, *Women's Works*, 47.

48. The first book edition of Nikolai Chernyshevsky's novel appeared in Geneva: *Chto delat'? Iz rasskazov o novykh liudiakh. Roman* (Geneva: Elpidin, 1867). The first edition to be published in Russia was Nikolai Chernyshevsky, *Chto delat'? Roman* (St. Petersburg: Tipografiia V. A. Tikhanova, 1905). In 1901–1902, the same title was used by no one less than Lenin for a book, which at the time he too could only publish abroad (in Stuttgart).

49. Forrester, "*Mother* as Forebear," 52.

50. "In both works," Forrester adds, "the son has a close friend, who becomes to some degree the mother's foster son," Forrester, 53. In *Sofia Petrovna* this role belongs to Kolya's Jewish friend and coworker, Alik Finkelshtein.

51. Forrester, 56.

52. Forrester, 53.

53. Chukovskaia, "Luchshaia moia kniga," 154. This lineage between Sofia Petrovna and Gogol's petty clerk was first noted in Kees Verheul, "Een Russische poging tot rekenschap," *Tirade* 13 (January 1969): 43. After Chukovskaia's novella was published in Russia in 1988, Natalia Ivanova likewise compared Sofia Petrovna to an "Akaky Akakievich of the 1930s of our century," Natalia Ivanova, "Khranit' vechno," *Iunost'*, no. 7 (1988): 87.

54. Nikolai Gogol, *The Collected Tales*, trans. Richard Pevear and Larissa Volokhonsky (New York: Vintage, 1999), 394.

55. Chukovskaya, *Sofia Petrovna*, 3–4.

56. Gogol, *Collected Tales*, 419.

57. Chukovskaia, *Zapiski*, 3: 202.

58. Quoted in Irina Obukhova-Zelin'skaia, *K. I. Chukovsky i Yu. P. Annenkov. "Nesmotria na razluchaiushchee nas rasstoianie i na istekshie gody . . ."* (Moscow: MIK, 2017), 84–85. Annenkov's correspondence with Chukovsky resumed in 1961.

59. In the 1910s and 1920s, Annenkov illustrated Chukovsky's *Krokodil* and *Moidodyr*. He also authored sketches and caricatures of Chukovsky and other writers (Yury Iurkun, Velimir Khlebnikov, Mikhail Zoshchenko, Nikolai Evreinov, Aleksei Tolstoy, and Alexander Blok, whose poem "Twelve" Annenkov illustrated). The sample copy of Chukovskaia's novella with Annenkov's cover art and illustrations is held among Chukovsky's papers at the Russian National Library (Fond 620). The cover is reproduced in Obukhova-Zelin'skaia, *Chukovsky i Annenkov*, 84.

60. Chukovskaya, *Sofia Petrovna*, 66; emphasis in the original. Cf., for example, Andrei Tarkovsky's film *The Mirror* (1975), whose protagonist Masha, a proofreader for a Soviet newspaper in the 1930s, rushes to the print shop in fear that a typo may have crept into Stalin's name. It is not made clear what the typo was, or even if there was a typo, since it may have been just a product of Masha's afflicted imagination (although it can be inferred that "Stalin" may have been misspelled as "Sralin"). As the title of Tarkovsky's film suggests, the political reality under Stalin was "mirrored" in the Soviet subject's psyche, much as the years of the Great Terror, the historical setting for this episode, were reflected in the post-Thaw reality of the late 1960s and early 1970s when Tarkovsky worked on his film.

61. Akhmatova, *Requiem* (Munich: Tovarishchestvo zarubezhnykh pisatelei, 1963), 17.

62. Fyodor Dostoevsky, *An Honest Thief and Other Stories*, trans. Constance Garnett (New York: Macmillan, 1923), 58.

63. Verheul, "Een Russische," 46.

64. Alexander Werth, "A Classic of the Purge," Review of *Opustelyi dom*, by Ludia Chukovskaya, *Times Literary Supplement*, February 16, 1967.

65. Gleb Struve, "A Classic of the Purge" [Letter to the Editor], *Times Literary Supplement*, March 9, 1967.

66. Annenkov's name is mentioned in this regard in Struve's letter to Alexander Bakhrakh on March 14, 1967, Alexandre Bakhrakh Papers, Box 4, Bakhmeteff Archive, Columbia University.

67. Struve, "Classic of the Purge." In his letter to Bakhrakh, Struve specifies, "I have a letter from Moscow written in late 1962 or early 1963 about this story, and in this letter both the novella itself and the heroine are called Sofia Petrovna," Alexandre Bakhrakh Papers, Box 4. Whose letter Struve had in mind remains unknown.

68. She could have communicated her objection to Annenkov personally or through her father, but their letters to Annenkov are unavailable.

69. Lydia Chukovskaia, "Otkrytoe pis'mo pisatel'nitsy Lidii Chukovskoi M. Sholokhovu," *Russkaia mysl'*, November 29, 1966. The letter, originally titled "Mikhailu Sholokhovu, avtoru 'Tikhogo Dona,'" was written on May 25, 1966, soon after the Twenty-third Congress of the Party held March 28–April 9, 1966, where Sholokhov, the Nobel Prize laureate for literature in 1965, infamously regretted that Sinyavsky's and Daniel's sentences of seven and five years, respectively, were perhaps too "lenient." The editorial preface to Chukovskaia's letter in *Russkaia mysl'* referred to her "courage and candor" as "a sufficient proof of the truthfulness of her novella," whereby the purges of the 1930s and the show trials of the 1960s, in public consciousness, remained intertwined. Chukovskaia's letter to Sholokhov was not her first public statement in defense of Sinyavsky and Daniel. On January 23, 1966, she and Vladimir Kornilov coauthored an open letter to the editor of *Izvestiia*, where the two writers on trial had been slandered in Dmitry Eremin's article "Perevertyshi" ("The Turncoats"). See Lydia Chukovskaia, *Otkrytoe slovo* (New York: Khronika Press, 1976), 15–17.

70. "Po povodu knigi 'Opustelyi dom,'" *Russkaia mysl'*, January 5, 1967.

71. For the publisher of Five Continents, the arrest, persecution, and trial of Sinyavsky and Daniel became "a complete revelation." Only then, in his own words, did he understand that "statements of the highest officials of the Soviet party and the state about the Soviet Union's invincible power do not correspond to reality—from this trial, it appeared that two or three books published in the West without the permission of Soviet censorship can in fact 'undermine the foundations of the Soviet system, weaken its power,'" "Po povodu knigi."

72. Lydia Chukovskaia, "Sofia Petrovna," *Novyi zhurnal* 83 (1966): 5.

73. Chukovskaia, "Luchshaia moia kniga," 159; diary entry on December 22, 1966. By contrast, three months earlier, when she first saw the Parisian edition, it left Chukovskaia with mixed feelings. "I received 'Sofia' under the title 'Opustelyi dom.' Cannot read it. Only peeked inside—nearly all the characters have been for some reason renamed. . . . They are some strangers. The heroine's name is Olga Petrovna. On the cover, there is a quote from 'Requiem' on a red wrapper. (Never have I imagined that a quote from AA may look unpleasant.) Still, despite everything, it is her, my Sofia. I am holding it in my hands. It is published." "Luchshaia moia kniga," 158–59; diary entry on September 24, 1966. The edition Chukovskaia is referring to appears to be yet another draft version, since there is neither a red wrapper nor a quote from *Requiem* on the cover of *Opustelyi dom* as released by Five Continents in Paris later that year.

74. Chukovskaia, *Opustelyi dom*, 6.

75. Struve, "Classic of the Purge."

76. See Chukovskaia's diary entries in late 1967 and early 1968 on the translations of *Sofia Petrovna* into English, French, German, and Dutch, as well as on the reviews of these foreign-language editions (Chukovskaia, "Luchshaia moia kniga," 159).

77. Alexander Werth, "A Classic of the Purge" [Letter to the Editor], *Times Literary Supplement*, March 23, 1967; emphasis in the original.

78. Werth, "A Classic of the Purge," *Times Literary Supplement.*

79. Chukovsky and Chukovskaia, *Perepiska*, 424.

80. The mystification was exposed by the émigré critic Leonid Rzhevsky seven years after both Chukovsky and Grynberg died in 1969. Rzhevsky first published their correspondence in Russian. Leonid Rzhevsky, "Zagadochnaia korrespondentka." Chukovsky's other American correspondent throughout the 1960s was the translator Mirra Ginzburg. See Tatiana Chebotarev, "'Vy—khudozhnik, ne remeslennik.' Perepiska Korneiia Chukovskogo i Mirry Ginzburg," *Arkhiv evreiskoi istorii* 4 (2007): 248–318.

81. Kornei Chukovsky, *Sobranie sochinenii v 15 tomakh* (Moscow: Agentstvo FTM, 2012), 15: 700–706. The first of both issues of *Novyi zhurnal* with *Sofia Petrovna* reached Chukovsky no later than November 14, 1967: "Reading an old report on the meeting at the Writers' Union a propos Pasternak," Chukovsky, *Dnevnik*, 387. The report on Pasternak's expulsion from the Writers' Union on October 31, 1958, was published in the same issue of *Novyi zhurnal*, no. 83, as the first installment of *Sofia Petrovna*.

82. Boris Filippov Papers, Gen Mss 334, Box 3, Folder 83, Beinecke Rare Book and Manuscript Library, Yale University.

83. Boris Filippov Papers, Gen Mss 334, Box 3, Folder 83.

84. Filippov's name was invoked in multiple Soviet publications on Sinyavsky and Daniel, including Dmitry Eremin, "Perevertyshi," *Izvestiia*, January 13, 1966, and Zoya Kedrina, "Nasledniki Smerdiakova," *Literaturnaia gazeta*, January 22, 1966. It was also mentioned at the trial. Other invectives exposed Filippov's real name, Filistinsky, and targeted him not only as a tamizdat publisher but also as a Nazi collaborator on the occupied territories during the war. See, e.g., A. Ivashchenko, "Podsadnaia utka: istoriia prestuplenii B. Filippova-Filistinskovo, v proshlom gestapovtsa, nyne izdatelia-klevetnika v Soedinennykh Shtatakh," *Komsomol'skaia pravda*, June 9, 1968.

85. The scandal involved other Western publishing ventures as well, such as Stephen Spender's *Encounter*. See, for example, Sylvan Fox, "Stephen Spender Quits *Encounter*," *New York Times*, May 8, 1967.

86. Chukovskaya, *Sofia Petrovna*, 119. The quote comes from Lydia Chukovskaia, *Protsess iskliucheniia* (Paris: YMCA-Press, 1979), 18.

87. Grigory Aronson, Review of *Novyi zhurnal* 83, *Novoe russkoe slovo*, June 19, 1966.

88. Yury Terapiano, Review of *Novyi zhurnal* 83, *Russkaia mysl'*, July 16, 1966.

89. Yury Terapiano, Review of *Novyi zhurnal* 84, *Russkaia mysl'*, November 12, 1966.

90. Yury Bolshukhin, Review of *Novyi zhurnal* 84, *Novoe russkoe slovo*, November 27, 1966.

91. Chukovskaia, *Sofia Petrovna*, 39.

92. Chukovskaia, 2.

93. Maia Muravnik, "'Rekviem' v proze," *Novoe russkoe slovo*, May 13, 1988.

94. Werth, "Classic of the Purge." Born in St. Petersburg in 1901, Werth emigrated to England in 1922. During World War II, he was stationed in Moscow as a foreign correspondent and subsequently traveled to the USSR more

than once. In June 1967 he visited Chukovskaia, among others, in Peredelkino. See his *Russia: Hopes and Fears* (New York: Simon & Schuster, 1969), 297–98.

95. David Gallagher, "Friends and Enemies," *Times Literary Supplement*, September 7, 1967. An exception to this pattern was Nikolai Belov's review of *Opustelyi dom*, where Chukovskaia's work is referred to as "a pearl amid the heap of memoirs" but is rather unexpectedly compared to Maupassant's debut novel *Une Vie*. Nikolai Belov, Review of *Opustelyi dom*, by Lydia Chukovskaia, *Russkaia mysl'*, December 22, 1966. Having read *The Deserted House* in English translation, Montague Haltrecht also noted that "the novel does not earn its praise merely on account of its subject matter." Montague Haltrecht, "A Nightmare of the Purses," *Sunday Times*, August 27, 1967.

96. Merle Fainsod, "One to Be Burned," *New York Times*, November 12, 1967.

97. Fainsod, "One to Be Burned."

98. Chukovskaia, *Opustelyi dom*, 5. David Gallagher disagreed: "*The Deserted House* is in some ways a more fascinating description of Stalin's purges even than Solzhenitsyn's *A Day in the Life of Ivan Denisovich*, because the action takes place not in some safely distant camp but in Leningrad." David Gallagher, "Somewhere in Leningrad," *Times*, August 28, 1967.

99. Evgeniia Ginzburg's memoir was published simultaneously in the Frankfurt-based Russian émigré journal *Grani* (nos. 64–68, 1967) and as a book in Italy (Milan: Mondadori, 1967). Allilueva's *Dvadtsat' pisem' k drugu* came out in New York the same year (New York: Harper & Row, 1967).

100. Saul Maloff, "Can Such Things Have Been?" *Chicago Tribune*, November 5, 1967.

101. Svetlana Allilueva, *Twenty Letters to a Friend*, trans. Priscilla Johnson (New York: Harper & Row, 1967), 59. In fact, Svetlana must have been twelve, since the described episode is preceded by the arrest of Stanislav Redens in November 1938.

102. Maloff, "Such Things."

103. Chukovskaia, *Sofia Petrovna*, 98, 104.

104. Nikolai Belov, "Vtoraia zhizn' Evgenii Ginzburg," *Russkaia mysl'*, July 13, 1967. Without discussing the specific discrepancies between *Opustelyi dom* and the *Novyi zhurnal* publication, Belov notes that the Milan book edition of Ginzburg's *Krutoi marshrut* happens to be less reliable than its serialized publication in *Grani*.

105. George Haupt, Review of *The Deserted House*, by Lydia Chukovskaya, and *Journey into the Whirlwind*, by Eugenia Ginzburg, *Russian Review* 28, no. 2 (April 1969): 243.

106. Harrison E. Salisbury, "Loyalty was the Error," *New York Times*, November 19, 1967. See also, Haupt, "Review," "While Chukovskaya engages in fine psychological analysis, Ginzburg gives a minute and factual account of her own vicissitudes and those of others who traveled with her from station to station on the road to Calvary."

107. Helen Muchnic, "Nightmares," *New York Review of Books*, January 4, 1968.

108. Serebriakova's memoir was first published in Paris in the Polish émigré journal *Kultura* 7–8 (1967): 47–50, and serialized the same year in Russian in *Novoe russkoe slovo* in New York (December 8–30, 1967). As one émigré critic noted, "Having written *Sandstorm*, Galina Serebriakova remained not a human but a party functionary." (Boris Domogatsky, "Zapiski iz ada," *Novoe russkoe slovo*, June 7, 1968).

109. See also, for example, Werth's description of *Sofia Petrovna* as "just as significant and, in its own way, fully as masterly as Alexander Solzhenitsyn's *One Day in the Life of Ivan Denisovich*. Like that book, it will rank as one of the classics of Russian 'purge literature.'" Werth, "Classic of the Purge." Merle Fainsod wrote, along the same lines, that "'The Deserted House' promises to take its place with 'Ivan Denisovich' as one of the most impressive examples of the genre of Russian 'purge literature.'" Fainsod, "One to Be Burned." See also "Sauberungs-Literatur. Artikel 58," review of *Journey into the Whirlwind*, by Eugenia Ginzburg, and *Kolyma Tales*, by Varlam Shalamov, *Der Spiegel*, no. 40 (September 25, 1967): 176–77.

110. Thompson Bradley, Review of *The Deserted House*, by Lydia Chukovskaya, *Slavic Review* 27, no. 4 (December 1968): 688.

111. Bradley, "Review," 688.

112. Herman Ermolaev, Review of *The Deserted House*, by Lydia Chukovskaya, *Slavic and East European Journal* 13, no. 1 (Spring 1969): 101.

113. Ermolaev, 99. Ermolaev was mistaken, however, in assuming that the Paris edition of *Opustelyi dom*, from which the English translation was made, "judging from various changes and improvements, is the more recent one," Ermolaev, 100.

114. Robert Granat, "The Great God Ninel," *New Leader* 51, no. 3 (January 29, 1968): 21.

115. Muravnik, "'Rekviem' v proze."

116. Chukovskaia continued to work on *Going Under* through 1957. On December 3, 1957, she wrote to Leonid Panteleev from Dubulty, Latvia, that she had "completed the novella" she had been writing "since 1949, two weeks at a time." Panteleev and Chukovskaia, *Perepiska*, 119. The same year Pasternak's *Doctor Zhivago* was published in Italy. The campaign against him, however, goes back years earlier and is reflected in *Going Under*. "I have seen enough of them in Maleevka," Chukovskaia wrote about Pasternak's adversaries, "and have described them accurately." Chukovskaia, *Zapiski*, 2: 323; diary entry of October 28, 1958.

117. Chukovskaia, *Zapiski*, 2: 299. Akhmatova was one of the first readers of Chukovskaia's novella, although her initial response to *Going Under* on April 21, 1958, when she read it in Chukovskaia's presence, was evidently more reserved than her response eighteen years earlier, when she first read *Sofia Petrovna* (299–303). A month later, *Going Under* was read by Leonid Panteleev, who found it too autobiographical. Panteleev and Chukovskaia. *Perepiska*, 123. "Autobiography, in my view," Chukovskaia wrote back, "is a natural source of any writer's work. And if you have an unpleasant feeling while reading it, I am afraid it is not because it is autobiographical, but because it is not masterful

enough from the literary perspective." Panteleev and Chukovskaia, 124. Later readers of *Going Under* in Russia included Lev Kopelev and Raisa Orlova, as well as theater critic Vera Shitova and translator Lenina Zonina, none of whom thought highly of the novella, whether because it was fiction or because the protagonist's ignorance of her husband's fate ten years after his death seemed too incredible. Lydia Chukovskaia, *"Dnevnik—bol'shoe podspor'ie . . ." (1938–1994)* (Moscow: Vremia, 2015), 234–35; diary entry of May 20, 1969.

118. In 1937, in conjunction with the Soviet centennial of Pushkin's death, Detskoe Selo was renamed Pushkin. Until 1918 the town had been called Tsarskoe Selo. Chukovskaia stayed in Maleevka in November and December 1948. The history of Maleevka, although less famous than Tsarskoe Selo, also goes back to the nineteenth century, when it belonged to Count Vorontsov, then to merchant Maleev, and later to the journalist and translator Vukol Lavrov. It became a Soviet writers' residence in the 1920s.

119. Cf., for example, Vasily Grossman's novel *Everything Flows* (*Vse techet*), which shares some of the subject matter with *Going Under* as it tells the story of a recent gulag returnee. Written in 1955–1963, the manuscript of *Everything Flows* was "arrested" together with Grossman's *Life and Fate* and did not appear abroad until after the author's death (Frankfurt: Possev, 1970).

120. Chukovskaia, *Sofia Petrovna*, 3.

121. Chukovskaia's memoir about her father was first published abroad, Lydia Chukovskaia, *Pamiati detstva*, with an afterword by Efim Etkind (New York: Chalidze Publications, 1983); Lydia Chukovskaya, *To the Memory of Childhood*, trans. Eliza Kellogg (Evanston, IL: Northwestern University Press, 1988).

122. Chukovskaia, *Byloe i dumy Gertsena*.

123. Although there is little discussion of Herzen's London-based publishing house and its role in fighting censorship in tsarist Russia, by working on Herzen throughout the 1950s and early 1960s Chukovskaia was "implicitly justifying the strategy that she has used in her own two novels." Alexis Klimoff, "In Defense of the Word: Lydia Chukovskaya and the Russian Tradition," introduction to Lydia Chukovskaia, *The Deserted House*, trans. Aline B. Werth (New York: Nordland, 1978), xxvi.

124. Before they were published together under one cover (Chukovskaia, *Otkrytoe slovo*), Chukovskaia's political statements appeared in Russian émigré and Western periodicals.

125. In June 1973 Michael Scammell, a British journalist, translator, and founder of *Index on Censorship* in London, was searched at the airport in Moscow after visiting Chukovskaia. The KGB confiscated his personal notes and a letter from Chukovskaia to Zhores Medvedev, Soviet scientist and dissident who had recently settled in London and whom she was asking to handle royalties from the sales of her books abroad. Medvedev specifies that while the incident took place in June 1973, it was not until Chukovskaia's expulsion from the Writers' Union that the newspaper *Sovetskaia Rossiia* decided to make this public, on January 12, 1974, falsifying facts about her publications in tamizdat. Zhores A. Medvedev, "The Attack on Lydia Chukovskaya," *New York Review of Books*, March 7, 1974. The statement first appeared in Russian in *Novoe russkoe*

slovo on January 25, 1974. In particular, the Soviet newspaper claimed that *Sofia Petrovna* and *Going Under* were brought out, respectively, not in New York and Paris, but in West Germany by Possev, a publishing house whose overt anti-Soviet agenda, ill-famed affiliation with the NTS, and support from the CIA made it especially ominous for a writer in Russia. In addition, *Sovetskaia Rossiia* stated that Scammell attempted to smuggle out Chukovskaia's "short stories," which, according to Medvedev, who saw the protocol of the search, was also a falsification.

126. Akhmatov, *Zapisnye knizhki*, 441.
127. Kudrova, *Russkie vstrechi*, 67. In June 1965 Norman was one of Akhmatova's hosts in England. Together with Amanda Haight, he prepared an English translation of *Requiem* that Akhmatova approved of as the most accurate although literal; this translation, however, remained unpublished. In March 1966 Norman was denied a visa to Russia to attend Akhmatova's funeral. See his account of meetings with Chukovskaia during his next trip to Russia in 1967, Kudrova, 67–71, when they discussed, in particular, the publication of Chukovskaia's *Akhmatova Journals* (*Zapiski*) in English, for which Norman translated Akhmatova's poems.
128. Kudrova, *Russkie vstrechi*, 70. By 1972 Chekhov Publishing House, spearheaded by Max Hayward, had brought out, among other titles, Brodsky's second collection of poetry, *Ostanovka v pustyne* (*A Halt in the Desert*), and Nadezhda Mandelshtam's first book of memoirs, *Vospominaniia*, both published in 1970. Hayward's Chekhov Publishing House is not to be confused with the old émigré press of the same name, which was active in New York between 1952 and 1956.
129. Chukovskaia, *Protsess iskliucheniia*, 71.
130. Chukovskaia, "Dnevnik," 274–75. In 1972 *Literaturnaia gazeta* seems to have held the record of open letters by Soviet writers protesting their publications abroad. Those included Bulat Okudzhava and Anatoly Gladilin (both published on November 29, 1972), Arkady and Boris Strugatsky (on December 13, 1972), and Varlam Shalamov (on February 23, 1972). On Shalamov's letter to *Literaturnaia gazeta*, see chapter 4. As an earlier example, Strekhnin invoked a similar letter by Tvardovsky, who contested the pirated publication of his *Vasily Terkin in the Otherworld* (*Vasily Terkin na tom svete*) in Munich almost ten years earlier, *Mosty* 10 (1963): 129–44. Accordingly, 1972 saw a spike in publications of contraband manuscripts from the USSR in tamizdat, which apart from Chukovskaia's *Going Under* included Gladilin's *Forecast for Tomorrow* (*Prognoz na zavtra*), Boris and Arkady Strugatskys' novels *Snail on the Slope* (*Ulitka na sklone*) and *The Ugly Swans* (*Gadkie lebedi*), Alexander Galich's *Generation of the Doomed* (*Pokolenie obrechennykh*), all published in Frankfurt by Possev, as well as Andrei Platonov's *Chevengur* and Nadezhda Mandelshtam's *Hope Abandoned* (*Vtoraia kniga*) by YMCA-Press, and Petr Yakir's *A Childhood in Prison* (*Detstvo v tiur'me*) by Macmillan.
131. Chukovskaia, "Dnevnik," 275.
132. Lydia Chukovskaya, *Going Under*, trans. Peter M. Weston (London: Barrie & Jenkins, 1972). See Chukovskaia's diary entry of July 15, 1972, which

references the edition, Chukovskaia, *"Dnevnik,"* 272. On August 20, 1972, her daughter Elena heard it announced on the radio, and in the next few days, Chukovskaia listened to three BBC broadcasts devoted to her novella's English translation. "The reviews are at a very low level. My book is about the word—but no word about it. . . . General evaluation: below 'Requiem' and Nadezhda Mandelshtam's memoirs. But why must it be compared to the 'Poem' and the memoirs? Extremely silly," *"Dnevnik,"* 272-73.

133. Kudrova, *Russkie vstrechi*, 70. It remains unclear whether "P. Winster" is Norman's own typo or Kudrova's, who published his memoirs in Russian.

134. Kudrova.

135. Lydia Chukovskaia, *Sofia Petrovna. Spusk pod vodu* (Moscow: Moskovskii rabochii, 1988). A copy of this edition, inscribed to Norman, reveals that even in 1988 Chukovskaia still did not know that sixteen years earlier *Going Under* had been translated by him. The inscription reads, "Dear Peter! Please be healthy to translate *Going Under* for me," Kudrova, *Russkie vstrechi*, 60.

136. Mikhail Koriakov, "'Rodina moia, Rossiia . . . '," *Novoe russkoe slovo*, April 2, 1972.

137. Cf., Chukovskaia, *Zapiski*, 2: 301. "She likes everything about the street lights [*nravitsia vse fonarnoe*]. Everything after it is better than what comes before." In Chukovskaia's manuscript, the inserted text was originally titled "Fonari na mostu" ("Street Lights on the Bridge"), but "in the American edition," as the author points out, the title "was removed by me," 301. In later editions, Nina Sergeevna's "manuscript" in *Going Under* was printed as "Bez nazvaniia" ("Untitled").

138. Koriakov, "Rodina moia."

139. Tolstoi, *Polnoe sobranie sochinenii*, 41: 345 ("Krug chteniia").

140. Koriakov, "Rodina moia." In the postscript to his review, Koriakov lashes out against the editors of Chekhov Publishing House for their "tasteless" and "redundant" note about Chukovskaia, her father, and the historical setting of the novella: "After all, the book is not published for some kind of Paraguayans!" Evidently, by "Paraguayans" Koriakov means the non-Russian cofounders of the press, Max Hayward and Edward Kline. Two years earlier Koriakov had attacked them for publishing "ignorant notes of some unknown person" as a preface to Brodsky's *Ostanovka v pustyne*, which were in fact written by Anatoly Naimain and edited by Edward Kline. "We have never yet witnessed such a desecration of Russian poetry and of Chekhov's name," Koriakov wrote, enraged by the "encroachment" of the sacred name of Chekhov by the trespassing "Paraguayans." Mikhail Koriakov, "Izdatel'stvo imeni Chekhova," *Novoe russkoe slovo*, June 25, 1970.

141. One exception was an anonymous review, which argued that *Going Under* "has not just hit on a 'theme' with built-in resonance, horror, moment; a real literary talent is at work, artistically illuminating a virtually incomprehensible experience," Review of *Going Under*, by Lydia Chukovskaya, *New York Times*, October 17, 1976.

142. "Down into the Past," *Times Literary Supplement*, August 11, 1972.

143. "Down into the Past." It is unlikely that by referring to the "Chekhovian" tone of *Going Under*, the critic could have implied the Chekhov Publishing House that brought out the Russian edition.

144. A fleeting reference to Dostoevsky is nevertheless made in one of the English reviews of *The Deserted House*, in which Chukovskaia's first work is referred to as "a document, a note from underground." Maloff, "Such Things."

145. Anatole Broyard, "A Matter of Literary Politics," *New York Times*, March 31, 1976.

146. The phrase belonged to Anatoly Safonov, twice laureate of the Stalin Prize for Literature and Art, who used it at the meeting of Soviet writers in Moscow on October 31, 1958, when Pasternak was unanimously expelled from their ranks. Chukovskaia was subjected to a similar procedure twelve years after Pasternak. This formula was also applied to Brodsky, as well as Sinyavsky and Daniel, during the campaigns against them in 1964 and 1966.

147. Broyard, "Literary Politics."

148. See, for example, an essay on Broyard by Henry Louis Gates, Jr., "White Like Me," *New Yorker*, June 17, 1996.

149. Broyard, "Literary Politics."

150. A similarly nostalgic sentiment is voiced in another pseudonymous review of *Spusk pod vodu*, E. B., "Review of *Spusk pod vodu*," *Novoe russkoe slovo*, November 19, 1972.

151. Broyard, "Literary Politics." Broyard's review pertained to the second printing of *Going Under* in 1976. On November 2, 1976, Chukovskaia heard his review broadcast in Russian translation over Voice of America: "I was lying in bed listening to the radio. . . . And suddenly I hear right over my ear, 'Lydia Korneevna Chukovskaia.' It turns out that *Going Under* has been published in the U.S. and the 'Voice' is broadcasting a review from the *New York Times*. Of course, I immediately forgot the name of the publishing house and the translator. Then I heard that the novella allegedly takes place in the Russian part of Finland. Enraged, I turned off the radio. . . . Apparently, it is the 'Finnish houses' that confuse them." Chukovskaia, "Dnevnik," 292–93.

152. Andrei Klenov, "Chudesnaia kniga," *Novoe russkoe slovo*, June 30, 1974.

153. Cf., the opening of Prishvin's short story "A Holiday" ("Prazdnik"), first published in *Literaturnaia gazeta* on May 1, 1941: "I confess that the words 'House of Creative Work' [*Dom tvorchestva*] (Maleevka) used to sound ridiculous to me. Never had I thought that the ideas of creativity and institution were compatible. But when I found myself in Maleevka, had a meal with everybody else, had a chat, read, played the billiard and wrote something or other, my notion of the House of Creative Work changed; it turned out it was not about the words, but about the work itself: everyone here works splendidly and meets each other at ease. Nowhere did I hear writers converse with each other so freely and soulfully as in Maleevka." Mikhail Prishvin, *Sobranie sochinenii v 8 tomakh* (Moscow: Khudozhestvennaia literatura, 1983), 5: 244.

154. Chukovskaia, *Going Under*, 25.

155. Chukovskaia, 48–50.

156. Shmuel Halkin, *Erdishe vegn* [Earthly Ways] (Moscow: Der Emes, 1945).

157. *Heymland* 1 (1947): 104–5. I owe this observation to Dr. Dov-Ber Kerler. I am also grateful to Barbara Harshav and Bogdan Horbal, Amanda Seigel, and Lyudmila Sholokhova for their help with the poem attribution.

158. Aron Kushnirov, "Tri stikhotvoreniia," trans. Ruvim Moran, *Novyi mir*, no. 4 (1947): 117. Cf. Chukovskaia's diary entry on April 10, 1947: "Nothing

interesting [in this issue of *Novyi mir*] except Kushnerev [sic!]." Lydia Chukovskaia, *Iz dnevnika. Vospominaniia* (Moscow: Vremia, 2010), 145. In 1948 *Father-Commander* (*Foter-Komandir*) served as the title of Kushnirov's book of poetry (Moscow: Der Emes, 1948).

159. See Joshua Rubenstein and Vladimir P. Naumov, *Stalin's Secret Pogrom: The Post-War Inquisition of the Jewish Anti-Fascist Committee*, trans. Laura Esther Wolfson (New Haven, CT: Yale University Press, 2005).

160. Chukovskaia, *Going Under*, 88.

161. See also Anna Akhmatova, *The Complete Poems*, ed. with an introduction by Roberta Reeder, trans. Judith Hemschemeyer (Boston: Zephyr Press, 1997), 414: "If only you knew from what rubbish / Poetry grows, knowing no shame, / Like a yellow dandelion by the fence, / Like burdock and goosefoot." In later editions of *Going Under*, only one quatrain of Akhmatova's 1922 poem is cited.

162. Chukovskaia, *Going Under*, 67.

163. Chukovskaia, 97.

164. Chukovskaia, 114.

165. Chukovskaia, 112.

166. Chukovskaia, *Procherk*. The book consists of eighteen chapters, as if to invoke the eighteen years between Bronshtein's death in 1939 and the year Chukovskaia obtained his death certificate in 1957.

167. Galkin was decorated with the Order of the Red Banner of Labor in 1958 and died in 1960. He is buried at the Novodevichy Cemetery. See Lev Ozerov's 1990 poem "Shmuel Halkin" ("He was in Maleevka, / When they came for him . . ."), in his *Portraits without Frames*, ed. Robert Chandler and Boris Dralyuk, trans. Maria Bloshteyn, Robert Chandler, Boris Dralyuk and Irina Mashinski (New York: New York Review of Books, 2018), 152–55. See also Chukovskaia's diary entries about Galkin in her *Zapiski*, 2: 193, 293, 652. In 1958 Akhmatova was introduced to Galkin by Maria Petrovykh and translated five of his poems. What drew Akhmatova to Galkin, other than poetry, was the fact that he had been serving his sentence at the same labor camp in Abez, Komi Republic, as her husband Nikolai Punin, who died there in 1953.

168. As Chukovskaia confessed years later, *Going Under* was based to a large extent on her own diary entries from 1948–1951 and was thus "very close" in genre to her Akhmatova journals. Chukovskaia, *Zapiski*, 2: 297.

169. Chukovskaia, *Going Under*, 98.

170. Chukovskaia, *Sofia Petrovna*, 109.

171. Chukovskaia, 106.

172. Chukovskaia, 1.

173. Chukovskaia, *Going Under*, 105.

174. Chukovskaia, 109–10.

175. Chukovskaia, 101–2.

176. Chukovskaia, 110.

177. Chukovskaia, 37.

178. Chukovskaia, 126–29.

179. Grigory Svirsky, *Na lobnom meste: literatura nravstvennogo soprotivleniia (1946–1976 gg.)*, with an introduction by Efim Etkind (London: Overseas

Publications Interchange, 1979), 91. This "definition" is missing from the English version of Svirsky's book, *A History of Post-War Soviet Writing: The Literature of Moral Opposition*, ed. and trans. Robert Dessaix and Michael Ulman (Ann Arbor, MI: Ardis, 1981). In his monograph on Azhaev, Thomas Lahusen points out, however, that Svirsky had known Azhaev personally and even thanked him in writing for standing to his defense in 1952. Thomas Lahusen, *How Life Writes the Book: Real Socialism and Socialist Realism in Stalin's Russia* (Ithaca, NY: Cornell University Press, 1997), 194–95. Not disclosing his personal acquaintance with Azhaev, Svirsky reports having met Chukovskaia in Maleevka more than once, particularly in the late 1940s, "gray-haired, silent, short-sighted, almost never smiling." Svirsky, *Na lobnom meste*, 309.

180. Vasily Azhaev, "Daleko ot Moskvy," *Dal'nii Vostok*, nos. 1–2 (1946), 4 (1947), and 2 (1948).

181. Vasily Azhaev, "Daleko ot Moskvy," *Novyi mir*, nos. 7–9 (1948). In 1949 *Far from Moscow* came out as a separate edition and was awarded the Stalin Prize of the First Degree. A film adaptation by Aleksandr Stolper was made the following year (awarded another Stalin Prize in 1951). From 1960 until his death in 1968, Azhaev was the editor in chief of *Soviet Literature*, a journal that published socialist-realist works in foreign-language translations for export. On Azhaev's novel, see Lahusen, *Life Writes*, 103–22.

182. Konstantin Simonov, "Predislovie k romanu V. Azhaeva," in Vasily Azhaev, *Vagon* (Moscow: Sovremennik, 1988), 6–7.

183. Coincidentally, the year Orwell's famous dystopia *1984* was first published in England (1949) overlaps with the historical setting of *Going Under*. When Chukovskaia came across a radio program about Orwell, broadcast by one of the foreign stations, she remarked that his thoughts on language, and the language of lies in particular in *1984* and *Animal Farm*, "are entirely consonant with the thoughts expressed in my *Going Under*." Chukovskaia, "Dnevnik," 266–67; diary entry of April 27, 1972.

184. Anne Hartmann, "'Ein Fenster in die Vergangenheit': Das Lager neu lesen," *Osteuropa* 57, no. 6 (June 2007): 79. Hartmann refers to another novel written in the gulag that became a Soviet bestseller, Robert Stillmark's *Heir from Calcutta* (*Naslednik iz Kal'kutty*, 1958). However, Stillmark's popular adventure novel is an example of Aesopian language rather than a product of *goszakaz* (ideological state commission): set in the eighteenth century, it is removed from the gulag both historically and geographically, retaining only indirect references to Stalin's Russia. Furthermore, *Heir from Calcutta* was "commissioned" to the author by the criminal foreman in his labor camp, not a high-ranking literary functionary such as Simonov. Vasilevsky, the foreman, hoped to send the novel to Moscow as "his" tribute to Stalin and earn himself an early release. In 1958 his name appeared on the title page of the first edition as Stillmark's coauthor.

185. Svirsky, *Na lobnom meste*, 308.

186. Svirsky, 311.

187. Among other Soviet writers like Azhaev, Svirsky lists Yaroslav Smeliakov, Aleksandr Rekemchuk, and Yury Smirnov, "all of whom wrote their own 'Gulag Archipelagos.'" Svirsky, 311.

188. Chukovskaia, *Going Under*, 129.

189. Chukovskaia, 134.

190. Chukovskaia, 135.

191. A passing reference to Azhaev is found in her father's diary entry on April 19, 1962: "I am reading Azhaev. I could not even imagine one could be such a talentless writer. It is beyond literature," Chukovsky, *Dnevnik*, 310. Two years before his death, in 1966, Azhaev wrote his second novel, *The Train Car* (*Vagon*), in which he told the story of a young prisoner in the gulag from a much more outspoken perspective. *Vagon* was not published in Russia until 1988.

192. Chukovskaia, *Going Under*, 37.

193. E. B., "Review." Another review, on the other hand, spoke not only of *Going Under*, but also of *Sofia Petrovna* and even Chukovskaia's *Zapiski ob Anne Akhmatovoi* as "internal emigration." Ekaterina Breitbart, "Khranitsel'nitsa traditsii," *Grani* 104 (1977): 172. It is likely that the review signed with the initials "E. B" could also have been authored by Breitbart.

194. Holmgren, *Women's Works*, 59.

195. While condemning the male "artists" for their conformism and abuse of the written word, the female characters in *Going Under* "exemplify an altogether different Stalinist vice. . . . They either serve or accompany the 'artists.' In Nina Sergeevna's critical reading, they too devalue culture but in a more physical way; she scorns them as the embodiment of vulgar materialism and sensual indulgence." Holmgren, 61.

196. Chukovskaia, *Going Under*, 62.

197. Holmgren, *Women's Works*, 56.

198. Lewis Carroll, *Alice's Adventures in Wonderland* (New York: Appleton, 1866), 5.

199. Kristin Brandser, "Alice in Legal Wonderland: A Cross-Examination of Gender, Race, and Empire in Victorian Law and Literature," *Harvard Women's Law Journal* 24 (2001): 221. Moreover, "in this closing episode of *Alice's Adventures in Wonderland* (1865), Lewis Carroll dramatizes what was to become an increasingly popular Victorian scene: a woman questioning and critiquing the law and claiming a place for herself within its institutions," 221.

4. Varlam Shalamov's *Kolyma Tales*

1. Varlam Shalamov, "O proze," in his *Sobranie sochinenii*, 5: 157. For the English translation of Shalamov's essay "On Prose" (1965), see *Late and Post Soviet Russian Literature: A Reader*, Book 2, *Thaw and Stagnation*, ed. Mark Lipovetsky and Lisa Ryoko Wakamiya (Boston: Academic Studies Press, 2015), 111–26.

2. Varlam Shalamov, *Kolymskie rasskazy* (1978).

3. Shalamov's lifetime collections of poetry include *Ognivo* (*Flint*, 1961), *Shelest list'ev* (*The Rustle of the Leaves*, 1964), *Doroga i sud'ba* (*Road and Fate*, 1967), *Moskovskie oblaka* (*Moscow Clouds*, 1972), and *Tochka kipeniia* (*The Point of Ebullience*, 1977). The short story "Stlanik" ("Elfin Wood") was published in *Sel'skaia molodezh'*, no. 3 (1965): 2–3. Like his poetry, which the Soviet critics thought

was mainly devoted to northern nature (although they still censored and edited it for publication), "Stlanik" also posed innocently as a short story about botany rather than the gulag.

4. Roman Gul', *Ia unes Rossiu. Apologiia emigratsii*, vol. 3: *Rossiia v Amerike* (New York: Most, 1989), 170.

5. Roman Gul', preface to "Kolymskie rasskazy," by Varlam Shalamov, *Novyi zhurnal* 85 (1966): 5. This first selection of *Kolyma Tales* included "Sententsiia" ("Maxim"), "Posylka" ("The Parcel"), "Kant" ("Pushover") and "Sukhim paikom" ("Field Rations"). Unless otherwise noted, the English titles are from Varlam Shalamov, *Kolyma Stories*, trans. with an introduction by Ronald Rayfield (New York: New York Review of Books, 2018). Gul''s definition of *Kolyma Tales* as "a human document" (a soubriquet he applied to other manuscripts from the USSR as well) may go back to an earlier review of his own 1921 account of the Russian Civil War, *Ledianoi pokhod (The Ice Campaign)*, which Fedor Ivanov referred to as "a human document of contemporaneity," quoted in Oleg Korostelev, *Ot Adamovicha do Tsvetaevoi. Literatura, kritika, pechat' russkogo zarubezh'ia* (St. Petersburg: Izdatel'stvo imeni Novikova, 2013), 245.

6. Gul', *Ia unes Rossiu*, 3: 179.

7. For example, "Kaligula" ("Caligula") and "Pocherk" ("Handwriting") in *Posev*, no. 1 (January 7, 1967): 3–4; "Dve vstrechi" ("Two Encounters") and "Chuzhoi khleb" ("Someone Else's Bread") in *Vestnik RSKhD* 89–90 (1968): 90–94; "Vizit mistera Poppa" ("Mr. Popp's Visit") and "Bol'" ("Pain") in *Novoe russkoe slovo*, July 14, 1974. Apart from *Novyi zhurnal*, the most representative selections of *Kolyma Tales* were published in two consecutive issues of *Grani* 76 (1970): 16–83, and 77 (1970): 15–48.

8. Mikhail Geller, introduction to *Kolymskie rasskazy*, by Varlam Shalamov (London: Overseas Publications Interchange, 1978), 6.

9. The four cycles of *Kolyma Tales* completed by 1966 are "Kolymskie rasskazy" ("Kolyma Tales"), "Levyi bereg" ("The Left Bank"), "Artist lopaty" ("The Spade Artist"), and "Voskreshenie listvennitsy" ("The Resurrection of the Larch"). *Novyi zhurnal* published individual short stories from each of them.

10. Osip Mandelshtam, *Sobranie sochinenii v 2 tomakh*, ed. Gleb Struve and Boris Filippov (Washington DC: Inter-Language Literary Associates, 1964–1966).

11. Clarence Brown, "Memoirs from the House of the Dead," *Washington Post*, November 2, 1981. Brown's name was first mentioned in this regard by John Glad, in Varlam Shalamov, *Kolyma Tales*, trans. with a foreword by John Glad (London: Penguin, 1994), xv. In his 1981 review, as if reliving his impressions of Shalamov, Brown described him in the present tense as a "tall, broad-shouldered, raw-boned modern instance of Protopop Avvakum, whose only conceivable habitat in America would be Appalachia. He is utterly gentle, cultivated, and courteous. Nothing in his nature testifies to the torments endured during those 17 years in Stalin's frozen hell, except, perhaps, for the restless contortions of his hands, the fingers of which seem like prehistoric creatures locked in endless combat on the table."

12. Clarence Brown Papers, Princeton University. Brown's travel diary details his stay in Moscow from February 10 to May 25, 1966. See also the diary entry of Aleksandr Gladkov, who visited Nadezhda Mandelshtam on May 24,

1966, together with Brown and Shalamov. Mikhail Mikheev, "Oderzhimyi pravdoi: Varlam Shalamov—po dnevnikam Aleksandra Gladkova," https:// shalamov.ru/research/215/. On March 24, 1966, in a letter to his Princeton colleague Nina Berberova, Brown wrote about Akhmatova, who had died earlier that month. "I have the sad distinction of having been her last visitor. On the evening of the 2nd she was exceedingly warm and gay. We laughed a great deal and I left with the buoyant feeling that we would have many more meetings. On the 5th I learned that she had died that morning. In her coffin, a plain pine box, she was extraordinarily beautiful," Nina Berberova Papers, Gen Mss 182, Box 5, Folder 90, Beinecke Rare Book and Manuscript Library, Yale University. In addition to *Kolyma Tales*, the other manuscript Brown smuggled out of Russia in 1966 was Nadezhda Mandelshtam's memoir, first published four years later—Nadezhda Mandelshtam, *Vospominaniia*; Nadezhda Mandelshtam, *Hope against Hope*, trans. Max Hayward, with an introduction by Clarence Brown (New York: Atheneum, 1970). In 1976 Brown assisted in transferring Osip Mandelshtam's archive to Princeton, where it is held to this day.

13. Irina Sirotinskaia, "Interview to John Glad, Washington D.C., April 19, 1990," RGALI, Fond 2595. I thank Anna Gavrilova for familiarizing me with this source.

14. *The New Review* Records, Box 2, Folder 14, Amherst Center for Russian Culture.

15. Shalamov's manuscript is not mentioned anywhere in Brown's correspondence with either Filippov or Struve: Boris Filippov Papers. Gen Mss 334, Box 3, Folders 41–42, Beinecke Rare Book and Manuscript Library, Yale University; Gleb Struve Collection, box 26, folders 3–4, Hoover Institution Archives, Stanford University.

16. John Glad, *Conversations in Exile: Russian Writers Abroad*, trans. Richard Robin and Joana Robin (Durham, NC: Duke University Press, 1993), 62.

17. *The New Review* Records, Box 2, Folder 14; Gul''s emphasis.

18. *The New Review* Records, Box 2, Folder 14. Incidentally, this was also how Shalamov's *Kolyma Tales* were perceived at the time by some of his fellow writers in Russia, for example, by Lydia Chukovskaia: "I can't understand why I don't like [Shalamov's short stories]. Some time ago Fridochka [Vigdorova] gave them to me—the entire book—as a typescript. I read about 5 stories and stopped, gave them to someone else. . . . They lack something. But what? A sense of measure? The ability to convert horror and chaos into harmony?" Chukovskaia, "*Dnevnik*," 346–47; diary entry of April 25, 1985. "Shalamov's 'Kolyma Tales' are impossible to read. It is an agglomeration of horrors—here is one, here is one more. An invaluable contribution to our knowledge of Stalin's camps. A relic. Nothing more." Chukovskaia, *Iz dnevnika*, 423; diary entry of January 17, 1995.

19. *The New Review* Records, Box 2, Folder 14; Gul''s emphasis.

20. *The New Review* Records, Box 2, Folder 14; Brown's emphasis. Mandelshtam died on December 27, 1938. See Nadezhda Mandelshtam, *Hope Against Hope*, 376–91 ("The Date of Death"), where she speaks of Shalamov's "Cherry Brandy": "Some people have written stories about M.'s death. The one by Shalamov, for example, is an attempt to convey what M. must have felt while

dying—it is intended as a tribute from one writer to another. But among these fictional accounts there are some which claim to provide authentic detail," 384–85. Abroad, the circumstances of Mandelshtam's death were also covered in mystery. According to one rumor recounted by Filippov to Brown on August 2, 1960, Mandelshtam's sentence had allegedly "been commuted . . . to EX-ILE, with mandatory check-ins once a week at the local NKVD bureau. He had been exiled to some small town near Voronezh (I cannot recall which one at the moment), where my acquaintance had visited him. In her words, Mandelshtam died there at the end of 1940 from tuberculosis. This is what I had heard from her, and she was a big friend of Mandelshtam's. But according to other sources, Mandelshtam was captured in that town by the Germans and exterminated as a Jew," Boris Filippov Papers, Gen Mss 334, Box 3, Folders 41–42. The "famous Soviet pianist" who had told this story to Filippov "in early March 1941" could be Maria Iudina (1899–1970). For details on Mandelshtam's death, see Pavel Nerler, *Con Amore: Etiudy o Mandelshtame* (Moscow: Novoe literaturnoe obozrenie, 2014), 451–502.

21. Osip Mandelstam, *50 Poems*, trans. Bernard Meares, with an introduction by Joseph Brodsky (New York: Persea Books, 1977), 70; Osip Mandelstam, *Sochineniia v 2 tomakh* (Moscow: Khudozhestvennaia literatura, 1990), 2: 170.

22. Shalamov, *Kolyma Stories*, 74; *Novyi zhurnal* 91 (1968): 8.

23. Yury Terapiano, Review of *Novyi zhurnal* 91, *Russkaia mysl'*, August 1, 1968.

24. See Pavel Nerler, "Ot zimy k vesne: rasskazy V. T. Shalamova 'Sherri-brendi' i 'Sententsiia' kak tsikl," in his *Con Amore*, 216–24. See also his "Sila zhizni i zmerti. Varlam Shalamov i Mandelshtamy (na poliakh perepiski N. Ya. Mandelshtam i V. T. Shalamova)," http://shalamov.ru/research/61/9.html, trans. from *Osteuropa*, no. 6 (June 2007): 229–37. Here and throughout this chapter, I am using the original title of Shalamov's short story "Sententsiia," which corresponds to "Sententious" in John Glad's early English translation and to "Maxim" in Donald Rayfield's.

25. Shalamov, *Kolyma Stories*, 70.

26. Shalamov, 448.

27. Shalamov, 74.

28. Shalamov, 70. I have amended the translation to better match the original "mir v doroge."

29. Shalamov, 69–70.

30. Quoted in Claire Cavanagh, *Osip Mandelstam and the Modernist Creation of Tradition* (Princeton, NJ: Princeton University Press, 1995), 42.

31. In 1949–1950, while still in Kolyma, Shalamov drafted a poem under the title "Silentium," which was among those he sent to Pasternak. While alluding to Tiutchev, Shalamov's poem, according to Esipov, "speaks of an entirely different measure of human pain, which is not only inexpressible verbally, but should not be articulated at all until death" (Varlam Shalamov, *Stikhotvoreniia i poemy v 2 tomakh*, ed., with an introduction and commentary by Valery Esipov (St. Petersburg: Pushkinskii dom—Vita nova, 2020), 2: 306, 562).

32. Cf., "What is our earthly tongue before delightful nature? / . . . / But can the living be represented in something lifeless? / Who could recreate creation

in words? / Is the inexpressible subject to expression? / . . . / All the infinite is crowded into one sigh, / And only silence speaks understandably" [*Chto nash iazyk pred divnoiu prirodoi? / . . . / No l'zia li v mertvoe zhivoe peredat'? / Kto mog sozdanie v slovakh peresozdat'? / Nevyrazimoe podvlastno l' vyrazhen'iu? . . . / . . . / Vse neob'iatnoe v edinyi vzdokh tesnitsia, / I lish' molchanie poniatno govorit?*], Vasily Zhukovsky, *Stikhotvoreniia* (Leningrad: Sovetskii pisatel', 1956), 235–36; quoted in Sofya Khagi, "Silence and the Rest: The Inexpressible from Batiushkov to Tiutchev," *Slavic and East European Journal* 48, no. 1 (Spring 2004): 44–45.

33. Shalamov, *Kolyma Tales*, 71.

34. On May 13, 1965, at the memorial reading devoted to Mandelshtam, organized by Ilya Ehrenburg and held at Moscow State University, before his first public reading of "Cherry Brandy," Shalamov spoke about "the principles of Acmeism [that] have proven so healthy and alive that the list of [its] members resembles a martyrology record. . . . These poets' verses have not become literary mummies. Had the same ordeals been faced by the Symbolists, it would have been an escape to the monastery, into mysticism." "Vecher pamiati Mandel'shtama v MGU," *Grani* 77 (1970): 86.

35. Nina Savoeva, *Ia vybrala Kolymu* (Magadan: Maobti, 1996), 10–11.

36. "Nach Auschwitz ein Gedicht zu schreiben, ist barbarisch," Theodor W. Adorno, *Prismen: Kulturkritik und Gesellschaft* (Baden-Baden: Suhrkamp, 1955), 31.

37. Shalamov, *Kolyma Stories*, 345.

38. "Sententsiia" is an attempt to revive not only the legacy of the poet, who had died "earlier than the date of his death," but also the entire movement of Acmeism which he advocated. Upon reading the manuscript of Nadezhda Mandelshtam's memoir, in his first letter to her on June 29, 1965, Shalamov described it as "Acmeism . . . that has survived to nowadays. . . . Acmeism was born . . . out of struggle for the living life and the earthly world against Symbolism, with its cult of the afterlife [*zagrobshchina*] and mysticism," Shalamov, *Sobranie sochinenii*, 6: 409. Having read Shalamov's "Sententsiia," Nadezhda Mandelshtam in turn praised it for its "accuracy, which is a million times more accurate than any mathematical formula" (6: 423).

39. Shalamov, *Kolyma Stories*, 435–36. Rayfield translates *zloba* as "malice," which I have amended to "anger."

40. Shalamov, 436.

41. Shalamov, 439.

42. Shalamov, 439–40. The translation has been modified to preserve the original word and the title of the short story ("Sententsiia").

43. Shalamov, 441.

44. Shalamov. This entire paragraph is also omitted in the first publication in *Novyi zhurnal* and Glad's English translation.

45. Valery Esipov, "Kommentarii k 'Kolymskim rasskazam,'" http://shalamov.ru/research/249/; emphasis in the original.

46. Shalamov, *Kolyma Stories*, 441–42.

47. Quoted in Cavanagh, *Osip Mandelstam*, 43.

48. Shalamov, *Kolyma Stories*, 442; *Novyi zhurnal* 85 (1966): 11.

49. Elena Mikhailik, *Nezakonnaia kometa. Varlam Shalamov: opyt medlennogo chteniia* (Moscow: Novoe literaturnoe obozrenie, 2018), 119–20.

50. On October 9 Brown acknowledged receipt of the manuscript, which "arrived yesterday," *The New Review* Records, Box 2, Folder 14.

51. Varlam Shalamov, "A Good Hand" and "Caligula," in *Russia's Other Writers: Selections from Samizdat Literature*, ed. Michael Scammell, with a foreword by Max Hayward (New York: Praeger, 1971), 152–58.

52. *The New Review* Records, Box 2, Folder 14. Two years earlier, in the spring of 1969, Brown wrote to Scammell that he had already shown a few sample translations of Shalamov's prose to "Bob Loomis at Random House [who] has asked to see more," but because Brown had "not had the time to get back to it," the question of publishing Shalamov in English was put on the back burner, Brown's letters to Scammell on April 19 and May 4, 1969. I thank Michael Scammell for allowing me to read them. Scammell, meanwhile, was busy translating Anatoly Marchenko's *My Testimony* (*Moi pokazaniia*), which was published in 1969.

53. See Michael Meyer Brewer, "Varlam Shalamov's *Kolymskie rasskazy*: The Problem of Ordering" (MA thesis, University of Arizona, 1995), https://repository.arizona.edu/handle/10150/190395, 87.

54. Irina Kanevskaia, "Pamiati avtora 'Kolymskikh rasskazov,'" *Posev*, no. 3 (1982): 47. Another manuscript of *Kolyma Tales* may have been sent to France around the same time by Natalia Stoliarova through her French friends, who "smuggled it out by gluing the pages underneath their clothes." Oleg Dorman, *Podstrochnik. Zhizn' Lilianny Lunginoi, rasskazannaia eiu v fil'me Olega Dormana* (Moscow: Corpus, 2009), 271. In 1977 Stoliarova facilitated the first book edition of *Kolyma Tales* by sending yet another manuscript to Geller in Paris.

55. Gleb Struve Collection, box 29, folder 16. In the same letter to Struve, Gul' wrote that Chekhov Publishing House, founded in New York in 1970 by Max Hayward, "would like to publish Shalamov's short stories that had appeared in *Novyi zhurnal*. And I still have quite many of them." The first book edition of *Kolyma Tales*, however, had to wait eight more years.

56. Jerzy Giedroyc Papers, Instytut Literacki, Maison Lafitte; Gul''s emphasis.

57. Giedroyc's letter to Gul' dated April 3, 1969; Giedroyc's original grammar and style preserved.

58. Shalamov, *Kolyma Stories*, 3. The last sentence has been amended. Inexplicably, Rayfield translates "the readers, not the writers" as "the bosses, not the underlings." See Anastasiya Osipova, "The Forced Conversion of Varlam Shalamov," review of *Kolyma Stories*, by Varlam Shalamov, *Los Angeles Review of Books*, July 11, 2019, https://lareviewofbooks.org/article/the-forced-conversion-of-varlam-shalamov/.

59. Toker, *Return*, 5.

60. Shalamov, *Sobranie sochinenii*, 5: 153. Thus the effect of *Kolyma Tales*, according to Toker, "largely depended on the pulsating deployment of the material, testimony to atrocities alternating with narratives of moments of

reprieve." Leona Toker, "Samizdat and the Problem of Authorial Control: The Case of Varlam Shalamov," *Poetics Today* 29, no. 4 (2008): 743.

61. Shalamov, *Sobranie sochinenii*, 4: 618 ("Pasternak").

62. First published in Aleksandr Ginzburg, *Belaia kniga*, 405–6. Shalamov's authorship of "Letter to an Old Friend" was kept secret until four years after his death, when it was disclosed by Aleksandr Ginzburg, the editor of *Belaia kniga*, on the occasion of the twentieth anniversary of Sinyavsky and Daniel's trial. Aleksandr Ginzburg, "Dvadtsat' let tomu nazad," *Russkaia mysl'*, February 14, 1986.

63. Irina Sirotinskaia, *Moi drug Varlam Shalamov* (Moscow: Allana, 2006), 41.

64. Varlam Shalamov, "V redaktsiiu 'Literaturnoi gazety,'" *Literaturnaia gazeta*, February 23, 1972.

65. These editions will be addressed below. Two drafts of Shalamov's letter to the German publisher, held among his papers in Moscow (RGALI, Fond 2595), contest the unauthorized publication of the book and demand that the honorarium be sent to the author, "if this is in fact stipulated by the laws of your country," quoted in Valery Esipov, *Shalamov* (Moscow: Molodaia gvardiia, 2012), 295. Another document recently discovered in Shalamov's archive is his autobiographical statement written in the third person and evidently in anticipation of the publication of a book edition of *Kolyma Tales* abroad. See Franziska Thun-Hohenstein, "Warlam Schalamow an den Leser im Westen. Ein Archivfund," *Blog des Leibniz-Zentrums für Literatur–und Kulturforschung*, January 10, 2022, https://doi.org/10.13151/zfl-blog/20220110-01.

66. Shalamov, "Pis'mo v redaktsiiu 'Literaturnoi gazety.'" Assailing *Posev*, Shalamov must have also meant *Grani*, another NTS-affiliated journal in Frankfurt, where fifteen of his short stories were published in 1970 (nos. 76–77). Note, however, that unlike *Novyi zhurnal*, neither *Posev* nor *Grani* seems to have edited Shalamov's short stories and published them with only minor discrepancies.

67. Shalamov, "Pis'mo v redaktsiiu 'Literaturnoi gazety.'"

68. This is how Shalamov explained it to Gladkov: "A conversation with Markov.—We will admit you [to the Writers' Union], but see, they are publishing you abroad. We know you don't send manuscripts there yourself, it is done without your permission, but why don't you write about it for me, and I will show your letter to the [Union's] admission committee." Gladkov, *O poetakh*, 273; Gladkov's diary entry of February 28, 1972.

69. Cf. his bitter remark in late 1971: "Samizdat is a ghost, the most dangerous of ghosts, a poisoned weapon in the struggle between two intelligence services, where a human life costs no more than in the battle for Berlin." Shalamov, *Sobranie sochinenii*, 5: 329; quoted in Toker, "Samizdat," 735–36.

70. Gladkov, *O poetakh*, 273.

71. See, for example, Boris Lesniak, "Varlam Shalamov, kakim ia ego znal," *Rabochaia tribuna*, March 14, 1994, and his "Vospominiia o Varlame Shalamove," *Na Severe Dal'nem*, no. 2 (1989).

72. Shalamov, *Sobranie sochinenii*, 7: 367.

73. Toker, "Samizdat," 752. As for the final sentence of Shalamov's letter— "The problematics of *Kolyma Tales* has been removed by life"—Toker traces it

back to Nikolai Bukharin's speech at the Fourteenth Congress of the Party in 1926, where he stated that one of the problems, debated five years earlier, "in its 1921 formulation has been removed by life [*vopros v toi formulirovke, v kakoi on stoial v 1921 godu, sniat zhizn'iu*]. It is interesting that in the preceding sentence . . . Bukharin says, 'I do not renounce the quotation from *Krasnaia nov*" [*ya ot tsitaty iz 'Krasnoi novi' ne otrekaius'*]. . . . Shalamov's reference to the camps not being the way they were under Stalin, 'the problematics' of his stories being 'removed by life,' may thus be, consciously or otherwise, also a way of saying with Bukharin (executed in 1938), 'I do not renounce.'" Toker, 752.

    74. Toker.

    75. Toker, 753.

    76. Toker, 744.

    77. "Uprazdnenie Kolymy?" *Russkaia mysl'*, March 23, 1972.

    78. In October 2015, I happened to meet the author of "Undoing Kolyma?" in Paris. He asked me not to disclose his name but said he felt sorry for what he had written about Shalamov in *Russkaia mysl'*.

    79. *Novyi zhurnal* 106 (1972): 31.

    80. Roman Gul', "Otchet redaktora," *Novoe russkoe slovo*, April 30, 1972. By the end of the year, the disagreement between Shakhovskaia and Gul' over Shalamov was exhausted, so much so that on November 7, 1972, she offered him the typescript of Shalamov's short story "A Book Dealer" ("Bukinist"), which she had received from a "loyal person" but was reluctant to publish in *Russkaia mysl'* "not only because Shalamov wants to join the Writers' Union, but also because it is too long for us." *The New Review* Records, Box 9, Folder 53. Apparently the short story was missing from both manuscripts of *Kolyma Tales* that Gul' had in New York. It appeared in *Novyi zhurnal* 110 (1973): 5–19.

    81. *The New Review* Records, Box 10, Folder 36; Struve's letter to Gul' on August 7, 1972. See also the response of the editor of *Posev* to Shalamov's letter, Lev Rar, "Otvet 'Literaturnoi gazete,'" *Posev*, no. 4 (April 1972): 9–10, as well as two open letters from Shalamov's "personal friends" in the same issue of the émigré journal (10–11).

    82. Aleksandr Dymshits, "Za chistotu printsipov," *Literaturnaia Rossiia*, February 11, 1972.

    83. By 1972 Okudzhava's three books had been published in Frankfurt by Possev: *Bud' zdorov, shkoliar!* (1964), *Proza i poeziia* (1968), and *Dva romana* (1970). An established poet, guitar singer, and script writer, Okudzhava was pressured to renounce these publications under threat of being expelled from the Party. On November 18 he wrote a letter protesting "the use of his name by foreign publishers in their own selfish interests" (*Literaturnaia gazeta*, November 29, 1972). The same issue of the newspaper ran a similar letter by Anatoly Gladilin, whose novel *Prognoz na zavtra* (*Forecast for Tomorrow*) had also been brought out in Frankfurt by Possev. The publication of Arkady and Boris Strugatskys' novels *Ulitka na sklone* (*Snail on the Slope*) and *Gadkie lebedi* (*The Ugly Swans*) by Possev in 1972 likewise forced them to have to "repent" publicly in *Literaturnaia gazeta* two weeks after Gladilin and Okudzhava (*Literaturnaia gazeta*, December 13, 1972). See Yury Bit-Iunan and Daria Pashchenko, "Protestnoe

pis'mo v 'Literaturnoi gazete' kak forma upravleniia sovetskim literaturnym protsessom," *Vestnik RGGU* 17, no. 8 (2016): 9–21.

84. Petr Iakir, *Detstvo v tiur'me* (New York: Macmillan, 1972); Pyotr Yakir, *A Childhood in Prison*, ed., with an introduction by Robert Conquest ([London]: Macmillan, 1972).

85. Quoted in Aleksei Makarov, "Pis'mo Petra Iakira Varlamu Shalamovu," *Acta Samizdatica. Zapiski o samizdate* 4 (2018): 287. Iakir's appeal to Shalamov was mentioned in the *Chronicle of Current Events* on March 5, 1972 (no. 24), but it must have never been sent out to the addressee and remained unpublished. See also Irina Galkova, "Pis'mo o pis'me," *Acta Samizdatica. Zapiski o samizdate* 4 (2018): 293–301.

86. Quoted in Makarov, "Pis'mo," 289. Iakir presumed that *Kolyma Tales* was published abroad "without any distortions."

87. Makarov, 290. An active member of the dissident movement, Iakir was arrested and imprisoned, together with Viktor Krasin, four months later. During the investigation, which lasted more than a year, he was broken by the KGB, repented, and gave out the identities of many dissidents, undermining the movement.

88. Aleksandr Solzhenitsyn, *Arkhipelag GULag. Opyt khudozhestvennogo issledovaniia. 1918–1956* (Paris: YMCA-Press, 1974), 2: 610; Solzhenitsyn, *Gulag Archipelago*, 623. The footnote was purged from later editions of *Gulag Archipelago*.

89. Shalamov, *Sobranie sochinenii*, 5: 365–66; 363. For Solzhenitsyn's perspective on his failed collaboration with Shalamov, see his essay "S Varlamom Shalamovym," *Novyi mir*, no. 4 (1999): 163–69.

90. For example, in his letter to Shalamov on June 23, 1967, Aleksandr Khrabrovitsky updated him on exactly which texts had been published in the first two issues of *Novyi zhurnal* (nos. 85–86). I thank Sergei Soloviev for pointing me to this information from Shalamov's archive (RGALI, Fond 2595). Moreover, Khrabrovitsky recalls that Shalamov himself showed him the issues of *Novyi zhurnal* with his short stories. Aleksandr Khrabrovitsky, *Ocherk moei zhizni. Dnevnik. Vstrechi* (Moscow: Novoe literaturnoe obozrenie, 2012), 209.

91. Quoted in Khrabrovitsky, *Ocherk moei zhizni*, 208.

92. Georgy Adamovich, "Stikhi."

93. Roman Gul', "Solzhenitsyn," 60.

94. On Shalamov's use of landscape, see Leona Toker, "Varlam Shalamov's Kolyma," in *Between Heaven and Hell: The Myth of Siberia in Russian Culture*, ed. Galya Diment and Yury Slezkine (New York: St. Martin's Press, 1993), 151–69.

95. Solzhenitsyn, *Ivan Denisovich*, 181.

96. Anatoly Dremov, "Retsenziia na rukopis' 'Kolymskikh rasskazov,'" by Varlam Shalamov, in *Shalamovskii sbornik* 3, ed. Valery Esipov (Vologda: Grifon, 2002), 36–37. The review is dated November 15, 1963. For a selection of other internal reviews of Shalamov's prose in Soviet publishing houses and periodicals, see Sergei Soloviev, "Pervye retsenzii na 'Kolymskie rasskazy' i 'Ocherki prestupnogo mira,'" in *Shalamovskii sbornik* 5, ed. Valery Esipov (Vologda: Common Place, 2017), 248–80.

97. Dremov, ""Retsenziia na rukopis'," 36–37.

98. Dremov, 37–38.

99. Dremov, 35.

100. *The New Review* Records, Box 2, Folder 14; Gul''s letter to Brown on September 29, 1966.

101. Shalamov, *Sobranie sochinenii*, 6: 277.

102. Shalamov, 6: 297.

103. Shalamov, *Kolyma Stories*, 97. See Shalamov's essay "Kak 'tiskaiut rómany'" ("How 'Novels' Are 'Printed'") in his *Sketches of the Criminal World: Further Kolyma Tales*, trans. Donald Rayfield, with an introduction by Alissa Valles (New York: New York Review of Books, 2020), 101–10. On "The Snake Charmer" and Dostoevsky's *Notes from the House of the Dead* (1862) as a "palimpsest" for gulag narratives, see Yasha Klots, "From Avvakum to Dostoevsky: Varlam Shalamov and Russian Narratives of Political Imprisonment," *Russian Review* 75, no. 1 (January 2016): 7–25. The name of Shalamov's character, Andrei Fedorovich Platonov, is clearly a reference to Andrei Platonovich Platonov (Klimentov), whose earlier works Shalamov may have known before writing "The Snake Charmer." As Robert Chandler points out, the name of the camp where Shalamov's Platonov used to "pull novels" for the local thieves, Dzhankhara, may even be an allusion to Platonov's "Dzhan." Robert Chandler, "Varlam Shalamov and Andrei Fedorovich Platonov," *Essays in Poetics: The Journal of the British Neo-Formalist Circle* 27 (Autumn 2002): 185. However, the name of Shalamov's character may also be a reference to Dostoevsky, whose first name, Fedor, he inherits as his patronymic, with the compositional schemes of Shalamov's and Dostoevsky's texts being too similar to ignore. According to Chandler, it may also refer to Nikolai Fedorov, whose utopian ideas of transhumanism and eternal life may have been important for Platonov, but much less so for Shalamov. Chandler, 187. On Gul''s editing of "The Snake Charmer" for publication in *Novyi zhurnal* 86 (1967): 10–15, and for the resulting deficiencies in the English translation by John Glad, see Lysander Jaffe, "Writing as a Stranger."

104. Shalamov, *Sobranie sochinenii*, 6: 279.

105. Shalamov, 6: 283–88.

106. Shalamov, 5: 148.

107. Shalamov, 5: 151.

108. Osip Mandelshtam, "Smert' romana," in his *Sobranie sochinenii v 4 tomakh* (Moscow: Art-Biznes-Tsentr, 1993): 2: 271–75.

109. See, for example, Shalamov's memoir "Dvadtsatye gody" ("The nineteen-twenties") in his *Sobranie sochinenii*, 4: 318–98, as well as Pavel Arseniev, "Literatura chrezvychainogo polozheniia," *Translit* 14 (2014): 40–52; Svetlana Boym, "'Banality of Evil,' Mimicry, and the Soviet Subject: Varlam Shalamov and Hannah Arendt," *Slavic Review* 67, no. 2 (Summer 2008): 342–63; Mikhailik, *Nezakonnaia kometa*, 92–123. Shalamov's principles of "new prose" are parallel, in this regard, to the concept of "intermediary literature" (*promezhutochnaia literatura*) introduced by Lydia Ginzburg, who wrote about the siege of Leningrad and was a member of OPOYAZ (Society for the Study of Poetic Language) in the 1920s. Cf. Lydia Ginzburg, *Zapisnye knizhki. Vospominaniia.*

Esse (St. Petersburg: Iskusstvo-SPB, 2002), 305: "It is useless to read novels because this kind of conventionality has stopped working." See Emily van Buskirk, *Lydia Ginzburg's Prose: Reality in Search of Literature* (Princeton, NJ: Princeton University Press, 2016) and Buskirk and Zorin, *Alternative Identities*.

110. Nikolai Chuzhak, *Literatura fakta: pervyi sbornik materialov rabotnikov LEFa* (Moscow: Federatsiia, 1929; reprinted Moscow: Zakharov, 2000), 6, 28.

111. Nikolai Chuzhak, "Pisatel'skaia pamiatka," in *Literatura fakta*, 21.

112. Chuzhak, 15.

113. Shalamov, *Sobranie sochinenii*, 5: 151.

114. Chuzhak, "Pisatel'skaia pamiatka," 21–23.

115. Sergei Tretiakov, "The Biography of the Object," *October* 118 (Fall 2006): 61–62.

116. Chuzhak, *Literatura fakta*, 33.

117. Shalamov, *Sobranie sochinenii*, 6: 284. See Elena Mikhailik, "Kot, begushchii mezhdu Shalamovym i Solzhenitsynym," in *Shalamovskii sbornik* 3, ed. Valery Esipov (Vologda: Grifon, 2002), 101–14; as well as Fabian Heffermehl and Irina Karlsohn, *The Gulag in Writings of Aleksandr Solzhenitsyn and Varlam Shalamov: Memory, History, Testimony* (Leiden: Brill, 2021).

118. Gul', *Odvukon'*, 81.

119. Sinyavsky, "Dissent," 153. At the symposium "Odna ili dve russkikh literatury" ("One or Two Russian Literatures") held in Geneva in 1978, Sinyavsky's wife and publishing partner, Maria Rozanova, claimed that it was no longer the political but the linguistic and stylistic barrier that came between two generations of Russian writers abroad. Maria Rozanova, "Na raznykh iazykakh," 207.

120. Although translations of *Kolyma Tales* into foreign languages is a separate topic, it is worth noting that the arbitrary ordering of the short stories, as well as the edits and typos, were replicated in Shalamov's English editions. In his foreword to the first volume, the translator specifies, "This book contains only a selection of Shalamov's stories. . . . Certainly, such a selection necessarily involves an element of arbitrariness, and I sincerely hope that the complete stories will eventually appear in English." Varlam Shalamov, *Kolyma Tales*, trans., with a foreword by John Glad (New York: Norton, 1980), 16–17. In the second volume, published a year later, the translator repeats, "Shalamov's stories cannot be judged as single entities. Each constitutes a piece of the total puzzle, and they impart an understanding and achieve an emotional impact in their totality." Varlam Shalamov, *Graphite*, trans., with a foreword by John Glad (New York: Norton, 1981), 13. In both editions, however, Shalamov's short stories are grouped into the following thematic rubrics: "Survival," "Hope," "Defiance," "The Criminal World," "The Jailors' World," "The American Connection," and "Release" (in *Kolyma Tales*), and even more straightforwardly, into "Living," "Eating," "Working," "Marrying" [sic!], "Stealing," "Escaping," and "Dying" (in *Graphite*, which borrows its title from Shalamov's eponymous short story placed last in the book). Nevertheless, "Shalamov's stories [are] sensitively collected and translated by John Glad," as Irving Howe naively claimed in "Beyond Bitterness," his review of *Kolyma Tales*, by Varlam Shalamov, *New York*

Review of Books, August 14, 1980. Moreover, on the dust jacket of *Graphite*, Shalamov's name was misspelled as "Shalamav." "Physically, the book is a lemon," wrote Clarence Brown, "and misprints are thicker than the lice on the pathetic slaves of Kolyma. . . . Reader, never buy a book edited in New York on a Monday." Brown, "Memoirs." The original composition of the cycles was partially restored only in 1994, although the translations remained the same: Varlam Shalamov, *Kolyma Tales*, trans., with a foreword by John Glad (London: Penguin, 1994). It took nearly another quarter of a century for Shalamov's prose to be finally retranslated by Donald Rayfield. However, see Osipova, "Forced Conversion."

121. The idea of publishing *Kolyma Tales* with Sveshnikov's camp drawings, "which fit the nature of Shalamov's prose very well," was suggested to Geller by Igor Golomshtok, an art historian who emigrated to England in 1972 (Michel Heller Papers, Box 6, Folder 7. Bibliothèque de Documentation Internationale Contemporaine, Nanterre; Golomshtok's letter to Geller on April 14, 1978). In the same letter, Golomshtok wrote, "One of my graduate students at Oxford, a very talented Englishman, started translating [Shalamov's] short stories printed in *Novyi zhurnal*," and it was "only the absence of manuscripts" that stood in the way of "publishing Shalamov here as a more or less comprehensive volume in good English translation." Golomshtok's student was Robert Chandler. In 1985 YMCA-Press brought out another volume of Shalamov's prose compiled by Geller, who specified in his introduction that it was based on manuscripts sent by Shalamov's friends abroad as "disjointed pages" after the author's death. Varlam Shalamov, *Voskreshenie listvennitsy*, ed., with a foreword by Mikhail Geller (Paris: YMCA-Press, 1985), 7. Among those manuscripts was Shalamov's poetry, which, according to Geller, was also being prepared for publication abroad as a book. No book of Shalamov's poetry, however, ever appeared in tamizdat.

122. Geller, Introduction, 6.

123. The German edition came first. *Artikel 58: Die Aufzeichungen des Häftlings Schalanow*, trans. Gizela Drohla (Cologne: Friedrich Middelhauve Verlag, 1967). That same year it was translated into Afrikaans: Varlam Šalanov, *Artikel 58: 'N Ooggetuie Verslag oor die Bannenlinge in 'n Siberiese Strafkamp*, trans. Johannes van der Merwe (Cape Town: Tafelberg-uit-gewers, 1967). The French volume, also translated from the German, followed two years later: *Article 58: mémoires du prisonnier Chalanov* (Paris: Gallimard, 1969). A different French publisher brought out *Kolyma Tales* with the name of the author and title corrected: Varlam Chalamov, *Récits de Kolyma*, trans. Olivier Simon (Jean-Jacques Marie) and Katia Kerel (Paris: Denoël, 1969). On the history of these foreign-language editions, see Mark Golovizin, "K voprosu o proiskhozhdenii pervykh zarubezhnykh izdanii 'Kolymskikh rasskazov' V. T. Shalamova," in *Shalamovskii sbornik* 4, ed. Valery Esipov and Sergei Soloviev (Moscow: Litera, 2011), 197–214.

124. Geller, Introduction, 6. Before compiling Shalamov's book in 1978, Geller dedicated an entire chapter to him in his monograph *Kontsentratsionnyi mir i sovetskaia literatura* (London: Overseas Publications Interchange, 1974),

281–99). Geller's monograph was published in French and in Polish: *Le monde concentrationnaire et la littérature soviétique* (Lausanne: L'Age d'Homme, 1974); *Świat obozów koncentracyjnych a literatura sowiecka,* tr. Michal Kaniowski (Paris: Instytut Literacki, 1974).

125. Gennady Andreev, "O knige V. Shalamova," *Russkaia mysl'*, April 12, 1979.

126. Compassion and humanism in *Kolyma Tales,* according to Andreev, are "moved . . . to a rear, unnoticeable plane as something ordinary and insignificant," as he could tell from the short story "The Exam" ("Ekzamen"), whose narrator is saved by being allowed to stay and work at the camp infirmary as a paramedic after failing the entrance exam in chemistry.

127. Shalamov, *Sobranie sochinenii,* 5: 148 ("On Prose"). Cf. "Why is that, Varlam Tikhonovich? Why is it that out of a clear sky it appears that you would refuse to become either a stoolie or a brigadier—if it is the case that no one in camp can avoid or sidestep that slippery slope of corruption? . . . Does it mean that you did nonetheless grasp at some branch sticking out? Does it mean that you found a footing on some stone—and did not slide down any further? And maybe, despite everything, anger is not really the most long-lived feeling there is? Do you not refute your own concept with your character and verses?" Solzhenitsyn, *Gulag Archipelago,* 2: 623.

128. Primo Levi, *The Drowned and the Saved,* trans. Raymond Rosenthal (New York: Simon & Schuster, 2017), 69. See Toker, *Gulag Literature,* and Boym, "Banality of Evil," 342–63.

129. Andreev, "O knige."

130. Shalamov, *Sobranie sochinenii,* 5: 299.

131. Mikhailik, *Nezakonnaia kometa,* 18.

132. Gul', *Ia unes Rossiiu,* 3: 179. By 1978 Overseas Publications Interchange had published *Delo o demonstratsii na Pushkinskoi ploshchadi 22 ianvaria 1967 goda,* edited by Pavel Litvinov (1968); *Kontsentratsionnyi mir i sovetskaia literatura* by Mikhail Geller (1974); *V teni Gogolia* and *Progulki s Pushkinym* by Abram Tertz (both in 1975); *Zapiski nezagovorshchika* by Efim Etkind (1977); and *SSSR i Zapad v odnoi lodke* by Andrei Amalrik (1978); among others. After Stypulkowski died in 1981, the director of OPI was Serafim Miloradovich.

133. George Ivask Papers, Box 3, Folder 75, Amherst Center for Russian Culture.

134. In her letter to Geller on November 3, 1977, Stoliarova wrote, "I have already obtained everything except four sketches, which I will send either separately or together with the rest." Michel Heller Papers, Box 26, Folder 1. The manuscript, according to Stoliarova, contained eighty-six short stories from three cycles (thirty-three from "Kolyma Tales," twenty-eight from "The Artist of the Spade," and twenty-five from "The Left Bank"). "The rest [of the short stories] are not so strong," she added. Her choice of the texts for Geller's edition of *Kolymskie rasskazy* was made in consultation with Leonid Pinsky. Eventually, however, the book comprised 103 short stories, seventeen of which must have been taken from other manuscripts available by that time in the West.

135. George Ivask Papers, Box 3, Folder 75.

136. Gennady Andreev, "V mertvom tsarstve (vmesto predisloviia)," Michel Heller Papers, Box 26, Folder 7.

137. Shalamov, *Kolyma Stories*, 462. Cf. Shalamov, *Sobranie sochinenii*, 5: 155: "Sterne's *Sentimental Journey* cuts off with a half-phrase and no one disapproves of such an ending. Why, then, do readers of my short story 'How It Began' try to finish the phase I have left unfinished, 'My eshcho rabo . . .,' correcting it in longhand? And how am I supposed to fight for the style, to protect my copyright."

138. Andreev, "V mertvom tsarstve."

139. Andreev, *Gor'kie vody* and *Trudnye dorogi.*

140. See Irina Galkova, "Rodion Vas'kov—geroi prozy Varlama Shalamova," in *Zakon soprotivleniia raspadu. Sbornik nauchnykh trudov*, ed. Lucas Babka et al. (Prague: *Slovanská knihovna*, 2017), 185-96, as well as Shalamov's own sketch "Vas'kov House" ("Dom Vas'kova"), in his *Sobranie sochinenii*, 4: 469-80.

141. Andreev, "V mertvom tsarstve."

142. Upon his release Khomiakov was restricted from living in forty-one larger cities of the Soviet Union. In the beginning of the war, he was drafted into the Red Army but was taken prisoner by the Germans in the Crimea in 1942. After several years as a Soviet POW in Norway, he avoided forced repatriation to the USSR and stayed in Germany, where he joined the NTS and embarked on his career as a writer and publisher.

143. Violetta Iverni, "Zerkalo pamiati," *Kontinent* 19 (1979): 379.

144. Iverni, 381-82. On name change and heteronymy in *Kolyma Tales*, see Leona Toker, "Name Change and Author Avatars in Varlam Shalamov and Primo Levi," in *Narrative, Interrupted: The Plotless, the Disturbing and the Trivial in Literature*, ed. Markku Lehtimäki, Laura Karttunen and Maria Mäkelä (Berlin: De Gruyter, 2012), 227-37.

145. Iverni, "Zerkalo pamiati," 380; Iverni's emphasis.

146. Andrei Sinyavsky, "Srez materiala," *Sintaksis* 8 (1980): 184.

147. Sinyavsky, 180-81.

148. Shalamov, *Kolyma Stories*, 442.

149. Geller, Introduction, 8.

150. Evgeny Zamiatin, "O sintetizme," in his *Sobranie sochinenii v 5 tomakh* (Moscow: Russkaia kniga, 2004), 3: 168.

151. Varlam Shalamov, "Pis'mo staromu drugu," in *Belaia kniga po delu A. Sinyavskogo i Iu. Danielia*, ed. by Aleksandr Ginzburg (Frankfurt: Possev, 1967), 409. The title of Shalamov's anonymous essay invokes Herzen's letters "To an Old Comrade" ("K staromu tovarishchu," 1869), addressed almost a century earlier to Mikhail Bakunin.

152. Shalamov, "Pis'mo staromu drugu," 406.

Epilogue

1. Sentenced to five years for "social parasitism" in March 1964, Brodsky was officially set free on September 23, 1965.

2. Iosif Brodsky, *Stikhotvoreniia i poemy*. See Yakov Klots, "Kak izdavali pervuiu knigu Iosifa Brodskogo," *Colta.ru*, May 24, 2015, https://www.colta.

ru/articles/literature/7415-kak-izdavali-pervuyu-knigu-iosifa-brodskogo; Ivan Tolstoi and Andrei Ustinov, "'Molites' Gospodu za perepischika.' Vokrug pervoi knigi Iosifa Brodskogo," *Zvezda*, no. 5 (2018): 3–22.

3. An even more striking contrast to the affair of Sinyavsky and Daniel was the case of Valery Tarsis, who was not only spared trial for publishing his novel *Ward 7 (Palata No. 7)* abroad under his real name (Frankfurt: Possev, 1966) but even managed to receive honoraria from his tamizdat publishers before being "allowed" to leave the country only weeks before Sinyavsky and Daniel were sentenced to years of hard labor for the same "crime." Earlier, however, Tarsis had been subjected to forced psychiatric treatment for publishing in tamizdat since 1962. One émigré critic went as far as to claim that "Tarsis does not exist," that he "has been invented by the Soviet secret police." Argus, "Tarsis i Sinyavsky," *Novoe russkoe slovo*, November 4, 1965. Days after Sinyavsky and Daniel's trial, Tarsis was stripped of Soviet citizenship while already in London.

4. In 1978 Sinyavsky and his wife, Maria Rozanova, cofounded their journal and publishing house Sintaksis as a tribute to Aleksandr Ginzburg's first samizdat poetry journal of the same name (1960–1962). In 1966 Ginzburg compiled *Belaia kniga po delu A. Sinyavskogo i Iu. Danielia.* He was arrested and put on trial two years later. See *Protsess chetyrekh*, ed. Pavel Litvinov (Amsterdam: Alexander Herzen Foundation, 1971) and Vladimir Orlov, *Aleksandr Ginzburg: russkii roman* (Moscow: Russkii put', 2017).

5. See, for example, Sergei Dovlatov's often humorous account of the rivalry and misunderstandings between the oldest Russian émigré newspaper, *Novoe russkoe slovo*, and the Third-Wave weekly, *Novyi amerikanets*, which he cofounded in New York in the early 1980s. Dovlatov, *Rech' bez povoda*.

6. Abram Tertz, *Progulki s Pushkinym* (London: Overseas Publications Interchange, 1975). See Roman Gul', "Progulki khama s Pushkinym," *Novyi zhurnal* 124 (1976): 117–29, and Michel Aucouturier, "Vtoroi sud nad Abramom Tertzem," *Toronto Slavic Quarterly* 15 (2006), http://sites.utoronto.ca/tsq/15/aucouturier15.shtml.

7. Tertz, *Trial Begins*, 218–19. While Tertz advocated for the grotesque and the fantastic, the Soviet critic Sinyavsky wrote his dissertation on the guru of socialist realism, Maxim Gorky, only several years earlier.

8. Catherine Th. Nepomnyashchy, *Abram Tertz and the Poetics of Crime* (New Haven, CT: Yale University Press, 1995).

9. While Arzhak's works were always published abroad under a pen name, Tertz's essay first appeared anonymously. "Le réalisme socialiste," *Esprit* 270, no. 2 (February 1959): 335–67; "On Socialist Realism," *Dissent* (Winter 1960): 39–66.

10. Gleb Struve Collection, box 94, folder 11, Hoover Institution Archives, Stanford University; Gennady Khomiakov's letter to Struve of January 11, 1962.

11. Boris Riurikov, "Sotsialisticheskii realizm i ego nisprovergateli," *Inostrannaia literatura*, no. 1 (1962): 191–200; quoted in Aleksandr Ginzburg, *Belaia kniga*, 20.

12. This version, however, appears undocumented, although it is mentioned in several sources, e.g., in Liudmila Sergeeva, "Triumvirat: Andrei Sinyavsky—Abram Terts—Maria Rozanova," *Znamia*, no. 8 (2017): 105–69.

13. It was published, however, as Filippov's afterword to Nikolai Arzhak, *Govorit Moskva. Povesti i rasskazy* ([Washington, DC]: Inter-Language Literary Associates, 1966), 161–66. See Yakov Klots, "'Osuzhdat' reku za to, chto v nei kto-to utopilsia . . .': pis'mo amerikanskogo izdatelia Tertsa i Arzhaka v redaktsiiu *Literaturnoi gazety*," *Colta.ru*, February 12, 2016, https://www.colta.ru/articles/literature/10100-osuzhdat-reku-za-to-chto-v-ney-kto-to-utopilsya.

14. Eremin, "Perevertyshi"; Kedrina, "Nasledniki Smerdiakova." By February 1966 Filippov's Inter-Language Literary Associates had published Tertz's novel *Liubimov* (*The Makepeace Experiment*, 1966) and four editions by Arzhak: *Govorit Moskva* (*This Is Moscow Speaking*, 1962), *Ruki. Chelovek iz MINAPa* (*Hands. A Man from MINAP*, 1963), *Iskuplenie* (*The Atonement*, 1964), and *Govorit Moskva. Povesti i rasskazy* (*This Is Moscow Speaking. Novellas and Short Stories*, 1966). Another book by Tertz, *Mysli vrasplokh* (*Thought Unaware*, 1966), was in the making throughout the investigation, as well as a collection of documents and speeches on the trial, including the closing statements of Sinyavsky and Daniel, which came out later that year (*Sinyavsky and Daniel na skam'e podsudimykh*, 1966).

15. Sinyavsky, "Dissent," 153.

16. Joseph Brodsky, "In Memory of Carl Proffer," Joseph Brodsky Papers, Gen Mss 613, Box 123, Folder 2772, Beinecke Rare Book and Manuscript Library, Yale University.

17. This is why, as Eugenie Markesinis has noted, "Tertz did not come about as the result of the Thaw, he had been maturing in Siniavskii's mind for some time previously: the change of political climate simply gave him the necessary opening to act." Eugenie Markesinis, *Andrei Siniavskii: A Hero of His Time?* (Boston: Academic Studies Press, 2013), 25.

18. Tertz continued to be published abroad after Sinyavsky was imprisoned. Moreover, in the camp Sinyavsky continued to write as Tertz. He did not renounce his pen name even after emigrating to Paris in 1973.

19. Matich, "Tamizdat," 33. In his conversation with Matich, Sinyavsky compared Tertz's writings to Gogol's "Nose," which split off from its owner's body and, according to the rumor, tried to escape across the border. Matich, 33.

20. Foucault, *Discipline and Punish*, 16–17. It was not until the turn of the eighteenth century that Jeremy Bentham's panopticon became a model for the modern prison as a place of observation, surveillance, and knowledge of the prisoners, to the extent their bodies permitted.

21. Nepomnyashchy, *Abram Tertz*, 64. Written only a year after his essay "On Socialist Realism," "Pkhentz" was not published—in *Encounter* (April 1966): 3–13—until after Sinyavsky and Daniel's trial. According to Maria Rozanova, Sinyavsky had read it to Sergei Khmelnitsky and thus exposed his authorship, making the short story "unpublishable." For this reason it was not included in Tertz's first book *Fantasticheskie povesti* (Paris: Instytut Literacki, 1961). Ivan Tolstoi, "Andrei i Abram. Puteshestvie po biografii Sinyavskogo. K 80-letiiu pisatelia," *Radio Svoboda*, October 8, 2005, https://archive.svoboda.org/programs/otbl/2005/otbl.100905.asp. As it happens, since the late 1940s Khmelnitsky had been an MGB and then a KGB informer. See his later article "Iz chreva kitova," *Dvadtsat'-dva* 48 (1986): 151–80, exposing Sinyavsky's own ties with the

Soviet secret police, as well as Sinyavsky's and Peltier's replies to Khmelnitsky, "O 'ruke KGB' i prochem," *Kontinent* 49 (1986): 337–42.

22. Abram Tertz, *Fantastic Stories* (Evanston, IL: Northwestern University Press, 1987), 243.

23. "This play with Pushkin's name," Nepomnyashchy notes, "also extends to the narrator's 'double,' the hunchback Leopold Sergeevich, who not only bears Pushkin's patronymic, but is described by his neighbors by analogy with Pushkin . . .: 'our hunchback is the spitting image of Pushkin.'" (Nepomnyashchy, *Abram Tertz*, 65.

24. Cf. "I found a leaky drainpipe and stationed myself under the stream. It ran right down my neck, cool and delicious, and in about three minutes I was damp enough. The people hurrying past, all of them with umbrellas and rubber soles, looked at me sideways, intrigued by my behavior. I had to change my position, so I took a stroll through the puddles. My shoes were letting water in nicely. Down below, at least, I was enjoying myself." Tertz, *Fantastic Stories*, 225.

25. Tertz, 238–40.

26. Tertz, 220. In the English translation of the short story quoted here, Veronika's name is changed to "Verochka."

27. Tertz.

28. Tertz, 223–24. A queer reading of "Pkhentz" has been undertaken by Anastasia Kayiatos: "This gynophobic passage lends the text a decidedly gay tone. . . . Rather than highlighting for him the beauty of femininity, that thing the socialist male must desire for the sake of socialist futurity, Andrei is horrified to see nothing 'female' there so much as 'an old man's face, unshaven and baring its teeth,' threatening castration as the cost of entering Veronika personally, or normative society symbolically." "It is hard not to be struck," Kayiatos adds, "by the (intended) strangeness of this rendition of the female reproductive organ as a violent 'apparatus,' a most personal catapult shooting out pre-fab babies for the sake of the socialist Purpose. In the present academic moment, we might place the 'apparatus' in a Foucauldian framework of biopower, as a discursive-institutional formation of the heteronormative state. We might also keep contemporary to 'Pkhentz,' and connect it to the official definition provided by *Pravda* in 1953, which defines the 'Soviet State Apparatus' as a 'mighty instrument' wedding the Communist Party to the Soviet people in the 'sacred' and 'historic task' of 'building a communist society.'" Anastasia Kayiatos, "Silence and Alterity in Russia after Stalin, 1955–1974" (PhD thesis, University of California, Berkeley, 2012), https://escholarship.org/content/qt1989594t/qt1989594t.pdf?t=odx9l7, 316–17.

29. Aleksandr Zholkovsky has traced Pkhentz's unconsummated encounter with Veronika to Jonathan Swift's *Gulliver's Travels*, whose titular character's misogyny and misanthropy Pkhentz inherits. Cf. "I must confess no object ever disgusted me so much as the sight of her monstrous breast, which I cannot tell what to compare with, so as to give the curious reader an idea of its bulk, shape, and colour. It stood prominent six feet, and could not be less than sixteen in circumference. The nipple was about half the bigness of my head, and the hue both of that and the dug, so varied with spots, pimples,

and freckles, that nothing could appear more nauseous," Swift, *Gulliver's Travels*, ed. with an introduction by Claude Rawson (Oxford: Oxford University Press, 2005), 82–83; Aleksandr Zholkovsky, "'Pkhentz' na randevu: niu, meniu, dezhaviu," *Novoe literaturnoe obozrenie*, no. 3 (2011): 210–28. Elion Borenstein, on the other hand, has observed that Pkhentz's "most horrible neighbor," who damages the bathtub in order to "murder" him, is named Kostritskaya—"with the 'o' in her name pronounced, according to the rules of Russian, as an 'a,' her name all but screams 'castration,'" Eliot Borenstein, "A Hothouse Flower in a Communal Apartment," February 7, 2019, https://www.eliotborenstein.net/soviet-self-hatred/a9szd5212pib5qvc6b91vcf21ygkwo.

30. Tertz's fiction in general, according to Markesinis, is free from "heroes or villains, establishment or dissident authors, positive or negative character judgments." Markesinis, *Andrei Siniavskii*, xi. However, Tertz's novel *Liubimov* features the characters of Kochetov and Sofronov, two Soviet literary functionaries referred to by their real last names (Kochetov's first name is changed from Vsevolod to Vitaly, but Sofronov's first name, Anatoly, is left intact).

31. Tertz, *Fantastic Stories*, 243.

32. Tertz, 244.

33. Gogol, *Collected Tales*, 419.

34. Tertz, *Fantastic Stories*, 244.

35. Tertz, 244–45.

36. Tertz, 243.

37. "Manuscripts don't burn," says Voland, Bulgakov's magical character from *The Master and Margarita*, before leaving Moscow and taking the Master and Margarita along. In the novel, however, it is not only the Master's manuscript that catches fire but the city itself and its various institutions, including the Massolit.

38. Nepomnyashchy, *Abram Tertz*, 74–75.

39. Shalamov, *Kolyma Stories*, 439.

40. Fyodor Dostoevsky, *The House of the Dead: A Novel in Two Parts*, trans. Constance Garnett (New York, 1915), 6. Cf. the title of Gustav Herling's gulag memoir, *A World Apart*, trans. Joseph Marek (London: Heinemann, 1951).

41. Tertz, *Fantastic Stories*, 229–31. "The promise of queer connection," Kayiatos sums up, "is foreclosed completely: the queer alien realienated as reproductive heterosexuality is restored as the human norm in the story and Soviet society." Kayiatos, "Silence and Alterity in Russia after Stalin," 319.

42. Tertz, 239.

43. Nostalgia, according to Svetlana Boym, "is a longing for a place, but actually it is a yearning for a different time. . . . Nostalgia is not always about the past; it can be retrospective but also prospective. Fantasies of the past determined by needs of the present have a direct impact on the realities of the future." Svetlana Boym, *The Future of Nostalgia* (New York: Basic Books, 2016), xvi.

44. On Russia after Stalin as the land of the "undead," including gulag returnees, see Alexander Etkind, *Warped Mourning: Stories of the Undead in the Land of the Unburied* (Stanford, CA: Stanford University Press, 2013).

45. Zinik, *Emigratsiia*, 16.

46. Zinik, 51.

47. Borenstein, "Hothouse Flower."

48. Abram Tertz, "Pkhentz," in *Tsena metafory, ili prestuplenie i nakazanie Siniavskogo i Danielia* (Moscow: Kniga, 1989), 263–78.

49. The most remarkable example so far of this new "tamizdat" is the online Russian Oppositional Arts Review (ROAR) launched by Linor Goralik in Israel. ROAR does not distinguish between authors in Russia and abroad, but the review itself, given its outspoken position, can only be hosted on a foreign server.

BIBLIOGRAPHY

Archival Materials

Amherst Center for Russian Culture, Amherst, MA
George Ivask Papers
The New Review Records

Bakhmeteff Archive, Columbia University, New York
Alexander Bakhrakh Papers

Beinecke Rare Book and Manuscript Library, Yale University, New Haven, CT
Boris Filippov Papers, Gen Mss 334
Joseph Brodsky Papers, Gen Mss 613
Nina Berberova Papers, Gen Mss 182
Roman Gul' Papers, Gen Mss 90

Bibliothèque de Documentation Internationale Contemporaine (BDIC), Nanterre
Michel Heller Papers

Center for East European Studies, Bremen
Lev Kopelev Papers, Fond 13
NTS Papers, Fond 98

Dom Russkogo Zarubezh'ia imeni Aleksandra Solzhenitsyna, Moscow
Gennady Khomiakov Papers, Fond 155

Hoover Institution Archives, Stanford University, Palo Alto, CA
Gleb Struve Collection, No. 85018

Instytut Literacki, Maison Lafitte, Paris
Jerzy Giedroyc Papers

International Institute of Social History, Amsterdam
Archief Alexander Herzen Foundation, ARCH02660

Library of Congress, Washington, DC
Vozdushnye Puti Records

Princeton University Library, Special Collections, Princeton, NJ
Clarence Brown Papers

Russian National Library, St. Petersburg
Kornei Chukovsky Papers, Fond 620

Russian State Archive of Literature and Art (RGALI), Moscow
Varlam Shalamov Papers, Fond 2595

References

Adamovich, Georgy. "Meetings with Anna Akhmatova." In *Anna Akhmatova and Her Circle*, edited by Konstantin Polivanov, translated by Patricia Beriozkina, 62–76. Fayetteville: University of Arkansas Press, 1994.

——. "Na poliakh 'Rekviema' Anny Akhmatovoi." *Mosty* 11 (1965): 206–10.

——. "'Podarok Pasternaku'. Al'manakh 'Vozdushnye mosty.'" *Novoe russkoe slovo*, December 6, 1959.

——. Review of *Odin den' Ivana Denisovicha*, by Aleksandr Solzhenitsyn. *Russkaia mysl'*, January 3, 1963.

——. "Stikhi avtora 'Kolymskikh rasskazov.'" *Russkaia mysl'*, August 24, 1967.

——. "Vstrechi s Annoi Akhmatovoi." *Vozdushnye puti* 5 (1967): 99–114.

Adorno, Theodor W. *Prismen: Kulturkritik und Gesellschaft*. Baden-Baden: Suhrkamp, 1955.

Adzhubei, Aleksei. "Ot okeana k okeanu." *Iunost'*, no. 2 (1956): 96–102.

Akhmatova, Anna. *Anna Akhmatova and Her Circle*. Edited by Konstantin Polivanov. Translated by Patricia Beriozkina. Fayetteville: University of Arkansas Press, 1994.

——. *Beg vremeni. Stikhotvoreniia 1909–1965*. Moscow: Sovetskii pisatel', 1965.

——. *The Complete Poems*. Edited, with an introduction by Roberta Reeder. Translated by Judith Hemschemeyer. Boston: Zephyr Press, 1997.

——. *Izbrannoe*. Tashkent: Sovetskii pisatel', 1943.

——. *Izbrannye stikhotvoreniia*. New York: Izdatel'stvo imeni Chekhova, 1952.

——. *Iz shesti knig*. Leningrad: Sovetskii pisatel', 1940.

——. "Mandelshtam. Listki iz dnevnika." *Vozdushnye puti* 4 (1965): 23–43.

——. *Poema bez geroia*. Ann Arbor, MI: Ardis, 1978.

——. "Poema bez geroia." *Vozdushnye puti* 1 (1960): 5–42; 2 (1961): 111–52.

——. *Poems of Anna Akhmatova*. Edited and translated, with an introduction by Stanley Kunitz and Max Hayward. Boston: Houghton Mifflin, 1973.

——. *Rekviem*. Munich: Tovarishchestvo zarubezhnykh pisatelei, 1963.

——. "Rekviem." *Grani* 56 (October 1964): 11–19.

——. *Requiem*. 2nd ed., revised by the author, with an afterword by Gleb Struve. Munich: Tovarishchestvo zarubezhnykh pisatelei, 1969.

——. "Rekviem." *Neva*, no. 6 (1987): 74–79.

——. *Requiem and Poem without a Hero*. Translated by D.M. Thomas. Athens: Ohio University Press, 1978.

——. *Sobranie sochinenii v 6 tomakh*. Moscow: Ellis Lak, 1998.

——. *Sochineniia v 3 tomakh*. Edited by Gleb Struve and Boris Filippov. [Munich]: Inter-Language Literary Associates, 1965–1983.

——. *Stikhotvoreniia. 1909–1960*. Moscow: Khudozhestvennaia literatura, 1961.

——. *The World That Causes Death's Defeat: Poems of Memory*. Edited and translated, with an introduction, critical essays, and commentary by Nancy K. Anderson. New Haven, CT: Yale University Press, 2004.

——. *Zapisnye knizhki Anny Akhmatovoi (1958–1966)*. Edited by K. N. Suvorova, with an introduction by Emma Gershtein. Torino: Giulio Einaudi Editore, 1996.

"A[khmatova] v Italii." *Russkaia mysl'*, January 9, 1965.

Aksenov, Vasily. "The Metropol Affair." *Wilson Quarterly* 6, no. 5 (1982): 152–59.

Allilueva, Svetlana. *Dvadtsat' pisem' k drugu*. New York: Harper & Row, 1967.

——. *Twenty Letters to a Friend*. Translated by Priscilla Johnson. New York: Harper & Row, 1967.

Andreev, Gennady [Gennady Khomiakov]. *Gor'kie vody*. Frankfurt: Possev, 1954.

——. "O knige V. Shalamova." Review of *Kolymskie rasskazy*, by Varlam Shalamov. *Russkaia mysl'*, April 12, 1979.

——. *Trudnye dorogi*. Munich: Tovarishchestvo zarubezhnykh pisatelei, 1959.

Andronikashvili-Pilniak, Boris. "Dva izgoia, dva muchenika: Boris Pil'niak i Evgeny Zamiatin." *Znamia*, no. 9 (1994): 123–53.

Anin, Nikolai [Nikolai Davidenkov]. "Leningradskie nochi." *Parizhskii vestnik*, August 21, 1943.

Annenkov, Yury. "Anna Akhmatova." *Vozrozhdenie* 129 (September 1962): 41–52.

——. *Dnevnik moikh vstrech. Tsikl tragedii*. Moscow: Khudozhestvennaia literatura, 1991.

Anrep, Boris. "The Black Ring." In *Anna Akhmatova and Her Circle*, edited by Konstantin Polivanov, translated by Patricia Beriozkina 77–92. Fayetteville: University of Arkansas Press, 1994.

Argus [Mikhail Aizenshtadt-Zheleznov]. "Tarsis i Sinyavsky." *Novoe russkoe slovo*, November 4, 1965.

Aronson, Grigory. Review of *Novyi zhurnal* 83. *Novoe russkoe slovo*, June 19, 1966.

Arseniev, Pavel. "Literatura chrezvychainogo polozheniia." *Translit* 14 (2014): 40–52.

Arzhak, Nikolai. *Govorit Moskva. Povesti i rasskazy*. Introduction and afterword by Boris Filippov. [Washington, DC]: Inter-Language Literary Associates, 1966.

Aucouturier, Michel. "Vtoroi sud nad Abramom Tertzem." *Toronto Slavic Quarterly* 15 (2006). http://sites.utoronto.ca/tsq/15/aucouturier15.shtml

Azhaev, Vasily. "Daleko ot Moskvy," *Dal'nii Vostok*, nos. 1–2 (1946), 4 (1947), and 2 (1948).

——. "Daleko ot Moskvy," *Novyi mir*, nos. 7–9 (1948).

——. *Daleko ot Moskvy*. Moscow: Sovetskii pisatel', 1949.

——. *Vagon*. Moscow: Sovremennik, 1988.

Baklanov, Grigory. "Chtob eto nikogda ne povtorilos.'" *Literaturnaia gazeta*, November 22, 1962.

Bannikov, Nikolai. "Vysokii dar." Afterword to *Izbrannoe*, by Anna Akhmatova, 535–56. Moscow: Khudozhestvennaia literatura, 1974.

Barghoorn, Frederick. *The Soviet Cultural Offensive: The Role of Cultural Diplomacy in Soviet Foreign Policy*. Princeton, NJ: Princeton University Press, 1960.

Basalaev, Innokenty. "Zapisi besed s Akhmatovoi (1961–1963)." Edited by E. M. Tsarenkova, I. Kolosov, and N. Kraineva. *Minuvshee: Istoricheskii al'manakh* 23 (1998): 561–92.

Bauman, Zygmunt. *Retrotopia*. Cambridge: Polity, 2017.

Belinsky, Vissarion. *Polnoe sobranie sochinenii v 13 tomakh*. Moscow: Izdatel'stvo AN SSSR, 1953–1959.

Beliutin, Elii. "Khrushchev v Manezhe." *Druzhba narodov*, no. 1 (1990): 139–42.

Belov, Nikolai. Review of *Opustelyi dom*, by Lydia Chukovskaia. *Russkaia mysl'*, December 22, 1966.

——. "Vtoraia zhizn' Evgenii Ginzburg." *Russkaia mysl'*, July 13, 1967.

Berberova, Nina. *The Italics Are Mine*. Translated by Philippe Radley. New York: Harcourt, Brace & World, 1969.

Bergman, Jay. "Soviet Dissidents on the Russian Intelligentsia, 1956–1985: The Search for a Usable Past." *Russian Review* 51, no. 1 (January 1992): 16–35.

Berlin, Isaiah. *Personal Impressions*. Edited by Henry Hardy, with an introduction by Noel Annan. 2nd ed. Princeton, NJ: Princeton University Press, 2001.

Bezsonov, Yury. *Dvadtsat' shest' tiurem i pobeg s Solovkov*. Paris: Imprimerie de Navarre, 1928.

——. *My Twenty-Six Prisons and My Escape from Solovki*. London: Jonathan Cape, 1929.

Bit-Iunan, Yury, and David Feldman. "Intriga i sud'ba Vasiliia Grossmana." *Voprosy literatury*, no. 6 (2010): 153–82.

——. "K istorii publikatsii romana V. Grossmana 'Zhizn' i sud'ba' ili 'Kak eto bylo' u B. Sarnova." *Toronto Slavic Quarterly* 45 (Summer 2013): 175–203.

——. *Vasily Grossman: Literaturnaia biografiia v istoriko-politicheskom kontekste*. Moscow: Neolit, 2016.

——. *Vasily Grossman v zerkale literaturnykh intrig*. Moscow: Forum, 2016.

Bit-Iunan, Yury, and Daria Pashchenko. "Protestnoe pis'mo v 'Literaturnoi gazete' kak forma upravleniia sovetskim literaturnym protsessom." *Vestnik RGGU* 17, no. 8 (2016): 9–21.

Bloom, Harold. *The Anxiety of Influence: A Theory of Poetry*. New York: Oxford University Press, 1973.

Bobyshev, Dmitry. "Akhmatova i emigratsiia." *Zvezda*, no. 2 (1991): 177–81.

Bogomolov, Nikolai. "Lydia Nord i inzhenery dush." *Toronto Slavic Quarterly* 34 (2010): 203–17.

Böll, Heinrich. *Missing Persons and Other Essays*. Translated by Leila Vennewitz. Evanston, IL: Northwestern University Press, 1994.

Bol'shukhin, Yury. Review of *Novyi zhurnal* 84. *Novoe russkoe slovo*, November 27, 1966.

Borenstein, Eliot. "A Hothouse Flower in a Communal Apartment." February 7, 2019. https://www.eliotborenstein.net/soviet-self-hatred/a9szd52 12pib5qvc6b9lvcf21ygkwo.

Bourdieu, Pierre. *The Field of Cultural Production*. New York: Columbia University Press, 1994.

Boym, Svetlana. "'Banality of Evil,' Mimicry, and the Soviet Subject: Varlam Shalamov and Hannah Arendt." *Slavic Review* 67, no. 2 (Summer 2008): 342–63.

——. *The Future of Nostalgia*. New York: Basic Books, 2016.

Bradley, Thompson. Review of *The Deserted House*, by Lydia Chukovskaia. *Slavic Review* 27, no. 4 (December 1968): 688.

Brandser, Kristin. "Alice in Legal Wonderland: A Cross-Examination of Gender, Race, and Empire in Victorian Law and Literature." *Harvard Women's Law Journal* 24 (2001): 221–54.

Breitbart, Ekaterina. "Khranitsel'nitsa traditsii (Lydia Korneevna Chukovskaia)." *Grani* 104 (1977): 171–82.

——. Review of *Sanya: My Life with Aleksandr Solzhenitsyn*, by Natalya Reshetovskaia. *Grani* 100 (1976): 505–11.

Brewer, Michael Meyer. "Varlam Shalamov's *Kolymskie rasskazy*: The Problem of Ordering." Master's thesis, University of Arizona, 1995. https://repository.arizona.edu/handle/10150/190395.

Brodsky, Iosif. *Ostanovka v pustyne*. New York: Izdatel'stvo imeni Chekhova, 1970.

——. "Pamiati Karla Proffera." Translated by Olga Voronina. *Zvezda*, no. 4 (2005): 122–25.

——. *Stikhotvoreniia i poemy*. With a foreword by Georgy Stukov [Gleb Struve]. Washington, DC: Inter-Language Literary Associates, 1965.

Brodsky, Joseph. Foreword to *This Prison Where I Live: The PEN Anthology of Imprisoned Writers*, edited by Siobhan Dowd, xi–xv. New York: Cassell, 1996.

——. "Geography of Evil." *Partisan Review* 44, no. 4 (1977): 637–45.

——. *Less Than One: Selected Essays*. New York: Farrar, Straus & Giroux, 1986.

Brown, Clarence. "Memoirs from the House of the Dead." Review of *Graphite*, by Varlam Shalamov. *Washington Post*, November 29, 1981.

Broyard, Anatole. "A Matter of Literary Politics." Review of *Going Under*, by Lydia Chukovskaya. *New York Times*, March 31, 1976.

Bulgakov, Mikhail. *The Master and Margarita*. Translated by Richard Pevear and Larissa Volokhonsky. New York: Penguin, 1997.

Burg, David. "O rasskaze Solzhenitsyna 'Psy,' padenii Khrushcheva i sud'be Tvardovskogo." *Posev*, December 18, 1964.

Buskirk, Emily van. *Lydia Ginzburg's Prose: Reality in Search of Literature*. Princeton, NJ: Princeton University Press, 2016.

Buskirk, Emily van, and Andrei Zorin, eds. *Lydia Ginzburg's Alternative Literary Identities: A Collection of Articles and New Translations*. Vienna: Peter Lang, 2012.

Carlisle, Olga. *Solzhenitsyn and the Secret Circle*. London: Routledge & K. Paul, 1978.

Carroll, Lewis. *Alice's Adventures in Wonderland*. New York: Appleton, 1866.

Cavanagh, Claire. *Osip Mandelstam and the Modernist Creation of Tradition*. Princeton, NJ: Princeton University Press, 1995.

Chalamov, Varlam. *Récits de Kolyma*. Translated by Olivier Simon [Jean-Jacques Marie] and Katia Kerel. Paris: Denoël, 1969.

Chandler, Robert. "Varlam Shalamov and Andrei Fedorovich Platonov." *Essays in Poetics: The Journal of the British Neo-Formalist Circle* 27 (Autumn 2002): 184–92.

Chandler, Robert, Boris Dralyuk, and Irina Mashinski, eds. *The Penguin Book of Russian Poetry*. London: Penguin, 2015.

Chebotarev, Tatiana. "'Vy—khudozhnik, ne remeslennik.' Perepiska Korneiia Chukovskogo i Mirry Ginzburg." *Arkhiv evreiskoi istorii* 4 (2007): 248–318.

Chernyshevsky, Nikolai. *Chto delat'? Iz rasskazov o novykh liudiakh. Roman.* Geneva: Elpidin, 1867.

——. *Chto delat'? Roman.* St. Petersburg: Tipografiia V. A. Tikhanova, 1905.

Chudakova, Marietta. "Po povodu vospominanii L. Feuera i R. Feuer-Miller." In *Tynianovskii sbornik: piatye Tynianovskie chtenia*, edited by Marietta Chudakova, 366–74. Moscow: Imprint, 1994.

Chugunov, T. "Kto on?. O 'druge detstva' Tvardovskogo." *Novyi zhurnal* 86 (1967): 78–93.

Chukovskaia, Lydia. *'Byloe i dumy' Gertsena.* Moscow: Khudozhestvennaia literatura, 1966.

——. *"Dnevnik—bol'shoe podspor'ie . . ." (1938–1994).* Moscow: Vremia, 2015.

——. *Iz dnevnika. Vospominaniia.* Moscow: Vremia, 2010.

——. *Opustelyi dom.* Paris: Cinq Continents, 1965.

——. "Otkrytoe pis'mo pisatel'nitsy Lidii Chukovskoi M. Sholokhovu." *Russkaia mysl'*, November 29, 1966.

——. *Otkrytoe slovo.* New York: Khronika Press, 1976.

——. *Pamiati detstva.* Afterword by Efim Etkind. New York: Chalidze Publications, 1983.

——. *Po etu storonu smerti (iz dnevnika 1936–1976).* Paris: YMCA-Press, 1978.

——. "Posle kontsa. Iz 'akhmatovskogo' dnevnika." *Znamia*, no. 1 (2003): 154–67.

——. *Procherk.* Moscow: Vremia, 2009.

——. *Protsess iskliucheniia.* Paris: YMCA-Press, 1979.

——. "Sofia Petrovna." *Novyi zhurnal* 83 (1965): 5–45; 84 (1966): 5–46.

——. "Sofia Petrovna." *Neva*, no. 2 (1988): 51–93.

——. *Sofia Petrovna. Spusk pod vodu.* Moscow: Moskovskii rabochii, 1988.

——. "'Sofia Petrovna'—luchshaia moia kniga. Iz dnevnika." *Novyi mir*, no. 6 (2014): 139–67.

——. *Zapiski ob Anne Akhmatovoi.* 3 vols. Moscow: Soglasie, 1997.

Chukovskaya, Lydia. *The Akhmatova Journals: 1938–1941.* Translated by Milena Michalski and Sylva Rubashova, with poetry translated by Peter Norman. London: Harvill, 1994.

——. *The Deserted House.* Translated by Aline B. Werth. New York: Dutton, 1967.

——. *The Deserted House.* Translated by Aline B. Werth. New York: Nordland, 1978.

——. *Going Under.* Translated by Peter M. Weston [Peter Norman]. London: Barrie & Jenkins, 1972.

——. *Sofia Petrovna.* Translated by Aline Werth. Evanston, IL: Northwestern University Press, 1994.

——. *To the Memory of Childhood.* Translated by Eliza Kellogg. Evanston, IL: Northwestern University Press, 1988.

Chukovsky, Kornei. *Dnevnik. 1930–1969.* Moscow: Sovremennyi pisatel', 1994.

——. "Literaturnoe chudo." In *Sobranie sochinenii v 15 tomakh.* Moscow: Agentstvo FTM, 2012.

Chukovsky, Kornei, and Lydia Chukovskaia. *Kornei Chukovsky—Lydia Chukovskaia. Perepiska. 1912–1969.* Edited by Zhozefina Khavkina and Elena Chukovskaia. Moscow: Novoe literaturnoe obozrenie, 2003.

Chuzhak, Nikolai, ed. *Literatura fakta: pervyi sbornik materialov rabotnikov LEFa.* Moscow: Federatsiia, 1929. Reprint, Moscow: Zakharov, 2000.

Clark, Katerina. "Socialist Realism *with* Shores: The Conventions for the Positive Hero." In *Socialist Realism without Shores*, edited by Thomas Lahusen and Evgeny Dobrenko, 27–50. Durham, NC: Duke University Press, 1997.

Conquest, Robert. "Solzhenitsyn in the British Media." In *Solzhenitsyn in Exile*, edited by John B. Dunlop, Richard S. Haugh, and Michael Nicholson, 3–23. Stanford, CA: Hoover Institution Press, 1984.

Curtis, J. *The Englishman from Lebedian': A Life of Evgeny Zamiatin.* Boston: Academic Studies Press, 2013.

——. "Istoriia izdaniia romana 'My', perevody i publikatsii." In *"My": Tekst i materialy k tvorcheskoi istroii romana*, edited by M. Yu. Liubimova and J. Curtis, 499–534. St. Petersburg: Mir, 2011.

Dalos, György. *The Guest from the Future: Anna Akhmatova and Isaiah Berlin.* Translated by Antony Wood. New York: Farrar, Straus & Giroux, 1999.

Darnton, Robert. *Censors at Work: How States Shaped Literature.* New York: Norton, 2014.

Dobin, Evgeny. *Poeziia Anny Akhmatovoi.* Leningrad: Sovetskii pisatel', 1968.

Dolinin, Aleksandr. "Karl Proffer i Vladimir Nabokov: k istorii dialoga." *Novoe literaturnoe obozrenie*, no. 1 (2014): 145–52.

Domogatsky, Boris. "Zapiski iz ada." Review of *Krutoi marshrut*, by Evgeniia Ginzburg. *Novoe russkoe slovo*, June 7, 1968.

Dorman, Oleg. *Podstrochnik. Zhizn' Lilianny Lunginoi, rasskazannaia eiu v fil'me Olega Dormana.* Moscow: Corpus, 2009.

Dostoevsky, Fyodor. *An Honest Thief and Other Stories.* Translated by Constance Garnett. New York: Macmillan, 1923.

——. *The House of the Dead: A Novel in Two Parts.* Translated by Constance Garnett. New York, 1915.

——. *Memoirs from the House of the Dead.* Translated by Jessie Coulson, with an introduction and notes by Ronald Hingley. Oxford: Oxford University Press, 2001.

——. *Zapiski iz mertvago doma.* St. Petersburg: Tipografiia Eduarda Pratsa, 1862.

Doubassoff, Irene. *Ten Months in Bolshevik Prisons.* Edinburgh: William Blackwood & Sons, 1926.

Dovlatov, Sergei. *Rech' bez povoda . . . Ili kolonki redaktora.* Moscow: Makhaon, 2006.

"Down into the Past." Review of *Going Under*, by Lydia Chukovskaya. *Times Literary Supplement*, August 11, 1972.

Dremov, Anatoly. "Retsenziia na rukopis' 'Kolymskikh rasskazov.'" In *Shalamovskii sbornik 3*, edited by Valery Esipov, 36–37. Vologda: Grifon, 2002.

Driver, Sam N. *Anna Akhmatova.* New York: Twayne, 1972.

Dudintsev, Vladimir. "Ne khlebom edinym." *Novyi mir*, no. 8 (1956): 31–118; no. 9 (1956): 37–118; no. 10 (1956): 21–98.

——. *Ne khlebom edinym.* Munich: Tsentral'noe ob'edinenie politicheskikh emigrantov iz SSSR, 1957.

——. *Ne khlebom edinym.* New York: Novoe russkoe slovo, 1957.

——. *Not by Bread Alone.* Translated by Edith Bone. New York: Dutton, 1957.

Dviniatina, Tatiana, and Natalia Kraineva, eds. "'Acumiana' P.N. Luknitskogo 1962 g. v fondakh IRLI i RNB." In *Ezhegodnik rukopisnogo otdela Pushkinskogo doma na 2011 god*, 753–90. St. Petersburg: Pushkinskii dom, 2012.

Dymshits, Aleksandr. "Za chistotu printsipov." *Literaturnaia Rossiia*, February 11, 1972.

E. B. Review of *Spusk pod vodu*, by Lydia Chukovskaia. *Novoe russkoe slovo*, November 19, 1972.

Eremin, Dmitry. "Perevertyshi." *Izvestiia*, January 13, 1966.

Ermolaev, Herman. Review of *The Deserted House*, by Lydia Chukovskaia. *Slavic and East European Journal* 13, no. 1 (Spring 1969): 99–101.

Esipov, Valery. "Kommentarii k 'Kolymskim rasskazam.'" http://shalamov.ru/research/249/.

——. *Shalamov*. Moscow: Molodaia Gvardiia, 2012.

Etkind, Alexander. *Warped Mourning: Stories of the Undead in the Land of the Unburied*. Stanford, CA: Stanford University Press, 2013.

Etkind, Efim. "Otets i doch'." *Vremia i my* 66 (May–June 1982): 168–83.

Evtushenko, Evgeny. "Nasledniki Stalina." *Pravda*, October 21, 1962.

Fainsod, Merle. "One to Be Burned." Review of *The Deserted House*, by Lydia Chukovskaya. *New York Times*, November 12, 1967.

Feuer, Kathryn. "Russia's Young Intellectuals." *Encounter* (February 1957): 10–25.

——, ed. *Solzhenitsyn: A Collection of Critical Essays*. Englewood Cliffs, NJ: Prentice Hall, 1976.

Feuer, Lewis S. "Cultural Scholarly Exchange in the Soviet Union in 1963 and How the KGB Tried to Terrorize American Scholars and Suppress Truths." In *Tamizdat: Publishing Russian Literature across Borders*, edited by Yasha Klots. Special issue of *Wiener Slawistischer Almanach* 86, 299–310. Berlin: Peter Lang, 2021.

Feuer Miller, Robin. "Double Diaries and Layered Memories. Moscow, 1963." In *Tamizdat: Publishing Russian Literature across Borders*, edited by Yasha Klots. Special issue of *Wiener Slawistischer Almanach* 86, 311–20. Berlin: Peter Lang, 2021.

——. "Vmesto nekrologa Kathryn Feuer." In *Tynianovskii sbornik: piatye Tynianovskie chtenia*, edited by Marietta Chudakova, 357–66. Moscow: Imprint, 1994.

Filippov, Boris. "Pis'mo v redaktsiiu 'Literaturnoi gazety.'" Afterword to *Govorit Moskva. Povesti i rasskazy*, by Nikolai Arzhak. 161–66. [Washington, DC]: Inter-Language Literary Associates, 1966.

——. "'Poema bez geroia' Akhmatovoi." *Vozdushnye puti* 2 (1961): 167–83.

——. Review of *Izbrannye stikhotvoreniia*, by Anna Akhmatova. *Novyi zhurnal* 32 (1953): 300–305.

Filistinsky, Boris [Boris Filippov, pseud.]. "Kak napechatali Akhmatovu." *Za Rodinu*, September 2, 1943.

Finn, Peter, and Petra Couvée. *The Zhivago Affair: The Kremlin, the CIA, and the Battle over a Forbidden Book*. New York: Vintage, 2015.

Fleishman, Lazar. "Iz akhmatovskikh materialov v arkhive Guverovskogo instituta." In *Akhmatovskii Sbornik* 1, edited by Sergei Dediulin and Gabriel Superfin, 165–93. Paris: Institute d'études slaves, 1989.

——. "Iz arkhiva Guverovskogo instituta. Pis'ma Iu. G. Oksmana k G. P. Struve."
    Stanford Slavic Studies 1 (1987): 16–70.
——. *Vstrecha russkoi emigratsii s "Doktorom Zhivago": Boris Pasternak i "kholodnaia
    voina."* Stanford, CA: Stanford Slavic Series, 2009.
Forrester, Sibelan. "*Mother* as Forebear: How Lidiia Chukovskaia's *Sof'ia Petro-
    vna* Rewrites Maksim Gorkii's *Mat'*." In *American Contributions to the 14th
    International Congress of Slavists*, edited by David M. Bethea, 51–67. Bloom-
    ington, IN: Slavica, 2008.
Foucault, Michel. *Discipline and Punish: The Birth of Prison*. Translated by Alan
    Sheridan. New York: Vintage, 1979.
——. "Of Other Spaces: Utopias and Heterotopias." In *Heterotopia and the City:
    Public Space in a Postcivil Society*, edited by Michiel Dehaene and Lieven de
    Cauter, 13–30. London: Routledge, 2008.
Fox, Sylvan. "Stephen Spender Quits *Encounter*." *New York Times*, May 8, 1967.
Frank, Viktor. *Izbrannye stat'i*. Edited by Leonard Shapiro. London: Overseas
    Publications Interchange, 1974.
Galkova, Irina. "Pis'mo o pis'me." *Acta Samizdatica. Zapiski o samizdate* 4 (2018):
    293–301.
——. "Rodion Vas'kov—geroi prozy Varlama Shalamova." In *Zakon soprotivleniia
    raspadu. Sbornik nauchnykh trudov*. Edited by Lucas Babka et al., 185–96.
    Prague: *Slovanská knihovna*, 2017.
Gallagher, David. "Friends and Enemies." *Times Literary Supplement*, September
    7, 1967.
——. "Somewhere in Leningrad." *Times*, August 28, 1967.
Galushkin, Aleksandr. "Delo Pil'niaka i Zamiatina. Predvaritel'nye itogi rassle-
    dovaniia." In *Novoe o Zamiatine*, edited by Leonid Geller, 89–148. Moscow:
    MIK, 1997.
Garanin, Evgeny. "Povest', posle kotoroi pisat' po-staromu nel'zia…Ob 'Odnom
    dne Ivana Denisovicha' A. I. Solzhenitsyna." *Posev*, December 23, 1962.
Garaudy, Roger. *D'un réalisme sans rivages: Picasso, Saint-John Perse, Kafka*. Preface
    by Louis Aragon. Paris: Plon, 1963.
Gates, Henry Louis, Jr. "White Like Me." *New Yorker* (June 17, 1996): 66–81.
Geller, Mikhail. Introduction to *Kolymskie rasskazy*, by Varlam Shalamov, 5–16.
    London: Overseas Publications Interchange, 1978.
——. *Kontsentratsionnyi mir i sovetskaia literatura*. London: Overseas Publications
    Interchange, 1974.
Genis, Aleksandr. "Tret'ia volna: primerka svobody." *Zvezda*, no. 5 (2010):
    205–14.
Ginzburg, Aleksandr, ed. *Belaia kniga po delu A. Sinyavskogo i Iu. Danielia*. Frank-
    furt: Possev, 1967.
——. "Dvadtsat' let tomu nazad." *Russkaia mysl'*, February 14, 1986.
Ginzburg, Eugenia. *Journey into the Whirlwind*. Translated by Paul Stevenson and
    Max Hayward. New York: Harcourt, Brace, & World, 1967.
Ginzburg, Evgeniia. "Krutoi marshrut." *Grani* 64–68 (1967).
——. *Krutoi marshrut*. Milan: Mondadori, 1967.
Ginzburg, Lydia. *Prokhodiashchie kharaktery. Proza voennykh let. Zapiski blokad-
    nogo cheloveka*. Edited by Emily van Buskirk and Andrei Zorin. Moscow:
    Novoe izdatel'stvo, 2011.

——. "Zapiski blokadnogo cheloveka." *Neva*, no. 1 (1984): 84–108.

——. *Zapisnye knizhki. Vospominaniia. Esse.* St. Petersburg: Iskusstvo-SPB, 2002.

Glad, John. *Conversations in Exile: Russian Writers Abroad.* Translated by Richard Robin and Joana Robin. Durham, NC: Duke University Press, 1993.

——. Foreword to *Kolyma Tales*, by Varlam Shalamov, ix–xix. London: Penguin, 1994.

Gladkov, Aleksandr. *O poetakh, sovremennikakh i—nemnogo o sebe . . . (Iz dnevnikov i zapisnykh knizhek).* Edited by Mikhail Mikheev. Moscow: YASK, 2018.

Glekin, Georgy. *Chto mne dano . . . Ob Anne Akhmatovoi.* Moscow: Ekon-Inform, 2011.

——. "Vstrechi s Akhmatovoi (iz dnevnikovykh zapisei 1959–1966 godov)." *Voprosy literatury*, no. 2 (1997): 302–24.

Glen, Nika. "Vokrug starykh zapisei." In *Vospominaniia ob Anne Akhmatovoi*, edited by V. Ia. Vilenkin and V. A. Chernykh, 627–39. Moscow: Sovetskii pisatel', 1991.

Glushanok, Galina, and Stanislav Shvabrin. "Perepiska Nabokovykh s Profferami." Translated, with a commentary by Nina Zhutovskaia. *Zvezda*, no. 7 (2005): 123–71.

Gogol, Nikolai. *The Collected Tales.* Translated by Richard Pevear and Larissa Volokhonsky. New York: Vintage, 1999.

Golovizin, Mark. "K voprosu o proiskhozhdenii pervykh zarubezhnykh izdanii 'Kolymskikh rasskazov' V.T. Shalamova." In *Shalamovskii sbornik* 4, edited by Valery Esipov and Sergei Soloviev, 197–214. Moscow: Litera, 2011.

Gorbanevskaia, Natalia. "Ee golos." In *Akhmatovskii sbornik* 1, edited by Sergei Dediulin and Gabriel Superfin, 233–43. Paris: Institute d'études slaves, 1989.

——. *Polden': delo o demonstratsii 25 avgusta 1968 goda na Krasnoi ploshchadi.* Frankfurt: Possev, 1970.

——. *Polden': delo o demonstratsii 25 avgusta 1968 goda na Krasnoi ploshchadi.* Moscow: Novoe izdatel'stvo, 2007.

Gotkhart, Natan. "Dvenadtsat' vstrech s Annoi Akhmatovoi." *Voprosy literatury*, no. 2 (1997): 261–301.

Granat, Robert. "The Great God Ninel." Review of *The Deserted House*, by Lydia Chukovskaya. *New Leader* 51, no. 3 (January 29, 1968): 21–22.

Grossman, Vasily. *Vse techet.* Frankfurt: Possev, 1970.

——. *Zhizn' i sud'ba.* Foreword by Efim Etkind. Lausanne: L'Age d'Homme, 1980.

Grot, Elena. "Anna Akhmatova." *Novoe russkoe slovo*, June 6, 1965.

Grynberg, Roman [Erge, pseud.]. "Chitaia 'Poemu bez geroia.'" *Vozdushnye puti* 3 (1963): 295–300.

Gul', Roman. "A. Solzhenitsyn, sotsrealizm i shkola Remizova." *Novyi zhurnal* 71 (1963): 58–74.

——. *Ia unes Rossiiu. Apologiia emigratsii.* Vol. 3, *Rossiia v Amerike.* New York: Most, 1989.

——. *Odvukon'. Sovetskaia i emigrantskaia literatura.* New York: Most, 1973.

——. "Otchet redaktora." *Novoe russkoe slovo*, April 30, 1972.

——. Preface to "Kolymskie rasskazy," by Varlam Shalamov. *Novyi zhurnal* 85 (1966): 5.

——. "Progulki khama s Pushkinym." *Novyi zhurnal* 124 (1976): 117–29.

——. "'Rekviem' Anny Akhmatovoi." *Novyi zhurnal* 77 (1964): 290–94.

Gumilev, Nikolai. *Sobranie sochinenii v 4 tomakh.* Edited by Gleb Struve and Boris Filippov. Washington, DC: Victor Kamkin, 1962–1968.

Gushchin, K. "Sobytie, o kotorom zagovorila vsia strana." *Posev*, December 14, 1962.

Haight, Amanda. *Anna Akhmatova: A Poetic Pilgrimage.* New York: Oxford University Press, 1976.

Halkin, Shmuel. *Erdishe vegn.* Moscow: Der Emes, 1945.

Haltrecht, Montague. "A Nightmare of the Purses." Review of *The Deserted House*, by Lydia Chukovskaya. *Sunday Times*, August 27, 1967.

Harkins, William E. *Dictionary of Russian Literature.* London: Allen & Unwin, 1957.

Hartmann, Anne. "'Ein Fenster in die Vergangenheit': Das Lager neu lesen." *Osteuropa* 57, no. 6 (June 2007): 55–80.

Haupt, George. Review of *The Deserted House*, by Lydia Chukovskaya, and *Journey into the Whirlwind*, by Eugenia Ginzburg. *Russian Review* 28, no. 2 (April 1969): 242–43.

Heffermehl, Fabian, and Irina Karlsohn, eds. *The Gulag in Writings of Aleksandr Solzhenitsyn and Varlam Shalamov: Memory, History, Testimony.* Leiden: Brill, 2021.

Heller, Michał. *Świat obozów koncentracyjnych a literatura sowiecka. Translated by Michał Kaniowski. Paris: Instytut Literacki, 1974.*

Heller, Michel. *Le monde concentrationnaire et la littérature soviétique.* Lausanne: L'Age d'Homme, 1974.

Herling, Gustaw. *A World Apart.* Translated by Joseph Marek [Andrzej Cioz-kosz]. London: Heineman, 1951.

Herzen, Alexander. *A Herzen Reader.* Edited and translated, with an introduction by Kathleen Parthe, and a critical essay by Robert Harris. Evanston, IL: Northwestern University Press, 2012.

——. *My Past and Thoughts: The Memoirs of Alexander Herzen.* Translated by Constance Garnett, with an introduction by Isaiah Berlin. Berkeley: University of California Press, 1982.

Holmgren, Beth. *Women's Works in Stalin's Time: On Lidiia Chukovskaia and Nadezhda Mandelshtam.* Bloomington: Indiana University Press, 1993.

Howe, Irving. "Beyond Bitterness." Review of *Kolyma Tales*, by Varlam Shalamov. *New York Review of Books*, August 14, 1980.

Hull, David Stewart. Review of *One Day in the Life of Ivan Denisovich*, by Aleksandr Solzhenitsyn. *Russian Review* 22, no. 3 (July 1963): 336–37.

Iakir, Petr. *Detstvo v tiur'me.* New York: Macmillan, 1972.

"'. . . Ia ne imeiu otnosheniia k Serebrianomu veku . . .' Pis'ma Odoevtsevoi V. F. Markovu (1956–1975)." In *"Esli chudo voobshche vozmozhno za granitsei . . ." Epokha 1950-kh v perepiske russkikh literatorov-emigrantov*, edited, with an introduction and commentary by Oleg Korostelev, 695–794. Moscow: Russkii put', 2008.

Iangirov, Rashit. "'Drebezzhan'e moikh rzhavykh strun . . . ': iz perepiski Vladimira i Very Nabokovykh i Romana Grynberga (1940–1967)." In *In Memoriam: Istoricheskii sbornik pamiati A. I. Dobkina*, edited by Vladimir Aloi and Tatiana Pritykina, 345–97. St. Petersburg: Feniks—Athenaeum, 2000.

——. "Druz'ia, babochki i monstry: iz perepiski Vladimira i Very Nabokovykh s Romanom Grynbergom (1943–1967)." *Diaspora: Novye Materialy* 1 (2001): 477–556.

——. "Roman Grynberg i Roman Iakobson. Materialy k istorii vzaimootnoshenii." In *Roman Iakobson: Teksty, Dokumenty, Issledovaniia*, edited by Henryk Baran, 201–12. Moscow: RGGU, 1999.

Israel, Nico. *Spirals: The Whirled Image in Twentieth-Century Literature and Art*. New York: Columbia University Press, 2015.

Iurasov, S. *Vasily Terkin posle voiny*. New York: Izdatel'stvo imeni Chekhova, 1953.

Ivanov, Georgy. *Peterburgskie zimy*. Paris: La Source, 1928.

Ivanova, Natalia. "Khranit' vechno." *Iunost'*, no. 7 (1988): 86–90.

Ivashchenko, A. "Podsadnaia utka: istoriia prestuplenii B. Filippova-Filistinskovo, v proshlom gestapovtsa, nyne izdatelia-klevetnika v Soedinennykh Shtatakh." *Komsomol'skaia pravda*, June 9, 1968.

Iverni, Violetta. "Zerkalo pamiati." Review of *Kolymskie rasskazy*, by Varlam Shalamov. *Kontinent* 19 (1979): 379–83.

Jaccard, Jean-Philippe. *Literatura kak takovaia. Ot Nabokova k Pushkinu*. Moscow: Novoe literaturnoe obozrenie, 2014.

Jacobson, Alexander. "Pirate, Book Artist: An Introduction to Alec Flegon." *Wiener Slavistisches Jahrbuch* 8 (2020): 240–53.

——. "Tamizdat as Masquerade: The Case of Aleksandr Solzhenitsyn's Four *Gulags*." In *Tamizdat: Publishing Russian Literature across Borders*, edited by Yasha Klots. Special issue of *Wiener Slawistischer Almanach* 86, 119–42. Berlin: Peter Lang, 2021.

Jaffe, Lysander. "'Writing as a Stranger': Two Translations of Shalamov's 'The Snake Charmer.'" https://shalamov.ru/en/research/207/.

Jauss, Hans Robert. *Toward an Aesthetic of Reception*. Translated by Timothy Bahti, with an introduction by Paul de Man. Minneapolis: University of Minnesota Press, 1982.

Jones, Polly. "The Thaw Goes International. Soviet Literature in Translation and Transit in the 1960s." In *The Socialist Sixties: Crossing Borders in the Second World*, edited by Anne E. Gorsuch and Diane P. Koenker, 121–47. Bloomington: Indiana University Press, 2013.

Julius, Annette. *Lidija Čukovskaja: Leben und Werk*. Munich: Otto Sagner, 1995.

Kanevskaia, Irina. "Pamiati avtora 'Kolymskikh rasskazov.'" *Posev*, no. 3 (1982): 46–47.

Kaverin, Veniamin. "Sem' par nechistykh." *Novyi mir*, no. 2 (1962): 142–77.

Kayiatos, Anastasia. "Silence and Alterity in Russia after Stalin, 1955–1974." PhD diss., University of California, Berkeley, 2012. https://escholarship.org/content/qt1989594t/qt1989594t.pdf?t=odx9l7.

Kedrina, Zoya. "Nasledniki Smerdiakova." *Literaturnaia gazeta*, January 22, 1966.

Khagi, Sofya. "Silence and the Rest: The Inexpressible from Batiushkov to Tiutchev." *Slavic and East European Journal* 48, no. 1 (Spring 2004): 41–61.

Khazan, Vladimir. "My sluzhim ne partiiam, ne gosudarstvu, a cheloveku": iz istorii zhurnala 'Opyty' i al'manakha 'Vozdushnye puti.'" *Toronto Slavic Quarterly* 29 (2009). http://sites.utoronto.ca/tsq/29/hazan29.shtml.

Khmelnitsky, Sergei. "Iz chreva kitova." *Dvadtsat'-dva* 48 (1986): 151–80.

Khrabrovitsky, Aleksandr. *Ocherk moei zhizni. Dnevnik. Vstrechi.* Moscow: Novoe literaturnoe obozrenie, 2012.

Khrushchev, Nikita. *Sluzhenie narodu—vysokoe prizvanie sovetskikh pisatelei.* Moscow: Gosudarstvennoe izdatel'stvo politicheskoi literatury, 1959.

Kim, Roman. "Kto ukral Punnakana?" *Oktiabr'*, no. 10 (1963): 41–92.

Kind-Kovács, Friederike. *Written Here, Published There: How Underground Literature Crossed the Iron Curtain.* Budapest: Central European University Press, 2014.

Kind-Kovács, Friederike, and Jessie Labov, eds. *Samizdat, Tamizdat, and Beyond: Transnational Media during and after Socialism.* New York: Berghahn, 2013.

Klebanova, Evgenia [N. N-ko, pseud.]. "Moi vstrechi s Annoi Akhmatovoi." *Novoe russkoe slovo.* March 13, 1966.

Klenov, Andrei. "Chudesnaia kniga." Review of *Spusk pod vodu*, by Lydia Chukovskaia. *Novoe russkoe slovo*, June 30, 1974.

Klimoff, Alexis. "In Defense of the Word: Lydia Chukovskaya and the Russian Tradition." Introduction to *The Deserted House*, by Lydia Chukovskaya, translated by Aline B. Werth, i–xliv. New York: Nordland, 1978.

——. "The Sober Eye: Ivan Denisovich and the Peasant Perspective." In *One Day in the Life of Ivan Denisovich: A Critical Companion*, edited by Alexis Klimoff, 3–31. Evanston, IL: Northwestern University Press, 1997.

Klots, Yakov. "Kak izdavali pervuiu knigu Iosifa Brodskogo." *Colta.ru* (May 24, 2015). https://www.colta.ru/articles/literature/7415-kak-izda vali-pervuyu-knigu-iosifa-brodskogo.

——. "'Osuzhdat' reku za to, chto v nei kto-to utopilsia . . . ': pis'mo ameri-kanskogo izdatelia Tertsa i Arzhaka v redaktsiiu *Literaturnoi gazety*." *Colta.ru* (February 12, 2016). https://www.colta.ru/articles/literature/ 10100-osuzhdat-reku-za-to-chto-v-ney-kto-to-utopilsya.

——. "'Rekviem' Akhmatovoi v tamizdate: 56 pisem." *Colta.ru* (June 24, 2019). https://www.colta.ru/articles/literature/21637-rekviem-ahmato voy-v-tamizdate-56-pisem.

Klots, Yasha. "From Avvakum to Dostoevsky: Varlam Shalamov and Russian Narratives of Political Imprisonment." *Russian Review* 75, no. 1 (January 2016): 7–25.

——, ed. *Tamizdat: Publishing Russian Literature across Borders.* Special issue of *Wiener Slawistischer Almanach* Band 86. Berlin: Peter Lang, 2021.

——. "The Way Back. Kathryn Feuer's and Gleb Struve's Letters on Academic Exchange, Yulian Oksman and Crossing the Soviet-Finnish Border (June 1963)." In *Across Borders: 20th Century Russian Literature and Russian-Jewish Cultural Contacts. Essays in Honor of Vladimir Khazan*, edited by Lazar Fleishman and Fedor Poljakov, 557–84. Berlin: Peter Lang, 2018.

Koehler, Ludmila. "Alexander Solzhenitsyn and Russian Literary Tradition." *Russian Review* 26, no. 2 (April 1967): 176–84.

Komaromi, Ann. "Ardis Facsimile and Reprint Editions: Giving Back Russian Literature." In *Samizdat, Tamizdat and Beyond: Transnational Media during and after Socialism*, edited by Friederike Kind-Kovács and Jessie Labov, 27–50. New York: Berghahn, 2013.

——, ed. *Project for the Study of Dissidence and Samizdat*. https://samizdat.library.
utoronto.ca.

——. "The Unofficial Field of Late Soviet Culture." *Slavic Review* 66, no. 4 (Winter 2007): 605–29.

Kopelev, Lev, "Pis'mo Solzhenitsynu." *Sintaksis* 37 (2001): 87–102.

Kopelev, Lev, and Raisa Orlova. *My zhili v Moskve. 1956–1980*. Moscow: Kniga, 1990.

Koriakov, Mikhail. "Izdatel'stvo imeni Chekhova." *Novoe russkoe slovo*, June 25, 1970.

——. "'Rodina moia, Rossiia . . ..'" *Novoe russkoe slovo*, April 2, 1972.

Korostelev, Oleg. "Merezhkovsky v emigratsii." *Literaturovedcheskii zhurnal* 15 (2001): 3–17.

——, ed. *Ot Adamovicha do Tsvetaevoi. Literatura, kritika, pechat' russkogo zarubezh'ia*. St. Petersburg: Izdatel'stvo imeni Novikova, 2013.

——, ed. "Perepiska G. V. Adamovicha s R. N. Grynbergom: 1953–1967." *Literaturovedcheskii zhurnal* 17 (2003): 97–181.

——, ed. "Zhurnal 'Opyty' (New York, 1953–1958). Issledovaniia i materialy." *Literaturovedcheskii zhurnal* 17 (2003): 97–368.

Kovalenko, Iu. "A. A. vo Frantsii." *Nedelia*, June 15, 1989.

Kovalenkov, Aleksandr. "Pis'mo staromu drugu." *Znamia*, no. 7 (1957): 165–73.

Kozlov, Denis. *The Readers of* Novyi Mir. *Coming to Terms with the Stalinist Past*. Cambridge, MA: Harvard University Press, 2013.

Krivosheina, Nina. *Chetyre treti nashei zhizni*. Moscow: Russkii put', 2017.

Kudrova, Irma. *Russkie vstrechi Pitera Normana*. St. Petersburg: Zhurnal "Neva," 1999.

Kushnirov, Aron. "Foter-Komandir." *Heymland* 1 (1947): 104–5.

——. "Tri stikhotvoreniia." Translated by Ruvim Moran. *Novyi mir*, no. 4 (1947): 117.

——. *Foter-Komandir*. Moscow: Der Emes, 1948.

Kuznetsov, Anatoly. "Baby Yar." *Iunost'*, no. 8 (1966): 6–42; no. 9 (1966): 15–46; no. 10 (1966): 23–51.

——. *Baby Yar*. Moscow: Molodaia Gvardiia, 1967.

——. *Baby Yar*. Frankfurt: Possev, 1970.

Lahusen, Thomas. *How Life Writes the Book: Real Socialism and Socialist Realism in Stalin's Russia*. Ithaca, NY: Cornell University Press, 1997.

——. "Socialist Realism in Search of Its Shores." In *Socialist Realism without Shores*, edited by Thomas Lahusen and Evgeny Dobrenko, 5–26. Durham, NC: Duke University Press, 1997.

Lakhman, Gizella. "Rodnaia zemlia. Otvet na stikhotvorenie Anny Akhmatovoi." *Novoe russkoe slovo*, April 7, 1963.

Lakshin, Vladimir. "Ivan Denisovich, ego druz'ia i nedrugi." *Novyi mir*, no. 1 (1964): 223–45.

Lambert, Bruce. "Frederick Barghoorn, 90, Scholar Detained in Soviet Union in 1963." *New York Times*, November 26, 1991.

Lesniak, Boris. "Varlam Shalamov, kakim ia ego znal." *Rabochaia tribuna*, March 14, 1994.

——. "Vospominiia o Varlame Shalamove." *Na Severe Dal'nem*, no. 2 (1989).

Levi, Primo. *The Drowned and the Saved.* Translated by Raymond Rosenthal. New York: Simon & Schuster, 2017.

Leving, Yury. "'Akhmatova' russkoi emigratsii—Gizella Lakhman." *Novoe literaturnoe obozrenie,* no. 5 (2006): 164–73.

——. "Zabytye imena russkoi emigratsii. Poet Gizella Lakhman." In *Russkie evrei v Amerike 2,* edited by Ernst Zaltsberg, 96–114. Jerusalem: Russkoe evreistvo v zarubezh'e, 2007.

Levi-Strauss, Claude. *Structural Anthropology.* Translated by Claire Jacobson and Brooke Grundfest Schoepf. New York: Basic Books, 1963.

Lipkin, Semyon. *Stalingrad Vasiliia Grossmana.* Ann Arbor, MI: Ardis, 1986.

Lipovetsky, Mark. "A Monument to Russian Modernism: The Ardis Vision of Contemporary Russian Literature." In *Tamizdat: Publishing Russian Literature across Borders,* edited by Yasha Klots. Special issue of *Wiener Slawistischer Almanach* 86, 203–23. Berlin: Peter Lang, 2021.

Litvinov, Pavel. "Political and Human Rights Tamizdat." In *Tamizdat: Publishing Russian Literature across Borders,* edited by Yasha Klots. Special issue of *Wiener Slawistischer Almanach* 86, 329–35. Berlin: Peter Lang, 2021.

Ljunggren, Anna. "Anna Akhmatova's *Requiem*: A Retrospective of the Love Lyric and Epos." In *Anna Akhmatova. 1889–1989. Papers from the Akhmatova Centennial Conference,* edited by Sonia I. Ketchian, 110–26. Oakland, CA: Berkeley Slavic Specialties, 1993.

Lopukhina-Rodzianko, Tatiana. *Dukhovnye osnovy tvorchestva Solzhenitsyna.* Frankfurt: Possev, 1974.

Loseff, Lev. *Joseph Brodsky: A Literary Life.* Translated by Jane Ann Miller: New Haven, CT: Yale University Press, 2011.

——. *On the Beneficence of Censorship: Aesopian Language in Modern Russian Literature.* Munich: Otto Sanger, 1984.

Losev, Lev. "Krestnyi otets samizdata." In his *Meandr. Memuarnaia proza,* 289–92. Moscow: Novoe izdatel'stvo, 2010.

Lourié, Arthur. "Olga Afanasyevna Glebova-Sudeikina." In *Anna Akhmatova and Her Circle,* edited by Konstantin Polivanov, 230–33. Fayetteville: University of Arkansas Press, 1994.

Lukács, Georg. "Solzhenitsyn and the New Realism." *Socialist Register* (1965): 197–215.

Lundblad-Janjić, Josefina. "Poetry and Politics: An Allegorical Reading of Varlam Shalamov's Poem 'Avvakum v Pustozerske.'" https://shalamov.ru/research/239/.

Magner, Thomas F. Review of *One Day in the Life of Ivan Denisovich,* by Aleksandr Solzhenitsyn. *Slavic and East European Journal* 7, no. 4 (Winter 1963): 418–19.

Makarov, Aleksei. "Pis'mo Petra Iakira Varlamu Shalamovu." *Acta Samizdatica. Zapiski o samizdate* 4 (2018): 285–92.

Makovsky, Sergei. *Na Parnase Serebrianogo veka.* Munich: Tsentral'noe ob'edinenie politicheskikh emigrantov iz SSSR, 1962.

——. "Nikolai Gumilev po lichnym vospominaniiam." *Novyi zhurnal* 77 (1964): 157–89.

——. *Requiem.* Paris: Rifma, 1963.

Maksimov, Vladimir. "Metropol' ili metropol'." Review of *Metropol*. *Russkaia mysl'*, May 17, 1979.

Malia, Martin. *Alexander Herzen and the Birth of Russian Socialism, 1812–1855.* Cambridge, MA: Harvard University Press, 1961.

Maloff, Saul. "Can Such Things Have Been?" Review of *The Deserted House*, by Lydia Chukovskaya. *Chicago Tribune*, November 5, 1967.

Malsagoff, S. A. *An Island Hell: A Soviet Prison in the Far North.* Translated by F. H. Lyon. London: A. M. Philpot, 1926.

Mancosu, Paolo. *Kontrabandisty, buntari, piraty: perepetii istorii izdaniia "Doktora Zhivago."* Moscow: Azbukovnik, 2017.

——. *Zhivago's Secret Journey: From Typescript to Book.* Stanford, CA: Hoover Institution Press, 2016.

Mandelshtam, Osip. *Sobranie sochinenii.* New York: Izdatel'stvo imeni Chekhova, 1955.

——. *Sobranie sochinenii v 2 tomakh.* Edited by Gleb Struve and Boris Filippov. Washington, DC: Inter-Language Literary Associates, 1964–1966.

——. *Sobranie sochinenii v 4 tomakh.* Moscow: Art-Biznes-Tsentr, 1993.

——. *Sochineniia v 2 tomakh.* Moscow: Khudozhestvennaia literatura, 1990.

Mandelstam, Nadezhda. *Hope against Hope.* Translated by Max Hayward, with an introduction by Clarence Brown. New York: Atheneum, 1970.

——. *Vospominaniia.* New York: Izdatel'stvo imeni Chekhova, 1970.

Mandelstam, Osip. *50 Poems.* Translated by Bernard Meares, with an introduction by Joseph Brodsky. New York: Persea Books, 1977.

Marchenko, Anatoly. *Moi pokazaniia.* Paris: La Presse Libre, 1969.

——. *My Testimony.* Translated by Michael Scammell. New York: Dutton, 1969.

Markesinis, Eugenie. *Andrei Siniavskii: A Hero of His Time?* Boston: Academic Studies Press, 2013.

Markov, Vladimir, ed. *Priglushennye golosa. Poeziia za zheleznym zanavesom.* New York: Izdatel'stvo imeni Chekhova, 1952.

Marshak, Samuil, "Pravdivaia povest'." *Pravda*, January 30, 1964.

Matich, Olga. *"Tamizdat:* The Spatial Turn, Textual Embodiment, My Personal Stories." In *Tamizdat: Publishing Russian Literature across Borders*, edited by Yasha Klots. Special issue of *Wiener Slawistischer Almanach* 86, 27–60. Berlin: Peter Lang, 2021.

——. *Zapiski russkoi amerikanki. Semeinye khroniki i sluchainye vstrechi.* Moscow: Novoe literaturnoe obozrenie, 2016.

Matich, Olga, and Michael Heim, eds. *The Third Wave: Russian Literature in Emigration.* Ann Arbor, MI: Ardis, 1982.

Mayakovsky, Vladimir. "Nashe otnoshenie." *Literaturnaia gazeta*, September 2, 1929.

Mayorova, Olga. Preface to "Ann Arbor v russkoi literature." *Novoe literaturnoe obozrenie*, no. 1 (2014): 130–37.

Medvedev, Zhores A. "The Attack on Lydia Chukovskaya." *New York Review of Books*, March 7, 1974.

——. "Lzhivyi detektiv v gazete 'Sovetskaia Rossiia.'" *Novoe russkoe slovo*, January 25, 1974.

Metropol: Literary Almanac. Translated by Kevin Klose. New York: Norton, 1982.

Metropol'. Literaturnyi al'manakh. Ann Arbor, MI: Ardis, 1979.

Mieželaitis, Eduardas. "Stikhi." *Novyi mir*, no. 11 (1962): 3–7.

Mihajlov, Mihajlo. *Leto moskovskoe 1964. Mertvyi dom Dostoevskogo i Solzhenitsyna.* Translated by Iaroslav Trushnovich. Frankfurt: Possev, 1967.

Mikhailik, Elena. "Kot, begushchii mezhdu Shalamovym i Solzhenitsynym." In *Shalamovskii sbornik* 3, edited by Valery Esipov, 101–14. Vologda: Grifon, 2002.

——. *Nezakonnaia kometa. Varlam Shalamov: opyt medlennogo chteniia.* Moscow: Novoe literaturnoe obozrenie, 2018.

Mikheev, Mikhail. "Oderzhimyi pravdoi: Varlam Shalamov—po dnevnikam Aleksandra Gladkova." https://shalamov.ru/research/215/.

Miłosz, Czesław. Introduction to *The Trial Begins. On Socialist Realism*, translated by Max Hayward and George Dennis, 131–45. Berkeley: University of California Press, 1982.

Moleva, Nina. *Manezh. God 1962.* Moscow: Sovetskii pisatel', 1989.

Monas, Sidney. "Ehrenburg's Life, Solzhenitsyn's Day." *Hudson Review* 16, no. 1 (Spring 1963): 112–21.

Moser, Charles. "U Anny Akhmatovoi." *Grani* 73 (1969): 171–74.

Muchnic, Helen. "From Russia with Candor." Review of *Metropol. New York Times*, February 27, 1983.

——. "Nightmares." Review of *The Deserted House*, by Lydia Chukovskaya, and *Journey into the Whirlwind*, by Eugenia Ginzburg. *New York Review of Books*, January 4, 1968.

——. Review of *Vozdushnye puti* 1. *Russian Review* 20, no. 1 (January 1961): 87–88.

Muravnik, Maia. "'Rekviem' v proze." *Novoe russkoe slovo*, May 13, 1988.

Nathans, Benjamin. "Talking Fish: On Soviet Dissident Memoirs." *Journal of Modern History* 87 (September 2015): 579–614.

Nayman, Anatoly. *Remembering Anna Akhmatova.* Translated by Wendy Rosslyn, with an introduction by Joseph Brodsky. New York: Henry Holt, 1991.

Neizvestnyi, Ernst. "Moi dialog s Khrushchevym." *Vremia i my* 41 (May 1979): 170–200.

Nepomnyashchy, Catherine Th. *Abram Tertz and the Poetics of Crime.* New Haven, CT: Yale University Press, 1995.

Nerler, Pavel. *Con Amore: Etiudy o Mandelshtame.* Moscow: Novoe literaturnoe obozrenie, 2014.

——. "Kraft für das Leben und den Tod. Varlam Šalamov und die Mandel'štams." *Osteuropa*, no. 6 (2007): 229–38.

——. "Sila zhizni i zmerti. Varlam Shalamov i Mandelshtamy (na poliakh perepiski N. Ya. Mandelshtam i V. T. Shalamova)." http://shalamov.ru/research/61/9.html, trans. from Osteuropa, no. 6 (June 2007): 229–37.

Nivat, George. *Soljenitsyne.* Paris: Seuil, 1980.

Nord, Lydia [Olga Olenich-Gnenenko]. "Tragediia Anny Akhmatovoi." *Bulleten' russkogo obshchestva pomoshchi bezhentsam v Velikobritanii*, September 6, 1951.

Novyi kolokol. Literaturno-publitsisticheskii sbornik. Edited by Natalie Belinkov. London, 1972.

Obolensky, Aleksandr. "Alesha Dostoevskogo i Solzhenitsyna." *Russkaia mysl'*, September 7, 1972.

Obolensky, Valerian [N. Osinsky, pseud.]. "Pobegi travy." *Pravda*, July 4, 1922.

Obukhova-Zelin'skaia, Irina. *K. I. Chukovsky i Iu. P. Annenkov. "Nesmotria na razluchaiushchee nas rasstoianie i na istekshie gody . . .".* Moscow: MIK, 2017.

Offord, Derek. "Alexander Herzen and James de Rothschild." *Rothschild Archive* (April 2005–March 2006): 39–47.

Oksman, Yulian. "Iz dnevnika, kotorogo ia ne vedu." In *Vospominaniia ob Anne Akhmatovoi*, edited by V. Ia. Vilenkin and V. A. Chernykh, 640–47. Moscow: Sovetskii pisatel', 1991.

Oksman, Yulian [N.N., pseud.]. "Donoschiki i predateli sredi sovetskikh pisatelei i uchenykh." *Sotsialisticheskii vestnik*, nos. 5–6 (May–June 1963): 74–76.

Orlov, Vladimir. *Aleksandr Ginzburg: russkii roman.* Moscow: Russkii put', 2017.

"O 'ruke KGB' i prochem." *Kontinent* 49 (1986): 337–42.

Osipova, Anastasiya. "The Forced Conversion of Varlam Shalamov." Review of *Kolyma Stories*, by Varlam Shalamov. *Los Angeles Review of Books*, July 11, 2019, https://lareviewofbooks.org/article/the-forced-conversion-of-varlam-shalamov/.

Oushakine, Serguei. "The Terrifying Mimicry of Samizdat." *Public Culture* 13, no. 2 (Spring 2001): 191–214.

Ozerov, Lev. *Portraits without Frames.* Edited by Robert Chandler and Boris Dralyuk. Translated by Maria Bloshteyn, Robert Chandler, Boris Dralyuk, and Irina Mashinski. New York: New York Review of Books, 2018.

Pallon, V. "Zdravstvuite, katvorang." *Izvestiia*, January 14, 1964.

Panteleev, Leonid, and Lydia Chukovskaia. *L. Panteleev—L. Chukovskaia. Perepiska. 1929–1987.* Foreword by Pavel Kriuchkov. Moscow: Novoe literaturnoe obozrenie, 2011.

Paperno, Irina. *Stories of the Soviet Experience: Memoirs, Diaries, Dreams.* Ithaca, NY: Cornell University Press, 2009.

Pavlovsky, Aleksei. *Anna Akhmatova: ocherk tvorchestva.* Leningrad: Lenizdat, 1966.

Petkevich, Tamara. *Memoir of a Gulag Actress.* Translated by Yasha Klots and Ross Ufberg. DeKalb, IL: Northern Illinois University Press, 2010.

Pinkham, Sophie. "*Zdesizdat* and Discursive Rebellion: The *Metropol* Affair." *Ulbandus Review* 17 (2016): 127–45.

Popova, Nina, and Tatiana Pozdniakova, eds. *V tom dome bylo . . .* St. Petersburg: Muzei Anny Akhmatovoi, 2019.

"Po povodu knigi 'Opustelyi dom.' " *Russkaia mysl'*, January 5, 1967.

Pospielovsky, Dimitry. "From Gosizdat to Samizdat and Tamizdat." *Canadian Slavonic Papers* 20, no. 1 (March 1978): 44–62.

Prishvin, Mikhail. *Sobranie sochinenii v 8 tomakh.* Moscow: Khudozhestvennaia literatura, 1982–1986.

Proffer, Carl R. *The Widows of Russia and Other Writings.* Ann Arbor, MI: Ardis, 1987.

Proffer Teasley, Ellendea. *Brodsky among Us: A Memoir*. Boston: Academic Studies Press, 2017.

Protsess chetyrekh. Edited by Pavel Litvinov. Amsterdam: Alexander Herzen Foundation, 1971.

Pushkin, Alexander. *The Bronze Horseman: Selected Poems of Alexander Pushkin*. Translated, with an introduction by D. M. Thomas. New York: Viking, 1982.

Ranchin, Andrei, and Nikita Sapov, eds. *Stikhi ne dlia dam: russkaia netsenzurnaia poeziia vtoroi poloviny XIX veka*. Moscow: Ladomir, 1994.

Rar, Lev. "Otvet 'Literaturnoi gazete.'" *Posev*, no. 4 (April 1972): 9–10.

Ravdin, Boris. *Na podmostkakh voiny. Russkaia kul'turnaia zhizn' Latvii vremen natsistskoi okkupatsii. 1941–1944*. Stanford, CA: Stanford University Press, 2005.

——. "Pamiatka chitateliu gazety 'Parizhskii vestnik': 1942–1944." In *Vademecum. K 65-letiiu Lazaria Fleishmana*, edited by Anrei Ustinov, 457–529. Moscow: Vodolei, 2010.

Ravdin, Boris, and Gabriel Superfin. "Lydia Nord kak istochnik." In *Kul'tura russkoi diaspory: emigratsiia i memuary*, edited by S. Dotsenko, 199–204. Tallinn: Tallinskii universitet, 2009.

Reeve, Franklin D. "The House of the Living." *Kenyon Review*, no. 2 (Spring 1963): 356–60.

——. *Robert Frost in Russia*. Boston: Little, Brown, 1964.

Reisch, Alfred A. *Hot Books in the Cold War: The CIA-Funded Secret Western Book Distribution Program behind the Iron Curtain*. Budapest: Central European University Press, 2014.

Reshetovskaia, Natalya. *Sanya. My Life with Aleksandr Solzhenitsyn*. Translated by Elena Ivanoff. New York: Bobbs-Merrill, 1975.

Review. *Going Under*, by Lydia Chukovskaya. *New York Times*, October 17, 1976.

Richmond, Yale. *Cultural Exchange and the Cold War: Raising the Iron Curtain*. University Park: Pennsylvania State University Press, 2003.

Riurikov, Boris. "Sotsialisticheskii realizm i ego nisprovergateli." *Inostrannaia iteratura*, no. 1 (1962): 191–200.

Rozanova, Maria. "Na raznykh iazykakh." In *Odna ili dve russkikh literatury?*, edited by Georges Nivat, 202–16. Geneva: L'Age d'Homme, 1981.

Rubenstein, Joshua, and Vladimir P. Naumov, eds. *Stalin's Secret Pogrom: The Post-War Inquisition of the Jewish Anti-Fascist Committee*. Translated by Laura Esther Wolfson. New Haven, CT: Yale University Press, 2005.

Rzhevsky, Leonid. "The New Idiom." In *Soviet Literature in the Sixties: An International Symposium*, edited by Max Hayward and Edward L. Crowley, 55–80. New York: Praeger, 1964.

——. *Prochtenie tvorcheskogo slova: literaturovedcheskie problemy i analizy*. New York: New York University Press, 1970.

——. "Zagadochnaia korrespondentka Korneia Chukovsogo." *Novyi zhurnal* 123 (1976): 98–164.

Salisbury, Harrison E. "Loyalty Was the Error." Review of *Journey into the Whirlwind*, by Eugenia Ginzburg. *New York Times*, November 19, 1967.

Saraskina, Liudmila. *Aleksandr Solzhenitsyn.* Moscow: Molodaia Gvardiia, 2008.

Sarnov, Benedikt. "Kak eto bylo. K istorii publikatsii romana V. Grossmana 'Zhizn' i sud'ba.'" *Voprosy literatury,* no. 6 (2012): 9–47.

"Sauberungs-Literatur. Artikel 58." Review of *Journey into the Whirlwind,* by Eugenia Ginzburg, and *Kolyma Tales,* by Varlam Shalamov, *Der Spiegel,* no. 40 (September 25, 1967): 176–77.

Savoeva, Nina. *Ia vybrala Kolymu.* Magadan: Maobti, 1996.

Scammell, Michael. *Solzhenitsyn: A Biography.* New York: W. W. Norton, 1984.

Schmemann, Alexander. "Anna Akhmatova." *Novyi zhurnal* 83 (1966): 84–92.

Semenov-Tian'-Shan'sky, Aleksandr (Episkop). "Den' Ivana Denisovicha." *Vestnik RSKhD* 106 (April 1972): 357–58.

Serebriakova, Galina. "Smiercz." Translated by Józef Łobodowski. *Kultura* 7–8 (1967): 47–50.

——. "Smerch." *Novoe russkoe slovo,* December 8–30, 1967.

Serebrovskaia, Elena. "Doch' svoei rodiny." *Zvezda,* no. 1 (1988): 178–83.

——. "Protiv nigilizma i vseiadnosti." *Zvezda,* no. 6 (1957): 198–202.

Sergeeva, Liudmila. "Triumvirat: Andrei Sinyavsky—Abram Terts—Maria Rozanova." *Znamia,* no. 8 (2017): 105–69.

Shalamov, Varlam. *Doroga i sud'ba.* Moscow: Sovetskii pisatel', 1967.

——. "A Good Hand" and "Caligula." In *Russia's Other Writers: Selections from Samizdat Literature,* edited by Michael Scammell, with a foreword by Max Hayward, 152–58. New York: Praeger, 1971.

——. *Graphite.* Translated, with a foreword by John Glad. New York: Norton, 1981.

——. *Kolyma Tales.* Translated, with a foreword by John Glad. New York: Norton, 1980.

——. *Kolyma Tales.* Translated, with a foreword by John Glad. London: Penguin, 1994.

——. *Kolyma Stories.* Translated, with an introduction by Ronald Rayfield. New York: New York Review of Books, 2018.

——. *Kolymskie rasskazy.* Edited, with an introduction by Mikhail Geller. London: Overseas Publications Interchange, 1978.

——. *Kolymskie rasskazy.* Edited, with a foreword by Mikhail Geller. 2nd ed. London: Overseas Publications Interchange, 1982.

——. "On Prose." In *Late and Post Soviet Russian Literature: A Reader.* Book 2, *Thaw and Stagnation.* Edited by Mark Lipovetsky and Lisa Ryoko Wakamiya, 111–26. Boston: Academic Studies Press, 2015.

——. "Pis'mo staromu drugu." In *Belaia kniga po delu A. Sinyavskogo i Iu. Danielia,* edited by Aleksandr Ginzburg, 405–15. Frankfurt: Possev, 1967.

——. *Sketches of the Criminal World: Further Kolyma Tales.* Translated by Donald Rayfield, with an introduction by Alissa Valles. New York: New York Review of Books, 2020.

——. *Sobranie sochinenii v 7 tomakh.* Moscow: Terra, 2013.

——. *Stikhotvoreniia i poemy v 2 tomakh.* Edited, with an introduction and commentary by Valery Esipov. St. Petersburg: Pushkinskii dom—Vita nova, 2020.

——. "Stlanik." *Sel'skaia Molodezh',* no. 3 (1965): 2–3.

——. *Voskreshenie listvennitsy*. Edited, with a foreword by Mikhail Geller. Paris: YMCA-Press, 1985.

——. "V redaktsiiu *Literaturnoi gazety*." *Literaturnaia gazeta*, February 23, 1972.

[Shalamov, Varlam]. *Artikel 58: Die Aufzeichungen des Häftlings Schalanow*. Translated by Gizela Drohla. Cologne: Friedrich Middelhauve Verlag, 1967.

[Shalamov, Varlam]. *Article 58: mémoires du prisonnier Chalanov*. Paris: Gallimard, 1969.

Šalanov, Varlam [Varlam Shalamov]. *Artikel 58: 'N Ooggetuie Verslag oor die Bannenlinge in 'n Siberiese Strafkamp*. Translated by Johannes van der Merwe. Cape Town: Tafelberg-uit-gewers, 1967.

Shapiro, Irina. Review of *One Day in the Life of Ivan Denisovich*, by Aleksandr Solzhenitsyn. *Slavic Review* 22, no. 2 (June 1963): 375–77.

Shelest, Georgy. "Samorodok." *Izvestiia*, November 5, 1962.

Shklovsky, Viktor. *Theory of Prose*. Translated by Benjamin Sher, with an introduction by Gerald L. Bruns. Elmwood Park, IL: Dalkey Archive, 1991.

——. *Zoo, or Letters Not about Love*. Translated by Richard Sheldon. Champaign, IL: Dalkey Archive, 2012.

Shneerson, Maria. *Aleksandr Solzhenitsyn. Ocherki tvorchestva*. Frankfurt: Possev, 1984.

Sholokhov, Mikhail. *Fierce and Gentle Warriors*. Translated by Miriam Morton. New York: Doubleday, 1967.

Shruba, Manfred, and Oleg Korostelev, eds. *Psevdonimy russkogo zarubezh'ia. Materialy i issledovaniia*. Moscow: Novoe literaturnoe obozrenie, 2016.

Simonov, Konstantin. "Predislovie k romanu V. Azhaeva," 6–7. Moscow: Sovremennik, 1988.

——. "O proshlom vo imia budushchego." *Izvestiia*, November 17, 1962.

Sinyavsky, Andrei. "Dissent as a Personal Experience." Translated by Maria-Regina Kecht. *Dissent* 31, no. 2 (Spring 1984): 152–61.

——. "Srez materiala." Review of *Kolymskie rasskazy*, by Varlam Shalamov. *Sintaksis* 8 (1980): 180–86.

Sirotinskaia, Irina. *Moi drug Varlam Shalamov*. Moscow: Allana, 2006.

Sjeklocha, Paul, and Igor Mead. *Unofficial Art in the Soviet Union*. Berkeley: University of California Press, 1967.

Slizskoi, Arkady. "'Odin den'.' Povest' Solzhenitsyna." *Russkaia mysl'*, December 25, 1962.

Slonim, Mark. "Predislovie (ko vtoromu izdaniiu)," in *"My": Tekst i materialy k tvorcheskoi istroii romana*, ed. M. Yu. Liubimova and J. Curtis, 313–16. St. Petersburg: Mir, 2011.

Soloviev, Sergei. "Pervye retsenzii na 'Kolymskie rasskazy' i 'Ocherki prestupnogo mira." In *Shalamovskii sbornik 5*, edited by Valery Esipov, 248–80. Vologda: Common Place, 2017.

Solzhenitsyn, Aleksandr. *Arkhipelag GULAG. Opyt khudozhestvennogo issledovaniia. 1918–1956*. 3 vols. Paris: YMCA-Press, 1973–1975.

——. *Between Two Millstones*. Book 1, *Sketches of Exile. 1974–1978*. Translated by Peter Constantine. Notre Dame, IN: University of Notre Dame Press, 2018.

——. *Bodalsia telenok s dubom. Ocherki literaturnoi zhizni*. Paris: YMCA-Press, 1975.

——. *Bodalsia telenok s dubom. Ocherki literaturnoi zhizni.* Moscow: Soglasie, 1996.
——. *The Gulag Archipelago, 1918–1956: An Experiment in Literary Investigation.* Translated by Thomas P. Whitney. 3 vols. New York: Harper & Row, 1973.
——. *In the First Circle.* Translated by H. T. Willetts. New York: Harper & Collins, 2009.
——. *The Love Girl and the Innocent.* Translated by Nicholas Bethell and David Burg. New York: Bantam Books, 1969.
——. "Matrenin dvor." *Novyi mir*, no. 1 (1963): 42–63.
——. "Nashi pliuralisty." *Vestnik RKhD* 139 (1983): 133–60.
——. *The Nobel Lecture on Literature.* Translated by Thomas P. Whitney. New York: Harper & Row, 1972.
——. *The Oak and the Calf: Sketches on Literary Life in the Soviet Union.* Translated by Harry Willetts. New York: Harper & Row, 1979.
——. *One Day in the Life of Ivan Denisovich.* Translated by Max Hayward and Ronald Hingley, with an introduction by Max Hayward and Leopold Labedz. New York: Praeger, 1963.
——. *One Day in the Life of Ivan Denisovich.* Translated by Ralph Parker, with an introduction by Marvin L. Kalb. New York: Dutton, 1963.
——. *One Day in the Life of Ivan Denisovich.* Translated by H. T. Willetts, with an introduction by Katherine Shonk. New York: Farrar, Straus & Giroux, 2005.
——. "Odin den' Ivana Denisovicha." *Novyi mir*, no. 11 (1962): 8–74.
——. "Odin den' Ivana Denisovicha." *Roman-gazeta* 277, no. 1 (1963).
——. *Odin den' Ivana Denisovicha.* Moscow: Sovetskii pisatel', 1963.
——. *Publitsistika v 3 tomakh.* Yaroslavl': Verkhniaia Volga, 1997.
——. *Stories and Prose Poems.* Translated by Michael Glenny. New York: Farrar, Straus & Giroux, 2014.
——. "S Varlamom Shalamovym." *Novyi mir*, no. 4 (1999): 163–69.
——. *V kruge pervom.* New York: Harper & Row, 1968.
——. *V kruge pervom.* Paris: YMCA-Press, 1969.
"Sovetskie zhurnalisty o G. P. Struve." *Russkaia mysl'*, January 19, 1956.
Spivakovsky, P. E., and T. V. Esina, eds. *Ivanu Denisovichu polveka. Iubileinyi sbornik. 1962–2012.* Moscow: Russkii put', 2012.
Strakhovsky, Leonid I. *Craftsmen of the Word: Three Poets of Modern Russia: Gumilev, Akhmatova, Mandelshtam.* Cambridge, MA: Harvard University Press, 1949.
Struve, Gleb. "After the Coffee-Break." *New Republic* 148 (February 2, 1963): 15–16.
——. "A Classic of the Purge." *Times Literary Supplement*, March 9, 1967.
——. "Kak byl vpervye izdan 'Rekviem.'" Afterword to *Rekviem*, by Anna Akhmatova, 2nd ed., 22–24. Munich: Tovarishchestvo zarubezhnykh pisatelei, 1969.
——. "Nikolai Nedobrovo and Anna Akhmatova." In *Anna Akhmatova and Her Circle*, edited by Konstantin Polivanov, 215–30. Fayetteville: University of Arkansas Press, 1994.
——. "O povesti A. Solzhenitsyna." *Russkaia mysl'*, February 12, 1963.
——. "Russia Abroad." *Russian Review* 35, no. 1 (January 1976): 94–102.

——. *Russian Literature under Lenin and Stalin, 1917–1953.* Norman: University of Oklahoma Press, 1971.

——. *Russkaia literatura v izgnanii.* New York: Izdatel'stvo imeni Chekhova, 1956.

——. *Soviet Russian Literature, 1917–1950.* Norman: University of Oklahoma Press, 1951.

Struve, Nikita. "Vosem' chasov s Annoi Akhmatovoi." In Akhmatova, *Sochineniia,* 2: 325–46. [Munich]: Inter-Language Literary Associates, 1968.

"Sudebnyi protsess Lydii Chukovskoi protiv izdatel'stva 'Sovetskii pisatel'.'" In *Politicheskii dnevnik. 1964–1970,* 51–58. Amsterdam: Alexander Herzen Foundation, 1972.

Svirski, Grigori. *A History of Post-War Soviet Writing: The Literature of Moral Opposition.* Edited and translated by Robert Dessaix and Michael Ulman. Ann Arbor, MI: Ardis, 1981.

Svirsky, Grigory. *A History of Post-War Soviet Writing: The Literature of Moral Opposition.* Edited and translated by Robert Dessaix and Michael Ulman. Ann Arbor, MI: Ardis, 1981.

——. *Na lobnom meste: literatura nravstvennogo soprotivleniia (1946–1976 gg.).* Introduction by Efim Etkind. London: Overseas Publications Interchange, 1979.

Swift, Jonathan. *Gulliver's Travels.* Edited, with an introduction by Claude Rawson. Oxford: Oxford University Press, 2005.

"Syn—ottsu." *Chasovoi* 442, no. 3 (March 1963): 17–18.

Tarsis, Valery. *Palata No. 7.* Frankfurt: Possev, 1966.

Tempest, Richard. *Overwriting Chaos: Aleksandr Solzhenitsyn's Fictive Worlds.* Boston: Academic Studies Press, 2019.

Terapiano, Yury. Review of *Novyi zhurnal* 83. *Russkaia mysl',* July 16, 1966.

——. Review of *Novyi zhurnal* 84. *Russkaia mysl',* November 12, 1966.

——. Review of *Novyi zhurnal* 91. *Russkaia mysl',* August 1, 1968.

Terras, Victor. *Belinskij and Russian Literary Criticism.* Madison: University of Wisconsin Press, 1974.

Tertz, Abram. *Fantastic Stories.* Evanston, IL: Northwestern University Press, 1987.

——. *Fantasticheskie povesti.* Paris: Instytut Literacki, 1961.

——. "Pkhentz." *Encounter* (April 1966): 3–13.

——. *Progulki s Pushkinym.* London: Overseas Publications Interchange, 1975.

——. *The Trial Begins: On Socialist Realism.* Translated by Max Hayward and George Dennis, with an introduction by Czesław Miłosz. Berkeley: University of California Press, 1982.

[Tertz, Abram]. "Le réalisme socialiste." *Esprit* 270, no. 2 (February 1959): 335–67.

[Tertz, Abram]. "On Socialist Realism." *Dissent* (Winter 1960): 39–66.

Thun-Hohenstein, Franziska. "Warlam Schalamow an den Leser im Westen. Ein Archivfund." *Blog des Leibniz-Zentrums für Literatur—und Kulturforschung.* January 10, 2022. https://doi.org/10.13151/zfl-blog/202201 10-01.

Timenchik, Roman. *Poslednii poet: Anna Akhmatova v 60-e gody.* 2 vols. Moskva: Mosty kul'tury—Gesharim, 2014.

Timenchik, Roman, and Vladimir Khazan, eds. *Peterburg v poezii russkoi emigratsii (pervaia i vtoraia volna)*. With an introduction and commentary by the editors. St. Petersburg: Akademicheskii proekt, 2006.

Todorov, Tzvetan. *Genres in Discourse*. Translated by Catherine Potter. New York: Cambridge University Press, 2001.

Toker, Leona. *Gulag Literature and the Literature of Nazi Camps: An Intercontextual Reading*. Bloomington: Indiana University Press, 2019.

——. "Name Change and Author Avatars in Varlam Shalamov and Primo Levi." In *Narrative, Interrupted: The Plotless, the Disturbing and the Trivial in Literature*, edited by Markku Lehtimäki, Laura Karttunen, and Maria Mäkelä, 227–37. Berlin: De Gruyter, 2012.

——. *Return from the Archipelago: Narratives of Gulag Survivors*. Bloomington: Indiana University Press, 2000.

——. "Samizdat and the Problem of Authorial Control: The Case of Varlam Shalamov." *Poetics Today* 29, no. 4 (2008): 735–58.

——. "Varlam Shalamov's Kolyma." In *Between Heaven and Hell: The Myth of Siberia in Russian Culture*, edited by Galya Diment and Yury Slezkine, 151–69. New York: St. Martin's Press, 1993.

Tolstoi, Ivan. "Andrei i Abram. Puteshestvie po biografii Sinyavskogo. K 80-letiiu pisatelia." *Radio Svoboda*. October 8, 2005. https://archive.svoboda.org/programs/otbl/2005/otbl.100905.asp.

——. *"Doktor Zhivago": novye fakty i nakhodki v Nobelevskom arkhive*. Prague: Human Rights Publishers, 2010.

——. *Otmytyi roman Pasternaka: "Doktor Zhivago" mezhdu KGB i TsRU*. Moscow: Vremia, 2009.

——. "Upravliaia tamizdatom. Oksfordskii epizod Akhmatovoi." *Radio Free Europe*. March 5, 2016. https://www.svoboda.org/a/27590977.html.

Tolstoi, Ivan, and Andrei Ustinov. "'Molites' Gospodu za perepischika.' Vokrug pervoi knigi Iosifa Brodskogo." *Zvezda*, no. 5 (2018): 3–22.

Tolstoi, Lev. *Polnoe sobranie sochinenii v 90 tomakh*. Moscow: Khudozhestvennaia literatura, 1928–1964.

Tolstoy, Leo. *Tolstoy's Short Fiction*. Edited, with revised translations by Michael R. Katz. 2nd ed. New York: Norton, 2008.

——. *War and Peace*. Translated by Richard Pevear and Larissa Volokhonsky. New York: Vintage, 2008.

Tol'ts, Vladimir. "Dekabr' 1962. Manezh. 50 let spustia." *Radio Svoboda*. December 1, 2012. https://www.svoboda.org/a/24786334.html.

Tretiakov, Sergei. "The Biography of the Object." *October* 118 (Fall 2006): 57–62.

Tribunsky, Pavel. "Fond Forda, fond 'Svobodnaia Rossiia' / Vostochnoevropeiskii fond i sozdanie 'Izdatel'stvo imeni Chekhova.'" In *Ezhegodnik Doma russkogo zarubezh'ia imeni Aleksandra Solzhenitsyna*, 577–600. Moscow: Dom russkogo zarubezh'ia, 2014.

——. "'Izbrannye stikhotvoreniia' A.A. Akhmatovoi (1952): istoriia izdaniia." In *Izdatel'skoe delo rossiiskogo zarubezh'ia (XIX–XX vv.)*, edited by Pavel Tribunsky, 321–28. Moscow: Russkii put', 2017.

——. "Likvidatsiia 'Izdatel'stva imeni Chekhova,' Khristianskii soiuz molodykh liudei i 'Tovarishchestvo ob'edinennykh izdatelei.'" In *Ezhegodnik Doma russkogo zarubezh'ia imeni Aleksandra Solzhenitsyna*, 646–715. Moscow: Dom russkogo zarubezh'ia, 2015.

Tribunsky, Pavel, and Vladimir Khazan. "'Tam nashi usiliia ne ostaiutsia tshchetnymi i prinimaiutsia s velichaishim vnimaniem' (piat' pisem iz perepiski redaktorov al'manakhov 'Mosty' i 'Vozdushnye puti')." In *Ezhegodnik Doma russkogo zarubezh'ia imeni Aleksandra Solzhenitsyna*, 386–402. Moscow: Dom russkogo zarubezh'ia, 2018.

Trubetskoi, Yury. "Ob Anne Akhmatovoi." *Russkaia mysl'*, June 23, 1964.

Tvardovsky, Aleksandr. Foreword to "Odin den' Ivana Denisovicha," by Aleksandr Solzhenitsyn, 8–9. *Novyi mir*, no. 11 (1962).

——. *Novomirskii dnevnik. 1961–1966*. Moscow: PROZAiK, 2009.

——. *Sobranie sochinenii v 6 tomakh*. Moscow: Khudozhestvennaia literatura, 1980.

——. "Vasily Terkin na tom svete." *Izvestiia*, August 18, 1963.

[Tvardovsky, Aleksandr]. "Vasily Terkin na tom svete." *Mosty* 10 (1963): 129–44.

Ulianov, Nikolai. "Zagadka Solzhenitsyna." *Novoe russkoe slovo*, August 1, 1971.

"Uprazdnenie Kolymy?" *Russkaia mysl'*, March 23, 1972.

"Vecher pamiati Mandel'shtama v MGU." *Grani* 77 (1970): 82–88.

Velikanova, E. M., ed. *Tsena metafory, ili prestuplenie i nakazanie Sinyavskogo i Danielia*. Moscow: Kniga, 1989.

Venclova, Tomas. *Pogranich'e*. St. Petersburg: Izdatel'stvo Ivana Limbakha, 2015.

Verheul, Kees. "Een Russische poging tot rekenschap." *Tirade* 13 (January 1969): 36–46.

Vinogradov, Vladimir. "O zadachakh stilistiki: nabliudeniia za stilem 'Zhitiia Protopopa Avvakuma.'" In *Russkaia rech': sbornik statei*, edited by Lev Scherba, 195–273. Petrograd: Foneticheskii institut prakticheskogo izucheniia iazykov, 1923.

Vladimov, Georgy. *Vernyi Ruslan. Istoriia karaul'noi sobaki*. Frankfurt: Possev, 1975.

V mire fantastiki i prikliuchenii. Edited by Evgeny Bradis and Vladimir Dmitrevsky. Leningrad: Lenizdat, 1964.

Voinovich, Vladimir. *Portret na fone mifa*. Moscow: Eksmo, 2002.

Volin, Boris [Iosif Fradkin]. "Nedopustimye iavleniia." *Literaturnaia gazeta*, August 26, 1929.

V. O. "'Odin den' Ivana Denisovicha.'" *Chasovoi* 441, no. 2 (February 1963): 15.

Wachtel, Andrew. "One Day—Fifty Years Later." *Slavic Review* 72, no. 1 (Spring 2013): 102–17.

Wachtel, Andrew, and Ilya Vinitsky. *Russian Literature*. Cambridge, MA: Polity, 2009.

Wells, David. "The Function of the Epigraph in Akhmatova's Poetry." In *Anna Akhmatova. 1889–1989. Papers from the Akhmatova Centennial Conference*, edited by Sonia I. Ketchian, 266–81. Oakland, CA: Berkeley Slavic Specialties, 1993.

Werth, Alexander. "A Classic of the Purge." Review of *Opystelyi dom*, by Lydia Chukovskaya. *Times Literary Supplement*, February 16, 1967.

——. "A Classic of the Purge." *Times Literary Supplement*, March 23, 1967.

——. *Russia: Hopes and Fears*. New York: Simon & Schuster, 1969.

Yakir, Pyotr. *A Childhood in Prison*. Edited, with an introduction by Robert Conquest. [London?]: Macmillan, 1972.

Zamâtin, Evgenij Ivanovic. *Nous autres*. Translated by B. Cauvet-Duhamel. Paris: Gallimard, 1929.

Zamiatin, Eugene. *We*. Translated by Gregory Zilboorg. New York: Dutton, 1924.

Zamiatin, Evgeny. *Litsa*. Washington, DC: Inter-Language Literary Associates, 1967.

——. *My*. New York: Izdatel'stvo imeni Chekhova, 1952.

——. "Pis'mo v redaktsiiu 'Literaturnoi gazety.'" *Literaturnaia gazeta*, October 7, 1929.

——. *Sobranie sochinenii v 5 tomakh*. Moscow: Russkaia kniga, 2004.

Zamjatin, Jevgenij Ivanovič. *My*. Translated by Václav Koenig. Prague: Štorch-Marien, 1927.

Zavalishin, Viacheslav. "Anna Akhmatova." *Novoe russkoe slovo*, April 27, 1952.

——. "Povest' o 'mertvykh domakh' i sovetskom krest'ianstve." *Grani* 54 (1963): 133–50.

Zezina, Maria. *Sovetskaia khudozhestvennaia intelligentsiia i vlast' v 1950–1960-e gody*. Moscow: Dialog, 1999.

Zholkovsky, Aleksandr. "'Pkhentz' na randevu: niu, meniu, dezhaviu." *Novoe literaturnoe obozrenie*, no. 3 (2011): 210–28.

Zhukovsky, Vasily. *Stikhotvoreniia*. Leningrad: Sovetskii pisatel', 1956.

Zinik, Zinovy. *Emigratsiia kak literaturnyi priem*. Moscow: Novoe literaturnoe obozrenie, 2011.

INDEX

Abramov, Fedor, 59, 222n101
Acmeism, 75, 95, 157, 262n34
Ada (Nabokov), 27
Adamovich, Georgy, 63, 69, 72, 74–75, 91, 102, 169–70
Adorno, Theodor, 158
Adzhubei, Aleksei, 43, 83
Aerial Ways, 71–72, 73, 89, 237n98
"Air" (Mieželaitis), 56
Akhmatova, Anna, 6–7, 8, 20, 26, 40–41, 68–105, 231n47
    personal life: death of, 68; health, 240n122; portrait (painting), 87, 236n86; travels, 91, 237n104, 238nn105–6; visitors, 71, 72, 91, 233n61, 240n122, 241n138
    publishers, 226n1, 226n3 (see also *Requiem* (Akhmatova)); relations with publishers, 71–74, 83–90, 96–97, 240–41n131
    reception: doubt about authorship, 95–96, 101; as martyr, 70, 76; misreading of poems, 96; as non-witness, 111; reaction to from Russian diaspora, 91, 95, 101; years of "silence," 70, 97
    relationships: relations with Chukovskaia, 77, 106, 108, 110, 118–19, 251n117; relations with Ivanov, 227n7; relations with Makovsky, 227n7; relations with publishers, 71–74, 83–90, 96–97, 227n7, 230n32, 240–41n131; relations with Solzhenitsyn, 78, 231nn48–50, 232n55
    themes and style: civic themes, 95–96; epigraphs, 238–39n109; exile in own land, 76; national feeling, 239n114; recyclization, 242n149; rejection of exile, 70, 91–105, 102
    works: *Beg vremeni*, 80, 232n56;

"Courage," 94, 95; *Izbrannoe*, 241n132; *Iz shesti knig*, 98; memoir about Mandelshtam, 234n71; "Native Land," 100–101; "Poem without a Hero," 7, 70, 71–77, 229n19, 229n22; *Requiem*, 6, 7, 8, 12, 40–41, 68–105 (see also *Requiem* (Akhmatova)); *Rosary*, 75; "Slava Miru," 240–41n131; "Song of Peace," 95–96; "The Sentence," 96–97, 241n132; "The Silent Don flows silently," 97; "They took you away at daybreak," 97
Aksenov, Vasily, 31
Aldanov, Mark, 150
Alexander Herzen Foundation, 20, 208n52
Alexander II, 17
Alice's Adventures in Wonderland (Lewis), 148
Allilueva, Svetlana: *Twenty Letters to a Friend*, 128
Amalrik, Andrei, 166
American Committee for Freedom for the Peoples of the USSR, 88
Andreev, Gennady. *See* Khomiakov, Gennady
Andropov, Yury, 212n90
Anin, N. *See* Davidenkov, Nikolai
Annenkov, Yury, 87, 91, 118–19, 236n86, 247n59, 247n68
Anrep, Boris, 91, 92, 239n111
Anxiety of Influence, The (Bloom), 45
Aragon, Louis, 67
Ardis Publishers, 12, 27–32, 210–11n74, 211n82, 212n87; logo, 28
Arkhipelag GULag. See *Gulag Archipelago, The* (Solzhenitsyn)
Aronson, Grigory, 126
"Art as a Device" (Shklovsky), 201
"Artificial Limbs" (Shalamov), 181

émigré reviewers. *See* literary criticism
Eremin, Dmitry, 191
Ermolaev, Herman, 129–30
Eugene Onegin (Pushkin), 214n10
Everything Flows (Grossman), 252n119
Evtushenko, Evgeny, 43; "Baby Yar," 45;
    "The Heirs of Stalin," 43
"Exam, The" (Shalamov), 270n126
Experiments (journal), 71

Facets (journal), 29, 89–90
Faithful Ruslan (Vladimov), 223n102
Fantasticheskie povesti (Sinyavsky), *195*
fantastic realism, 189, 193
Far Far Away (Tvardovsky), 41
Far from Moscow (Azhaev), 144–45
fascism, 243n156
Fate of a Man (Sholokhov), 44
Favorsky, Vladimir, 28
Feuer, Kathryn. *See* Beliveau, Kathryn
Feuer, Lewis S., 83–84
Feuer, Robin, 83, 84
"fields of cultural production" (Bourdieu),
    10, 15
Filial (Dovlatov), 213n103
Filippov, Boris, 29, 88, 96, 97–98, 99,
    125, 152, 187, 191, 249n84; letter to
    editor *Literaturnaia gazeta*, 191
Filistinsky, Boris. *See* Filippov, Boris
Five Continents publishing house, 119,
    121, 248n71
Flegon Press, 222n100
Forrester, Sibelan, 116, 244n8
Foucault, Michel, 14, 193
Free Russian Press, 17–18, 206–7n35
Free Word (publishing house), 21
Frost, Robert, 68

Galkin, Samuil, 138, 142, 256n167
Garanin, Evgeny, 65
Garaudy, Roger: *Realism without Shores,* 67
Geller, Mikhail, 152, 178
gender, 102–3, 104–5, 258n195, 258n199;
    women authors, 43, 111
geography, 14–15, 19, 24, 32, 33, 65, 66,
    67, 102, 176, 188; boundaries, 15,
    187, 189; deterritorialization, 94,
    188, 189; geographical other, 192–93
Giedroyc, Jerzy, 162, 193
"Gimn utru." *See* "Hymn to Morning"
    (Mieželaitis)
Ginzburg, Aleksandr, 25, 203n2
Ginzburg, Evgenia, 41, 42, 250nn104–6;

Journey into the Whirlwind, 42,
    128, 129
Ginzburg, Lydia: *A Day of the Besieged City,*
    45; *Blockade Diary,* 45–48
Ginzburg, Mirra, 249n80
Gippius, Zinaida, 70, 102
Gladkov, Aleksandr, 96, 165, 229–30n31
glasnost', 31, 244n8
Glazkov, Nikolai, 2, 203n2
Glebova-Sudeikina, Olga, 101
Glen, Nika, 78
Glikin, Isidor, 109
"Gnev naroda." *See* "People's Wrath"
    (Chukovskaia)
Gody i voiny. See *Years of My Life*
    (Gorbatov)
Gogol, Nikolai: "The Overcoat," 117–18,
    197–98, 213–14n7
Going Under (Chukovskaia), 131–48
history of publication: book cover, *134*;
    publication in New York, 131, 133;
    publication in Russia, 131, 132; title,
    254n137; translation, 135, 254n135
reception: audience, 135; reception
    by Soviet authorities, 135; reviews,
    135–37, 251–52nn116–117,
    253–54n132, 254n141, 255n151
themes and style: characters, 138–44;
    compared to *Alice's Adventures,* 148;
    compared to *Sofia Petrovna,* 131–32;
    diary style, 131–32; as part of cycle,
    131; revisiting *Great Terror,* 106;
    setting, 138; theme of motherhood,
    143; theme of nature, 136, 137
Gorbatov, Alexander: *Years of My Life,* 129
Gorky, Maxim, 116, 117; *Mother,* 116
gosizdat (state publishing), 2, 7, 27, 172,
    192; editorial stage of, 214–15n15;
    One Day in the Life of Ivan Denisovich
    (Solzhenitsyn), 9, 11–12; quality
    considerations, 4; *Requiem,* 93
"Gothic Horror Novel of Emigration,
    The" (Zinik), 201
Govorit Moskva. Povesti i rasskazy
    (Daniel), *196*
Granat, Robert, 130
Grani. See Facets (journal)
Granin, Daniil, 90
Great Patriotic War, 44–45
Great Terror, 10, 42, 106; in fiction,
    106–48 *passim*
Gribachev, Nikolai, 82
Grossman, Vasily, 211n87; *Everything*

9 781501 768958